Cernăuți

BUKOVINA

Dniester (Nistru) River

BESSARABIA

U.S.S.R.

MOLDAVIA

Siret

river

Iași

Chișinău

Prut River

CARPATHIANS

Brașov

Galați

river

MUNTENIA

Danube

Brăila

river

Ploești

WALLACHIA

DOBROGEA

Bucarest

Constanța

BLACK SEA

river

BULGARIA

RUMANIA:

POLITICAL PROBLEMS OF
AN AGRARIAN STATE

Rumania

POLITICAL PROBLEMS OF
AN AGRARIAN STATE

BY HENRY L. ROBERTS

ARCHON BOOKS
1969

SBN: 208 00651 6
LIBRARY OF CONGRESS CATALOG CARD NUMBER: 69-13629
PRINTED IN THE UNITED STATES OF AMERICA

PREFACE

RUMANIA is economically one of the relatively backward regions of the world. It is not as backward as vast areas of Asia and Africa, but like them it is faced with the problems of an agrarian society in the twentieth century. How are such societies to adapt themselves to the demands and challenges of the industrial world economy? This is perhaps the most interesting and compelling reason for a study of Rumanian politics and agriculture. A further reason is that since the end of the Second World War Rumania has been "behind the Iron Curtain" and has therefore acquired a certain immediate significance as part of the complex of issues dividing the Soviet Union and the United States. Finally, literature in English on Rumania is comparatively limited and unsatisfactory. Hence, this study of a country rather remote from the interests of most Americans may shed some light in a dark corner.

The premise of this book is that an understanding of Rumania's recent history requires familiarity with the depressed status of its peasantry, whose plight has been a chronic source of alarm, anxiety, or despair since the time of Tudor Vladimirescu, who in 1821 raised a popular revolt against the boyars. Discussions I heard in Bucarest in the winter of 1944–45 echoed to a surprising extent the manifestoes of 1848, the debates on the emancipation of 1864, the polemics evoked by the 1907 uprising, and the Peasant party's radical pamphlets of 1920.

To be sure, between 1821 and 1944 Rumania underwent tremendous changes which might make one question whether the same problems were involved. An independent kingdom was created from the principalities of Moldavia and Wallachia, which had formerly acknowledged the Turkish sultan as their suzerain; after the First World War this kingdom doubled its area. World commerce came to Rumania; industry, if not large, expanded rapidly in the twentieth century. The population multiplied many times over. In agriculture itself there were important developments. From a semipastoral land, where stock raising was more important than farming, Rumania became, for a time, one of the great wheat and maize exporters of the world.

Agrarian problems, too, seemed to change during this period. Initially the chief sources of social discontent were servile dues and labor obligations which bore heavily upon the peasant. Later the unequal distribution of land, a great part of which was monopolized by huge latifundiary estates, seemed the root of the trouble. Still later the spokesmen of the peasants complained of the lack of credit and capital and claimed that industry was growing parasitically at the expense of agriculture. Finally, rural overpopulation appeared to supersede all other causes of agrarian distress.

Different efforts at reform, however, failed to overcome these evils, which seemed to be interlinked. For example, servitudes, in the guise of labor contracts, reappeared after their formal abolition because of the unequal distribution of property. The manifestations of overpopulation were only in part a consequence of demographic pressure; they also arose from the low level of output and from the estate owners' control over large areas of land. It was as though Rumania were suffering from one of those maladies which display varying symptoms at different times but continue to waste the victim. The peasantry remained poor and abased throughout, agricultural technique stayed at an exceedingly primitive level, and Rumanian society was marked by a deep chasm between capital and countryside, between peasant and ruler. In 1944 it was obvious that this changing yet persistent affliction was still present, still serious despite the extensive land reforms of 1918–21 which were to have led to a prosperous peasant agriculture by the extensive distribution of estate land to the small cultivators.

Since 1945, of course, with the progressive absorption of the country into the Soviet economic and political sphere, Rumania and its problems must be considered in the vastly more complex context of the Soviet system and in that sense cease to be an altogether intelligible field for independent investigation. While many elements of the agrarian problem remain the same—under any system demographic pressure, level of productivity, and organization of farming are objective data not to be conjured away—control of policy now lies largely in Moscow and is presumably designed for an enormous territorial and economic unit.

The aim of this book is to investigate the agrarian question and its political implications: the effect of a depressed peasantry and a retrograde agriculture upon political life, and, conversely, the attitudes and actions of the major political groups in regard to peasant poverty and agrarian reform. In general terms, the conclusion reached is that the all-pervading influence of the West in the course of the last century or more is the decisive element in this problem. Not only do the outstanding features of the agrarian crisis in Rumania stem directly or indirectly from this influence, but the domestic political activity is understandable only as a variety of responses, involving the copying, modification, or rejection of Western political and ideological models, to the social and economic dislocation which growing contact with the West has brought about.

Consequently, the eventual resolution of the agrarian problem in its broader implications depends not upon certain specific technical or political reforms but upon the much more extensive task of adjusting the total relations of Rumanian society to the Western industrial civilization which has enveloped the globe. Present Soviet domination, while reducing the possibility of Rumania's continued direct and uninhibited contact with the West, complicates and amplifies but does not alter this conclusion, for the Soviet system itself appears to be a response—on an overwhelming scale and in a particularly dynamic manner—of a society subject to the same Western influence. In this respect a study of the Rumanian agrarian question may help to clarify what seems to be the central and most fateful issue of our times.

In working out this conclusion I have attempted to combine political analysis and economic survey. Too frequently in works on Rumanian history and on the agrarian question in general I have noticed a tendency to separate politics and economics. For purposes of simple narrative or economic theorizing such a separation has its advantages. But studies dealing with the economics of the agrarian problem are apt to sidetrack the political elements and then conclude by saying, "Such-and-such would be the best economic cure for these difficulties but the unfavorable political situation has prevented its application." Similarly, a straight political narrative of the bewildering confusion of Rumanian public life is likely to conclude with the sentiment, "After all, what more could be expected under such depressed economic conditions?" In each case the picture is incomplete, the question of final responsibility evaded. Obviously, there is a continuous and reciprocal relationship between the political and the economic, and both must be constantly in mind in the search for practical solutions.

I must confess, though, that this study, too, has certain limitations with respect to scope, period covered, and precision of information. Apart from the currently decisive fact of Soviet domination, much of Rumanian history must, if my general conclusion is correct, find its explanation in the impact of external influences over which the Rumanians have had little or no control. Yet it was clearly impossible here to trace the ultimate origins and significance of such external influences as the European industrial and commercial revolution or the manifold political and imperialist interests making up the so-called Eastern question. By limiting myself to a relatively close study of Rumania in its reaction to these influences I hope, however, to have achieved a concreteness not attainable in a more extensive survey. As William James said, "A large acquaintance with particulars often makes us wiser than the possession of abstract formulas, however deep."

With regard to the period covered, I have concentrated primarily on the years between 1922 and 1945. I have discussed only briefly the historical background and the important land reforms of 1918–21 since they have been treated in elaborate detail by Dr. David Mitrany in *The Land and the Peasant in Rumania*. While I have written at some length on events since the Communists came to power, I prefer to regard that section as a tentative postscript. My personal observations ceased in the summer of 1945, the many important subsequent developments are highly controversial and cannot be handled satisfactorily without reference to all of eastern Europe, and the information concerning them has become increasingly difficult to obtain or assess.

A third limitation, which affects the precision of my analysis, arises from the inaccuracy, unreliability, and incompleteness of Rumanian statistics, which have been a source of anguish to all who have attempted any quantitative appreciation of the Rumanian situation. Three principal reasons account for these statistical difficulties:

a) the absence of a sound basis for statistical information because of the relative immaturity of the country's economy and administration;

b) the distortion of statistics for political or propagandistic reasons;

c) the apparent inability of many Rumanians to handle the simplest arithmetical operation, a perplexing but frequently noted phenomenon. The last two difficulties, while exasperating, are in most cases amenable to a degree of criticism and correction. The first, however, is more fundamental and limits any effort to obtain a precise picture.

In 1940 the Rumanian economist and former finance minister, Virgil Madgearu, gave an accurate description of Rumanian statistical sources at that date:

The principal difficulty of research on the Rumanian economy is the inadequacy of official statistics. . . . Thus, we have at our disposal only one census of the population of the country since it has been united in its ethnic frontiers—that of 1930. We have the most rudimentary knowledge of the agricultural sector, which is the most important in the Rumanian social-economic organization. We lack statistics on agricultural exploitations, and even the statistics on the extent and division of agricultural terrain, on inventory, livestock, etc., are defective. We lack statistics on agricultural laborers. Although there is more information on the industrial sector, statistical data are limited to manufacturing industries. Data on extractive industries are incomplete, and are non-existent for crafts and domestic industries.[1]

As Madgearu observed, agricultural statistics are particularly weak. For several years after the First World War estimates of the distribution of agricultural property were based on information gathered in 1905 or before. Plans were laid for a thorough agricultural census in 1930, but only a brief summary for the whole of Rumania was published. In 1941 the government organized a much more scientific agricultural census, but unfortunately only a provisional summary of the results was published, plus detailed studies of a few districts. Another drawback was that the frontiers of Rumania in 1941 did not correspond with those before 1940 or with those after 1945, and as the director of the Rumanian Central Institute of Statistics said, "Our results cannot be compared with preceding situations." The relatively few statistics which have been published by the Groza regime since 1945 are highly tendentious and suspect.

In short, any attempt at rigorous quantitative precision in discussing Rumanian agriculture seems hopeless. Although in the pages that follow a good deal of numerical data has been included, I have used it cautiously and with a painful awareness of its weaknesses and dangers.

Undoubtedly, my general attitude toward Rumania has been fundamentally determined by my own experiences while in that country during the first year after the armistice of September, 1944. To balance these subjective impressions, which have led to bias and unwarranted generalizing in so much of the writing about eastern Europe and the Balkans, I have checked my conclusions with as many primary sources as possible. These are discussed in a bibliographical note at the end of this study. Needless to say, the events of the past five years have compelled modification and in some cases rejection of my earlier opinions. But then, the writer of contemporary history can scarcely hope to build his house upon a rock.

1. Virgil Madgearu, *Evoluția economiei românești după războiul mondial.* (Bucarest, 1940), p. v.

I have a number of people to thank for their advice and assistance in the preparation of this book. It was originally written as a dissertation and submitted to the Faculty of Social Studies of Oxford University in 1948. To Mr. Hugh Seton-Watson, my supervisor, and Mr. C. A. Macartney and Dr. David Mitrany, my examiners, I owe great thanks for their careful reading of the manuscript. Dean John Krout of Columbia, Professors Philip Mosely of Columbia, and Sherman Kent of Yale were also kind enough to read this study and to offer numerous scholarly and editorial suggestions. Professor Abram Bergson of Columbia was most helpful on matters relating to Soviet economic and agrarian policy. Mr. Seton-Watson, Dr. Mitrany, Mr. F. W. D. Deakin, Mr. Mihail Farcaşanu, and Mr. Şerban Vallimarescu put at my disposal some indispensable Rumanian books, pamphlets, and newspapers which would otherwise have been unavailable to me. I am indebted to the librarians of the Royal Institute of International Affairs in London and the Bibliothèque de Documentation Internationale in Paris for aiding me in the use of their collections. I owe much to my American colleagues in Bucarest, especially Louis E. Madison, for endless conversations, discussions, and arguments concerning Rumanian affairs. Above all, I have a great and unpayable debt to one Rumanian friend, now dead, whose clear vision and intellectual integrity—rarities in these times and in that land—have been a source of profound and continued inspiration to me.

Note on Proper Names, Spelling, and Conversion of Weights and Measures

It seems impossible to follow a consistent method in the spelling of Rumanian proper names without producing awkward results. As a general rule I have employed the Rumanian spelling except where a name is most familiar in an anglicized form.

The name of the country itself presents difficulties. "România," the true spelling, does not indicate the English pronunciation at all (as pronounced by the Rumanians, the accent is on the third syllable, and the "â" resembles the difficult Russian vowel "ы"). "Roumania" comes from the French, but the "ou" is unnecessary in English, so I have employed "Rumania," a generally accepted variant. I have used the anglicized forms of the regional names, Moldavia (Moldova), Bessarabia (Basarabia), and Transylvania (Transilvania). Dobrogea, however, is given its Rumanian spelling rather than the older Turkish forms.

"Wallachia," which I use, is a foreign word not used by the Rumanians and rather disliked. On the other hand, of their words for this region between the Danube and the Carpathians, "Ţara Românească" might be misleading, and I preferred to restrict "Muntenia" to its narrower meaning as the region east of the Olt River, in contrast to Oltenia to the west. Bucarest (Bucureşti) is the only city which I have anglicized, though I might have used Jassy instead of Iaşi (the capital of Moldavia). With regard to personal names, I attempted to follow the most familiar usage and avoid odd-sounding distortions. Thus, King Michael instead of Mihai, but Carol, Ion, and Iuliu rather than Charles, John, and Julius.

I have spelled Rumanian words with their diacritical marks. The following English equivalents may serve as a guide to pronunciation:

â, î = have no English equivalent; like the Russian "ы"; one grammar suggests pronouncing a back "u" without rounded lips

ă = like the "e" in "suffer" or the "u" in "burn"

i = final "i" is usually not pronounced but softens the preceding consonant

u = "oo" as in "food"

c = before "e" or "i" like English "ch" or "tch"; otherwise like "k"

g = before "e" or "i" like English "j" or "g" in "gentle"; otherwise hard as in "garden"

ş = "sh"

ţ = "ts" as in "hats"

The following are the American equivalents to the weights and measures used in this book:

1 kilometer (km.) = 0.62 mile
1 square kilometer (km.²) = 0.386 square mile
1 hectare (ha.) = 2.47 acres
1 cadastral yoke (used in Transylvania) = 1.4 acres = 0.58 hectare
1 pogon = approximately ½ hectare (5012 square meters)
1 kilogram (kg.) = 2.20 lbs. avoirdupois
1 quintal = 220.46 lbs. avoirdupois
1 metric ton = 1.1023 short tons
1 hectoliter = 2.84 U.S. bushels

In the measurement of crop yields it is difficult to convert quintals into bushels, since the first is a measure of weight and the second of capacity. The weight of the bushel varies according to the crop. Roughly, one U.S. bushel is equivalent to 60 lbs. of wheat, 56 lbs. of shelled corn, or maize, 48 lbs. of barley, 56 lbs. of rye, and 32 lbs. of oats. Hence one quintal of wheat is approximately 3.67 bushels, and a yield of 10 quintals per hectare equals 14.9 bushels per acre. A quintal of corn is about 3.94 bushels, and a yield of 10 quintals per hectare equals 16.0 bushels per acre.

Because of the instability of Rumanian money it is difficult to make satisfactory conversions of the *leu* to the dollar. Before the First World War the leu at par was equal to 19.3 cents U.S. gold (old parity), the value of all currencies in the Latin Monetary Union to which Rumania belonged. After the postwar inflation the leu was stabilized in 1929 at 10 milligrams of gold, .900 fine; one leu was equal to .598 U.S. cents. In 1936 the gold content was reduced, and the leu was equal to 1.0127 U.S. cents (new parity). In August, 1947, after a terrific inflation, the leu was restabilized at 6.6 milligrams of gold, or .66 U.S. cents.

CONTENTS

PART I

HISTORICAL BACKGROUND AND
ECONOMIC FRAMEWORK

I

PEASANT AGAINST LANDOWNER

The Peasant Revolt of 1907

IN MARCH, 1907, the peasants in northern Moldavia, not far from the Russian frontier, arose in revolt.[1] Initially the uprising was directed, perhaps as a result of anti-Semitic instigation, against certain Jewish tenants renting large estates, but in its rapid extension south and west into Muntenia and along the Danube into Oltenia it became an increasingly violent assault upon all large tenant farmers and absentee landowners. The peasants not only demanded an amelioration of their labor contracts but in some districts seized land and organized revolutionary bands. The poorer peasants, those with insufficient holdings to support themselves, seem to have been the first to revolt, but they were soon joined by the more prosperous villagers. Indeed, subsequent investigations revealed that the active heads of the movement, in so far as it received any direction, had been village leaders, ex-army sergeants, clerks, and schoolteachers.[2]

For a time neither the central authorities in Bucarest nor the local administrations were able to cope with the spreading unrest, but after the dismissal of the Conservatives a Liberal government, perhaps under the threat of foreign intervention by Austria, took vigorous countermeasures. Troops under General Averescu, later a war hero and political figure, descended on the countryside and after some sharp conflicts restored order. Reprisals in districts where there had been peasant violence were extremely severe. It has been estimated that upward of 11,000 peasants were killed in the course of the revolt and its suppression.

Although the uprising lasted less than a month and was completely subdued, it was, and was felt to be, an event of frightening significance. Here was no by-product of foreign invasion, the frequent

1. For an account of the revolt see Radu Rosetti, *Pentru ce s'au răsculat țăranii* (Bucarest, 1908). A recent novel by Leo Katz, *Seedtime* (New York, 1947), is based on this uprising. Many aspects of the revolt are obscure, and the dossiers relating to its suppression are reported to have disappeared subsequently from the Ministry of War. In 1948, however, under the auspices of the Groza government, Mihail Roller edited a collection of state documents regarding the 1907 uprising. This new material, which may contain important additional information, was not available when this chapter was written.
2. C. Dobrogeanu-Gherea, *Neoiobăgia* (Bucarest, 2d ed., n.d.), p. 204.

occasion of many of Rumania's woes, nor a national revolt against an alien dominant class, but the unmistakable sign of a deep cleft within Rumanian society. The explosive culmination of a situation which had been building up during the preceding half-century, it rendered explicit and obvious the political dangers of the unresolved agrarian question. The outbreak had been foreshadowed by local uprisings in 1888, 1889, 1894, and 1900, and a few observers had predicted trouble. On the whole, however, an atmosphere of optimism and complacency had prevailed in the years following Rumania's emergence as a united and independent state. In 1906 the Minister of Domains had proudly declared in the Rumanian senate: "Gentlemen, you know that Rumania is one of the countries in Europe in which the small holding is more widespread than elsewhere, where the relation between the large and the small proprietor is more to the advantage of the latter than even in democratic France." [3]

The brief but intense convulsion of 1907, which in the eyes of terrified contemporaries had threatened Rumania's existence as a state and had nearly become a civil war, broke this complacency and gave rise to some soul searching. Politicians and writers ardently debated the causes of the revolt. Indeed, the stimulus of this unsettling event produced some of the most original social writings that have appeared in Rumania. For those who were unwilling or unable to see the full import of the uprising, it was most simply explained as the result either of "instigation" or of "peasant misery." The Conservatives accused the Liberal party of instigating the revolt to overthrow the Cantacuzino government. Despite the vagaries of Rumanian politics, it seems unlikely that the Liberals, many of whom were large landowners themselves, should wittingly have used such a dangerous device, although there is evidence of Liberal agitation directed against the Jewish *fermiers*.

The Liberals in turn charged that the revolt was the work of foreign revolutionaries: "The Rumanian authorities have discovered that the peasant uprisings are the fruits of a secret propaganda carried on among the peasants by a revolutionary group, in which teachers, priests, and Russian seamen of the cruiser "Potemkin" are taking part." [4] They expelled from the country some 880 persons, in-

3. Quoted in G. D. Creangă, *Grundbesitzverteilung und Bauernfrage in Rumänien*, 3 Teile, in *Staats- und Sozialwissenschaftliche Forschungen*, Hefte 129, 140 (Leipzig, 1907, 1909), I, 25.

4. Const. Titel Petrescu, *Socialismul în România* (Bucarest, n.d.), p. 198. In 1905 the Russian cruiser "Potemkin," after the mutiny, eventually sailed to Constanța, where the crew debarked as political refugees.

cluding Christian Rakovsky, one of the leaders of the Rumanian socialist movement.

Although signs of revolutionary activity and organization had been observed in certain districts, and some inflammatory pamphlets from Bessarabia had circulated in Rumania, the spontaneous spread of the revolt and the lack of evidence of careful preparation would argue against any important significance of such activity. The Rumanian socialists, who were in an extremely weak position, opposed the uprising. In 1892 the party program had declared that a backward country like Rumania was in no position to initiate a social revolution, and in 1907 the party advised the peasants against revolting: "Uprisings benefit only the boyars. The peasants afterward become even weaker and more depressed. . . . Peasants, you will not be delivered by uprisings, you will achieve profitable and lasting results not through violence and plundering but through seeking to destroy the political power of the boyars, landowners, and tenants." [5] In any event, the charge of instigation is a superficial one which, if sustained, explains the spark, not the conflagration.

Neither is peasant misery, while clearly a necessary ground for the revolt, a sufficient explanation. Extreme misery "dulls the mind, numbs the soul, destroys energy and the spirit of revolt, and leads to resignation and blind submission—a state of mind diametrically opposed to that which leads to revolt." [6] Moreover, the 1906 harvest had been exceptionally good. The important part played by village leaders and wealthy peasants would indicate that the revolt was more than a simple reaction to misery.

Certain contemporaries, notably G. D. Creangă, Radu Rosetti, Constantin Garoflid, and C. Dobrogeanu-Gherea, made more penetrating analyses of the problem. Creangă, by his statistical studies of property holdings, provided concrete evidence of the high percentage of land occupied by great estates. Rosetti, after an extensive historical survey of the agrarian question, concluded that "the latifundia is the enemy," that the true instigators of the rising were not Liberals or foreign agents but the "egoism, greediness, lack of scruple and lack of foresight on the part of the ruling classes both old and new." [7] Garoflid, an agrarian expert and himself a landowner, held that the acknowledged maldistribution of land was a consequence of a basic crisis in the system of agricultural production. The socialist

5. *Ibid.*, p. 196.
6. Dobrogeanu-Gherea, *op. cit.*, p. 179.
7. Rosetti, *op. cit.*, p. 624.

Dobrogeanu-Gherea argued that a state of permanent crisis in Rumania was being effected by the impact of Western political and economic forms upon the traditional Rumanian pattern. The result was an unfortunate hybrid, *neoiobăgia* (neoserfdom), the form of liberal-bourgeois institutions superimposed upon a feudal reality. Although Dobrogeanu-Gherea placed excessive trust in neoiobăgia as an all-inclusive explanation, he correctly realized that Rumania's contact with the Western world had a dynamic and by no means simple effect upon the existing economic and social structure.[8]

Economic and Social Roots of the Agrarian Problem [9]

An extreme concentration of land in large estates, an excessive fragmentation of small holdings, and the insignificance of medium-sized properties were the most obvious elements of the Rumanian agrarian problem at that time. In 1905 the disparity between large and small holdings probably exceeded that of any state in Europe, including Russia. On the basis of his investigations, which are probably the most accurate available, G. D. Creangă estimated that Rumanian properties were divided in the following manner: in the terminology of the time, small properties (0–10 hectares), comprising over 95 per cent of all properties, covered 40 per cent of the arable and grazing land; medium properties (10–100 hectares), comprising 4 per cent of all properties, occupied 11 per cent; whereas about 5,000 large and latifundiary estates held nearly 50 per cent.[10] If forests, orchards, and vineyards are included, the area covered by large property exceeded 57 per cent. These figures on property do not, of course, include the landless peasants. Creangă estimated that there were at that time about 300,000 peasants without land and

8. For a further analysis of Dobrogeanu-Gherea's ideas in connection with Rumanian Social Democracy, see below, pp. 276–280.

9. More extensive, and in some respects conflicting, discussions of the economic background of the agrarian problem are given in David Mitrany, *The Land and the Peasant in Rumania,* Carnegie Endowment for International Peace, "Economic and Social History of the World War" (London; New Haven, Yale University Press, 1930), and Marcel Emerit, *Les Paysans Roumains depuis le traité d'Andrinople jusqu'à la libération des terres (1829–1864)* (Paris, 1937).

10. In numbers the division was as follows:

Size of holdings in hectares	Number of holdings	Area in hectares
0–10	920,939	3,153,645
10–100	38,723	862,800
Over 100	5,385	3,810,351
	965,047	7,826,796

For more detailed figures on the distribution of property see the Appendix.

another 200,000 who held property jointly and were not included in his computations.

On the assumption that a holding of less than 3 hectares was totally inadequate, at the Rumanian level of production, to provide a family with even the bare means of subsistence, Creangă concluded that over 60 per cent of the peasant cultivators (landless peasants plus those with less than 3 hectares), "for the most part heads of families, find themselves in unconditional dependence upon landowners and tenants." [11] If peasants owning between 3 and 5 hectares —holdings certainly on the margin of subsistence—are included, it appears that nearly 85 per cent of the peasants were unable to earn a secure living from the produce of their soil and had to seek additional income elsewhere.

The concentration of land in great estates does not, of course, necessarily imply an agrarian crisis; English and Prussian agriculture developed successfully on large properties. Nor does the peasant's need to go beyond his own holding to earn a living necessarily spell misery for him. The reason the large estate appeared at this time to be the central feature of the Rumanian agrarian problem lies in the particular development of rural property and labor relations in the course of the eighteenth and nineteenth centuries.

Unfortunately, the background of Rumanian agrarian history is still extremely obscure. The original social function and source of privilege of the landowning nobles, the boyars, have been the subject of several notable but inconclusive controversies among Rumanian scholars. It is not certain when and to what degree the mass of Rumanian cultivators were reduced to a servile status. Evidence provided by villages of *răzeşi* and *moşneni*—free peasant communities with a form of common landholding, which have survived as relics in the hilly districts—suggests that they at one time were a prevalent form of rural organization, but scientific investigation of these villages has been undertaken only in recent years.[12] There is no question, however, that by the eighteenth century the boyars—and the monasteries—had come to control a great deal of the land, to which

11. Creangă, *op. cit.*, I, 189.
12. The term *boier* has been the popular, if historically inaccurate, name for all large landowners. The problem of ascertaining the boyar's original role resembles in some respects the confusion in Russian history between allodial hereditary landowners and the nobility of service. The villages of free peasants (*răzeşi* in Moldavia and *moşneni* in Wallachia) pose, in respect to their nature and origins, questions similar to those relating to the Russian *mir* and the South Slav *zadruga*. Illuminating discussions of these points may be found in H. H. Stahl's article, "Organizarea socială a ţărănimii," in *Enciclopedia României* (4 vols., Bucarest, n.d.), I, 559–576, and in his recent book, *Sociologia satului devălmaş românesc* (Bucarest, 1946), I.

the majority of the peasants were bound as *rumâni* (the most common term for serfs). In its form as in its relatively late flowering the Rumanian servile system more nearly resembled that of Russia than that of western Europe.

The life of the Rumanian serfs was bitter and squalid, as is illustrated by periodic mass flights across the Danube or into Transylvania. Their burdens resulted from their being on the bottom of the social structure of a state first fighting and then subservient to the Ottoman Empire and from the task of supporting, in a relatively self-sufficient economy, the needs of the boyars and their retainers. Although the growing boyar domination was a gradual process and apparently accompanied an internal breakdown of the village community, the act of binding the peasant to the land, carried out as a general measure by Michael the Brave (*ca.* 1558–1601), had, in large part at least, a military and political purpose: to insure a settled population able to provide military supplies. However, while the tax burden and the tributes owing the Turks were transmitted from prince and boyar to the back of the peasant, servile labor obligations, the *clacă*, were relatively light. The population was sparse, and the boyars were not reluctant to grant the peasants land, of which there was an abundance, provided, of course, they paid their tithes in kind.

Toward the middle of the eighteenth century two new elements appear: increasing state legislation, superseding or codifying customary practices, and the growth of commercial activity. The twin action of these two factors becomes ever more important right through the nineteenth century, and on their interrelation hangs much of the agrarian problem. Both were destructive of the old closed society of traditional rights and a relatively static economy; both were introduced from without. Sometimes they reinforced one another in promoting change; sometimes one held the other in check.

Around 1750 the Phanariot prince, Constantin Mavrocordat, formally abolished serfdom in an act anticipating and resembling the Habsburg Emperor Joseph II's emancipation of 1781. Although this act, in principle, relieved the peasant of personal bondage and of being tied to the land, it did not rid him of labor obligations or dues to the boyar for the use of the land he cultivated. Indeed, at about the same time the boyars initiated a persistent and successful effort to increase the number of days of the clacă and to define a working day in terms which greatly exceeded what a peasant could actually accomplish in one day. Simultaneously, they began to establish and extend seigneurial monopolies on such activities as milling and the sale of wine.

Both actions clearly arose from the growing commercial possibilities of these years. The Turks were increasing their imports of grain from the principalities, and despite Turkish restrictions trade was developed with neighboring states. Hence it was in the interest of the boyars to increase the amount of labor available to them and to monopolize profitable commercial undertakings. One direct consequence of this new commercial pressure on the peasant was the revolt led by Tudor Vladimirescu in 1821 "against the boyars who have devoured our rights."

The next step is signalized by the Treaty of Adrianople of 1829, which opened Rumanian ports to world commerce, and the Organic Statutes of 1831–32, which gave the principalities their first constitutional documents. The effect of the first was vastly to accelerate the pace of commercial expansion. At the beginning of the nineteenth century raising livestock had been the principal occupation, but it was now replaced by the cultivation of cereals, for which the acreage nearly doubled in the thirty years betwen 1829 and 1859. This expansion of commerce in cereals continued until by the outbreak of the First World War Rumania ranked fourth among the world's cereal exporters and fifth among the wheat exporters. As a result, the relative value of land steadily increased. As early as 1805 the boyars undertook to limit the peasants' right to pasture, and in 1828 Prince Sturdza announced that the peasants had no right to exploit more than two-thirds of the lord's domain.

This trend was reinforced by the Organic Statutes. Introduced during the period of Russian occupation, these acts attempted to codify, in somewhat different terms for the two principalities, the relations between boyar and peasant. In so far as they reduced arbitrary action and made precise and definite the peasant's obligations, they were to his benefit. This gain, however, was largely canceled by the fact that for the first time the lord of the land was defined as a full proprietor of his estate. The traditional concept of "master of the land" was replaced by legal ownership. In return for set labor obligations and tithes, the peasants were granted use of land not in excess of two-thirds of the estate, the remaining third being totally in the lord's hands.[13] Under this system, while the peasants had life use of

13. The extent of the lord's demesne land—the land actually cultivated under his direction—before the nineteenth century is not certain. Mitrany, *op. cit.*, p. 21, points out that early village maps show no separate reserve for the master of the land, but

land, it was not passed on from father to son but reverted to the land-owner, who was in turn responsible for providing newly married young cultivators with a holding. In fixing the extent of land to be held by each cultivator, these acts, especially the one for Moldavia, reduced the amount customarily enjoyed for pasturage and restricted the peasants' forest rights. Although the peasant was theoretically free to move, he was in fact tied to his community by a net of regulations.

With a few modifications Rumanian agrarian relations were determined by the Organic Statutes for the next third of a century. Under them, as a contemporary observer remarked, "The principalities took on a new life"; there was a marked increase in economic activity. That the benefits of this activity were not generally shared by the peasants, however, is shown by their continued exodus across neighboring frontiers. They were being forced out of their old semipastoral habits, and the very increase of cereal exports could work to their disadvantage. For example, the entire 1847 wheat crop was sold in advance because of the urgent demands in other European states suffering from food shortages in the late 1840's. As a result of these premature sales, made largely through the boyars, the principalities experienced a food crisis which contributed greatly to the peasant unrest in the turbulent year 1848.

Apart from the abortive attempts at reform during the short-lived Wallachian revolution in 1848 and a moderate revision of the Organic Statutes in 1851, the next major change was the Act of 1864, which paralleled the 1848 emancipation in the Habsburg lands and the Russian emancipation of 1861. This act, promulgated for the united principalities by Prince Cuza, for political and social rather than for economic reasons, abolished the clacă and other servitudes. The peasants obtained full title to the land they had in use, based upon earlier regulations, and the landowners were given a compensation for the loss of their labor. The law followed the now recognized provision that peasant property could not exceed two-thirds of the former lord's estate. The new holdings could not be sold or alienated for a period of thirty years.

By this act, so it seemed, the remnants of the old servile system had been abolished. Possession and use of land were transformed into absolute property rights; the peasant holder was now a free proprietor, owing no servile obligations, and, indeed, the translation of the clacă and other dues into a redemption payment does seem to have dimin-

Emerit, *op. cit.*, p. 45, doubts if there is sufficient evidence to permit a positive declaration that the peasants traditionally had had the use of all the land.

ished his burdens.[14] Yet a quarter of a century after the Act of 1864 there began those peasant disturbances which culminated in the 1907 uprising. In some way, as Dobrogeanu-Gherea said, "The year 1864 carried in its womb the terrible year 1907."

The connection, however, is not a simple one and is paradoxical in several respects. Between 1864 and 1907 Rumania continued its rapid expansion in agriculture and commerce. Exports of grain, for example, increased from about 1,400,000 tons per year in the early 1880's to nearly 2,500,000 tons in 1905. Hence it is necessary to explain how under such circumstances there should have been growing peasant discontent. Was there, to repeat that old and difficult question, increasing poverty in the midst of expanding national wealth?

In the first place, while the Act of 1864 was passed against the wishes of the boyars, by a coup d'état on the part of Prince Cuza, the administration of the country, especially local administration, was still largely under their control, and they had ample opportunity to twist the provisions of the law to their advantage. Undoubtedly many injustices were committed in its application: often the landowner was able to distribute the worst land to the peasants, holding the best in his own estate; in a number of cases false measuring standards were used, an easy trick in a country lacking basic ground surveys; sometimes the landowner so divided the holdings that the peasants were unable to reach their property without paying a toll. As a cumulative result of these malpractices it is possible that although by the law the peasants were to receive the land they had in use before the reform, they actually received less and of lower quality. Local studies of a few districts indicate that such may have been the case, but statistics are lacking to make a general conclusion.

Another criticism of the law has been that while the peasants' claims to land could not exceed two-thirds of the lord's estate, the excess demand being met by grants of state land, in those regions where the peasants' quota was less the lord was able to retain as absolute property, with no future obligation, well over the minimal one-third. Moreover, under the Organic Statutes the lord was responsible for providing newly married peasants with a holding, while the new act made no adequate provision for subsequent generations. Peasant holdings now became inheritable property to be passed on from father to children. Since the new holdings were virtually inalienable and

14. This point, as in Russia, has been much disputed, and some authors have maintained that the peasants' burdens actually increased. The comparative figures, however, which are provided by Emerit, *op. cit.*, p. 516, if they are accurate and representative, show a considerable falling off of the amount owed by the peasant.

since the practice was to distribute land equally among heirs, there was an inevitable tendency, on many peasant holdings at least, toward a progressive subdivision of the property. This tendency has been regarded as one of the worst consequences of the reform: "At the end of three generations, the land distributed by Cuza to the rural workers was dispersed into an impalpable dust." [15] Unquestionably the fragmentation of holdings constituted a major obstacle to the introduction of rational agricultural techniques. Further, the reform did not grant land to a number of peasants, those who previously had not performed the clacă or who were listed as free proprietors. Finally, an examination of the size of the lots granted to the peasants reveals that a large number of cultivators did not receive enough land in the first place to enable them to establish a self-supporting holding on the level of cultivation then prevailing.[16]

It is clear, then, that the peasants' gains were limited, that in most cases they were not in a position to set up an independent farm, that the lord was relieved of all future responsibility, and that a number of categories of peasants were not taken care of. Such certainly were the drawbacks. The basis of Rumanian agriculture was not really altered. The reform of 1864 neither set Rumanian agriculture on the path of small peasant farming on the western European model—whether that was even theoretically possible, given the general nature of the Rumanian economy, will be discussed later—nor fostered large-scale farming based upon agricultural wage labor in the English or Prussian pattern.

In addition to the limitations of the 1864 reform, two other factors have been adduced to explain growing peasant dissatisfaction: the laws on agricultural contracts of 1866 and 1872, which are said to have reintroduced serfdom, and the land hunger of an increasing population. The immediate effect of the reform was to create a crisis in production and a great decline in the area sown, largely because the peasants preferred to cultivate their new holdings and refused to work for the landowners, who were faced with a serious labor shortage. The boyars attempted to compensate for this by passing special laws governing agricultural contracts, which unquestionably put the peasant at the landowner's mercy in matters regarding the fulfill-

15. Emerit, *op. cit.,* p. 519.

16. The allotments were based on an earlier threefold division of the peasants, determined by the number of oxen they possessed. Though the figures are only approximate, peasants having four oxen received roughly 6 hectares; those with two oxen 4½ hectares; and the so-called "tail-end" peasants, 2½ hectares. At the prevailing level of cultivation it was estimated that only the first class, a rather small minority of the peasantry, could obtain an assured surplus.

ment of labor contracts and even permitted the employment of military force to drive the peasant to work. Although the harsher aspects of these laws were later abandoned, they permanently affected landlord-peasant relations and did much to justify the term neoserfdom, "the confirmation of the old servitudes in contractual form."

Yet these laws, while harsh on the peasant once he fell into the power of the landowner, would be significant only on the assumption that the peasants were increasingly obliged to go to the landowner for assistance. That is, the laws of contracts merely accelerated the relapse into a servile system—one lacking the paternalistic protection of the old order—but were not in themselves the cause of a deteriorating situation. Moreover, the peasant uprisings did not occur when the laws were at their harshest but later when some of the worst provisions had been abrogated.

Land hunger, in general, results from an excess of population relative to the amount of land available. As has been noted, at the beginning of the nineteenth century the Rumanian principalities were not thickly settled, though even at the time of the Organic Statutes it was not possible to give adequate grants of arable land to the peasants in the old and relatively thickly settled mountainous districts. By the middle of the century the boyars were invoking population pressure to explain the high cost of land. There is no question that in the second half of the nineteenth century Rumania's population expanded at a very rapid rate.

At the same time, however, the expansion of land under cultivation appears to have been increasing even more rapidly, as the plough was put to untilled pastures, waste, and meadow.[17] The extent to which the peasants were able to benefit from this expansion of cultivated area cannot be estimated with any precision. Undoubtedly much of it took place on large estates under the control of the landowners. To some extent, too, it resulted from the peasants converting their pasture land to arable. The act of 1864 had made no provision for communal pasturing; the small peasant holdings were inadequate for both grain and livestock, and from 1864 there is a notable decline in animal husbandry. It is estimated that whereas in 1860 meadows and pasture comprised 33 per cent of the total surface of Rumania, they were reduced to 17 per cent in the years 1901–5, thus offsetting to a considerable degree the gain in land under cultiva-

17. According to Constantin Garoflid, *Chestia agrară în România* (Bucarest, 1920), p. 128, between 1859 and 1899 the population of Rumania increased by 54 per cent, whereas the area of land under cultivation increased by 85 per cent between 1862 and 1905.

tion.[18] Hence it may be concluded that much of the expansion of the arable either took place outside the peasant lands or at the expense of pasture. Against this, however, was the periodic doling out of state land, which, while only a palliative, did serve to balance in some measure the growing pressure of population.[19]

The most that may be said is that the growth of population was beginning to become an important element, one that would become increasingly troublesome in the twentieth century, and that while the plight of the Rumanian peasant at this time cannot really be attributed to rural overpopulation, the ratio of land to labor was shifting to his disadvantage. Given this tendency plus the fact that many peasants never had enough land to begin with, one can see how the landowners, controlling much of the land and armed with the laws on agricultural contracts, were able to preserve a quasi-servile system of social and labor relations.

Another development contributing greatly to social friction in the countryside was the increase, from the middle of the nineteenth century on, of absenteeism on the great estates, as the landowners found it pleasanter to live abroad or to engage in politics in Bucarest. By 1900, 56 per cent of the area of properties over 50 hectares and more than 72 per cent on the vast estates over 5,000 hectares were being leased, for the most part not to individual peasants but to large tenants.

The effects of absenteeism were particularly unfortunate in Rumania. To some extent the tenant may have been performing a useful entrepreneurial function in initiating economic activity,[20] but in most cases he merely sublet the greater part of the land to the peasants, who cultivated it in the old manner. The tenant was inclined to regard his lease, which was usually for a short term, as a speculative venture to provide quick gains not by improved cultivation but by

18. Ministère de l'Agriculture, de l'Industrie, du Commerce et des Domaines, *La Roumanie, 1866–1906* (Bucarest, 1907), pp. 267–268.

19. According to Creangă, *op. cit.*, I, 80, the state, in addition to some 572,000 hectares granted in 1864, had parceled out approximately 930,000 hectares by 1905.

It is apparently impossible to make a comparison of the average size of peasant properties at these two dates. The average size of the peasant allotments in 1864 was about 3.8 hectares, whereas by the end of the century the average size of peasant properties under 10 hectares was 3.4 hectares. But the first figure does not include peasant properties already held in full ownership in 1864.

20. The entrepreneurial character of the tenant is reflected in the fact that the larger the lease the higher was the percentage of foreign tenants. The problem of foreign tenants was closely associated with Rumanian anti-Semitism, and it was the common charge that Jewish tenants were grinding the peasant and ruining the country. While Jewish tenants were important on the largest estates of Moldavia, the great majority of tenants (73 per cent) were Rumanians.

making greater demands upon both the land and the peasant. Since his profits tended to be in direct proportion to the area he was able to lease, there was a marked inclination to build up vast agricultural trusts, some of which covered more than 100,000 hectares. Although ultimately the large tenant was a consequence rather than a cause of the agrarian problem, he was the focus of hatred and abuse: hated by the peasants because he dealt directly with them, verbally abused by the landowner-politicians who made him their scapegoat. Certainly some of the more spectacular injustices and preposterous labor contracts can be found on lands operated by tenants.

This speculative interest on the part of the tenant in acquiring more land contributed to a rapid rise in rents. Between 1870 and 1906 rents mounted between 100 and 200 per cent for a third of the properties and over 200 per cent for another third. The peasants consequently were obliged to pay more dearly for the use of land. In 1870 they generally retained from two to four parts of the produce of rented land and delivered one part to the landowner or large tenant; by 1906 in over half the cases studied in an investigation, the ratio was one to one.[21]

The rise in the value of land was not accompanied by an equivalent improvement in agricultural techniques. Most of the peasants were both inexperienced in the careful cultivation of small holdings and financially unable to improve their methods, and the large landowners and tenants had little incentive. By the working of the 1864 reform the peasants remained attached to their strip of land, lacking even the free mobility of the farm laborer. They continued to own most of the means of production: over 90 per cent of the draft animals, ploughs, and harrows in Rumania belonged to the peasants.

Under these conditions the distinction between large-scale and small-scale farming was blurred, and it was characteristic of the latifundiary cultivation prevailing in Rumania that the size of an undertaking was not determined by an organized integration of the productive factors of a given area but was rather the arithmetical sum of a large number of peasant cultivations. The peasant, in return for a piece of land, contracted either to cultivate another piece of land for the proprietor or tenant or to share the produce in a form of metayage. Money payments were uncommon except in Moldavia.[22]

21. Creangă, *op. cit.*, II, 18–22.

22. It must be observed, however, that while the great estates did not, in most cases, utilize progressive farming methods, the output of the large farms was consistently higher than that of the peasant holdings. The reasons for this difference have been the occasion of much dispute. Supporters of large-scale cultivation have held that despite

From a consideration of all these factors the peculiar nature of the Rumanian agrarian crisis emerges. The poorer peasant, who had been forced to go to the landowner or tenant for additional land, was in an increasingly bad bargaining position. The landowners or tenants, in responding to commercial incentives, could increase production with little cost to themselves merely by demanding more of him, since he supplied the implements and draft animals as well as the labor.[23] Clinging to his little plot of ground and doggedly refusing to become a migrant wage laborer, the poor peasant could see no possible relief to his situation except to have more land. On the other hand, the richer peasant, whose land was sufficient to produce a surplus, likewise found himself restricted by the relative monopoly in land, the high rents, and the speculation of the large tenants: the system was an obstacle to the further improvement of his position.[24]

In general, then, the economic background of the 1907 revolt lay not in peasant poverty alone but in the protracted dislocating effect of commerce upon a previously "natural economy" and a society involved in the ambiguities of neoserfdom. This dislocation has occurred in many forms throughout the globe where modern industry and commerce have impinged upon traditional social and economic patterns. The particular form it took in Rumania, increasing agrarian tension in the midst of a flourishing foreign commerce in cereals, was a product not only of economic and demographic factors but of Rumania's particular social structure, which was dominated by a boyar oligarchy.

Socially and economically Rumania resembled tsarist Russia in several ways. As Dobrogeanu-Gherea observed: "We are the only country in Europe, with the exception of Russia, which has the sad privilege of peasant revolts—neither the Western countries, superior to us in culture, nor those of the East, such as Serbia and Bulgaria, which are inferior to us, have them." [25] In both countries the history

---

the prevalence of unprogressive latifundiary cultivation, large property was making technical advances and was paving the way toward more scientific farming. Advocates of peasant farming have replied that the large owners had kept the best land to themselves and that the peasants were unable to give adequate attention to their own fields. As one peasant is reported to have said: "Do you think this beautiful maize is mine? It belongs to the Jewish tenant. I haven't even hoed my own once yet, his twice. He didn't allot us the land till late." Creangă, op. cit., I, 14.

23. This curious fact, that under the prevailing agrarian relations prosperity seemed to sharpen social tensions, may explain why the 1907 revolt should have followed the excellent 1906 harvest.

24. This grievance of the richer peasants may serve to explain why the minor uprising of 1888 had been most violent in the district of Ialomița, a sparsely populated region having a comparatively prosperous peasantry, but in which an exceptionally high percentage of the land (69 per cent) was in the hands of large proprietors, who leased out more than 70 per cent of their estates.

25. Dobrogeanu-Gherea, op. cit., p. 177.

of property relations followed a different course from that in the West, and in both countries contact with the West created a steadily increasing crisis which the legislative measures of the nineteenth century did not solve and in some respects exacerbated. In neither case did peasant emancipation lead to the healthy development of small holds but rather to the appearance of the land-hungry cultivator still in a position of dependence on the landowner.[26]

While there were these similarities in Russian and Rumanian social and economic life, and more than a casual parallel in the development of agrarian relations, the political and international positions of the two states were entirely different. This difference explains in part some of the very great divergences in the recent history of these countries.

Political Aspects of the Agrarian Question

Although Rumanian economic and social relations were such as to create a dangerous tension in the countryside, politically, in marked contrast to tsarist Russia, there was relatively little revolutionary activity. This difference has often been attributed to the lethargy and supineness of the Rumanian peasant or to his Daco-Roman stability and love of order and hard work. National qualities may have played some part, though the violence of the 1907 revolt was damaging to many such theories. A more substantial reason would appear to lie in the contrast between the political and international situations of the two states.

Russia, a great empire, was assured of its independence as a nation. Existing institutions were firmly fixed. Russian social reformers could direct their energies toward internal issues without being preoccupied with the question of national survival. For these reasons the climate was favorable to a revolutionary spirit. Quite opposite conditions obtained in Rumania, a newly created state whose position in the community, or anarchy, of nations was by no means secure. Many Rumanians were not as yet included within the country's

26. The sensitivity in Rumania to developments in Russia would suggest the presence of common characteristics. The Russian emancipation of 1861 was followed by Prince Cuza's Act of 1864. There is evidence that the Rumanian rising of 1889 was aroused by a rumor that the tsar had ordered land to be divided among the peasants. The Russian Revolution of 1905 found a reflection in the 1907 revolt in Rumania, and of course the Russian Revolution of 1917 had a direct bearing upon the Rumanian agrarian reforms of 1918–21. The correlation of these events is certainly more than a chronological coincidence. It might be added that Stolypin's program to reform Russian agriculture by creating a class of strong peasant holdings resembles some of the recommendations put forward by the Conservative agrarian expert Constantin Garoflid.

boundaries. Consequently, national aims and ambitions tended to receive first attention from all articulate Rumanians.

Whatever may be the answer to the much debated question of Rumanian origins, the two principalities, Moldavia and Wallachia, did not make their appearance until the thirteenth and fourteenth centuries. After a couple of centuries of precarious independence they fell under the domination of the Ottoman Empire. For a time native princes maintained some degree of internal authority; later Phanariot Greeks became the *hospodars* of the principalities; but the two provinces were not united until 1862, and the remnants of Turkish suzerainty were not shaken off until the Russo-Turkish War of 1877. While the Rumanians did contribute to achieving their national independence, the rise of a united Rumania was largely conditioned by events beyond their control: the decline of the Ottoman Empire, the repulse of Russia in the Crimean War, and the equilibrium established by the Concert of Europe at the Congress of Berlin. Rumania's independence and existence as a national state were thus externally determined, at least in the negative sense of permitting the Rumanians to enjoy some freedom of action in the nineteenth century.

The national progress of Rumania did not correspond with the social or material progress of the peasantry. On the contrary, the high points in Rumanian history from the national point of view often marked a decline in the peasant's status. The process of social differentiation which followed the foundation of the principalities seems to have led to a further subjugation of the peasant to the boyar. Under Michael the Brave, who for a short period ruled over all Rumanian lands, the peasants were definitely bound to the land. The Organic Statutes represented an advance constitutionally but also granted full proprietorship to the boyars and rendered the peasants' tenure even more precarious. To be sure, such a process is not unusual; in a society which is becoming more articulated the emerging ruling elements, which from a national aspect represent an advance by strengthening and organizing the state, may achieve their position at the expense of the more amorphous body of that society.

Because of the weakness and precarious position of the Rumanian state, preoccupation with national prestige outweighed and often ran counter to concern for social reform. In the abortive revolution of 1848 the young revolutionaries, educated in France, were undoubtedly fired by ideals of freedom and the rights of man, but more from desire to create in Rumania a proper modern state than from direct interest in the sufferings of the peasant. The manifestoes issued by the Muntenian revolutionaries promised land but at the same time, partly out of fear of Russian intervention, enjoined the peasants to shun violence and to continue working for the boyars.

Similarly, critics of conditions provoking the 1907 revolt show concern for Rumania's position as a nation. Radu Rosetti, for example, believed the threat of foreign intervention which such an outbreak might produce to be one of the most dangerous features of the peasant uprising. Despite his sympathy for the peasants and desire for reform, he pressed for a strong army and an increase in the village gendarmerie, to prevent a repetition of the disorders of 1907 and to show the peasants that the law would be enforced.[27] The socialist Dobrogeanu-Gherea, approaching the question from a different point of view, was equally anxious to maintain Rumania's independence. Fearing that the many similarities between Rumania and tsarist Russia might lead the latter to "regard the Moldo-Wallachian provinces as an easy prey," [28] he urged that Rumania must be protected from tsarist advances by the introduction and preservation of liberal institutions, completely unlike those of Russia. The populist Constantin Stere flatly stated that Rumania could not afford the "luxury of a revolutionary party," since in Rumania's uncertain position such activity invited foreign intervention.[29]

Consequently, although many economic and social tensions disturbed Rumania, and it was obvious that the boyars would not on their own initiative undertake any reforms likely to change the established order, there was little organized revolutionary activity or even revolutionary thinking. On the other hand, the prevalent sense of national insecurity also made the ruling groups more cautious in the exercise of power. King Carol I, a German prince who had been called to the throne in 1866, could not pretend to be an autocratic tsar. On more than one occasion the king, for reasons of national interest, advocated reform and undertook to soften the obstinacy of the boyars, who were likewise sensitive to real pressure from above or below and frequently showed themselves accommodating and flexible when threatened with serious resistance.

Rumania's weak power position led many of its political leaders to seek both political and ideological support from the West. Western political and constitutional forms were adopted wholesale: the Constitution of 1866 was based on Belgium's model, the legal system was taken from the Code Napoléon. Imitation of Western institutions had two different and contrary results. On one level, many

27. Rosetti, *op. cit.,* p. 668.
28. Dobrogeanu-Gherea, *op. cit.,* p. 45.
29. Constantin Stere, "Socialdemocratism sau poporanism," *Viaţa românească* (January, 1908), p. 50.

of these institutions naturally became mere façades to conceal a much cruder reality. Party politics, for example, bore a very superficial resemblance to those of nineteenth-century England: two principal parties, the Liberals and the Conservatives, alternated in office. But the reality behind this two-party system was altogether different. Politics were based on a very narrow franchise,[30] the parties themselves tended to be coteries surrounding a dominant personality or family, and there were constant factions and party splits. Both the Conservatives and the Liberals obtained their support from the landowners, the principal distinction between them being that the Conservatives were usually the explicit spokesmen of the large agrarian interests, whereas the Liberals were increasingly interested in making Rumania a strong modern (i.e., commercial and industrial) state and held the controlling positions in the growing financial institutions.

In the field of law the Rumanians demonstrated what Dobrogeanu-Gherea correctly called a "mania for legislation." A flood of laws was continually being passed—elegantly rendered by men who had taken their law course at Paris—but with remarkably little effect. Some were inapplicable at the outset, few were administered properly, and most were soon forgotten by all concerned, with no effort made to examine their consequences. Other examples could be cited from the fields of public finance, civil rights, and the press to illustrate the abyss lying between political and constitutional forms and actual practice. The persistence of this dualism right up to the 1940's has undoubtedly had a corrupting effect upon Rumanian politics and society.

Notwithstanding these contradictions, which have struck all foreign observers in the past century, the very introduction of Western paraphernalia had certain important positive effects. A peasant who had been inducted, under universal conscription, into the army, who could read in the press (or have read to him) about agrarian disturbances in Sicily, Ireland, or Russia, or who heard the charges and countercharges of the political parties, however rhetorical these may have been—such a peasant was moving out of the closed circle of the village. This is evidenced in the active role played by ex-army sergeants, clerks, and schoolteachers in the 1907 uprising. Moreover, the mere existence of constitutional and legal devices, however inoperative they may have been, provided potential channels for change and increased the flexibility of the existing order. Thus, in spite of the fact that changes were apt to prove illusory rather than real,

30. A system of electoral colleges, rather like that of Prussia before 1918, assured a preponderant strength in the assembly to the landowners and the wealthy urban groups.

that an endless series of palliatives and half-measures would take the place of real reforms, even so vigorous a critic of Rumanian institutions as Dobrogeanu-Gherea held that the presence of liberal institutions set Rumania in favorable contrast to tsarist Russia.[31]

In short, while economic and social tensions precipitated the 1907 revolt, the political situation prevented it from becoming more than a social eruption. It remained a revolt and not the initial stage of a revolution.

The Aftermath of 1907

The peasant uprising frightened the rulers of Rumania into attempting some measures of reform. A law on agricultural contracts was designed to protect the peasant by regulating agreements between him and the landlord or tenant, by prohibiting certain forms of rent in labor, by instituting communal grazing lands, and by establishing regional committees to fix agricultural wages and rents. This law was never really applied and quickly fell altogether into disuse. The proprietors preferred informal and unwritten agreements, which the law did not cover, and few peasants dared to demand application of the law for fear of being driven from the estate.[32]

A second law created a state-supported Rural Office to aid in the transfer of land from large properties to the peasants. Up to the beginning of 1912, however, the Rural Office had bought only 76,000 hectares, had divided up 15,000 hectares, and had sold to the peasants only 6,500 hectares.[33] A third law, by limiting the size of leases to 4,000 hectares of cultivable land, attacked the large agricultural trusts held in lease. A fourth law established cooperatives for renting land. It was probably the most successful; between 1908 and 1916 the land rented by the cooperatives increased from 133,000 hectares to 410,000 hectares.[34]

Although these laws were heralded as introducing a new conception into Rumanian life, *socialism de stat*—state intervention on behalf of the peasants—they really provide only examples of Rumanian legislative escapism. They but scratched the surface of the problem and were "fated to disappear without trace in the quicksand of Rumanian public life." [35] The state socialism proclaimed by the Liberals had very little to do with socialism in any Western sense of the term but more closely resembled the paternalistic policies of mercantilism.

31. Dobrogeanu-Gherea, *op. cit.*, p. 46.
32. Ilie S. Diaconescu, *Chestiunea ţărănească în România* (Bucarest, 1928), p. 115.
33. *Ibid.*, p. 120.
34. *Ibid.*, p. 124.
35. Mitrany, *op. cit.*, p. 89.

II

WAR AND AGRARIAN REFORM, 1913–21

The Balkan and First World Wars

THE relative calm and the economic revival which followed the 1907 revolt were interrupted shortly by the outbreak of war. Rumania's part in the Second Balkan War was a brief excursion across the Danube into Bulgaria to obtain Southern Dobrogea, but that campaign had an important effect on the agrarian question. Rumanian troops saw in Bulgaria a land of small holdings, without great landowners or large tenants, where the villages were better built and the fields more successfully tilled than in Rumania. The Liberal leader Ion I. C. Brătianu, returning from Bulgaria, published an article in the party organ *Indépendance Roumaine* in the autumn of 1913, in which he advocated a reform of the franchise and an expropriation of large properties to provide the peasants with land. This statement marked an abrupt shift in Liberal party policy, as in the years immediately after 1907 the Liberal leaders had declared themselves opposed to expropriation. Whether Brătianu was reading the signs of the times or whether he was making a calculated political move to oust the Conservatives, then in power, the question of land reform by expropriation had at last been taken up by one of the major political parties.

The Liberals were called to power in December, 1913. Elections were held in February, 1914, and the new Liberal assembly voted for the principle of revising the articles of the Constitution of 1866 relating to the inviolability of property and to the franchise. A constituent assembly, elected in June, 1914, appointed two commissions to prepare the reforms. At this point the First World War broke out and became the exclusive object of attention. The national interest outweighed the social. The constituent assembly was not reconvened until three years later; the commission for land reform met twice, but according to one of its members, "No work was done at all. In 1914 —nothing; in 1915—nothing; that was all its preparatory work." [1]

The history of Rumania in the First World War is an exceedingly complex intermingling of international, national, and social crosscurrents. When war came Rumania remained neutral, although it had

1. Quoted in Mitrany, *The Land and the Peasant in Rumania,* p. 98.

been party to the Triple Alliance (by a treaty which had been kept a complete secret from the Rumanian people). For two years it held this position while the Allies and the Central Powers attempted to outbid one another in promises of territory. The Allies, however, were in the better bargaining position: they could offer the Habsburg lands, Transylvania and Bucovina, as against Russian Bessarabia. The entry of Bulgaria on the side of the Central Powers and the initial successes of the Russian 1916 offensive tipped the balance in favor of the Allies. On August 27, 1916 the government declared war on Austria-Hungary.

Rumania immediately met military disaster. The Russian offensive came to a halt, and the anticipated Allied offensive in the Balkans, sufficient to occupy the Bulgarians, failed to materialize. The Rumanian assault on Transylvania was repulsed; the German General Mackensen successfully counterattacked from Bulgaria. With the German occupation of Bucarest in December, 1916, the Rumanian government withdrew to Iași, the capital of Moldavia. After a brief period of calm, the entire situation on the Eastern Front was altered by the Russian Revolution.

The February Revolution had an immediate effect upon the Rumanian situation. Russian and Rumanian troops were in close contact on the Moldavian front; the revolutionary ferment spreading among the Russian soldiers, the organization of soldiers' councils, and the agitation for taking over the land could easily have been communicated to the Rumanians. This revolutionary atmosphere, combined with military defeat and the occupation of much of the kingdom by the Germans, rendered the Rumanian government's position extremely precarious. At this critical juncture King Ferdinand [2] visited the front in April, 1917, and made the following declaration to the troops: [3]

Sons of peasants, who, with your own hands, have defended the soil on which you were born, on which your lives have been passed, I, your King, tell you that besides the great recompense of victory which will assure for every one of you the nation's gratitude, you have earned the right of being masters, in a larger measure, of that soil upon which you fought.

Land will be given you. I, your King, am the first to set the example; and you will also take a larger part in public affairs.

That there was need for such a move to bolster the morale of the troops and to ward off imminent danger of revolution is shown in a

2. King Carol I died in October, 1914, and was succeeded by his nephew Ferdinand I.
3. Mitrany, op. cit., p. 101.

speech of May 27, 1917 by Professor N. Basilescu, who had been one of the few to foresee the 1907 uprising: "This is the state of mind in the country: disbelief in the government, disbelief in Parliament, disbelief in the constituted authority. . . . Today as yesterday revolution appears to the Rumanian peasant the only possible means for him to resolve the great case between him and the proprietors of estates." [4] The eleventh-hour move by the king, which was supported by both the parties, seems to have been instrumental in averting trouble and in encouraging the troops. In the final Russian offensive of July, 1917, the Rumanian troops made a brave showing against the Germans and fought valiantly at the battles of Mărăşti (July 28) and Mărăşeşti (August 12–19).

The paternalistic tone of the king's address was also apparent, however, in the steps taken to carry out his proclamation. No peasant delegate participated in the constituent assembly which convened in 1917, and the bill passed by that assembly was simply a compromise worked out by the leaders of the Liberal and Conservative parties. Under Article 19 of the 1866 Constitution, property was inviolable; it could be expropriated only for reasons of public utility, narrowly defined as communications, public health, and national defense. Hence, to expropriate land for the purpose of distributing it to the peasants, it was necessary to amend the constitution.

The 1917 amendment extended the definition of public utility to include expropriation for the purpose of increasing peasant holdings. Cultivable land belonging to the crown and to public and private institutions and all rural properties belonging to foreigners and absentee owners were to be expropriated in their entirety. In addition, 2,000,000 hectares of cultivable land were to be expropriated from private properties (including absentee holdings) of over 100 hectares, the expropriation to be based on a progressive scale which was not defined. Thus, no maximum limit was set to properties. The figure of 2,000,000 hectares was not based on any agricultural criteria but represented a compromise between the amounts proposed by the Liberals and the Conservatives. The chief fault of this amendment was that it was not itself a law for expropriation but only set forth the principles of such a law. Section 5 of the amended Article 19 provided for the promulgation of a law to be passed six months after the national liberation by a two-thirds majority, usually required only for constitutional amendments. If this law were not passed, there would be no land reform.

With the October Revolution, Russia's withdrawal from the war,

4. Quoted in Diaconescu, *Chestiunea ţărănească în România*, p. 141.

and the collapse of the Eastern Front, Rumania was in a hopeless military position, and in March, 1918, it sued for peace. The pro-German Alexandru Marghiloman, who had remained behind in Bucarest, was entrusted with a new government. This government dissolved the constituent assembly, and Marghiloman declared that "the whole agrarian problem must be taken up anew from the beginning."

During the brief term of the Marghiloman government, Constantin Garoflid, Minister of Agriculture, introduced a series of agrarian measures: obligatory leases, the reorganization of the Ministry of Agriculture, and the organization of agricultural workers. Garoflid, though a Conservative and a landowner, had long been opposed to the latifundiary system in Rumania and desired to build up a prosperous medium peasantry. He regarded the 1917 amendment as "not a scientific work but an electoral manifesto." Although previously recognizing the need for expropriation, he considered such an extreme measure unsuited to wartime conditions and advocated forced leases of land to the peasants as a temporary solution. Much in Garoflid's program was conducive to a rational development of Rumanian agriculture. He may even have had in mind a progressive series of reforms, but his proposals were open to the criticism that in Rumania a policy advocating such moderation and gradualness most often meant doing nothing at all. His program, however, was not even to be begun.

The collapse of the Central Powers in the autumn of 1918, Rumania's reentry into the war, and the withdrawal of Mackensen's forces again reversed the situation. The Marghiloman government was dismissed and its laws declared null and void. With the breakdown of the Central Powers, chaos spread through eastern Europe. Revolutionary conditions prevailed in Russia, Austria, Hungary, and Bulgaria. In Rumania a dry year, combined with the dislocations caused by the war and the German occupation, left the peasants hard pressed for food. The action of the Marghiloman government in dissolving the constituent assembly had increased their doubts in the good faith of any government. Tension was heightened by the revolutionary activity among the Rumanians in the neighboring regions of Transylvania, Bucovina, and Bessarabia, which had been or were shortly to be incorporated in Greater Rumania.

The Agrarian Reforms of 1918–21

Immediately after the armistice, on November 12, 1918, King Ferdinand issued a new proclamation reaffirming his pledge of 1917.

Under the pressure of events the government did not bother to follow the formalities prescribed in the 1917 amendment but quickly drafted a decree-law, to be ratified subsequently by the parliament. This decree-law of December 15, 1918, laid down the norms under which land was immediately to be expropriated. Some of the leading provisions were as follows: [5]

a) As in the constitutional amendment, arable crown and mortmain land as well as foreign and absentee properties were completely expropriated.

b) The amount of 2,000,000 hectares was to be expropriated on a sliding scale from private properties of over 100 hectares. This rather arbitrary scale did represent an advance upon the 1917 amendment in limiting all properties to 500 hectares, but it made no provision for geographical differences, relative land hunger, or rational organization of estates. The law based the expropriation on properties rather than on proprietorship, to the benefit of the landowner with multiple holdings. Moreover, the relation between the scale of expropriation and the 2,000,000 hectares to be obtained was not accurately computed, and the expropriation actually fell short by some 450,000 hectares.

c) Compensation for expropriated land was to be based on a number of factors: price of sale in the region for five years prior to 1916, regional level of rent, evaluation by credit institutions, net income per hectares, etc., but was not to exceed twenty times the regional rental rate. Payments to proprietors were to be made by 5 per cent state bonds, redeemable in fifty years. The state was to contribute up to 35 per cent of the cost.

d) Peasant associations were to be created to serve as temporary recipients of the transferred land. The law went into little detail as regards resettlement, which was covered later by the law of 1921.

Ion I. C. Brătianu, who had headed the government on December 14, 1918, resigned on September 27, 1919, in a dispute with the Allies on the peace settlement. King Ferdinand accepted the resignation and formed a nonparty cabinet under General Vaitoianu to hold a general election. This election, virtually the first to be uncontrolled in Rumanian history, produced surprising results. The Liberals lost most of their seats in the Old Kingdom, and after some delay a bloc made up of the newly formed Peasant party and the National party of Transylvania assumed office.

During its brief term this government, with the Transylvanian Vaida-Voevod as Premier and Ion Mihalache as Minister of Agricul-

5. Full summaries of this and the subsequent agrarian law of 1921 are given in Diaconescu, *op. cit.,* pp. 148–334, and Mitrany, *op. cit.,* pp. 111–182.

ture, introduced a bill for the resettlement of the peasants as well as for an extension of the expropriation. According to Mihalache, the Vaida government sought to make a new agrarian reform which was not based on the limited concept of the constituent assembly at Iași.[6] Although this bill was not passed, it is of importance as an early expression of the agrarian program of what was to become the National Peasant party.

The *exposé de motifs* of the bill granted that when promulgated the acts of 1917 and 1918 represented the only workable formulae, given the composition of parliament and the state of the nation, but stated that the incorporation of Bessarabia and the other provinces in Greater Rumania now made imperative further action on behalf of the peasants in the Old Kingdom, since the new provinces were enjoying extensive land reforms. By the terms of this bill expropriation was to be based on the total holdings of a proprietor, not on separate properties, and was extended to include property continuously rented for ten years prior to 1916. Private property in excess of 100 hectares of cultivable land was to be expropriated; in this the framers of the bill consciously followed the provisions of the relatively radical Bessarabian land reform. Exceptions, however, were made for estates organized as farms with a significant capital investment; these were limited to 250 hectares in densely populated regions and to 500 hectares in regions of sparse population. Property remaining after expropriation was not to be leased except to peasant cooperatives. In general, the bill was more radical than its predecessors in the Old Kingdom and represented a peasant point of view, both as regards the expropriation and the organization of agriculture, rather than a political compromise formulated by the landowners to avert peasant revolt.

As soon as the nature of Mihalache's bill became known, the old parties took steps to block it. The Minister of Agriculture was unable to obtain an audience with the king, allegedly as a result of Liberal intrigue. On March 12, 1920, after failing to obtain the king's approval to present the bill as a government measure, Mihalache presented it to the assembly as a private member's bill. At that session he warned: "But it should be known that if parliament has to leave, or if the government has to leave, it is because of a conspiracy by the whole oligarchy of all the boyar political parties." His prediction was realized; on the following day the government, which still held a substantial parliamentary majority, was dismissed by the crown in

6. For the text of this bill and the debate at its introduction, see the pamphlet published by the Federația Democrației, *Proectul legei de improprietărirea țăranilor* (Bucarest, 1920).

what has been called "the most questionable act of King Ferdinand's reign." [7] Although peasant disturbances, general instability, and the inexperience of the Vaida government have been cited as reasons for its downfall, it seems clear that its dismissal stemmed directly from the hostility of the landowners to the proposed agrarian bill.[8] Thus, the effort of the Peasant party to carry through a more radical reform by legal means was defeated.

The new premier, General Averescu, was selected because he was a popular military hero. He immediately ordered new elections and by the usual controls was able to obtain a majority for his People's party. Mihalache was replaced by Constantin Garoflid. Garoflid, as has been seen, was by no means opposed to land reform, but he did not approve of the emphasis upon large-scale expropriation and the creation of a multitude of small holdings. It was his task, however, to complete a measure based upon principles he had always attacked.

The second land reform law for the Old Kingdom was promulgated on July 17, 1921. Although primarily concerned with allotting land and resettling the peasants, it also extended expropriation to obtain the 450,000 hectares lacking after the 1918 decree-law. Expropriation was now based on proprietors rather than properties, and the old sliding scale was abandoned in favor of a more elastic measure which took account of regional geographic differences and relative land hunger.[9] Land left to the proprietor was to be determined at once,

7. R. W. Seton-Watson, *History of the Roumanians* (Cambridge, 1934), p. 551.

8. The attitude of the landowners at this time is shown in a circular distributed by the Union of Syndicates of Moldavian Landowners: "We, landowners, are firmly determined to oppose by all means, and especially by impeaching before the Court of Cassation, all those provisions of the decree-law of 1918, of the law for communal grazing, and of any future law or decree, which may conflict with the letter of the Constitution regarding the expropriation of land . . . To re-consecrate the intangible right of property, we demand that a law shall be passed which shall punish with hard labor for life whomsoever shall speak of expropriation again." Quoted in Mitrany, *op. cit.*, p. 114.

9. Land was left to the proprietors on the following basis:

	Land cultivated by owner (hectares)	Land cultivated by owner with important capital investments (hectares)
In highlands and hills	100	100
In plains, where demand for land was great	150	200
In plains, where demand for land was moderate	200	300
In plains, where demand for land was satisfied	250	500

but land to be expropriated was not to be taken over until it could be utilized. Thus expropriation was to be gradual, keeping pace with resettlement.

The 1921 law established a list of priorities of claims to receive land, determined primarily by war service rather than by economic considerations. Land to be distributed was divided into complementary lots for peasants with less than 5 hectares, full lots of 5 hectares, and colonization lots of 7 hectares. Provisions for grazing land had been made by a special act of September 24, 1920; these were supplemented by Article 23 of the law of 1921. Nothing was done with respect to woodlands and forest.

The problem of compensation created much confusion. The acts of 1917 and 1918 had merely limited compensation to not more than twenty times the regional rent for 1916. With the decline of the leu after the war, this compensation was deemed inadequate, and the 1921 law raised the rate to forty times the 1916 regional rent. Half the price was to be paid by the state. The peasants' payments were to extend over a period of twenty years, on condition of a 20 per cent payment at the outset.

The scattered distribution of peasant holdings in uneconomic strips was one of the chief hindrances to rational cultivation. Garoflid had always regarded consolidation as indispensable for a more productive agriculture, and Article 136 of the 1921 law stated that measures for consolidating holdings would be provided for in a special act. This act, however, never appeared, and scattered strips remained characteristic of Rumanian farming. One reason for inaction on such an important issue was that the peasants themselves were not striving for consolidation as they were for more land. Mihalache, while granting that "none of us could be against consolidation on principle," feared that the dangers of misapplication under existing circumstances were greater than the probable benefits.[10]

A related problem was the practice of dividing holdings equally among heirs. The law of 1864 had made peasant allotments inalienable but had not prevented their fragmentation through inheritance. Article 126 of the 1921 law limited the splitting of allotted land by succession to a minimum of two hectares in the plains and one hectare in the hills and highlands. Article 127 permitted the owner of a property to leave it to only one heir, with a money payment to the others. Under Article 133 a landowner was allowed to declare indivisible an area up to 50 hectares. Article 120 reversed previous practice by

10. I. Mihalache, *Dreptul țăranilor la pământ, islazuri și paduri* (Bucarest, 1922), pp. 129–130.

permitting the sale of small property, on certain conditions and after five years. Article 122, however, limited purchases to 25 hectares in the hills and 100 hectares in the plains.[11]

In general, the 1921 law was more carefully drafted than that of 1918 and did attempt to remedy some of the technical errors of previous legislation. The economic effects of these land reforms, which together were reported officially to have expropriated nearly 2,800,-000 hectares of land in the Old Kingdom, will be discussed in a later chapter.[12] The acts of 1918 and 1921 were, however, essentially defensive political rather than economic measures. As Mihalache said in his critique of the decree-law of 1918,

it is not the work of a social concept, not the response to a social ideal, not the work of conviction; under the threat of the events of 1917, it is the continuation of a series of land settlements on the model of 1881 and 1889, it is the over-simplified concept that a new equilibrium between large property and small property must be stabilized in order that there be future peace.

In his opinion, "The ruling class has made only such concessions as were necessary to assure its own existence. The reforms have been a kind of safety valve." [13]

The safety valve, however, was successful. Despite its very precarious position, Rumania passed through the revolutionary storm in eastern Europe without an overthrow of the established order. Several reasons explain this success. A decisive factor, doubtless, was the flexibility of the ruling groups. Notwithstanding the obduracy of many members of the landed oligarchy and in spite of efforts to avoid or delay the reform, the landowners did at least yield sufficiently to prevent an outbreak. Their recalcitrance between 1917 and 1921 was in inverse ratio to the amount of peasant unrest. Moreover, the king, although conservative socially, was able to take the correct steps at two critical moments, in April, 1917, and in November, 1918.

Apart from the flexibility of the landowners, certain other forces were at work. Among the Conservatives, the stronghold of the landed interests, there were such men as Garoflid who recognized the failings of Rumanian agriculture and desired to make thorough-going changes, though along lines different from those followed. In the

11. For subsequent modifications, in 1925 and 1929, of these provisions for sale, see below, p. 125 and pp. 156–157.

12. The difficult task of discovering just what the land reforms accomplished in redistributing property is discussed below, pp. 48–49, and in the Appendix.

13. Mihalache, op. cit., pp. 5, 29.

Liberal party, the primary interest was in the expansion of industry, commerce, and finance, and since 1913 the party had officially stood for expropriation. In several respects the Liberal position was unfortunate since it had neither the reforming zeal of the new Peasant party nor the Conservatives' interest in the improvement of agriculture. The Liberals tended to regard land as a bone to be thrown to the peasants when the howls of the latter seemed menacing or detrimental to the national interest. Such a view was apt to neglect the economic aspects of the agrarian problem and to reduce it to a question of finding more land for distribution. Nevertheless, this Liberal attitude did make for change. Finally, once the question of land reform became the order of the day, the mere pressure of politics led the parties, if only for electoral reasons, to make the appearance of favoring reform.

A second factor was that the land laws, despite delays and omissions, were sufficiently extensive to pacify the peasants. A great deal of land changed hands, and the Rumanian reform was the most far-reaching of all the postwar agrarian measures in eastern Europe (excluding Russia, of course).

A third factor was concern for the national interest, which, as noted above, has usually been of primary importance in determining Rumanian internal policy. Notwithstanding military defeats, enormous human losses, and devastation of land, Rumania emerged from the war a victorious power with doubled population and territory.[14] The mere fact of being victorious and having achieved the national aim of Greater Rumania undoubtedly served to mitigate social tensions. The parties were in agreement in glorifying and protecting the new national unity; since Rumania was surrounded by states from which it had obtained territory, the defense of the new frontiers was a major concern of all postarmistice governments.

The very violence of the Russian Revolution, particularly the Bolshevik Revolution, served to create an opposing reaction in Rumania, heightened by the territorial dispute over Bessarabia. The political parties, including the Peasant party, were exceedingly hostile to bolshevism, which became the ultimate term of abuse in political debates. Mihalache had been sent to Bessarabia during the war to carry on antibolshevist propaganda, and one of his appeals for a more extensive land reform was that in the future the peasants should not be tempted to look beyond Rumania's frontier on the Dniester for better conditions. Fear of Soviet communism was one of the cardinal fea-

14. The area of Rumania in 1915 was 137,900 square kilometers; in 1919, 294,000 square kilometers. Its population in 1913 was 7,625,000; in 1919, 15,500,000.

tures of Rumanian policy for the next twenty-five years, and in the international councils Rumania was to stress its role as the European bulwark against bolshevism.[15]

Agrarian Reform in the New Territories

Thus far only the agrarian reform in the Old Kingdom has been considered, and it does provide the central thread of the agrarian question in the interwar period. But as a result of the war Rumania also acquired Bessarabia from Russia, Bucovina from Austria, and Transylvania from Hungary. The agrarian problems in these three provinces were different in several respects from that of the Old Kingdom; the separate laws passed for each of the provinces further increased the complexity of the Rumanian agrarian situation after the First World War.

1. BESSARABIA

Bessarabia, which had formed a part of the principality of Moldavia, was ceded by the Turks to Russia in 1812 at the Treaty of Bucarest, in return for the evacuation of the remainder of Moldavia and Wallachia.[16] Three southern districts were returned to Moldavia after the Crimean War, but reverted to Russia after the War of 1877. The population was predominantly Rumanian, though large numbers of Ukrainians and Bulgarians inhabited the southern districts. In the last decades of the nineteenth century the tsarist regime undertook to Russify Bessarabia but without marked success. The Moldavian boyars in Bessarabia were notoriously obscurantist, and the province was a "natural breeding ground of such movements as the Black Hundreds." [17]

15. F. Borkenau, in his study, *The Communist International* (London, 1938), p. 99, attaches great importance to the Rumanian agrarian reform in this connection: "The agrarian reform in Rumania was perhaps the strongest single obstacle that opposed the advance of Bolshevism towards the West. It was very far from solving all problems, even for the peasantry, but for a decade it took the sharp edge off them. Revolutionary trends among the proletariat remained, but the proletariat alone was nothing in Rumania, and revolutionism among its members was more of a convulsion than a clearly defined movement."

16. The current Soviet interpretation of this event appears to be that in the eighteenth century the Moldavian and Wallachian boyars had sought the incorporation of the principalities in Russia as the sole means of escaping the Turkish yoke. This act of liberation was taking place during the Turko-Russian war of 1806. The threat of Napoleon, however, forced Tsar Alexander to come to terms with the Turks, so that only Bessarabia was fortunate enough to be liberated and incorporated in the tsarist empire. See A. Dolnik, *Bessarabiya pod vlastyu Rumynskikh boyar, 1918–1940 gg.* (Moscow, 1945), p. 5.

17. R. W. Seton-Watson, *op. cit.*, p. 563.

Although the general agrarian structure of Bessarabia resembled that of the Old Kingdom, certain differences developed during the century of Russian control. The emancipation of 1861 corresponded roughly to the Cuza reform, but the allotted land, *nadyel*, was given over not to the peasant but to the peasant commune, the mir. While the Bessarabian allotments at the time of the emancipation were greater than for most parts of Russia, there was, as in Rumania, an increasing land hunger arising from the nature of the reform and the rapidly expanding population. The Stolypin reforms, after the 1905 revolution, worked to increase individual peasant ownership and to break up the mir, but by the outbreak of the war nadyel land still constituted the largest category of property. In Russia after 1907 the sale of land to the peasants by the large landowners was widespread and especially so in Bessarabia. Although a comparison of the pre-1914 distribution of property in Bessarabia with that in Rumania is difficult to make since the Russian returns were based upon distinctions between types of ownership rather than size, the general order of the problem was similar in the two regions.[18]

The history of Bessarabia's incorporation into Rumania is still bitterly controversial. Only the major developments can be sketched here. Immediately after the February Revolution, two political currents began to emerge in Bessarabia, an agrarian-revolutionary (which tended to be hostile to Rumania as a land dominated by boyars) and a nationalist-Moldavian. From July, 1917, the peasants began to seize land, and by the end of the year some two-thirds of the large property had been taken over. A military committee, representative of the Moldavian element, convoked a congress which, on October 21–23, 1917, passed a resolution in favor of the "historical and political autonomy" of Bessarabia and decided to convoke a national council (*Sfatul Țării*). The situation was utterly disorganized by the October Revolution and the Ukrainian break with the Bolsheviks. The *Sfat*, which was strongly Moldavian nationalist, was opposed to the centralism of the new Bolshevik regime. On December 2, 1917, it announced the formation of a Democratic Moldavian Republic as a self-governing unit in the Federative Democratic Russian Republic.

A crisis was reached in January, 1918, when Rumanian troops, sent to Bessarabia at the request of the Sfat, ousted the Bolshevik Soviets which had gained power in several cities and had attempted to supersede the Sfat. Shortly thereafter, the Sfat proclaimed the independence of the Moldavian republic. When Rumania sued for peace in March, 1918, the Germans favored the Rumanian interest

18. For statistics on land distribution in Bessarabia see the Appendix.

in Bessarabia. On April 9, 1918, the Sfat by open vote—86 to 3, with 36 delegates abstaining—declared for the union of Bessarabia with Rumania, but with important reservations: the Bessarabian land reform was to be maintained and the province was to have administrative autonomy.[19]

In Bessarabia, unlike the Old Kingdom, the redistribution of land was achieved by the direct action of the peasants. As a consequence, there were doubts, to say the least, among the cultivators as to the desirability of uniting with Rumania. Mihalache reported that the Bessarabian peasants said to him, "We will not unite with Rumania, since Rumania belongs to the *ciocoi*, who have fleeced the peasants." [20] Before Bessarabia was united with Rumania, however, there was a retreat from the first wave of land seizures. The Sfat succeeded in retaining 50 hectares for each proprietor, and subsequently the area was increased to 100 hectares. The land reform law proposed by the Sfat was subsequently ratified in Rumania by the decree-law of December 22, 1918, but 47 of the 73 articles of this decree-law were later modified by the law adopted by the Rumanian assembly in 1920.

The Bessarabian reform as finally drafted expropriated in full: former state and crown domains, mortmain estates, monastic properties (except one-half hectare for each monk), estates belonging to towns (except land reserved for town planning), estates of foreigners, and estates farmed out for five successive years. One million hectares were to be expropriated from private property, including all properties above 100 hectares (multiple holdings were counted as one property). Peasant allotments were set at 6–8 hectares, with complementary lots for peasants lacking the minimum. Compensation was based on rent obtained in the period 1910–14, capitalized at 5½ per cent. The price of the land, in general, was set at 800 lei per hectare, over the protests of the peasants who maintained that they had obtained the land through the revolution. The state assumed 25 per cent of the price. According to official Rumanian statistics, the total area expropriated was about 1,492,000 hectares.[21]

19. The Bessarabian controversy has centered on the actions of the Sfat: whether it was representative and whether its decisions reflected the wishes of the people. In the Soviet view, the Sfat was merely the tool of the landlord counterrevolutionaries, and the ousted Soviets the true representatives of the peasant masses. Dolnik, *op. cit.*, p. 20. There have been doubts as to the validity of the vote of April 9, 1918, and assertions that it was made under Rumanian military pressure. The high number of abstentions and the open vote would lead to the suspicion that it was scarcely an ideal referendum.

20. *Proectul legei de improprietărirea ţăranilor,* (Bucarest, 1920), p. 54. Ciocoi was the peasant's term for the boyar's pack of retainers.

21. For further statistics on the Bessarabian land reform see the Appendix.

It has been held that Bessarabia provided a revolutionary leaven for the rest of Rumania. To a degree this is true. Even before the First World War both socialist and populist theories were transmitted from Russia to Rumania through Bessarabia. The Bessarabian land reform had an effect upon the policy of the nascent Rumanian Peasant party; the exposé de motifs of the Peasant party's reform bill of 1920 argued that the law passed by Sfatul Țării for Bessarabia made equally extensive measures mandatory for all of Rumania. Mihalache, in defending his bill, pointed out that the Bucarest assembly was unwilling to accept for the Old Kingdom measures they had previously ratified for Bessarabia, and asked whether the impression was to remain that the Bessarabian peasant had achieved more for himself through revolution than had the peasant of the Old Kingdom through the good offices of the parliament.[22]

But the radical influences coming from Bessarabia were less than the contrary influence of Rumania upon Bessarabia. Successive formulations and arrangements regarding Bessarabia progressively reduced the extent of the agrarian reform, took away the administrative autonomy of the province, and extended the centralized administration of Bucarest. As a result, regardless of the original sentiment favoring incorporation in Rumania, Bessarabia was a disaffected area throughout the interwar period, with much the most corrupt administration of any Rumanian province.

2. BUCOVINA

Bucovina, which had formed the northern portion of the principality of Moldavia, was ceded by the Turks to Austria in 1775. The population was originally largely Rumanian; in 1848 Rumanians numbered 209,000 as against 108,000 Ruthenians. This proportion altered in subsequent decades until by 1910 the Ruthenians were the largest group, though not a majority, outnumbering the Rumanians 305,000 to 233,000. There were also some 102,000 Jews and 66,000 Germans at that date. In general, the Ruthenian population was concentrated in the northern part of Bucovina, the Rumanian in the south.

By the treaty of alliance of August 17, 1916, between the Allies and Rumania, the latter was to receive all of Bucovina to the Prut River. At the time of the peace conference, it was suggested that part of northern Bucovina be included, for ethnic reasons, in eastern Galicia. This suggestion was dropped with the collapse of Galician au-

22. *Proectul legei de improprietărirea țăranilor*, pp. 29 and 58.

tonomy because of the desire not to increase the number of Ukrainians under Polish rule. The incorporation of Bucovina had none of the turbulence that accompanied Bessarabia's. A general congress met on November 28, 1918, and voted for union with Rumania.

Before the First World War, of the cultivable area of Bucovina, holdings over 100 hectares occupied 25 per cent, holdings between 10 and 100 hectares 27 per cent, and small holdings 48 per cent. (If the very extensive forest lands are included the holdings over 100 hectares covered more than 60 per cent of the surface of the province.) Large properties were less dominant than in the Old Kingdom and medium properties much more important, partly because of German colonization and efforts by the Austrian government to foster this category of holding.

The decree-law of September 7, 1919, for the Bucovina land reform was ratified by the law of July, 1921, which modified the decree in favor of the landowners and reduced the extent of land to be expropriated. Land reform in Bucovina was made under more peaceful circumstances than elsewhere and was more carefully worked out. The state was given a right to reserve land for general needs, and the landowner was allowed continued use of his land until it was actually taken over. The reform expropriated in full: estates of foreigners and absentees, mortmain estates, estates of persons who had lost their civil rights, and estates farmed out for more than nine years. Expropriation of private properties was on a sliding scale beginning at 100 hectares and permitting a maximum of 250 hectares on properties having considerable inventory and equipment. Scattered properties belonging to the same owner were counted as one. The allotment of land was made in lots of 4–8 hectares, colonization lots of 5 hectares, and complementary lots of not less than ¼ hectare for peasants having less than 4 hectares. Compensation to landowners was approximately the same as in the Old Kingdom, and the state assumed 50 per cent of the cost. The peasant could pay in whole or in part, the remainder becoming a mortgage payable in 50 years at 5 per cent. According to official statistics the total area expropriated in Bucovina was about 76,000 hectares.[23]

3. Transylvania

The disputed history of Transylvania and the endless controversy that has raged between the Rumanians and the Hungarians

23. For further statistics on the distribution of land in Bucovina and the effects of the land reform see the Appendix.

are far too complex for inclusion here. Whatever the origins of the Transylvanian population, at the outbreak of the First World War the Rumanians constituted a majority of the inhabitants of this region; with the collapse of Austria-Hungary, the Transylvanian Rumanians, along with the other ethnic groups in the empire moved to break away. On October 12, 1918, the Rumanian National party of Transylvania drafted a resolution demanding the right of self-determination. A national assembly was called at Alba Iulia on December first and passed a resolution in favor of the union of all Rumanians. The basis of this union was to be:

1) full national liberty for all races;
2) full autonomy for all regions;
3) a democratic regime with general, direct, equal, and secret elections;
4) complete liberty of press, assembly, and association;
5) radical agrarian reform;
6) equitable conditions for industrial workers.

A Governing Council (*Consiliul Dirigent*), under Iuliu Maniu, was established as the temporary administration. The Treaty of Trianon assigned Transylvania and the adjacent regions of Maramureș, Crișana, and the Banat to Rumania.

Servile tenures had been abolished somewhat earlier in Transylvania than in the Old Kingdom, and the relative importance of medium properties reflected the generally higher level of cultivation. Nevertheless, there was a great disparity between large and small properties, a disparity intensified by the national question. The Rumanians were almost entirely peasants, and most of the large estates belonged to Hungarians. Reliable information, however, is lacking regarding the distribution of land either by size of property or by nationality; according to Hungarian critics of Rumanian statistics, no exact figures have ever been available for the land distribution in 1919 in the total area annexed by Rumania.[24] The Rumanians have claimed that they held only 24 per cent of the total area and that 98 per cent of the properties over 100 cadastral yokes (the yoke, used in Transylvania, equals .58 hectares) were held by non-Rumanians. While this claim may have been extreme, Hungarian sources grant that 87 per cent of the owners of properties exceeding 100 yokes were Magyars.

The project for the land reform, prepared in thirty-two sittings of the Governing Council, became a decree-law on September 12,

24. C. A. Macartney, *Hungary and Her Successors* (Oxford University Press, 1937), p. 316, n. 2.

1919, and was subsequently ratified by the law of July 23, 1921. In Transylvania, where economic life was more advanced and extensive cereal cultivation played a less dominant role than in the Old Kingdom, the agrarian reform while radical in intent was more broadly conceived and had numerous exceptions and exemptions. It expropriated in full: estates of foreigners, estates of certain public and private institutions, estates which had been leased for more than twelve consecutive years, and any estate land of more than 500 cadastral yokes. Below 500 yokes, land was expropriated on a sliding scale down to an exempted minimum of 200 yokes. If, however, further land were needed, property below 200 yokes could be expropriated. Multiple holdings by one proprietor were considered one. The size of allotments was not fixed. The order of preference was determined primarily by war service rather than by land need, but peasants owning more than 5 yokes were not to receive land until other demands had been satisfied. The Transylvanian reform went beyond the others in its provisions for communal woodlands, which were not created for the Old Kingdom, Bessarabia, and Bucovina until a law for the expropriation of forests was passed in 1924. Compensation for expropriated land was subject to less rigid limits and the payment to the landowner was prompter. According to official statistics about 1,664,-000 hectares were expropriated in Transylvania.[25]

The Rumanian land reforms, in the years 1918–21, did not, then, represent a unified program but varied considerably, depending upon geographical differences, previous agrarian conditions, and political circumstances. The reforms in Bessarabia and Transylvania reflected the more revolutionary spirit in those provinces; the complexities of the Transylvanian law and the attempt to relate it to the whole economy correspond to the generally higher level of Transylvanian agriculture and the presence of a nascent industry.

Notwithstanding these differences, however, which make it impossible to give a simple summary of the agrarian reform, the laws have certain common features: they were all based on expropriation in the "public interest" for the purpose of increasing peasant properties and communal pastures; although the decline of the leu in the 1920's almost destroyed the value of the compensation, the reforms were not planned as confiscations; and despite economic provisions of varying merit, the laws were not primarily economic reforms but social measures designed to appease the peasants' land hunger. More-

25. For further statistics on the effects of the reform in Transylvania see the Appendix.

over, the process of incorporating the new provinces into Greater Rumania did tend to level out the differences in the laws. The reform in the Old Kingdom was altered somewhat by the more radical atmosphere in the provinces. On the other hand, the Bessarabian, Bucovinan, and Transylvanian reforms were considerably modified by the time the parliament ratified them in 1921. National interest, as conceived of in Bucarest, demanded equilibrium, if not complete similarity, between the various agrarian laws.

An element of xenophobia, in the form of discrimination against foreign landowners and minorities, also appeared in the agrarian reforms and was the subject of the interminable case of the Hungarian optants, which was before the Council of the League of Nations throughout the 1920's. Unquestionably certain of the expropriation provisions were directed against the non-Rumanian minorities, and in Transylvania and Southern Dobrogea the execution of the reforms had a decidedly nationalist tinge. On the other hand, since the Rumanians in the new provinces usually included the poorest strata of the population, and many of the larger landowners were members of the minorities, it was inevitable that the leveling process of the land reforms should have benefited the Rumanians at the expense of the minorities. In any event, nationalist discrimination was a by-product of the land reforms, not a primary incentive.

At the conclusion of the First World War Rumania, in spite of terrible human and material losses, seemed to be entering a new and promising era. By an extraordinary combination of circumstances a united Greater Rumania had been achieved. The acquired territories with their resources and industry promised to add a new dimension to the Rumanian economy. The passage of the land reforms gave hope for greater social stability and the eventual growth of a prosperous peasant agriculture. The revolutionary fever subsided, the peasants had not revolted, a general strike of workers in 1920 had been successfully suppressed, and although new parties and politicians appeared on the scene, the continuity of the Rumanian monarchy and government stood unique in eastern Europe. But the two basic problems of Rumanian history remained: a weak power position and a backward economy. The first did not present an immediate threat because of the exhaustion of neighboring great powers through war and revolution. The task of adjusting the economy to a more advanced and rapidly changing world economy faced the nation immediately as Rumania began to repair the damage caused by the war.

III

AGRICULTURAL POPULATION AND PRODUCTION

T HE course of Rumanian politics between the wars can be understood only in its economic setting; urgent economic problems constantly demanded the attention of all governments, and at the same time the prevailing poverty and economic backwardness undermined political life and contributed powerfully to the emergence of the dictatorships. This and the following chapter sketch the general features of the economic framework, with particular emphasis upon agriculture and the demographic problem. Industry, commerce, and finance are considered primarily in their relation to the agrarian question.

Population [1]

According to the 1930 census, Rumania had a population of 18,057,028 persons, the largest of any state in eastern Europe with the exception of Poland. While the density, 61 persons per square kilometer in 1930, was less than that of the more highly industrialized states of western Europe, the population was increasing at a rapid rate. Rumania had one of the highest birth rates in non-Russian Europe as well as the highest death rate. In general, its population pattern resembled that of the other states of eastern Europe, especially Bulgaria, Yugoslavia, and the Soviet Ukraine, and was in marked contrast to the stable or declining populations of the West.

Eastern Europe is now passing through the phase of great population growth which began in England and western Europe in the eighteenth century and has since radiated eastward. This phenomenon, one of the most important in European history, appears to have followed a definite sequence: first, a high death rate and a high birth rate, more or less in balance, giving a stable or only slightly expanding population; then the death rate dropped rapidly; finally the birth rate dropped down to or below the death rate. The lag between the fall in the death rate and the subsequent fall in the birth rate produced the great expansion of population. From current evidence

1. More complete statistical information on the population is given in the Appendix.

it appears that in eastern Europe the birth rate has begun to decline, but its effect will not be reflected in the population for a number of years.

The decline of the death rate in the West resulted from the numerous social, hygienic, and nutritional improvements gradually introduced and disseminated over the last two centuries, all of which were slow in reaching eastern Europe. The subsequent fall in the Western birth rate appears to have been largely a conscious social restriction and not any decline in "national virility." [2] It generally accompanies a rise in living conditions and has shown a direct correlation with class differences.

The extent to which those factors bringing about the growth of population in the West apply to eastern Europe is not known with certainty. The fall in the eastern European death rate after the middle of the nineteenth century appears to have corresponded with the introduction of some of the social and hygienic improvements from the West, but it may also have resulted from a moderate improvement in internal and external security at a somewhat earlier date.[3]

Birth and death rates for Greater Rumania showed a decline during the interwar years, largely a result of drops in the rural rates. The rural birth rate in 1936, however, was still well above that of the towns (33.8 per thousand as against 21.4). The rate of natural increase, the excess of births over deaths, also displayed a perceptible decline, from over 14 per thousand inhabitants in the early 1920's to about 11 in the late 1930's. The birth rate fell greatly during the Second World War (to a low of 19.9 in 1945) and seems to have increased only slightly in the postwar years. The death rate having remained approximately the same, the rate of growth of Rumania's population has diminished tremendously under the exceptional conditions of the past decade.

Agricultural Overpopulation

While Rumania's over-all density of population is not very high as compared with that of western Europe, most of the people live on the land, and the agricultural population is quite dense. In 1941 the agricultural population of Rumania (minus Bessarabia, Northern Bucovina, Northern Transylvania, and Southern Dobrogea) represented 71.4 per cent of the total population and 94.4 per cent of the

2. Dudley Kirk, *Europe's Population in the Interwar Years* (League of Nations, 1946), p. 38.

3. A. M. Carr-Saunders, *World Population: Past Growth and Present Trends* (Oxford University Press, 1936), p. 80.

rural population.[4] There were 94.3 inhabitants of the agricultural population for every 100 hectares of agricultural land in private hands (including arable surface, meadow, vineyards, orchards, and pastures). Agricultural population was densest in the poor mountainous areas, in contrast to total population which was densest in the plains; in the Oltenian and Muntenian Carpathians 121.5 agricultural inhabitants occupied every 100 hectares of agricultural land in private hands, 112.8 in the Moldavian Carpathians and 108.3 in Bucovina.

That the density of Rumania's agricultural population was relatively high is shown in the following table, comparing Rumania (on the basis of earlier and somewhat different statistics) with other eastern European and some of the western European countries: [5]

Country	Density of population dependent upon agriculture per square kilometer of "arable-equivalent" * agricultural land, ca. 1930.
RUMANIA	79.7
Old Kingdom	79.9
Bessarabia	69.7
Bucovina	145.9
Transylvania	81.3
Bulgaria	95.4
Greece	86.7
Yugoslavia	100.1
Hungary	63.1
Poland	86.9
Austria	64.2
Czechoslovakia	69.4
Italy	53.4
Germany	52.1
France	28.8
Netherlands	81.7
Denmark	37.5
England and Wales	33.8

* "Arable-equivalent" is a statistical device to achieve a rough comparability between different types of land (arable, pasture, vineyards, etc.) used for agricultural purposes. A hectare of pasture land is clearly not equivalent to a hectare of arable.

The director of the Rumanian Central Institute of Statistics, in interpreting the results of the 1930 census, concluded that "These

4. Institutul Central de statistică, *Recensământal agricol al României din 1941* (Bucarest, 1945), Table 21.
5. Wilbert E. Moore, *Economic Demography of Eastern and Southern Europe* (League of Nations, 1945), pp. 197–204.

figures permit one to affirm that our country has arrived at the saturation point, and even at an agricultural overpopulation." [6] The term "overpopulation," however, has been subject to numerous interpretations and must be used cautiously.[7] In particular, in Rumania the issue of overpopulation has been too frequently brandished as a political weapon for contending parties.

Surplus population is sometimes defined in terms of an "optimum" population, one that achieves the maximum per capita real income. In such a case overpopulation would mean that a withdrawal of population from the land would increase per capita income since the marginal productivity of the surplus cultivators, given the law of diminishing returns, is less than the average per capita productivity. Apart from the manifold difficulties of determining such an optimum, this approach is somewhat artificial in the case of eastern Europe, where the problem of overpopulation is concerned not with any ideal optimum but with a possible Malthusian nightmare of mass suffocation. To be meaningful in this connection overpopulation must indicate that in some way more people are engaged in agriculture than are required for the type of cultivation prevailing, that they could be withdrawn from the soil without loss in agricultural production, the output of the surplus population being less than the loss occasioned by their presence (soil destruction, irrational holdings, etc.).[8]

It is clear that density alone does not determine overpopulation in this sense, since the Netherlands, for example, had a slightly higher agricultural density than Rumania but with entirely different social and economic consequences because of an intensive form of cultivation. The level of agricultural productivity, expressed in yield per unit of area is also a factor. That is, output per capita (C), which ultimately determines the level of existence, is equivalent to yield per unit of area (Y) divided by the density of agricultural population

$$(D): C = \frac{Y}{D}.$$

Now for purposes of general orientation it is possible to make a rough comparison of this equation for Rumania with that for non-

6. Sabin Manuila, *Structure et évolution de la population rurale* (Bucarest, 1940), p. 17.

7. For discussions of the definition of overpopulation see Moore, *op. cit.*, pp. 55–77; Carr-Saunders, *op. cit.*, pp. 330–331; and "The Problem of Surplus Agricultural Population," *International Journal of Agrarian Affairs, 1,* No. 1 (October, 1939); the entire issue is devoted to articles on the question.

8. If overpopulation is not defined in some such sense as this, it is necessary to consider alternative means of employment for the surplus population, unless the surplus is to be physically liquidated. This problem will be discussed presently in connection with town and country relations.

Russian Europe as a whole.[9] If we take Europe to be the norm,
$C = \dfrac{Y}{D}$, then the equivalent equation for Rumania is, very roughly,

$.48C = \dfrac{.69Y}{1.44D}$. That is, Rumania's per capita output in agriculture
is only 48 per cent of the European average because the yield is only
69 per cent as great and the density of agricultural population is 44
per cent greater. There are, however, marked regional differences
within Rumania. The situation in the Old Kingdom is approximately
the same as in Greater Rumania as a whole, but in Bucovina per
capita output is only 45 per cent of that for Europe, although yield
is 17 per cent above the European average $(.45C = \dfrac{1.17Y}{2.60D})$ because
of the extreme density of the population, over two and a half times
that of Europe. On the other hand, in Bessarabia the per capita output is low because of the low yield although the density of agricultural
population is only 24 per cent greater than that for Europe $(.45C =$
$\dfrac{.56Y}{1.24D})$. In Transylvania the per capita output is the highest in Rumania $(.51C = \dfrac{.74Y}{1.45D})$, a reflection of the generally more advanced
level of agriculture in that region which more than compensates for
the density of the population.

Some efforts were made in Rumania to calculate the hidden unemployment resulting from overpopulation. In 1933 A. Frunzanescu
and C. Vasiliu, after calculating the number of man-days required
to carry on a year's agricultural activity in Rumania, estimated that
only 43.66 per cent of the potential energy of agricultural labor
was actually employed in direct agricultural work, and not over 55
per cent in all farm activities.[10] An investigation of 200 peasant
farms of less than 3 hectares and of 100 farms between 3 and 5 hec-

9. See Wilbert E. Moore's work, *op. cit.*, which undertakes to convert European agricultural output and agricultural land into "crop units" and "arable equivalents,"
statistical devices to render commensurate different kinds of agricultural produce and
land. Relying on his basic figures I have used them here in a somewhat different manner.
See also Table VII in the Appendix.

10. A. Frunzanescu, *Munca omenească în actuală conjunctura agricolă* (Bucarest,
1935), cited in Madgearu, *Evoluţia economiei româneşti*, p. 48. Estimating an agricultural working population of 9,990,000 men, women, and children to be equivalent to
7,900,000 men, and assuming 235 working days a year, they arrived at a working potential of 1,865,100,000 man-days per year. They then calculated that the total man-
days necessary to achieve the various agricultural works in Rumania required only
814,400,000 man-days.

tares reached the conclusion that on farms under 3 hectares only 38 per cent of the available labor was being utilized and on farms between 3 and 5 hectares, only 60 per cent.[11]

Other indications of overpopulation during the interwar period were the continued expansion of arable at the expense of meadow and pasture (which is reflected in the decline of the number of cattle between 1921 and 1935 from 34 to 24 per 100 inhabitants), the increasing fragmentation of small properties and the extension of holdings under 3 hectares, and the emigration of peasants' sons to Bucarest, especially from the hilly and mountainous districts.[12] Thus there appears to be ample evidence of crowding, land hunger, and widespread hidden unemployment. What were the causes for this appearance of surplus population?

In a study of agricultural overpopulation, written in 1939, H. M. Conacher suggested that a surplus agrarian population could arise in a variety of ways:

1. Under conditions where the Malthusian theory has come true, and the pressure of population on subsistence is severe, usually through excessive fragmentation of land;

2. Under conditions less severe than in (1), where the cultivation of land has come under the formula of diminishing returns through straining a system of husbandry, and this has gone on over a widening area;

3. In cases where the distribution of returns among the different classes of producers is inequitable, with the result that the laborers are much in the same position as might be reached under (2) if they had been landholders;

4. In cases where, apart from the foregoing causes, a rural economy producing for export suffers from a considerable fall in demand, especially if such an economy has been using up its capital in the soil.[13]

In Rumania all these conditions have contributed in varying measure in the different regions. The first condition, in which pressure of population growth is the primary factor, operates as a tendency throughout most of Rumania, but appears to be of particular importance in Bucovina and the Carpathian districts. In 1941 the agricultural population per 100 hectares reached 164.7 in the *judeţ* of Dâmboviţa in the Wallachian Carpathians, 123.4 in Baia in the

11. Madgearu, *op. cit.*, p. 49.

12. Nicolae M. Dunăre, *Fii de ţărani vânzători ambulanţi în capitală*, Institutul Central de Statistică, Biblioteca Statistică, No. 22 (Bucarest, 1945), p. 6.

13. Contribution by H. M. Conacher in "The Problem of Surplus Agricultural Population," *International Journal of Agrarian Affairs, 1*, No. 1 (October, 1939), 27.

Moldavian Carpathians, 161.1 in Suceava in Bucovina, and 126.3 in
Bihor in western Transylvania. Dwarf holdings of less than 3 hectares are most numerous in these județe. The mountainous regions
represent an economic dead end; the land is poor and much of it unsuitable for cultivation; the pressure of population has forced the
multiplication of dwarf holdings; and social inertia and poverty have
limited emigration to less congested areas.

Such extreme population pressure is mainly limited, however, to
the mountainous and hilly regions. As has been indicated by the equa-
tions already given, agrarian overpopulation for the greater part of
Rumania is only in part a demographic problem. The rapid growth
of population from the middle of the nineteenth century did not
initially cause trouble because of the sparsity of inhabitants in the
Danube plain and the great extension of land put under the plough.
However, the relatively late emergence of the peasant as a proprietor,
the general lack of capital, and the predominant position of large
properties under neoserfdom combined to maintain the primacy of
extensive grain cultivation. This form of husbandry eventually began
to undermine Rumanian agriculture, especially after the expansion of small-scale farming, which was ill-suited to such an emphasis
upon cereals. Pasture land was reduced without the substitution of
forage crops, livestock declined, and the primitive wheat-maize rotation threatened to deplete even the rich soil of the plains. In the plains
regions, then, overpopulation is to some extent the result of the prevailing type and level of agriculture, although the constant increase
of population has undoubtedly aggravated the problem.

The fourth way in which a surplus agrarian population arises—
through a decline in exports—is only indirectly related to overpopulation and is primarily an economic maladjustment. The general decline of European cereal exports in the face of overseas competition,
and particularly the world grain crisis after 1929, intensified the
manifestations of overpopulation by depressing the whole agrarian
sector of the Rumanian economy. This, however, is a special case.

There remains to be discussed the third way in which a surplus
agrarian population arises: through inequitable distribution of returns. In regions dominated by great landowners who control a large
part of the soil, the peasants are likely to give the appearance of
overpopulation, since they lack sufficient land of their own to support themselves. There is no question that in nineteenth-century Rumania the concentration of land in large estates created land hunger
and the symptoms of overpopulation. It should be noted, however,
that even by 1907 it was becoming evident that the over-all density of

agricultural population in relation to the total agricultural land and the level of production was approaching a critical point.

To what extent was distribution a significant factor in overpopulation after the 1918–21 land reforms? To answer this question it is necessary to attempt an investigation of the effects of these reforms upon distribution.

The Distribution of Land [14]

Although the distribution of agricultural land in Rumania has been, if not the core of the agrarian question, at least the focus of attention, and although innumerable books, pamphlets, and articles have dealt with it, it is still difficult to provide a satisfactory picture of land distribution and impossible to give an exact account of its development in time. The incompleteness and irregularity of statistics, the intrusion of wars and the frequent changes of territorial boundaries, the unsettling effect of the agrarian reforms themselves, and on occasion the warping of figures to fit a political thesis have combined to obscure the real situation.

Before proceeding to an analysis of the available statistics it is necessary to be as clear as possible about the use of certain categories and definitions, since confusion over these has been the source of numerous erroneous conclusions. In particular it is indispensable to know what types of land are being included in the term "agricultural," and whether the distribution of land is on the basis of properties or of farming units.

During the interwar years the Rumanian Central Institute of Statistics came to classify land in the manner shown by the table on the following page (the 1936 areas of the respective types of land are included to indicate their comparative size).[15] Earlier Rumanian statistics frequently employed different classifications, and the inclusion or exclusion of pasture and woodland seriously alters the pattern of land distribution.

The second important distinction is between *properties*, based upon legal ownership of the land, and *exploitations*, defined in 1941 as "the area comprising all the land effectively cultivated under the direction and participation of the head of the exploitation." Exploitations and properties are obviously not identical, since an exploita-

14. For a more detailed discussion of the statistics of Rumanian land distribution see the Appendix.

15. Petre Onica, *Tehnica statisticii agricole,* Institutul Central de Statistică, Biblioteca Statistică, No. 9 (Bucarest, 1945), p. 17.

			Hectares (in 1936)	Per Cent
A. Agricultural area	1.	Arable	13,940,000	47.3
	a.	Cereals	11,609,000	
	b.	Alimentary plants	532,000	
	c.	Industrial plants	493,000	
	d.	Cultivated or artificial meadows (forage crops)	783,000	
	e.	Fallow	523,000	
	2.	Natural meadows	1,410,000	4.7
	3.	Grazing and pasture	2,448,000	8.3
	4.	Vineyards	328,000	1.1
	5.	Orchards	233,000	0.8
B. Nonagricultural area	1.	Woods and forests	6,449,000	21.9
	2.	Occupied land (yards, houses, streets and roads, cities, industrial and commercial land) and nonproductive	4,697,000	15.9

Total area 29,505,000 hectares

tion may be held on lease or in metayage. The statistics always show some difference between the two; in most cases large properties are more extensive than large exploitations, an indication that a portion of the large properties is being leased. A secondary distinction between privately owned and state or publicly owned properties is also important, and here again Rumanian statistics are often inconsistent.

Although official accounts of the results of the 1918–21 land reforms were issued by the Rumanian government, they are not a very reliable guide to the effect of these reforms on the distribution of agricultural property. About 6,000,000 hectares were reported to have been expropriated, of which about 3,900,000 hectares were distributed to some 1,393,000 peasants, or 69.5 per cent of those having a claim to land.[16] But while the land reform was supposed to have been completed around 1929–30, in 1940 it was officially announced that the reform was not yet terminated: 3,900 estates were still in possession of land which was to have been expropriated; 434,000 hectares of expropriated land had not even been surveyed for distribution; 440,000 hectares had not yet been divided; 900 law cases re-

16. Alexander Nasta, "La Réforme agraire en Roumanie," report presented to the Fourteenth Congress of the International Congress of Agriculture (Bucarest, June 7–10, 1929), p. 16; Biblioteca de Sociologie, Etică şi Politică, condusă de D. Gusti, 60 Sate româneşti (5 vols., Bucarest, 1941–43), II, 10.

garding the agrarian reform still awaited adjudication.[17] This belated but damaging announcement naturally throws in doubt many of the earlier statistics which painfully calculated the final effects of the reform to two decimals.

Similarly, it is not possible to make any satisfactory comparisons between prereform and postreform figures, even for the Old Kingdom. The official estimates of the post-1921 situation, which have been generally used in most studies of Rumanian agriculture, are suspect: they merely subtracted from Creangă's estimate of large properties in 1905 the amount of land presumed to have been expropriated and added it to the area of small properties, a method taking no account of twenty years' unofficial changes in property relations. The results were naturally most impressive: large property had been reduced from 40 per cent of the agricultural area to 10 per cent, whereas small peasant properties, which had previously covered about 60 per cent of the land, now accounted for 90 per cent. This was undoubtedly an inflated estimate of the consequences of the reform.

Statistics available for the years between 1921 and 1945 do not, unfortunately, altogether clarify the picture. Between 1921 and 1929 there was both a progressive resettlement of peasants on land acquired through the reforms and a natural division and dispersion of properties through inheritance and, to a lesser degree, through sale. The only sources to give an indication of the results of these developments are some fiscal censuses prepared by the Ministry of Finance. Since these were gathered for tax purposes and employ different categories for dividing land holdings, they are not comparable with other available figures on land distribution. A comparison of the 1923 and 1928 censuses does, however, indicate certain trends. The number of agricultural taxpayers increased more rapidly than the extension of arable land, indicating an increasing density of agricultural population and a reduction of the average size of holdings from 3.6 hectares to 3.5 hectares.[18] There was a marked decline in the area of properties over 250 hectares, partly as a result of the continued application of the land reforms, although the increase in average size of properties between 50 and 250 hectares might mean that some of the land of large properties was falling into the hands of the larger peasant owners. The area of properties under 10 hectares and especially of those under 5 hectares increased greatly.

17. Quoted in Madgearu, *op. cit.,* p. 77, n. 1.
18. These censuses are discussed in *60 Sate romănești*, II, 12–15 and are given in the Appendix below.

Although this increase may have been to some extent the result of the subdivision of holdings through inheritance, it was largely the reflection of allotments granted under the reform, since the situation in Bessarabia, which had completed its reform at an early date, was almost stationary, while there was a marked increase in the area of small properties in Transylvania, where the reform had been more gradually applied.

Only a very general summary of the distribution of land was published after the 1930 census, and even this summary is sufficiently ambiguous to prevent a comparison with earlier or later figures. According to this census, exploitations over 100 hectares in size still occupied almost 28 per cent of the total agricultural area (presumably also including some forest land) and nearly 15 per cent of the arable, the difference resulting from the high percentage of nonarable land possessed by large properties. Exploitations of less than 3 hectares, which amounted to 52 per cent of the total number, occupied less than 13 per cent of the total area and 16.5 per cent of the arable. Exploitations between 10 and 100 hectares occupied almost 25 per cent of the total agricultural area and over 25 per cent of the arable, a marked increase over the prewar situation in the Old Kingdom. This change reflects in part, however, the inclusion in the 1930 census of Transylvania and Bucovina, where medium holdings had been more numerous. In general, this census would show that large properties had not been reduced to the extent called for by the agrarian reforms, that holdings under 3 hectares still constituted the majority of the exploitations, and that medium holdings had increased in number and extent, although the agrarian reforms had made no provision for them.

The census of 1941 was the first careful attempt to analyze the distribution of land. Although its usefulness for present purposes is impaired by the omission of Bessarabia, Northern Bucovina, Northern Transylvania, and Southern Dobrogea, which had been lost in 1940, its summary results are the best information available. This census, which covered only individual and private exploitations, comprising 52 per cent of the total area of Rumania at that date, appears to show to an even greater extent the characteristics noted in the 1930 summary:

1) The group of exploitations and properties [19] between 3 and

19. The number of properties and exploitations were not identical for all categories; there were more properties than exploitations in holdings below 3 hectares and above 20 hectares, and more exploitations between 3 and 20 hectares. These differences merely reflect the fact that agricultural exploitations are not based solely on properties but also involve the use of property through lease or metayage.

5 hectares, which the 1918–21 land reforms considered as the basis of Rumanian agriculture in the allotment of land, actually constituted in 1941 only 19.5 per cent of the exploitations (18.4 per cent of the properties), occupying 16.4 per cent of the area of exploitations (16.1 per cent of the area of properties). On the other hand, exploitations under 3 hectares constituted 54.1 per cent of the total number (properties under 3 hectares constituted 58.4 per cent of the total number of properties).

2) The largest category of exploitations in terms of area was that between 5 and 10 hectares, i.e., above the average size for all holdings.

3) Despite the agrarian reforms, exploitations over 100 hectares occupied 14.2 per cent of the area; 8 per cent of the area was occupied by properties over 500 hectares.

Regionally, exploitations under one hectare were most numerous in mountainous districts and in industrial areas, where factory workers had small plots of land. Exploitations between one and 3 hectares were most common in the Carpathians and Bucovina. The large holdings were concentrated mainly in the southeast.

The 1941 census also provides the first comprehensive statistical picture of the way in which the land was farmed. More than 58 per cent of all exploitations properly speaking (that is, excluding the minute plots of land of less than one hectare of arable) were cultivated exclusively by family labor; and an additional 24.9 per cent utilized only part of the family's labor (the family also had recourse to other sources of income). Thus, 83 per cent of all exploitations proper were purely family cultivations. Exploitations using no family labor but employing workers, whether on a daily or yearly basis or in return for a piece of land, accounted for only 1.5 per cent of the total, although they covered 12.1 per cent of the land. For the most part these exploitations represented the residues of the expropriated estates. The fourth category, using both family and employed labor, represented intensive peasant farms, and comprised 15.3 per cent of the number of exploitations and 24.8 per cent of the area.

Over 71 per cent of the exploitations were owned by the cultivator, 28 per cent included additional land held in lease or metayage, and less than one per cent of the exploitations were entirely on rented land. If these criteria are combined with those above, the most prevalent form of peasant cultivation, accounting for 41.6 per cent of all exploitations proper, was one owned in its entirety by the cultivator and employing only family labor.

Unfortunately, the information on agricultural labor in 1941 has not been fully organized and published. According to a statistical bulletin issued in 1947, on the 2,300,000 odd agricultural exploitations in 1941, 813,546 "members of families," after completing work on their own holding, worked for others, either for money or for produce. Of these, 748,821 worked in the same village and 64,725 took the road to work in other villages. On September 1, 1940, there were 191,199 permanently hired agricultural workers, of whom 103,-353 were men, 68,325 women, and 19,521 children. As might be expected, the practice of seeking additional work was most extensive in the Carpathian regions of Oltenia and Muntenia, where for every 100 family exploitations, 50 members of families sought work, as against 35.3 for all Rumania. The same area had the least number of permanent hired workers, 4.7 per 100 exploitations as against 8.3 for all Rumania.[20]

The general results of the 1941 census, as published thus far, do not correlate size of exploitation with type of labor and holding. However, a special study for the judeţ of Argeş, "which by the variety of the soil and the nature of the exploitations constitutes one of the most representative judeţe of our country," [21] gives such a correlation, which may be a fair sample for all of Rumania. This correlation is what might be expected. Large farms, especially those over 100 hectares, were cultivated mainly by hired labor. Farms between 10 and 50 hectares were most frequently cultivated by a combination of family and hired labor. Peasant farms between 1 and 5 hectares used only family labor, and in about one-third of the cases the labor of the family was not completely utilized. Cultivators with holdings of less than one hectare fell into the class of agricultural laborers.

What conclusions may be drawn from these scattered and not altogether comparable figures regarding: (a) the effect of the agrarian reforms upon the distribution of land; (b) land distribution as a cause of agricultural overpopulation; (c) trends in land distribution during the interwar period?

(a) While there is no doubt that the agrarian reforms of 1918–21 greatly reduced the amount of land held by property owners of over 100 hectares, they did not bring about the virtual disappearance of large landed estates, as was so often proclaimed in the years after the First World War. In 1941 properties over 100 hectares still

20. Institutul Central de Statistică, *Comunicari statistice Nr. 16,.15 ianuarie 1947*, p. 3. In 1930 the Rumanian National Bank estimated that there were 464,000 agricultural workers, 16.7 per cent of the total agricultural active population of 2,773,769. *60 Sate româneşti*, II, 18.

21. Roman Cresin, *Agricultura din Judeţul Argeş* (Bucarest, 1945), p. 11.

occupied over 16 per cent of the privately owned land.[22] The extent of leasing and cultivation in metayage decreased considerably, however, and reflected the reduction of differences in the size of properties. As has been seen in the first chapter, before the First World War leasing and subleasing in a variety of forms was extremely widespread in the Old Kingdom. While the 1941 statistics do not present a clear picture of the exact amount of land let out, 71.8 per cent of the exploitations proper were owned by their cultivators, and only 0.4 per cent were cultivated entirely by tenants or in metayage. Of the 225,890 hectares covered by the census in the judeţ of Argeş, only 21,591 were rented. Properties in Argeş let out by their owners in rent or in metayage comprised 9.5 per cent of the total area of properties and 16.2 per cent of the arable terrain. These percentages are somewhat higher than the estimate made by the Rumanian Ministry of Finance in 1927 that 8.4 per cent of the land (based on taxpayers) in the Old Kingdom was let out.[23]

The agrarian reforms were not successful, however, in creating a satisfactory peasant agriculture based upon small properties of between 3 and 5 hectares.[24] In 1941 over 58 per cent of the properties were below 3 hectares, a perilous minimum for a self-sustaining cultivation; properties between 3 and 5 hectares amounted to only 18.4 per cent of the total number and covered only 16 per cent of the area. The reasons for this failure will be discussed shortly.

(b) The unequal distribution of land was not a primary cause of agrarian overpopulation during the interwar period. The 1941 census does not provide decisive evidence on this question, as it covered only a little over half the total area of Rumania in its 1941 frontiers. It included, however, over 87 per cent of the total arable, and is therefore fairly reliable as regards cultivable land. According to this census, the average size of all properties under 5 hectares was

22. This figure, it must be repeated, is not comparable with the pre-1914 figures. In the first place, geographical area is not the same. Moreover, Creangă in his 1905 estimate included state and public properties and grazing land but excluded forests. The 1941 census included whatever forest and grazing land was owned privately but omitted communal and state controlled pastures and forests.

23. Quoted in Mitrany, *The Land and the Peasant in Rumania*, p. 246.

24. In 1945 the Danish agricultural economist, M. Gormsen, who had been employed by the Rumanian government, stated that in its practical consequences, "the transformation of estate land into peasant land in Rumania in 1918–1921 meant in spite of everything only the continuation on a much larger scale of the old short-sighted policy of the past. This policy consisted in leaving as little land as possible to the peasants without taking into consideration whether it was sufficient or not for a rational and independent peasant agriculture." M. Gormsen, *Short Introduction to the Principal Structural Problems of the Agriculture in Roumania* (Bucarest, 1945), p. 40.

2.0 hectares. If all land in excess of 100 hectares were distributed to properties below 5 hectares, their average size would rise to 2.7 hectares; if all property in excess of 50 hectares, the average size would be 2.9 hectares. (This computation does not, of course, take into account regional differences in land distribution, which would considerably reduce the gains to small properties unless the farm population were far more mobile than it has been in the past.) Actually, the increase in arable would be less than the figures indicate because a fairly large proportion of big properties was forest land. In Argeș, for example, although it has more forest land than most judeţe, forests accounted for 57.1 per cent of the land of exploitations over 100 hectares, and 40. 9 per cent of the land of exploitations between 50 and 100 hectares.[25] According to a sampling of a number of villages throughout Rumania, 26 per cent of the land of properties over 25 hectares was forest.[26]

In short, while a further redistribution of the land would have some effect in increasing the size of peasant holdings and would provide a temporary relief for a number of peasants, it could not in itself remedy, even temporarily, the more fundamental problems connected with agricultural overpopulation. This point must be born in mind in connection with the land reform of 1945, to be discussed in a later chapter.

(c) While the changes in land distribution during the interwar period are not altogether clear, one principal development is discernible. Properties between 3 and 5 hectares, which are statistically the average size, failed to become the predominant type of holding. Instead, there appears to have been an increase in the number of submarginal holdings under 3 hectares and in the extent of medium peasant properties between 5 and 20 hectares. In the judeţ of Argeș, the renting of supplementary land was most widespread in exploitations between 5 and 10 hectares and between 10 and 20 hectares, a fact which would indicate relative economic strength. In 1940, Madgearu observed that after 1929 there had been a strengthening of middle properties on the one hand and the formation of an agricultural proletariat on the other.[27]

The investigation of sixty villages in 1938 showed in what way land reform contributed to this development. According to this sampling, the initial effect of the agrarian reform had been a leveling of the difference between poor and rich peasant households, an effect

25. Roman Cresin, *op. cit.,* p. 26.
26. *60 Sate românești,* II, 49.
27. Madgearu, *op. cit.,* p. 34.

more marked in the plains than in the mountains. However, the evolution of the two categories of peasant households—those which had received land under the reform and those which had not—was quite different. Holdings which had been either created or supplemented by allotments under the agrarian reform had a much lower resistance to the process of fragmentation of land than the nonallotted holdings; sale of holdings was more frequent among peasants who had received land by the reform.[28] The conclusion is that the agrarian reforms had not established the new properties on a firm basis, which would enable the poor peasant to maintain himself, and had only temporarily checked a tendency toward inequality in the village.

In general, the unequal distribution of land, as a purely economic factor, was not the primary cause for the agrarian difficulties of the interwar period. For a more complete explanation of these difficulties it is necessary to turn to the question of agricultural productivity and the relations of agriculture to the whole of the Rumanian economy.

Agricultural Production [29]

During the interwar years Rumanian agriculture was still largely devoted to the cultivation of cereal crops, which in 1938 occupied 82.1 per cent of the total arable surface: [30]

	In 1,000 hectares	Per cent of arable
Total arable	13,873.8	100.0
Cereals	11,387.3	82.1
Wheat	3,926.9	28.3
Maize	5,033.6	36.3
Barley	1,250.8	9.0
Oats	648.7	4.7
Rye	478.3	3.4
Alimentary plants	494.3	3.6
Industrial plants	487.6	3.5
Forage crops	734.3	5.3
Fallow	770.3	5.6

A slight shift in emphasis occurred during this period; the percentage of arable land under cereals dropped from 87 to 82 per cent, although the area under the principal grains, wheat and maize, in-

28. *60 Sate românești,* II, 33, 41.
29. Statistical material supporting and illustrating the conclusions of this section is included in the Appendix.
30. *Statistica agricolă a Românie: în 1938,* p. 2.

creased. Certain industrial plants, such as sunflower and soybean, showed a rapid rate of growth, especially in the second half of the 1930's, but they represented a very small percentage of the total acreage.

Considerable regional variations corresponded to differences in soil and terrain. Cereal cultivation was most widespread in the Old Kingdom and Bessarabia, especially in the plains of the Siret, Prut, and Danube rivers, and in Dobrogea; it was of much less importance in the Carpathian regions, Transylvania and Bucovina. In a few districts, of which the most notable was Țara Bârsei in southeastern Transylvania, the peasants carried on an intensive cultivation and had a standard of production well above the average for the country.

In the village investigations of 1938 it was discovered that cereal cultivation was predominant in all categories of holdings. It was most extensive in properties between 5 and 25 hectares, but even on dwarf holdings of under one hectare more than half the land was devoted to cereals.

With respect to the general volume of production, maize, which the peasants preferred to cultivate and which formed the major element in their diet, rose above the pre-1914 level, but wheat, which had been grown principally by large cultivators, never achieved the prewar level. Exports of both wheat and maize declined greatly below the prewar level.

PRODUCTION AND EXPORT OF CEREALS, 1909–39 [31]

(1909–13 production and export = 100)

	Wheat		Maize	
	Production	Export	Production	Export
1909–13 (1919 boundaries)	100	100	100	100
1928–32	67.7	15.9	104.1	58.1
1933–37	70.5	19.3	101.7	42.8
1935–39	88.7	39.8	108.8	32.5

The slump in cereal production was primarily the result of low yield per hectare, since by 1924 the area under cultivation had recovered from the immediate postwar decline and surpassed the average area cultivated between 1909 and 1913.

31. U.S. Department of Agriculture, "Wartime Agricultural Surpluses of the Danube Basin," *Foreign Agriculture, 4*, No. 12 (December, 1940), 712.

INDEX OF AREA, YIELD, AND PRODUCTION OF CEREALS [32]
(1909–13 = 100)

	1909–13	1920	1922	1924	1925	1926	1933–37
Area	100	84.4	94.5	101.2	103.5	102.8	114.3
Yield	100	86.7	77.5	60.0	71.7	99.2	81.7
Production	100	72.9	73.6	60.6	74.6	101.6	93.1

In the discussion of overpopulation it was seen that the productivity per hectare in Rumania was exceedingly low. For the four-year period 1928–32 the Rumanian wheat yield was below that of any Balkan state except Greece, averaging 9.5 quintals per hectare, as contrasted with a French yield of 14.8 and a Danish yield of 29.4 quintals per hectare during the same years. Although the Rumanian peasant has been more successful with maize, his output of that grain is also very low. This low rate of yield has been the most striking symptom of the unhealthy condition of Rumanian agriculture. The records of the past half century give little evidence of improvement, and there has been a noticeable decline in comparison with the pre-1914 figures.

Technical and material factors provide an immediate explanation for Rumania's poor output, but beyond these are more general causes which inhibit the improvement of agriculture and the introduction of more efficient techniques. On the whole, physical conditions in Rumania do not prevent a satisfactory agriculture. The hilly regions are somewhat deficient in humus but the soil of the plains is unusually fertile. The plains are exposed to extremes of rainfall and temperature, and the irregularity of the rainfall, the most serious threat to crops, is conducive to a wide fluctuation in output. Nevertheless, these conditions would present no serious obstacle to an increase in production if farming methods were adapted to the soil and climate.[33]

The principal material reasons for the low productivity are the extremely limited use of manure and fertilizers, absence of which is causing gradual depletion of the soil, even in the best plains regions; the lack of moisture-conserving measures; a primitive crop-rotation system; the low quality of livestock; backward techniques of cultivation and the shortage of agricultural equipment; and the prevalence of strip farming. The two last points require additional explanation.

32. League of Nations, *Agricultural Production in Continental Europe* (1943), p. 73.
33. U.S. Department of Agriculture, *op. cit.*, p. 715.

The low level of productivity is clearly a function of the investment in agricultural inventory, which is exceptionally small in Rumania: [34]

	Value of agricultural inventory in lei/hectare	Average production of wheat in kilograms/hectare
Rumania	1,000	860
Bulgaria	2,000	1,320
Poland	3,000	1,440
Germany	15,000	2,070
Switzerland	42,000	2,250

While there is a great dearth of investment in agricultural equipment, there is also an overinvestment in certain items because of the
large number of small holdings, each with its primitive inventory.
According to the 1941 census on agricultural equipment—the first
adequate estimate—though there was less than one plough to every
two exploitations, there was one plough for every seven hectares of
arable land. But since one plough was capable, according to Rumanian estimates, of turning over fifteen hectares, there were about
twice as many ploughs as were necessary in terms of technical requirements.[35]

The division of agricultural exploitations into numerous small
plots or strips is, of course, intimately related to the question of
agrarian reform and to the pressure of population, although strip
farming was prevalent before 1918. The agrarian reforms contributed to its extension, not only because they omitted any provisions
for consolidation, but also because the land of the expropriated
estates was usually divided into a number of small, narrow strips of
land of from ½ to 5 hectares, which were given either to landless
peasants or to those with inadequate holdings. These strips were often
several kilometers away from the peasant's village or his other holdings. In 1941 the average area of all exploitations was 4.5 hectares,
with an average of 5 plots per exploitation. Frequently these plots

34. Madgearu, *op. cit.,* p. 69.
35. Census of agricultural equipment, 1941 (*Recensământul agricol din 1941,* p. 56):

	Number	Number per 100 exploitations	Number per 100 hectares arable land
Ploughs	1,083,018	48.0	14.5
Harrows	752,063	33.3	10.0
Seed drills	58,589	2.6	0.8
Reapers	39,345	1.7	0.5
Tractors	8,416	0.4	0.1
Carts	1,191,254	52.7	15.7

of less than one hectare were several hundred meters long and only 5 to 10 meters wide. The strips were at a great distance from one another, some authorities estimating the average distance to be from 4 to 7 kilometers.[36] The division of farming units into such small strips is obviously an impediment to any rationalization of agriculture.

Primitive techniques and irrational organization of holdings, while directly responsible for low productivity, are really manifestations rather than causes of the stagnation of Rumanian agriculture. What has inhibited the introduction of technical and organizational improvements? Poverty and "lack of capital" merely describe the situation; they do not explain it. Nor can this stagnation be ascribed to the natural inertia of a primitive agricultural society: the Rumanian economy has been in the midst of a dynamic process of change for over a century.

The fall in yield after the agrarian reforms of 1918–21 naturally raised the question whether the expropriation of the large estates was responsible for the critical state of Rumanian farming. This question is likely to be misleading if it is reduced to a comparison of the theoretical merits of large scale and peasant agriculture. Criticism that the agrarian reforms are responsible for the decline in agricultural productivity is apt to assume that the pre-1914 estates were well-organized large farms, whereas for the most part they were latifundiary cultivations, farmed out to the peasants who cultivated them with their own animals and equipment.[37] To be sure, some of the large farms were relatively well managed (although the yield even on the big estates was low in comparison with western European standards), and it may be that certain other controls employed by the large farms—notably the selection of seed and the regulation of the date at which sowing should begin [38]—were sufficient to account for the higher yield of the large properties. During the interwar years, as before 1914, large farms continued to have a higher cereal

36. M. Gormsen, *op. cit.,* p. 15.

37. For example, the U.S. Department of Agriculture, in a study of Rumanian agriculture, cites the great annual fluctuation in the wheat yield, a result of the variation in rainfall, as an example of the inability of the small peasant to take appropriate moisture conservation measures. "Managers of the large estates knew how to overcome this handicap to a considerable extent." U.S. Dept. of Agriculture, *op. cit.,* p. 715. A comparison of pre-1914 yields, however, indicates that while the yield of large properties was higher than that of small properties, the fluctuation in yield was practically the same for both categories. Cf. Mitrany, *op. cit.,* p. 271.

38. Doreen Warriner, *The Economics of Peasant Farming* (Oxford University Press, 1939), p. 153.

yield than the small peasant holdings,[39] though there appear to be no satisfactory statistics on this point.

On the other hand, defenders of the agrarian reform and small peasant properties have tended to assume that the Rumanian small holder was on his way to becoming an independent peasant proprietor, a doubtful assumption in view of the prevalence of dwarf holdings and the continued excessive cultivation of cereals. In 1937 G. Ionescu-Sişeşti and N. Cornăţeanu upheld the reform and peasant farming on the following grounds:

The reform was an economic necessity under the conditions of devastation after the First World War; it was only by giving land to the peasants that they were induced to make the great effort necessary for agricultural recovery. Peasant farming became more intensive and less devoted to cereal cultivation. The peasant was better able to withstand agricultural crises, largely because the large farmer lacked his ability to reduce expenses and increase family labor. Finally, peasant agriculture should not be judged in terms of its contribution to the national income but by its ability to "assure the existence of the greatest possible number of citizens." It is therefore erroneous to "establish a comparison between peasant agriculture and the system of large property." [40]

The necessity of the agrarian reforms need not be argued, although they could be defined more convincingly as a social than as an economic imperative (i.e., the peasants would have refused to continue to work under the old system). It may also be true that peasant farming cannot be judged by narrow profit-and-loss accounting methods, since it is a manner of living as well as a form of livelihood. But Sişeşti's and Cornăţeanu's supporting arguments do not appear relevant to the actual Rumanian situation. There is no indication that peasant cultivation did become to any significant degree more intensive and varied. The examples they give, taken from a survey of a number of farms between 1930 and 1934, to illustrate the viability of peasant farming are not representative but comprise farms well above the average size for Rumania. Hence the real problem of dwarf holdings is avoided. The argument that small holdings are more resistant to crises because the peasant is able to restrict his consumption and increase family labor is not altogether reassuring in face of the growing pressure of population, regardless of its dubi-

39. M. Gormsen, *op. cit.*, p. 46.

40. G. Ionescu-Sişeşti and N. Cornăţeanu, *La Réforme agraire en Roumanie et ses conséquences* (Bucarest, 1937), pp. 42–53.

ous merits from the point of view of social welfare. The effort to ignore the importance of national income as a criterion for judging the advantages of peasant farming is unrealistic, given the existence of a modern Rumanian state with its manifold requirements. Finally, for all their optimism, Sișești and Cornățeanu admit the serious menace of continued subdivision of the land and urge the creation of a "peasant bourgeoisie." They do not indicate, however, what is to become of the poor peasants displaced in such a creation except to appeal for a further expansion of a national industry. The appeal to national industry, as a *deus ex machina*, at once undermines the whole argument for the viability of the Rumanian peasant proprietor.

Actually, such discussions of the merits and defects of peasant agriculture have only a limited relevance in Rumania. For example, in a study of 275 peasant households made in 1938, it was discovered that in general both the gross income per hectare (the total agricultural product of the holding, whether consumed or sold) and the agricultural income per hectare (gross income minus expenses for agriculture—labor payments, inventory, buildings, seed, etc.) tended to be higher on the small (under 3 hectares) than on the larger holdings. This higher net yield would appear to substantiate the contentions of the advocates of small farming.[41] In fact, however, the majority of the small holdings in this investigation operated at a deficit because the consumption needs of the household, largely food and clothing, were greater than the farm could produce. Only 14 per cent of the holdings between 1 and 3 hectares had an agricultural income greater than consumption, whereas in 86 per cent of the cases consumption was greater. Only 30 per cent of the holdings between 3 and 5 hectares had agricultural incomes greater than consumption. On the larger farms, between 10 and 20 hectares, 59 per cent had an agricultural income sufficient to meet consumption needs.[42] Therefore, the relative net incomes of farms of different sizes were of less

41. This higher rate of agricultural income among the small holdings is not, as it might appear, in contradiction to the statement that the cereal yield is higher on large farms than on small. A much smaller proportion of the income of the small holdings is derived from cereals; most of it comes from the sale of animals, fowls, fruits, etc. This, however, does not really represent a turn to intensive farming, since it is conducted on a very primitive level and only reflects the dwarf holder's efforts to maintain himself at a subsistence level.

42. *60 Sate românești*, II, 292. It should be noted that this investigation did not include large farms but only peasant holdings up to 40 hectares. Moreover, the results of the investigation showed an extremely wide range of variation, both regionally and among farms of the same size. Hence, the sampling may not have been extensive enough to permit confident generalization.

importance than the fact that the general level of productivity was so low that a great number of the small farms simply did not produce enough to support themselves.

The effect of the 1918–21 land reforms upon production is also obscured by the numerous other factors which worked to reduce output: the destruction caused by the First World War, the economic policy of the postwar governments, the agrarian crisis and the "price scissors" of the 1930's.[43] While one cannot dismiss the effect of the redistribution of land as of only historical interest, since the leading feature of the 1945 agrarian reform was a further expropriation of large properties, it should be stressed that the reforms of 1918–21 were passed because of a pressing political and social necessity for a redistribution of the land; they were not primarily designed to increase production, and whatever their effect upon yield, it should be regarded as incidental to the aims of the reforms.

In general, it seems fair to say that the redistribution of land in Rumania—except in so far as it contributed to a further extension of uneconomic strip farming—had only a marginal direct effect upon productivity. The decline in yield, even if it was caused by the expropriation of the large estates, was only a modest contribution to the generally low level of Rumanian productivity. A comparison with the yield per hectare in neighboring countries reveals that states with more extensive large properties than Rumania (Hungary and Poland) as well as states in which small holdings predominated (Bulgaria and Yugoslavia) all had a yield well below that of western and central Europe.[44]

If the reforms of 1918–21 failed to bring about a more efficient organization of Rumanian agriculture, what were the principal organizational defects which, by preventing the introduction of more rational techniques, maintained a low level of productivity?

A Danish agricultural economist, M. Gormsen, who came to Rumania in 1939 at the request of the Rumanian government, has made

43. For an extensive discussion of these factors and their effect upon productivity to 1930 see Mitrany, *op. cit.*, pp. 306–331.
44. Moore, *op. cit.*, pp. 35, 82.

	Per cent of land held in undertakings of over 50 ha. (ca. 1930)	Yield in crop units per ha.
Rumania	32.2	17
Hungary	51.3	21
Poland	47.3	18
Bulgaria	1.6	19
Yugoslavia	9.7	17
Europe (excluding U.S.S.R.)		24

a useful distinction between "agrarian reforms," which affect the organization of farming, and "agricultural reforms," which seek to improve the techniques.[45] In his opinion the agrarian reforms must be applied first or the agricultural reforms will be fruitless. Moreover, agrarian reforms can be carried out only by some superior body, such as the state, as the result of a conscious act of decision, whereas agricultural reforms are more gradual and can be applied by the farmers themselves. Among the main agrarian reforms indispensable for a prosperous agriculture he would include:

1) The abolition of servile relations—binding the peasant to the land, forced labor, feudal property relations, tithes, and the common utilization of the land. This reform was achieved in principle by the emancipation of 1864.

2) The transformation of estate land into peasant land. This was largely achieved by the reforms of 1918–21. Gormsen feels that a further transfer would yield positive but limited benefits.

3) The consolidation of individual peasant farms and, as a corollary, the partial evacuation of the villages and the establishment of farmhouses on the consolidated holdings. Gormsen regards this as the most important reform still to be carried out in Rumania.

4) The limitation of divisibility and expansion of holdings, to prevent the undoing of consolidation.

5) The introduction of a land register, definite property demarcations, and enclosures if necessary.

Under agricultural reforms he would include all such measures as the rationalization of farming methods; soil, seed, and livestock improvement; organization of agricultural credit and cooperation; the development of experimental stations; and so on.

In Gormsen's opinion, the Rumanian governments between the wars made the very serious mistake of devoting all their attention to efforts, often quite expensive, to introduce agricultural reforms. These were of little permanent value so long as the necessary agrarian reforms had not been made. An example is the complete failure of attempts to establish agricultural credit and peasant cooperatives, which have been the perennial promise of every new Rumanian government.

An effective permanent system of organized credit for peasant agriculture in Rumania does not exist although a number of institutions have been created from time to time to that purpose, as a rule with the assistance of the state or the national bank, but they only worked for a

45. M. Gormsen, *op. cit.*

short time and then died out or were transformed into something else. The lack of a land register, the small size of the peasant holdings, the whole backwardness of the system of agricultural exploitation, and, of course, the lack of really available capital, are the main reasons for the failure of the organization of agricultural credit in Rumania.[46]

To be sure, the shortage of the supply of credit is merely a sign of the lack of capital in Rumania. Such funds as there were found greater attractions in fields other than agriculture. But, as M. Gormsen says, not only was there a shortage of credit but peasant agriculture was not able to utilize greater quantities of investment properly under existing agrarian conditions. "As a matter of fact, a considerable part of the limited quantity of capital invested in peasant agriculture in the past has simply been lost, as was to be foreseen, without doing agriculture much good." [47]

The various cooperatives, in which the active participation of the peasants was extremely limited, have been of little real value, and at times they did more harm than good. The management quite frequently exploited the peasants' ignorance and inexperience to its own benefit. The cooperatives were not really cooperative ventures but rather official institutions, financed, directed, and controlled by the state and therefore completely subject to political vicissitudes. But most important a poor peasant is not in a position to be very useful in a cooperative. "The causal relationship between cooperative organizations and peasant prosperity is reciprocal, not unidirectional," [48] or, as a Rumanian economist remarked in this connection, "How are you to ring the bell if you do not have a bell?"

In the first chapter of this study it was observed that the structure of Rumanian society had led to a certain legislative "escapism"— an endless tinkering with laws and decrees, most of which had very little consequence. The numerous laws for the creation of agricultural credit and cooperatives are splendid examples. Why should there have been this resort to ineffective, though often expensive, experiments? To some extent they can be dismissed as efforts to solve a problem by means of sleight of hand rather than face the rigors of a more radical reform. They also reflect the Rumanian practice of copying Western procedures without ascertaining whether they are appropriate.

There is, however, the more serious question whether even appropriate agrarian reforms, along the lines suggested by Gormsen,

46. *Ibid.,* p. 57.
47. *Ibid.*
48. Moore, *op. cit.,* p. 112.

would be sufficient to rescue Rumanian agriculture. Gormsen himself, while believing that if the reforms he outlined had been applied in times past they might have set Rumanian agriculture on the right path, admits that it is now too late for them to be effective alone.

In other words, thanks above all to the disastrous delay in the realization of some of the most important agrarian reforms in Rumania . . . we have the paradox that the Rumanian peasant and agriculture cannot in fact be entirely saved from the temporary but very serious crisis even by the most rapid accomplishment of these very reforms, but one further and special means must be employed, namely the continuation of the rapid expansion and progress of another national occupation, industry.[49]

Once again, the solution to Rumania's agricultural crisis is seen to lie beyond agriculture,[50] suggesting, however, that failure to solve it is not solely the consequence of delay in carrying out necessary agrarian reforms. For while it is true that such reforms are a prerequisite to an improved peasant agriculture, conditions in Rumania have not been conducive to their successful application. Servile relations, which were legally abolished in 1864, reappeared immediately in the form of neoserfdom. The 1918–21 agrarian reforms attempted to limit the subdivision of properties below a certain minimum, but they clearly failed of their purpose. Constantin Garoflid, in 1921, strongly recommended a law for the consolidation of peasant properties but it was never passed, partly because the peasants themselves mistrusted such a measure. In other words, the difficulty is not simply, as Gormsen suggests, that agrarian reforms have been delayed too long to be wholly successful, since some early efforts were made and miscarried.[51]

49. Gormsen, *op. cit.*, p. 65.

50. Moore, *op. cit.*, p. 118, reaches the same general conclusion for all the peasant countries of eastern and southern Europe: "The net conclusion, accordingly, is that marked improvements in the levels of production and consumption in Eastern and Southern Europe cannot be expected from those measures that would place first and most emphasis upon agricultural production."

51. The difference here is largely one of emphasis but is quite important in judging the Rumanian situation. Gormsen approaches the question as an agricultural economist seeking to define the conditions necessary for a successful peasant agriculture. Quite naturally, he sees in the absence of agrarian reforms the basic structural defect in Rumanian farming; observing correctly that even these reforms are now inadequate to rescue Rumanian agriculture he concludes that if they had been achieved at an earlier stage the present crisis could have been avoided. While this may be true, the fact is that the reforms were not applied, and in those cases where they were attempted they did not achieve the desired effect. The necessity of creating independent peasant properties has been a cliché of Rumanian writers for the last half century at least and, as Mihalache said in 1921, no one was opposed to consolidation on principle. The danger of a purely structural analysis is that it underestimates the importance of the numer-

The agrarian problem is not rooted solely in agriculture. As was shown in the historical introduction, contact with the West had an unsettling effect upon the whole of Rumanian society. Among the dislocations, the following were of particular importance to agriculture:

1) The expansion of the population, which was one of the fundamental results of the contact with the West, made a "stable" agriculture impossible; there must be either a corresponding improvement in productivity or a decline in the level of consumption.[52]

2) The emphasis upon cereal cultivation, brought about by the possibility of profits in commerce, led to the creation and maintenance of extensive cultivation which persisted even after the expropriation of the great estates.

3) The social and economic relations of neoserfdom, which was a hybrid of Western and traditional practices, gave an excessive importance to the possession of land and a false emphasis to land distribution as the solution of the peasants' difficulties. As more and more land was distributed, it provided a decreasingly adequate remedy. The ultimate causes of these conditions lay outside Rumania but produced a profound modification in the internal structure of the agrarian economy.

While these manifestations of Western influence continue to have their effect upon Rumanian agriculture, they are largely an inheritance of the last century. More dynamic influences can be seen in the relations of agriculture to industry and commerce during the interwar years.

---

ous historical influences which have shaped Rumanian agriculture and is apt to place all the blame upon irresponsible legislators, selfish landowners, and unenlightened peasants.

52. A League of Nations study, *Industrialization and Foreign Trade* (1945), p. 63, mentions the danger of a backward country being involved in a "false start" in its efforts to catch up with the industrial states: "It has become increasingly clear, however, that undeveloped countries utilizing certain results of western knowledge and technique but not ready to assimilate western civilization with their own, run the risk of paying a heavy price for the influences to which they are subjected. The risk materializes if these influences fail to bring about the process of self-propelling development so characteristic of the western type of civilization. The most obvious cases of such a 'false start' occur when the impulses received tend to raise the population at the same or a higher rate than the national product."

IV

TOWN, COUNTRY, AND FOREIGN TRADE

Rumanian Industry

INDUSTRY has a Jekyll and Hyde role in the minds of many Rumanians. It is regarded as the potential savior of the economy through its ability to increase national productivity and to absorb surplus agricultural population. At the same time it is accused of exploiting the countryside and of gaining all the rewards. These two views are not necessarily mutually exclusive.

Before the First World War industry in the Old Kingdom was relatively undeveloped; the two most important industries were petroleum production and lumbering, both largely financed by foreign capital and both producing principally for export. Industrialization was naturally restricted by the scarcity of local capital and the lack of a trained labor force. Although the economy was predominantly agricultural, the Rumanian government, in 1887, inaugurated a policy of encouraging national industry by means of a high protectionist tariff, partly to avoid the complete destruction of household industries by foreign competition, partly for nationalist reasons.

The acquisition of new territories after the First World War—especially Transylvania with its mineral resources, metallurgical industry, and more highly developed economy—provided additional impulse to industrial expansion. Greater Rumania was moderately well endowed with raw materials: petroleum, fair lignite reserves, some iron, lead, zinc, and salt. Nevertheless, Rumania remained a predominantly agrarian country; in 1930 only 10 per cent of the active population was engaged in industry.

The growth of industry in the Old Kingdom in the first third of the twentieth century is shown by the following figures: [1]

	Number of industrial enterprises	Personnel	Horsepower in enterprises
1901	62,188	168,198	60,744
1930	58,892	279,897	623,442

The decrease in the number of establishments and the increase in horsepower show a concentration of industry in larger undertakings

1. Madgearu, *Evoluţia economiei româneşti*, p. 138.

and the decline of small shops. Against the increase in personnel employed must be set the growth of population from 5,957,000 in 1899 to 8,791,000 in 1930.

The rate of growth was somewhat slower in Transylvania, which had a more important industry at the beginning of the century than the Old Kingdom: [2]

	Under-takings	Personnel	Undertakings with less than 20 employees		Undertakings with more than 20 employees	
			No.	Personnel	No.	Personnel
1900	94,112	212,599	93,651	153,223	461	59,376
1930	59,040	269,623	58,000	123,260	1,040	146,363

According to the 1930 census there were 140,948 industrial enterprises in all of Rumania employing 616,743 persons; 130,433 were small shops employing between 1 and 5 persons. The chemical industry, including of course the petroleum industry, had the greatest capital investment, followed by the food, metallurgical, and textile industries. The food industry was most important in terms of value of output, followed by the textile, chemical, and metallurgical industries.

Except for a slump in the depression years, which was overcome by 1934, Rumanian industry experienced a fairly constant growth during the interwar period. The years 1921–26 were spent in recovering from wartime destruction, but by 1938 manufacturing production stood at 177.9 as against 100 for the year 1913: [3]

INDEX OF MANUFACTURING PRODUCTION (Base: 1913 = 100)

1913	100	1927	118.8	1934	167.8
1921	47.2	1928	131.8	1935	165.2
1922	73.2	1929	136.9	1936	175.0
1923	73.2	1930	132.5	1937	182.0
1924	89.0	1931	140.6	1938	177.9
1925	92.2	1932	111.9		
1926	103.7	1933	136.2		

The recovery and expansion of Rumanian industry after the depression was quite marked; the rate of growth was somewhat above

2. *Ibid.*, p. 140.
3. League of Nations, *Industrialization and Foreign Trade*, p. 137.

that for world manufacturing as a whole.[4] This recovery was accompanied by a further concentration of undertakings and an elimination of smaller establishments. The emphasis shifted from consumer goods toward capital goods: between 1927 and 1937 the volume of output of capital goods increased by 57.4 per cent, that of consumer goods by 45 per cent. In 1937 the value of the output of capital goods was only slightly less than that of consumer goods.

The rapid expansion of industry, especially of the capital goods industries, contrasts strangely with the backward state of Rumanian agriculture and the generally low level of consumption. In fact, however, the expansion of industry was not closely integrated with the development of the whole of the economy, but was the result of very special circumstances. The growth of capital goods industries did not correspond to the development of an internal market: two of the most important items, petroleum and wood, were primarily for export; the rapid growth of the metallurgical industry was caused by increasing state demands, above all for armaments. (In 1938, 70 per cent of the metallurgical output was consumed by the state.) The growth of the consumers goods industries did not lead to an equivalent increase in consumption. Indeed, in 1937 per capita consumption of most consumers goods was below the 1927 level, since the increase in production was matched by a decline in imports. While it is meaningless to consider the development of an industry as "artificial," since industry almost by definition is the essence of artificiality, nevertheless Rumanian industry was a forced growth, aided by high tariff production, state support, and a relatively high degree of cartelization.

In certain respects the precocious maturity of Rumanian industry resembles the development of Rumanian agriculture in the nineteenth century, in that both were molded by external economic forces of the more advanced West. Agriculture was driven into extensive cereal cultivation by the expansion of commerce; industry, instead of developing gradually from commerce and small crafts, rapidly assumed the Western form of large cartelized undertakings. To be sure, there is no reason why Rumanian industrial development should have repeated the historical stages of Western industry; on the contrary, the fact that the West had evolved a high level of industry made it both unnecessary and impossible for Rumanian industry to pursue the same path; but this hurried adoption of alien industrial patterns was bound to lead to economic dislocations.

4. *Ibid.,* p. 95. Rumanian manufacturing in 1936–38 was 45 per cent above that in 1926–29; for world manufacturing as a whole the increase was 33 per cent.

What was the effect of this industrial expansion upon Rumanian agriculture? In the first place, it did little to intensify farming, provide it with improved equipment, or lead to the creation of agricultural industries.

With all the accelerated rhythm of the process of industrialization, the cultivation of the soil and the raising of livestock have not received any notable stimulus toward intensification; food industries based upon agricultural produce have not developed; the textile industry, while well advanced, has neglected native textile plants—flax and hemp—it has stimulated the cultivation of cotton only in the last years, and has provided no incentive for improving the quality of wool; the oil industry has been unable to cause an increase in the production of oleaginous plants, and the introduction of the soy bean in recent years is the result solely of the influence of foreign commercial relations. Finally, the rudimentary and insufficient technical investment in agriculture and the minimal importance of chemical fertilizers illustrate the absence of any positive influence in this direction by the metallurgical and chemical industries.[5]

In the second place, industry in the interwar years, while growing rapidly, was in no position to absorb the excess labor force which was accumulating in agriculture in the absence of a more intensive cultivation. Between 1929 and 1938 personnel engaged in manufacturing industries increased by 90,000 or by about 10,000 a year, whereas the annual rural excess has been estimated at between 100,-000 and 200,000.[6] Rumanian industry at its existing level was clearly unable to provide much relief to agricultural overpopulation.

It may be concluded, then, that the development of Rumanian industry was of little direct benefit to agriculture, either in improving or intensifying cultivation or in absorbing surplus labor. It has been maintained, on the contrary, that the advance of industry was at the expense of agriculture, a common complaint in most agrarian communities. Two preliminary observations should be made in this connection. In a society which is advancing there is a natural tendency for agriculture to play a relatively smaller part, the proportion of income spent on food is less, and agriculture's share in the total income declines. Moreover, since agricultural supply is less elastic than the supply of industrial products, agriculture is more apt to suffer in the event of price fluctuation. In a depression a price scissors is likely to occur; in the period 1929–39 this effect was very strong in

5. Madgearu, *op. cit.*, p. 190.
6. *Ibid.*, p. 32.

Rumania and undoubtedly served to maintain agriculture in a depressed condition.[7] These, however, are general tendencies which, in theory at least, should adjust themselves in time; in the long run, and on the assumption of mobility in the factors of production, an equilibrium should be reached between agriculture and industry. But apart from such general factors, did the specific form of the development of Rumanian industry work to the disadvantage of agriculture?

A Yugoslav rural health worker, in describing the relations between town and country in the Balkans, concluded that agriculture was losing in the exchange of goods: [8]

A survey undertaken in several rural countries on the nutritional status of the population showed that there exists undernourishment among a large number of the rural population, and that agricultural products are exported from rural countries without consideration of the nutritional requirements of the people. The reasons are purely commercial. The industrial products imported into the rural countries in exchange serve merely the urban population and industrial establishments from which the farming population derives comparatively small benefit. To cover their money requirements, the farmers owning small holdings are usually compelled to sell the best products of their farms to the town people. Thus they are helping the cities and industries, themselves remaining far in the rear in regard to sanitation, housing, health, and general education.

The Rumanian economist Manoilescu undertook to demonstrate that in the Rumanian trade triangle between countryside, town, and foreign market, the countryside received far less in the way of goods

7. Madgearu, *op. cit.*, p. 80:

(1929 prices = 100)

	Price of agricultural products	Price of industrial products used by agriculture	Relation
1929	100.0	100.0	100.0
1930	68.2	98.0	69.6
1931	50.8	86.6	58.7
1932	47.7	80.9	59.0
1933	44.9	81.1	55.4
1934	44.1	82.6	53.4
1935	48.4	90.2	53.7
1936	54.0	95.4	56.6
1937	64.6	101.8	63.9
1938	67.1	99.2	67.6
1939	72.7	112.5	64.6

8. Andreya Stampar, "Observations of a Rural Health Worker," quoted in *International Journal of Agrarian Affairs, 1,* No. 1 (October, 1939), 71.

and services than it gave, the difference being gained by the towns.[9] According to these views, trade relations were actually detrimental to the rural areas, which were being drained by the towns and industries.

It is not necessary here to discuss the theoretical question whether there is any absolute disadvantage to the countryside in its commerce with the towns. If during a period of change toward industrialization the countryside's position declines in relation to the town, it is quite possible for a number of other factors—which may be "short term" or even noneconomic—to convert this relative disadvantage into an absolute loss in income. Such factors may include the inelasticity of agricultural supply, the immobility of agricultural labor, and the increase in agricultural population. Finally, governmental and political policies may favor industry at the expense of agriculture. This last point requires further elucidation, as it was quite important in Rumania.

Rumanian industry was created in the shelter of high protective tariffs, which undoubtedly served to increase the costs of agriculture and to benefit industry at its expense. These tariffs have been justified by the "infant industries" argument, and in part they were brought about by the agricultural protectionist policy of the European industrial states. But the combination of protectionism and the development of cartels did give industry a monopolistic position in the internal Rumanian market which worked to the disadvantage of agriculture. In addition to tariff protection, Rumania had a long tradition of direct encouragements to industry—such as exemptions from taxation and special transport rates—which persisted in the interwar period and were expanded in the 1930's.

The protective tariffs, by restricting foreign imports, had the effect of bringing in foreign capital for investment in local industry. But while foreign capital has been of great importance in the development of Rumania's larger industries and in the creation of its transportation system, the effect on the total economy has been somewhat one-sided, partly because the capital was naturally attracted to industries working for export: "Without depreciating the influence of foreign capital in stimulating industrialization, it is to be underlined that the benefits of invested foreign capital do not for the most part serve to create purchasing power in the national market

9. M. Manoilescu, "Das wirtschaftliche und soziale Dreieck der Agrarstaaten: die Stadt, das Dorf, das Ausland," *Internationale Agrarrundschau,* No. 6 (Berlin, 1940), also cited in Hugo Böker, "Agriculture's Share in the National Income and the Agricultural Situation," *International Review of Agriculture, 32,* No. 1 (January, 1941), 22. For a discussion of M. Manoilescu's views, see below, pp. 193–197.

and do not contribute to increasing the supply of capital, since they are exported." [10]

A comparison of industrial manufacture, industrial imports, and consumption of manufactured goods between 1927 and 1938 shows that while the percentage of industrial consumption which was provided for by Rumanian industry rose from 63.5 per cent to 78.6 per cent, the total consumption of industrial products dropped from about 93 billion lei in 1927 to 88 billion lei in 1938. That is, the increase in industrial production (from 59 to 69 billion lei) was more than balanced by the fall in industrial imports (from 34 to 19 billion lei). [11]

From this the conclusion might be drawn that Rumanian industrialization, instead of increasing purchasing power, was reducing it. Such indeed was Madgearu's opinion: "It is certain that the position of quasi-monopoly created by the system of protection of the national industry is the principal cause of the state of inferiority into which agriculture in general and peasant agriculture in particular have been driven." [12]

If the desirability of a policy of industrialization is granted, it is clear that since industries do not materialize from thin air and are not created by amiable fairy godmothers energy and resources must be diverted from other fields to the creation of industry, at least during the period of its inception and establishment. But the ultimate effect, presumably, is to raise the whole level of the economy; perhaps the agricultural sector will not advance as rapidly or as far, but in the long run at least the whole community should benefit. If Madgearu's conclusion is correct, such was not the result of Rumanian industrialization; instead, the industrial sector pulled away from the rest of the economy, was not directed to satisfying its needs, and may actually have reduced the over-all power of consumption.

Admittedly, twenty-five years may be too brief a period in which to judge such a development. Moreover, as has been mentioned before, a great many external influences had a powerful effect upon the Rumanian economy. The first years after 1921 were spent in recover-

10. Madgearu, *op. cit.,* p. 204. In this connection see also Jozo Tomasevich's chapter on "Foreign Economic Relations," in *Yugoslavia,* ed. Robert J. Kerner (Berkeley; Los Angeles, 1949), which expresses substantially the same view regarding the role of foreign investment in Yugoslavia.

11. Madgearu, *op. cit.,* p. 257.

12. Madgearu, *op. cit.,* p. 259. Madgearu's conclusions, however, are not altogether disinterested. As an old National Peasant who had attacked the protectionist policy of the Liberal party and had lowered tariffs when he was Minister of Finance, he was always of the opinion that industrial development in Rumania had been artificially forced and was battening on the peasant.

ing from the very extensive devastations of the war; the agrarian crisis and the world depression hurt agriculture all over the world; the agricultural protectionism of the European industrial states drove the east European nations toward industrial protection; from the middle of the 1930's the increasing menace of war led to a growing demand for heavy industries to supply armaments.

But despite all these external influences, there is still reason to believe that the relation of Rumanian agriculture to industry worked to the disadvantage of the former. Politically, of course, there is abundant evidence that industry was a far more promising source of funds than agriculture, and undoubtedly political and private interests worked to the benefit of industry. In 1927, G. D. Creangă observed, "The situation which before the war existed on the land, where a number of latifundiary owners retained the greater part of the agricultural revenue has now passed into the domain of trade and industry." [13] No doubt Rumania's need for industrialization was often used to camouflage private financial motives; in 1932 an English observer maintained that the high protectionist policy was not really designed to protect Rumania from the ravages of foreign capital but had been introduced "mainly because the Brătianu party aimed at reserving for themselves the monopoly of such profits as could be made through the exploitation of the national resources." [14]

In Rumania one can never be sure that such aims are not dominant. Nevertheless, the tension between industry and agriculture certainly involves more than the personal scramble for wealth and profits. The impulse toward industry was also intimately connected with Rumania's foreign commercial relations.

Commerce

Economic tensions on two levels have already been observed: between the peasant and the estate owner in the countryside, especially before 1914, and between agriculture and industry. Both were in some measure a consequence of Rumania's increasing involvement in the complex of world industry and commerce. It is now necessary to examine these external relations.

Rumanian foreign commerce was on a relatively small scale; in 1929, for example, the total value of imports and exports per capita was only one-tenth as great as that for Great Britain in the same

13. Quoted in Mitrany, *The Land and the Peasant in Rumania*, p. 575.
14. George Clinton Logio, *Rumania, Its History, Politics, and Economics* (Manchester, 1932), p. 126.

year. While the principal Rumanian imports were manufactured goods—textiles, iron and steel products, and machinery—the nature of these imports does show a fairly important shift between 1920 and 1938. Increasing imports of raw materials and semifinished goods (from 2 to 20 per cent of total value of imports) and a decline in finished manufactured goods (from 88 to 74 per cent) reflect the move toward industrialization. Rumania's principal exports were agricultural products (chiefly grain), timber, and petroleum products.[15] During the interwar years petroleum became the most important export, replacing cereals, which never regained their pre-1914 position.

The significance of petroleum in Rumania commerce was, of course, very great; Rumania had a more favorable balance of trade than the other Balkan states, thanks largely to its oil shipments. In addition to its importance as an export the oil industry provided the state in normal years with nearly one-third of its revenue, not including benefits to the railways which were state-operated. But while petroleum meant a great deal to Rumania's balance of trade, its importance to the whole economy should not be overemphasized. A large part of the industry was owned by foreigners, and a considerable proportion of the proceeds from exports did not reach the country in terms of foreign exchange. Moreover, the petroleum industry, being something of a lucky windfall and detached from the rest of the Rumanian economy, did not greatly influence the pattern of exports, though it added to their total value. Except for oil, Rumania's exports resembled those of the other eastern European agrarian states, with perhaps a greater emphasis upon cereals.

What were the disadvantages of this form of commerce which should have driven Rumanian governments to strain the economy in an effort to industrialize? In recent years there has been a widespread reaction against the classical theory of the international division of labor and an increasing belief that agricultural countries are trading at a disadvantage, regardless of the doctrine of comparative costs. This reaction has taken a number of forms, ranging from a reaffirmation of Friedrich List's ideas to an advocacy of economic autarky. Without becoming involved in the theory of international trade, one may observe at least three concrete ways in which the principle of international division of labor fails to satisfy an agrarian state.

In the first place, the existing international division of labor and

15. In 1928–30 the principal exports, in percentage of total value of exports, were: grain, 29.2; livestock, 6.0; timber, 14.3; petroleum, 33.0.

the distribution of industry were determined by a number of historical contingencies and are not an accurate reflection of the allocation of natural resources.[16] In the second place, historical evidence seems to indicate that the international division of labor has not, in fact, been successful in providing the more backward countries with manufactured goods. "Non-industrial countries can profit from such division of labor only to the extent they enjoy a surplus of their production that can be exported in exchange for foreign manufactures. Figures analyzed . . . clearly indicate that in the majority of non-industrial countries this surplus is not large enough to ensure them a plentiful supply of manufactures." [17] In the third place, regardless of the original reasons for a country's backwardness, the mere fact of backwardness in a competitive international system can serve to impede the country's advance toward industrialization.[18]

In addition to these general disadvantages which face undeveloped agrarian countries in world commerce, certain specific factors during the interwar years damaged Rumania's position as an exporter of agricultural products. The overseas cereal exporters, with their vast extent of land and mechanized agriculture, could produce grain more cheaply than Rumania with its peasant husbandry. The agricultural protectionism of the European industrial states had a very serious effect upon Rumania and all the eastern European states. Finally, the world agrarian depression after 1929 greatly reduced the value of Rumanian exports and created a price scissors.[19]

16. For a defense of the industrialization of agrarian states as a means of achieving a closer correspondence between the distribution of industry and the allocation of natural resources, see S. N. Prokopovicz, *L'Industrialisation des pays agricoles et la structure de l'économie mondiale après la guerre* (Neuchâtel, 1946).

17. League of Nations, *Industrialization and Foreign Trade*, p. 34.

18. K. Mandelbaum, *The Industrialization of Backward Areas* (Oxford, 1945), p. 4.

19. Royal Institute of International Affairs, *The Balkan States: I. Economic* (Oxford University Press, 1936), p. 65:

Price per Metric Ton of Rumanian Imports and Exports
(in Swiss francs)

	Exports	*Imports*
1922–30	121.3	815.8
1931	68.5	853.9
1932	57.0	823.4
1933	49.3	768.5
1934	46.5	629.6
1935	49.4	547.0
Percentage fall between 1922–30 average and lowest point, 1931–35	62	33

It is obvious, of course, that the real impulse toward industrialization in backward countries has been only in part economic; nationalism and the demands of state security have probably been more important in forming the actual decisions to create national industries. National interests, moreover, have a way of making relative economic differences appear absolute. Thus, if two countries are making economic progress, but one at twice the rate of the other, from the purely economic point of view both countries are gaining and the whole situation is on the positive side of the ledger. But if these two states are also involved in power politics, the relative economic disadvantage of the one state appears, and may in fact prove to be, an absolute loss. Consequently, when power relations enter into the picture, and in the Balkans that is axiomatic, economic disadvantages, which may be only relative or "temporary" in theory, appear much more menacing.

For all these reasons, in which economic and national interests are intermingled, foreign commerce or, more broadly, Rumania's economic contact with the West served as a spur to the creation of industry. Since unregulated commerce did not seem to bring this about but rather underlined Rumania's role as an agricultural nation, with all the real and imagined disadvantages that implied, industrialization was forced. While, as has been said before, there is no reason to regard this development as unnatural, that does not mean there was no dislocation. One does not know how Rumania's traditional institutions might have developed if left undisturbed. On the other hand, the superimposition of Western industrial, financial, and commercial organizations and techniques upon the undeveloped Rumanian economy did create a strain, one which is shown clearly in the financial and monetary difficulties that hounded Rumania throughout the interwar period.

Money and Finance

Rumanian finances and monetary policy have been notoriously wobbly. The cause is frequently ascribed to official graft and corruption, of which, no doubt, there was a great deal, some of it theatrically extravagant. Foreign advisers had occasion to be very critical of the use of foreign loans, state speculation in commodities, and laxness in the tax system. These shortcomings, however, were symptoms as well as causes, though they certainly exacerbated the financial troubles and contributed to a generally low standard of official ethics.

Before the First World War, Rumania's balance of payments was conditioned by the fact that it was an agricultural country developing with the aid of foreign capital. A positive balance of trade was usually devoted to covering the invisible exports—interest on state borrowings and returns on foreign capital invested in the country. Under postwar circumstances, the fairly stable situation which had obtained before 1914 was thrown out of equilibrium as a consequence of war losses, the incurrence of war debts, and the decline in cereal exports. German investments, which had been of major importance before the war, were cut off and were not replaced by an equivalent influx from the West. Despite Rumania's generally favorable balance of trade, the balance of payments was negative.

Rumania's financial position was further weakened by the chronic instability of the leu. Following the First World War the leu depreciated until 1927. It was legally stabilized in 1929 with the aid of an international loan of $100 million. This effort, however, was wrecked by the depression and the collapse of central European finance in 1931. In the 1930's Rumania, though at a somewhat later date than the other Balkan states, was forced to introduce exchange controls and suspend a considerable portion of the foreign debt payment. The gradual move toward increasing financial and commercial controls was largely a consequence of exchange difficulties. Despite the relatively favorable commercial position, Rumania was even less successful than the other Balkan states in achieving monetary stability, and the value of the leu continued to decline. By 1939 the Rumanian monetary situation was altogether chaotic, and the diversity of the rates of the leu made it impossible to ascertain the real value of the money.[20]

It is beyond the scope of this study to analyze the tortuous course of Rumanian financial and monetary policy, which was extremely complicated, subject to frequent change, and not successful in achieving its aims. In general, the financial field showed Rumanian administration at its worst. While the real difficulty was basically that of an immature economy attempting to catch up with a world economy —itself in serious crisis—the fact that Rumania, although in a somewhat better commercial position than the other Balkan states, was even less successful in its financial policy must be attributed largely to the political circumstances of the 1930's.

To some extent Rumania's financial vicissitudes by-passed the peasant in so far as he was leading a self-subsistent, nonmonetary life. He was principally affected in his requirements for credit. Although, as has been mentioned above, the Rumanian peasant was not in a

20. Madgearu, *op. cit.,* p. 325.

position to utilize credit very effectively, he was burdened with debts. These debts, for the most part, had not been contracted for capital investment in improved agricultural equipment but rather to meet his deficit of net income or to enable him to purchase land.[21] The supply of credit to agriculture was not sufficient to ease this burden. The underlying difficulty, of course, was the general lack of capital in Rumania; the available supply moved toward industry, a more remunerative and less precarious field than agriculture. It is not easy to determine whether credit discrimination in favor of industry was greater than the difference in risk between agriculture and industry. Certainly Rumanian agriculture offered very little security to loans, especially since many of the new allotments of land were legally inalienable.

But just as industry was being consciously fostered, so the diversion of credit away from agriculture was not solely the result of economic factors. For one thing, credit institutions were primarily designed for the benefit of industry; in 1925 the governor of the National Bank remarked that while Rumania had a national bank to help trade and a Society for Industrial Credit to help industry, there was no organized agricultural credit on a similar scale.[22] In any event, by 1938 industry was receiving double the amount of credit going to agriculture, not including foreign credit. Between 1928 and 1938 the National Bank's discounts to industry rose from 32.02 to 55.95 per cent of the total, whereas discounts for agriculture dropped from 22.97 to 4.94 per cent.[23] Under these circumstances it is not surprising that many a peasant was forced to go to the usurer to whom he had to pay exorbitant rates of interest, and went on from year to year falling deeper and deeper into debt.

Standard of Living

Unfortunately, there are no sound official evaluations of the Rumanian national income. Certain estimates have been made but they can serve only as a rough guide. Colin Clark has put the Rumanian income per head of working population, between the years 1925 and 1934, at 243 international units (i.e., the amount of goods and services that could be purchased for $1 in the United States over the

21. In 1928 the interest charge on debts equalled 10 to 11 per cent of the average gross income on 6,000 farms; after the agrarian depression, in 1931, this rose to 35 per cent. N. Cornățeanu, "Effects of the Agricultural Crisis on Peasant Farms in Rumania," *International Review of Agriculture, 22,* No. 7 (Rome, 1931), 208E.
22. Quoted in Mitrany, *op. cit.,* p. 424.
23. Madgearu, *op. cit.,* p. 353.

decade 1925–35). In Mr. Clark's opinion, this represented a drop
from a pre-1914 level of 298 international units and set Rumania
at the bottom of the eastern European states: [24]

INCOME PER HEAD OF WORKING POPULATION,
1925–34 (IN INTERNATIONAL UNITS)

Rumania	243
Bulgaria	284
Yugoslavia	330
Hungary	359
Poland	352
Czechoslovakia	455
Great Britain	1,069

It is very difficult, however, to make a satisfactory comparison
of Rumania's national income before and after the First World
War because of the addition of new territories which doubled the area
and population and because of the depreciation of the leu. A comparison of the per capita consumption of certain manufactured articles in 1913 and 1927 shows a slight improvement: [25]

ANNUAL PER CAPITA CONSUMPTION IN KILOGRAMS

	1913	1927
Sugar	4.59	5.94
Cotton goods	2.26	2.82
Paper	1.41	2.50
Soap	0.20	0.41

On the other hand, the per capita consumption of cotton goods, which
is a fairly good measure of the purchasing power of the peasant,
showed no steady advance over the last sixty years. Local consumption of cereals, especially of wheat, increased after the agrarian reforms, although at the expense of exports. Peasant housing appears
to have improved through the introduction of better building ma-

24. Colin Clark, *The Conditions of Economic Progress* (London, 1940), pp. 40, 132.
The method used to reach this conclusion was, by necessity, quite complicated. The
pre-1914 national income estimate for the Old Kingdom was taken from Dresdener
Bank figures; estimates for Bucovina and Transylvania were taken from studies on
Austria-Hungary by Waizner and Fellner. The figure for Bessarabia was established
arbitrarily. In addition to the task of combining these three estimates, it was necessary to take into account the enormous depreciation of the leu from its pre-1914 level
and the change in the level of prices. Given the ultimate uncertainty of Rumanian
statistics, it seems impossible to judge the probable accuracy of Mr. Clark's estimate.
25. Madgearu, *op. cit.*, p. 186.

terials and wooden floors, and it is quite possible that there were other improvements in village conditions which would not appear in statistics.

The depression greatly reduced the Rumanian income, and by 1937 the per capita real income had not yet regained the 1927 level.

In the chapter on population it was seen that Rumania had an extremely high death rate. This was matched by an extraordinarily high infant mortality rate, the highest in Europe. Between 1931 and 1938 infant deaths showed no sign of declining, but ranged between a maximum of 19.2 per 100 living births in 1935 and a minimum of 17.4 in 1933.

The low standard of living implicit in the vital statistics is also reflected in the dietary deficiencies of the Rumanian peasant. A number of surveys taken in the 1930's reached the same general conclusions: [26] while the caloric content of the diet was usually adequate, its quality was very poor; an excessive consumption of grains, especially maize in the form of corn meal (*mămăligă*) and not enough animal products or protective foods. Seasonal consumption, as might be expected, varied widely. The prevalence of pellagra has been an obvious indication of an unbalanced diet.

Statistics on housing, disease, medical service, education, and illiteracy confirm the impression that the Rumanian peasant had one of the lowest standards of living in Europe. Admittedly, the statistically average Rumanian is an abstraction. Peasants with holdings over 5 hectares lived better and were healthier than peasants on dwarf holdings. The husbandman with an intensively cultivated farm in Țara Bârsei in Transylvania had about three times the income of the small holder in Dobrogea. Nevertheless, the flat picture of widespread poverty and squalor presented by the statistics is not far from the truth. The colorful costumes and picturesque folk dances of the Rumanian peasantry should not obscure the fact that in 1930 nearly half the population was illiterate and in 1938 one child in five died before it was a year old.

Accompanying this peasant poverty was a marked inequality in the distribution of the total income. Rumanian statistics do not permit an exact estimate of its extent, but it was perfectly obvious to anyone who visited Bucarest. The unmistakable signs of luxury spending

26. D. C. Georgescu, *L'Alimentation de la population rurale en Roumanie* (Bucarest, 1940); W. Aykroyd, I. Alexa, I. Nitulescu, "Étude de l'alimentation des paysans dans la région à pellagre de Moldavie," *Archives roumaines de pathologie expérimentale et de microbiologie* (Paris, 1935); Ioan Claudian, *Alimentația poporului român* (Bucarest, 1939).

—palatial villas and flats in the residential sections, large automobiles, yachting clubs, and Parisian fashions—were in startling contrast to the conditions in the countryside. While the employment of surpluses in unproductive expenditure is a characteristic of undeveloped economies, this tendency was somewhat aggravated in Rumania by the inheritance of boyar extravagance and by the traditional social chasm between the peasant and the ruling groups. To some extent the unequal distribution of income was derived from the pre-1914 oligarchic agrarian society, but a great deal of the actual wealth was gained through industry and finance and through state connections.[27] Unequal distribution was not reduced by the tax structure, which depended largely upon indirect taxes on consumption goods and only to a limited degree upon income taxes.[28]

The economic importance of this distribution of income is difficult to measure. Obviously a mere leveling out of incomes would not make the Rumanian peasant significantly wealthier. On the other hand, the diversion of the nation's relatively limited surpluses into nonproductive expenditure undoubtedly restricted much-needed investments in agriculture and industry. In general, the social significance of this inequality—its reflection of the deep abyss between town and country—was more important than the immediate economic effects.

In its broad features the Rumanian economy during the interwar years resembled that of the pre-1914 Old Kingdom. The addition of new territories increased the internal market and provided important resources and industries. With these advantages came the task of unifying the economies of the different provinces and of recovering from the war. On the international level, the situation was less favorable than before; world trade was more restricted, especially after 1931; the industrial states protected their agriculture; the supply of foreign credit was limited and fell off greatly in the depression. For these reasons, plus a mixture of economic and nationalist mo-

27. The importance of politics and government connections in the acquisition of wealth in Rumania is proverbial, partly because the government played such an important role in economic undertakings. In 1939 the capital invested in state economic enterprises was considerably larger than the total capital investment of all private commercial and industrial undertakings. Madgearu, *op. cit.*, p. 360.

28. In 1935/36 22.8 per cent of the total tax revenue came from income and other direct taxes; 12.3 per cent from taxes on property transactions; 12.1 per cent from turnover taxes; 44.9 per cent from consumption taxes; and 7.9 per cent from customs duties. PEP study (Political and Economic Planning), *Economic Development in S.E. Europe* (London, 1945), p. 21.

tives, industrial expansion was fostered and while industry remained relatively small it displayed a rapid rate of growth.

In agriculture, on the contrary, there was general stagnation resulting from the interplay of a number of factors:

1) the growing pressure of population, which tended, in some regions at least, to nullify reforms and kept the per capita income at a low level;

2) the decline in European cereal commerce and the fall in grain prices after 1929;

3) the relative and perhaps absolute disadvantage of agriculture in internal commerce, allocation of capital, and government support;

4) what may be called the "residues" of the old landlord system: the persistence despite the land reforms of strip farming, extensive cereal cultivation, and, in an attenuated form, large estates, metayage, and labor contracts.

A vicious circle resulted. The peasant was unable to obtain credit because agriculture was a poor field for investment and was bound to remain so until it became more productive. Low yields were a function of primitive techniques, which in turn could not be improved without a reform in the organization of farming. The rational organization of farming was thwarted by the pressure of population as well as by government policy.

Despite the agrarian reforms of 1918–21, an independent small peasantry was not established; instead, dwarf holdings, insufficient to sustain a peasant family, predominated. So long as there was no alternative field of employment for peasants driven below the margin of subsistence, the appearance of a larger class of medium peasants by no means compensated for the increasing fragmentation and subdivision of the majority of peasant holdings. On the other hand, industry, which was regarded as a means of raising the level of productivity and of draining off surplus agrarian population, seems to have had the effect of reducing purchasing power and of aggravating the difficulties of the countryside. In general, one receives the impression that the Rumanian economy in attempting to lift itself by its bootstraps had merely driven the feet through the soles.

To be sure, it is uncertain just how much of this discouraging situation was a consequence of an internal maladjustment. Both in 1929 and in 1938–39 there was some promise of general improvement, but in both cases it was broken off, first by the depression and then by the outbreak of the Second World War. Perhaps under more propitious external circumstances these incipient improvements might have lasted and led to a general amelioration of the whole economy. It should be observed, however, that in each case the show of prosperity was based on a gamble. In 1929–30 it depended upon a high or rising level of prices, an unrestricted market for agricultural exports, and access to foreign capital. As soon as these conditions disappeared, the peasant as a debtor and Rumania as a debtor nation fell into serious difficulties. Similarly, the improvement in 1938–39 was intimately related to the economic advance of Hitler Germany, which was clearly directed to preparation for war.

The depressed condition of the Rumanian economy, which probably appears bleaker in retrospect with the sad knowledge of the disastrous culmination of the interwar period, had a twofold effect upon political activity. First, the chronic poverty and low level of economic life of the majority of the Rumanian people unquestionably undermined the fragile parliamentary foundations and fostered the survival of the traditional vices of political corruption. While Rumania was poor, its poverty was not simply that of a primitive community: sectors of the economy were advancing rapidly, partly at the expense of agriculture. Consequently, there was a great temptation to snatch at the available wealth through speculation, through monopoly, and through political influence.

Moreover, the obstinacy of the agrarian question and the difficulty of finding a satisfactory way out of the impasse contributed to the multiplicity of parties and programs. That is not to say that the confusion of Rumanian politics can be wholly explained by the economic problem or that the parties can be defined as consistent standard-bearers of different economic schools of thought; Rumanian politics were shot through with opportunism. But the complexity of the factors producing the agrarian problem led to a variety of opinions as to its solution. Since the agrarian reforms had not produced a healthy agriculture, had they gone too far or not far enough, or had they merely been mismanaged? Was further industrialization the ultimate solution, or had the forced growth of industry been responsible for the plight of agriculture? Was foreign capital indispensable to Rumanian recovery or was it a threat to the country's economic independence? Was agrarian overpopulation remediable through higher productivity or was emigration the only answer? [29] The dif-

29. Although the National Peasant party is reported to have contemplated mass emigration in 1929 (Logio, *op. cit.,* p. 165), this solution did not play a very important part in local politics, partly because it so flatly contradicted the ethnic nationalism of Greater Rumania. It has been regarded by some foreign observers, however, as the only adequate solution. Doreen Warriner (*The Economics of Peasant Farming,* p. 199), for example, concluded that "Without a redistribution of farm populations to regions

ferent responses to these questions provide at least a thread of meaning to the welter of political controversies during the interwar period.

---

outside Europe, Europe's farm problem cannot be solved in a way which can be reconciled with economic progress and political stability." Whatever the merits of emigration, it is a rather academic solution, given the increased barriers to immigration since the First World War. It is also doubtful in any event whether it could be on a scale large enough to balance population growth.

PART II

POLITICS AND THE AGRARIAN QUESTION

V

POLITICS IN GREATER RUMANIA

THE political history of Rumania since 1922 has been extraordinarily involved and unstable, frequently verging on the absurd but ultimately tragic. Economic circumstances as outlined in the preceding section have contributed to the continuing instability both through the tangle of political issues which they have produced and through the demoralizing effect upon political life of widespread and chronic poverty. Two important qualifications must be made, however.

While it is true that the task of finding remedies to Rumania's economic difficulties was forced upon all successive administrations, the governments rarely acted on the basis of purely economic considerations. A strong economic nationalism, in part arising from the desire to defend the acquisitions of Greater Rumania against Hungarian, Bulgarian, and Russian irredentism, determined policy during most of the years after the First World War.[1]

The unhealthy condition of politics stemmed not merely from the poverty of the peasants but from the fact that they were not really included in the political life of the nation. In 1924 Professor Rădulescu-Motru observed that "The passivity of the peasantry has been the principal cause of Rumania's immorality." [2] Even the Peasant party had its ideological origins in a literary movement, and the leaders of the party were, in the main, professional men and intellectuals. To be sure, in all countries there is a divergence between the direction and active membership of a political party and the mass of the electorate, but it was carried to an extreme in Rumania because of the vast gulf which had existed for centuries between the peasant and his rulers. Parliamentary politics, including even the names of parties, had been copied from the West in the nineteenth century by sections of the ruling groups anxious to modernize Rumania. Since these imported parties had little to do with the great majority of the

1. For a discussion of the effects of national interests upon the economic policy of all the Danubian states in the 1920's see Leo Pasvolsky, *Economic Nationalism of the Danubian States* (New York, 1928). Antonin Basch, *The Danube Basin and the German Economic Sphere* (London, 1944), gives a sympathetic appreciation of the difficulties confronting these states in shaping their economic policy.

2. C. Rădulescu-Motru, *Țărănismul, un suflet și o politică* (Bucarest, 1924), p. 37.

inhabitants, they had remained a field for partisan skirmishes among the different factions of the boyars and the growing financial and industrial interests. The limited ambit of politics was not, however, altogether the responsibility of the boyars, though most of them certainly cannot be charged with equalitarian leanings.

Much has been written in Rumania on the primitive state of the peasant, his inability to govern himself, and the necessity for his gradual, supervised initiation into the mysteries of government. While such writings often conceal an *arrière pensée*, they contain one element of truth: the economic role of the peasant, as a relatively self-contained and self-sufficient producer, does confine the orbit of his interests to his village. This limitation of interests has nothing to do with any shortcomings on the part of the peasant, but merely means that his economic and social life does not extend into many of the fields which comprise the necessary activities of modern governments. The immediate and obvious wishes of the peasant—such as more land, more lenient credit, and lower taxes—cannot be the satisfactory basis of a political program unless they can be related to some means of realizing them. The possibility of their direct and immediate fulfillment in Rumania was limited; the indirect measures which could ultimately improve his status—the over-all increase of the nation's productivity and capital—involved questions quite beyond his understanding as a peasant, if not as an individual.

In all states there is a gap between the desires of the average voter and the complexities of economic and administrative activity; in Rumania this gap was accentuated by the fact that almost four-fifths of the population was of the peasantry. Moreover, since such a large percentage of the population was devoted to one occupation, there was relatively little scope for the diversified play of economic and social interests in politics such as characterizes a more advanced society. Rumanian writers, regretting the division of their society between a formless mass of peasants and an oligarchic ruling group, have perennially pined for the emergence of a middle class. During the interwar period the base for political activity broadened somewhat through increasing industrialization, through the growth of a more numerous middle peasantry, and through strong regional interests in the new provinces, but the great bulk of the electorate was still the poor peasantry, whose chief historical means of declaring its wishes had been in sporadic and unsuccessful uprisings.

Partly for these reasons the extension of the suffrage after the First World War did not lead to political democracy. Politics, which retained a distinctly Phanariot flavor, was the art of taking advantage of the amorphous character of the peasantry. Rumanian elections were notorious for their corruption, ballot stuffing, and general unreliability as measures of public sentiment. Perhaps only two elections in the entire period were at all free and fair, and both produced a marked upset in political life. In most cases elections were "made" in advance. Many governments were in power through no popular mandate whatsoever but merely through political arrangements; dismissals were equally arbitrary and only occasionally resulted from the loss of popular confidence. It would be futile and misleading to attempt to explain the course of Rumanian politics by an analysis of the elections.

The most notable shifts in the political pattern in the years immediately after the First World War were the disappearance of the Conservative party and the rise of a number of new political formations, some of which were very short-lived. The position of the Conservatives had been declining even before the war, partly because of periodic crises in the selection of leaders.[3] The question of land reform and Rumania's participation in the war completely split the party; after 1918 there were two principal factions, the Conservative Democrats under Take Ionescu and the Progressive Conservatives under Alexandru Marghiloman. Ionescu participated in the Averescu cabinet of 1920–21, and after its fall attempted unsuccessfully to form a government; he died in 1922 and his followers subsequently joined Maniu's National party. Although Marghiloman confidently declared in 1923 that the "conservative doctrine is enjoying a flowering and an extraordinary vigor throughout the world," [4] his party disappeared shortly and was absorbed by other groups.

Perhaps too much social significance has been attributed to the disappearance of the Conservatives as a sign of the uprooting of the old boyar class through the land reform and the extension of the suffrage. Considering the ease with which Rumanian parties were concocted from thin air and parliamentary majorities obtained, equal emphasis should be placed upon internal party weaknesses and schisms and upon the consequences of the Germanophile attitude of many Conservatives during the war. To be sure, the Conservative doctrine, if there was such, had little to offer. Marghiloman could insist that *natura non facit saltum* and urge the importance of tradition and natural development, but in plain fact Rumania was pro-

3. "The history of the Conservative Party in Rumania has been the history of struggles for chiefs." Rădulescu-Motru, *op. cit.*, p. 36.
4. A. Marghiloman, "Doctrina conservatoare," in Institutul Social Român, *Doctrinele partidelor politice* (Bucarest, n.d.), p. 111.

gressing by irregular leaps and everyone was inclined to ridicule and revile the unhappy past. The Young Conservatives (Junimists) in the latter years of the nineteenth century had broken with the old-fashioned traditions of the great boyars, and before the war the party had included an increasing number of nonlandholding elements. In short, "conservatism" ceased to be a particularly promising political label.

A multitude of new parties made their appearance, ranging from the quickly outlawed Communists to a variety of fascist and anti-Semitic groups. Some of the parties, such as General Averescu's People's party and the historian Nicolae Iorga's National Democratic party, were little more than a coterie around a prominent man; some, notably the Peasant party and the Rumanian National party of Transylvania, had a relatively broad popular basis. Small parties represented the Jewish, German, Magyar, and Ukrainian minorities.

As the years passed the number of parties increased, often through schisms and regroupings, and the significance of political activity came to be in inverse proportion to the multiplicity of parties. The weak popular support of most of the parties, together with the extravagance of interparty squabbles, had the inevitable consequence of increasing political indifference among the mass of the people and of lending a certain plausibility to the claims of those who stood "above politics." From the beginning of the period there were appeals to "social harmony" and "solidarism" which were to reconcile political differences. Two institutions in particular served as foci for this "nonpolitical" current: the crown and the army. Although Rumania was a constitutional monarchy the crown had a strong position in both the Constitution of 1866 and the Constitution of 1923. From the days of Prince Cuza and Carol I there had been a tradition of the king father to his people, protecting them against the machinations of politicians; under Carol II this paternalism was to reach an extreme form in a monarchist dictatorship. The army played perhaps a less prominent role in Rumania than in the other Balkan states, but it was always in the background as a defender of law and order. In times of crisis or of transition, a general often appeared as head of the government; the Antonescu dictatorship was the culmination of the army's participation in politics.

Despite the multitude of parties and the general political confusion, five major currents, which successively dominated Rumania, can be discerned: the Liberal, the Peasantist, the Carolist, the Fascist, and the Communist. Chronologically, these currents overlapped and all were present throughout the period. In general, however, the

Liberals dominated the years between 1922 and 1928. The National Peasants came to power in the latter year and were in complete control for about two years. After 1930, although they formed a government as late as 1933, their position was completely undermined by the depression, by Carol II's activities, and by internal weaknesses. Carol reigned from 1930 to 1940. The first three years, during which he was establishing himself, were altogether muddled politically; eight cabinet crises arose between June, 1930, and December, 1933. From 1933 to 1937 the Liberals, under Gheorghe Tătărescu, were again in power, but they were scarcely the party they had been under the Brătianus and were overshadowed by the king. After 1937 Carol broke up the political parties and instituted a royal dictatorship. He was ruined by the international developments which led to the loss of Bessarabia, Northern Bucovina, Northern Transylvania, and Southern Dobrogea. Marshal Ion Antonescu came to power in 1940, initially with the support of the Iron Guard, and maintained a military and fascist dictatorship until Rumania's defeat in 1944. The first governments following the armistice were coalitions, but after March, 1945, the Communists held effective power in the nominally coalition cabinet of Petru Groza.

This division of the years since 1922 into five periods, each with its dominant political current, is, of course, somewhat arbitrary. It oversimplifies the complexity of the actual political scene, and at the same time is apt to give a false impression of coherence and distinctness to these selected currents. All the parties had certain points in common, arising from the nature of Rumanian society. Parties out of power tended to raise the same objections and complaints; when they came into office they began to pursue the same practices as their predecessors. The same clichés—and this is especially the case in the agrarian question—reappear in the literature of all parties. In addition, there was a steady flow of individuals, for opportunist or other reasons, from one party to another. Nevertheless, with all these limitations, the division used here does appear to correspond to the main lines of development in the segment of Rumanian history under consideration.

VI

THE LIBERAL PERIOD, 1922–28

Survey of Political Events

RUMANIAN politics did not really "return to normal" until Ion I. C. Brătianu and the National Liberal party took
office in January, 1922. The coalition government under
Vaida Voevod, which had come in as a result of the first postwar
elections in the autumn of 1919, had been arbitrarily ousted by the
king in March, 1920,[1] and the war hero General Averescu was called
to form a government. Averescu, who had widespread popularity
among the troops and was of peasant origin, appears to have played
a double role. In 1918 he had formed his People's League as a rallying point against the established corruption and inefficiency of the
old parties; he had even engaged in negotiations with the extreme
Left.[2] In 1919 he had temporarily joined the Vaida government; on
his political campaigns he had promised five hectares of land to every
peasant cultivator, a demagogic promise quite impossible of fulfillment. When he came to power, however, as leader of his People's
party, it was as the restorer of order, or, as he said, "the last reserve
of the Rumanian bourgeoisie." [3]

If the Averescu movement can be said to have had any leading
idea at all, it was, as General Cantacuzino put it, that the reforms
which were required could not be carried out by the old Liberal party

1. For the circumstances surrounding the fall of the Vaida government see above,
p. 27. According to the Liberals in 1922, the Vaida government collapsed because of
a rising bolshevist current: "public opinion demanded General Averescu." *Istoricul
Partidului Național Liberal de la 1848 și până astazi* (Bucarest, 1923), p. 226. While
there was doubtless a great deal of social unrest at this time, especially since the Socialists had refused to recognize the 1919 elections, there seems to be no reason to doubt
that the downfall of the Vaida government was a direct result of collusion between
King Ferdinand and the landowners to check Mihalache's proposed agrarian bill.

2. According to the socialist Titel Petrescu (*Socialismul în România*, p. 314), after
the armistice Averescu had consulted with the socialists on the prospects of collaboration and had even discussed the possible overthrow of the monarchy.

3. L. Trotsky and Ch. Rakovsky, *Ocherki politicheskoi rumynii* (Moscow, 1922),
p. 126. In a debate in the chamber Mihalache inveighed against Averescu's group:
"Your party is a heterogeneous conglomeration, without a program, without a clear
vision, and without consistency. Your party is based solely on the popularity of General
Averescu, and will last only as long as that popularity endures. . . . You are purely
and simply covering troops for the old parties of the ruling classes." Mihalache,
Partidul Țărănesc în politica țărei (Bucarest, 1925), pp. 17–18.

but only by a new and popular force united around a man representing the "principle of discipline." [4] This yearning after discipline and order usually manifested itself in all parties when once they came to power, but was especially noticeable in those men or groups who were in office, not through the operation of the electoral system— however unreliable it may have been—but through some special circumstance. General Radescu, who was Prime Minister in the winter of 1944–45, was the last and most pathetic example. This call for discipline was an attempt to compensate for Rumania's underlying political instability. In most instances it was directed against the Left and the doctrine of class warfare.

Elections were held in May, 1920, and produced, not unexpectedly, a resounding success for Averescu's party, which obtained 209 out of 369 seats in the chamber. Averescu had made an electoral pact with Take Ionescu and had been joined by a splinter group of Transylvanians under the poet and subsequent fascist, Octavian Goga. He was also supported by a number of Conservatives and Liberals who, it was unkindly observed, felt the need of finding new bottles for their old wine. There is also evidence, however, that he did attract a fairly large popular vote from the peasants.[5] The new cabinet included Take Ionescu as Foreign Minister, and Nicolae Titulescu, well known later in the League of Nations, as Minister of Finance. The Conservative landowner Constantin Garoflid was Minister of Agriculture and Domains, and the sinister and cynical Constantin Argetoianu, an accomplished election manipulator, was Minister of the Interior. The position of the National Liberal party at this time is not altogether clear. While Averescu had attacked the Liberals, they were willing to accept his election. Doubtless they were not reluctant to stay in the background until the storms of popular discontent had been subdued.

The two principal actions of the Averescu government were the agrarian reform law of 1921, already discussed, and the suppression of Left-wing activity. In October, 1920, an abortive general strike was crushed, and the socialists who had voted for affiliation with the Third International arrested.[6] Tension aroused by the general strike and its suppression was augmented by a bomb explosion in the Ru-

4. *Ibid.,* p. 18. The position of some of the men in Averescu's group, notably Manoilescu, came to be known as neoliberalism and provided a transition from the policy of the old Liberals to the leading ideas of the Carolist period.

5. Mihalache admitted as much, saying that in 1919 a great many peasants had confused General Averescu with the Peasant party and thought that he was working with the peasants against the landlords. *Ibid.,* p. 17.

6. For further discussion of socialist activities at this time see below, pp. 246–247.

manian senate on December 9, 1920, which killed several persons and led to a temporary state of siege in Bucarest. This type of violence was less characteristic of Rumanian than of Bulgarian or Serbian political life, but was a foreshadowing of the political degeneracy of the 1930's.

Having served his purpose as man of the hour, Averescu's position gradually deteriorated in 1921, partly because of blunders in the cabinet but largely because the various groups which had installed him now deserted and turned against him. The Liberals, who had accepted him, withdrew their support and retired from parliament, on the rather disingenuous grounds that the government was not representative and had mishandled the Liberals' land reform. Whatever the occasion, it was apparent that with the passing of the postwar turmoil the Liberals were prepared to resume their traditional leadership. General Averescu resigned on December 17, 1921. Take Ionescu attempted to form a cabinet but failed to obtain a vote of confidence. On January 19, Ion I. C. Brătianu took over the government.

With the exception of an interlude between March, 1926, and June, 1927, the Liberals were in office from 1922 to 1928. They retained a hold on the key administrative and financial posts and exerted a decisive influence over King Ferdinand in his last years. Perhaps their strongest bulwark was the dominating personality of Ion I. C. Brătianu. This masterful old politician, who had fought stubbornly throughout the war and the peace negotiations for the realization of Greater Rumania, ruled his party and the country in an arbitrary patrician manner, and until his death the Liberals were firmly established.

On the other hand, there is little evidence that they commanded extensive popular support during these years, practically none outside the Old Kingdom. Part of their success lay in the failure of the other parties to create or maintain a united and effective opposition. Although the Liberals did resort to crude electoral manipulations and to repressive police measures, usually in connection with periodic Communist scares, they were still an old-fashioned party and had not developed these procedures to the unhappy perfection now so familiar.[7] Under sufficient pressure they preferred to retire rather than to overthrow the constitution. But it required several years for the National party of Transylvania and the Peasant party of the Old Kingdom to form the consolidated opposition which ultimately dislodged them.

7. A somewhat sensational glimpse of the dark side of the Liberal administration is given in C. G. Costa-Foru's *Aus den Folterkammern Rumäniens* (Vienna, 1925), an exposé of the terrorist methods employed by the Rumanian secret police, the *Siguranţa*.

In March, 1922, the Liberals made an election in which they contrived to win 260 seats, as against 17 in the 1920 elections (General Averescu's party dropped to 11 seats). The opposition parties challenged the validity of the elections and withdrew from parliament.

A sharp controversy arose over the coronation of King Ferdinand on October 15, 1922. The opposition parties contended that the coronation should be sponsored by a coalition of all parties. Despite the fact that the coronation was held in the Transylvanian town of Alba Iulia to celebrate the unity of all Rumanian lands, the Transylvanian National party boycotted the ceremony.[8]

When the Liberals called for the March, 1922, elections they announced that one of the main tasks of the new assembly would be the preparation of a new constitution. Following the coronation, they proceeded to push through this act in the session opening in November. The legality of such a one-party procedure was denied by the opposition as contrary to the guarantees of autonomy in the original contracts made between the representative bodies of the new territories and the government of the Old Kingdom.[9] The opposition parties temporarily attended the parliamentary debates on the constitution, but the tumultuous sessions did not block its passage in March, 1923.

The 1923 Constitution was based on that of 1866, which it followed in many respects.[10] Because of the acquisition of such extensive new territories, a new constitutional document was deemed necessary. The following are some of its more controversial points: [11]

8. It is illustrative of the antagonism created by the centralizing policy of the Liberals that none of the chief figures responsible for the union of the new provinces with the Old Kingdom was present at the Coronation.

9. The arbitrary action of the Liberals was particularly resented in Transylvania, where the National party was undoubtedly the strongest political group. The regional autonomy of the province had already been infringed upon when General Averescu quite illegally abolished the Transylvanian Consiliu Dirigent in 1920.

10. The 1866 Constitution, closely patterned after the Belgian model, had been significantly amended on three occasions before 1923: 1) In 1879, in accordance with the stipulations of the Congress of Berlin, religious beliefs were removed as an obstacle to naturalization. This amendment was introduced to prevent the exclusion of Jews from citizenship. 2) In 1884 the number of electoral colleges for the chamber was reduced from four to three, thus broadening the franchise somewhat for the benefit of the growing urban middle class. 3) In 1914 the Liberals initiated measures for electoral and agrarian reforms. This work, which was delayed by the war, was carried out by the constitutional assembly in Iaşi in 1917. Article 19 was amended to permit land expropriation for purposes of agrarian reform; Articles 57 and 67 established universal suffrage and proportional representation for the chamber.

11. For a French translation of the text with commentary see F. R. and P. Dareste, *Les Constitutions modernes* (4th ed., 6 vols., Paris, 1928–34), II, 355 ff.; for a bibliography of Rumanian commentaries, *ibid.*, III, 223–226. An examination of some of its shortcomings was made by David Mitrany, "The New Rumanian Constitution," *The*

1) The first article ("The Kingdom of Rumania is a unitary and indivisible state") set the key for the centralist tendency of the constitution, which showed little evidence of the respect for local autonomy demanded by the new provinces.

2) Universal suffrage was limited to males. Article 6 stated that special laws would determine the conditions under which women could exercise political rights, but women did not receive the franchise for national elections until 1946.

3) The usual civil and political liberties were assured, but in many instances the assurances were qualified in such a manner as to permit their infringement, either by reference to state security or to special laws to be passed subsequently. For example, the right of association was guaranteed in Article 29, but the right of association did not imply the right to create legal entities. The conditions under which legal personality could be established were laid down in a separate law. In practice this severely limited the value of association, especially in trade union activities.[12]

4) Rural property could be owned only by Rumanian citizens (Article 18). Subsoil resources belonged to the state (Article 19). The latter article occasioned a great deal of foreign criticism as an example of the Liberals' economic xenophobia; it was also attacked by the peasant representatives as a means of defrauding the owner of land.

5) All power, according to the constitution, was derived from the nation through its delegates. The national assembly was bicameral: a senate and a chamber, the members of which were elected for a term of four years. All legislation had to pass both bodies. The chamber was elected by universal male suffrage, but the senate was composed of elected members and members by right. Senators were elected by citizens over forty years of age and by various professional bodies (municipal councils, chambers of commerce and agriculture, universities, etc.). Senators by right included: the heir to the throne, high church dignitaries, former presidents of the Council of Ministers, certain former senators and deputies who had served long terms, presidents of the supreme court of cassation, certain high military officers, and former presidents of the provincial national assemblies which had preceded the union.

Journal of Comparative Legislation and International Law, 3d Ser., *6,* P. 1 (February, 1924), 110–119.

12. See the article by the International Labor Office, *Freedom of Association, Vol. IV: Italy, Spain, Portugal, Greece, Serb-Croat-Slovene Kingdom, Bulgaria, Rumania,* Studies and Reports, Ser. A: Industrial Relations, No. 31 (Geneva, 1928), pp. 376–388.

6) District and local councils had both elected members and members introduced by the national assembly. The ratio of the two types of members was not fixed (in the original draft of the new constitution, appointed members were limited to one-fifth the total) and permitted an indeterminate amount of central control over local councils.

7) The powers of the crown, while confined to those enunciated in the constitution, were considerable and included the right to summon, prorogue, and dissolve the assembly, appoint and dismiss ministers, and sanction or veto laws. In many constitutional monarchies the crown has similar powers, which are formalized or limited by custom; in Rumania the crust of tradition was quite thin and the crown was actually in a position to exert a great deal of influence.

8) "In case of danger to the state, martial law, partial or general, may be established by means of a bill" (Article 128).

In summary, the constitution was relatively brief (138 articles), vague on many points, and left important details to be determined by subsequent laws. There were a number of loopholes whereby civil rights guarantees could be evaded and arbitrary executive action imposed. To be sure, in most constitutions qualifying clauses recognize the state's right to take exceptional measures for its own preservation, but whereas these exceptional measures are usually understood to be applicable only in cases of emergency, the situation in Rumania was such as to make exceptional measures—arrests without warrant, violation of privacy of correspondence, and prolonged states of siege —more or less standard practice. The omissions and evasions in the Rumanian constitution were of less importance than the spirit in which the document was interpreted.

Although the opposition parties hotly attacked the Liberals, denounced the new constitution, and boycotted the assembly, they were by no means united in their actions or purposes; in 1924 and 1925 there was a frequent regrouping of party alignments. The most important question was the course to be taken by the National party of Transylvania. All parties desired to gain the support of this well-organized body; since it had been formed as a regional Rumanian party in opposition to the Magyars, rather than on a social basis, its position in the political system of united Rumania was somewhat ambiguous. In 1920 General Averescu had tried without success to gain its adherence; when Brătianu came to power in 1922 he offered Maniu three portfolios in the cabinet but Maniu refused the offer.

In June, 1924, it was announced that the National party of Transylvania and the Peasant party had officially united, but shortly thereafter they drifted apart again.[13] In January, 1925, the National party of Transylvania temporarily fused with the historian Iorga's National Democratic party (to which Argetoianu now belonged). In May, 1925, a United Opposition, including Iorga's group, Maniu's Transylvanians, and the Peasant party, was temporarily established and demanded the resignation of the government. Averescu did not join the opposition bloc and it was rumored that he had a secret understanding with the Liberals to succeed them. In elections to the newly created Chambers of Agriculture,[14] 44 out of 75 districts were won by the United Opposition, 27 by the government, and 4 by the People's party. The tide seemed to be turning against the Liberals.

One reason the Liberals were able to maintain their position in the face of a growing if uncoordinated opposition during the years from 1922 to 1925 was the perennial fear of bolshevism, which in turn served to weaken or discredit all radical or reformist movements. On the international level Soviet-Rumanian relations were very bad because of the unresolved Bessarabian dispute. A conference held in Vienna in April, 1924, failed to bring any agreement between the two disputants.[15] Each side accused the other of plotting aggression and each took measures which aggravated the tension. The creation in 1924 of a Moldavian Soviet Republic on the left bank of the Dniester and ominous Soviet speeches forecasting the ultimate reunion of all Moldavians increased Rumanian anxiety. At the same time, in February, 1925, Vintilă Brătianu, Minister of Finance and brother of Ion I. C. Brătianu, stated his opposition to returning Wrangel's fleet to the U.S.S.R. because of the danger of a strong Soviet Black Sea fleet, and announced that negotiations were in progress for the cooperation of British, French, and Rumanian capital in the establishment of an armaments and munitions factory in Rumania.[16] Such an announcement obviously matched the Soviet thesis that the Western bourgeois powers were using the eastern European states as advanced bases for an assault upon the U.S.S.R.

13. For a discussion of the union of the Transylvanian National party and the Peasant party see below, pp. 140-141.

14. Chambers of agriculture were established in each district in 1925, with a mixed membership of elected and appointed members. In addition to their agricultural functions, they elected members to the senate. They soon became political instruments and were of very little value in the improvement of agriculture.

15. According to Louis Fischer, on the basis of information obtained from Christian Rakovsky, Litvinov and Trotsky were willing to accept the loss of Bessarabia, but Stalin, Rakovsky, and Chicherin were not. The latter hoped that by means of the Bessarabian issue they could "keep Rumania perennially on tenterhooks." Louis Fischer, *Men and Politics* (New York, 1941), pp. 134–135.

16. *Times* (London), February 7, 1925.

In July, 1924, by order of the Commander of the Second Army Corps, the Communist party in Rumania and its associated organizations were dissolved for having violated state of siege regulations and for endangering the security of the state.

Bessarabia naturally suffered badly in the conflict; reports of foreign observers in these years present a desolate picture of rotting commerce, depressed agriculture, miserable administration and widespread fear and disaffection. The province had been continuously under martial law since 1919. The Rumanians reported frequent Soviet raids, plots, and instigations to violence; the Russians reported brutally suppressed peasant uprisings. Both were taking place. In the notable rising at Tatar Bunar in 1924, which involved a whole village, there is ample evidence of Communist agitation, yet an entire community does not participate in a revolt without serious occasion.

Tension was not limited to Bessarabia; in December, 1924, some 400 persons described as Communist terrorists were arrested throughout Rumania. In September, 1925, 28 members of committees of "red" unions were arrested in Bucarest. Disturbances, however, were not solely the result of Left-wing activity. Several anti-Semitic outbreaks occurred, with the usual attacks on synagogues and Jewish shops. On October 27, 1924, Corneliu Zelea Codreanu, later the leader of the Iron Guard movement, achieved his first prominence by shooting the chief of police of Iași; he was subsequently acquitted.[17]

Under these circumstances, in which opposition to the government could so convincingly be depicted as anti-Rumanian, the Liberals, self-appointed guardians of Rumanian patriotism, were somewhat strengthened, whereas the Peasants were continually forced to protest their loyalty and to defend themselves against the charge of bolshevism.

At the beginning of 1926, however, the opposition to the Liberals became more intense. The announcement on December 28, 1925, of Prince Carol's renunciation of his right to the crown in favor of his infant son Michael [18] brought protests from the Transylvanian Nationalists and the Peasants. While expressing their continued loyalty to King Ferdinand, they refrained from voting on the bill of renunciation on the grounds that they had not been consulted on the appointment of the regency which was to govern during Michael's minority. It was widely known that Brătianu and Carol had not got

17. For the origins of the Iron Guard movement see below, pp. 226–228.
18. Carol had gone abroad with Mme Lupescu. Upon King Ferdinand's demand that he return, without her, Carol refused and renounced his right to the throne.

on well together, and it was generally believed that Brătianu had forced the king to exclude Carol.

Communal elections were held in February in an atmosphere of political excitement. The government, for all its electioneering techniques, did badly, especially in the larger towns. It won only one-third of the seats in the Bucarest municipal council. In Bessarabia the United Opposition won all lists. The government was defeated in most Transylvanian towns, notwithstanding its pact with the Magyar party; it won most of the rural Transylvanian communes through official pressure and the aid of the gendarmerie.

In March the Brătianu cabinet reached the end of its four-year term. In the last session of parliament it passed a new electoral law, whose unusual provisions were to make Rumanian elections even less representative of public opinion. Deputies had previously been elected on a proportional basis. According to the new act, modeled on Mussolini's law of January 7, 1923, the party gaining a plurality and at least 40 per cent of the votes was declared the majority party: it was to receive, as a premium, half the seats in the chamber plus a number of the remaining seats corresponding to its percentage of the total vote. Thus, a party gaining 40 per cent of the votes would occupy 70 per cent of the seats in the chamber (50 per cent plus two-fifths of the remaining 50 per cent). The remainder of the seats was divided proportionally among the other parties; a party failing to gain 2 per cent of the total votes obtained no representation.

According to the Liberals, there was nothing extraordinary about this law. A bill for electoral reform had been part of the Liberal program and had been stipulated in the 1923 Constitution.[19] In a country with such a multitude of unstable parties it might be argued that the "premium," as it was called, was a necessary device to give the party in office a sufficiently strong parliamentary majority to enable it to carry on its business.

Nevertheless, given the idiosyncrasies of Rumanian politics, the law had two very unfortunate effects. Since it was the practice for the crown to summon a government, which then proceeded to hold, or "make," elections with the aid of the administrative apparatus, the electoral law increased the opportunity for the selected group to swing the elections in its favor. On the other hand, the failure of a party obtaining less than 2 per cent of the votes to gain any repre-

19. According to Article 138 of the constitution, the current national assembly (i.e., the Liberal majority) could function after the promulgation of the constitution until the expiration of its mandate. During that period an electoral law was to be passed in accordance with the principles laid down in the constitution.

sentation was a natural incentive for such parties to abandon the parliamentary track altogether. The timing of the law led the opposition parties to charge that it was merely part of the Liberals' plan of grooming General Averescu to replace them, since his party was obviously weak in popular support. There is no question that in 1924 and 1925 Averescu had not cooperated with the other opposition parties but had worked in some measure with the Liberals.

On March 27, 1926, Brătianu resigned amid rumors that he favored General Averescu as his successor. The opposition was still fumbling in its efforts to unite; negotiations between the Transylvanian Nationalists and the Peasant party had broken down again on March 22 over a disagreement on the distribution of cabinet posts. The king, on March 29, consulted the leaders of the Transylvanian National, Peasant, and People's parties and requested a coalition cabinet; apparently the Peasants and the Nationalists agreed. But on the following day, much to their chagrin, King Ferdinand called on General Averescu to form a government.

The reasons for the king's action are not altogether clear. The Nationalists and the Peasants had blundered in not mending their differences earlier and achieving a solid coalition. On the other hand, the king had been responsible for their dismissal in 1920 and was probably quite doubtful of their ability to govern properly and likely to accept the advice of Brătianu. Brătianu of course denied that his party had any agreement with General Averescu but his disclaimer is not convincing. "All we did," he said, "was to prepare the atmosphere in order to bring into power a government which would present a guarantee for the continuity of the work accomplished by us. Apart from this we are the declared opponents of the present government." [20] It was generally believed, and probably correctly, that Brătianu had strongly urged the king to install General Averescu.

Averescu held elections in May. The National party and the Peasants, still unable to achieve fusion, agreed to collaborate in the election. Despite the premium Averescu faced quite a task in overcoming his party's numerical weakness, but he acted resolutely and altogether successfully in one of the more outrageous Rumanian elections. Military officers on active service were appointed as prefects of a number of districts. Circulation of vehicles and persons was strictly controlled. The leaders of the opposition were unable to get in touch with their constituents; even Ion Brătianu was blocked on one trip, and Mihalache was arrested by gendarmes in his own electoral district. Gendarmes supervised public gatherings and were directed to intervene

20. *Times* (London), April 21, 1926.

if anyone attempted "to excite the people." Political manifestoes and
slogans required the approval of the prefect. On the day of the election, numerous opposition delegates were arrested and not permitted
to supervise the voting or the counting. There was some violence and
a few deaths.[21] Averescu, by these means, obtained 52 per cent of the
votes, but under the premium he gained 292 out of 387 seats in the
chamber, the Opposition block held 69 seats, the Liberals 16, Cuza's
League of Christian Defense (an anti-Semitic formation) 10; the
socialists and the Communist-sponsored workers' bloc, having obtained less than 2 per cent of the votes, were not represented.

After the election the National and Peasant parties continued their
efforts to unite. In September delegates of the two parties voted for
fusion into a National Peasant party with Maniu as president and
Mihalache as vice-president. Iorga, however, declined to vote, and the
Peasant leader Dr. Lupu opposed the decision. The fusion was confirmed by the general congress held on October 10.

A new crisis arose with the serious illness of King Ferdinand in
November, 1926, and the renewed controversies over the succession,
Carol's renunciation, and the regency. The National Peasants, who
believed that King Ferdinand had been an instrument of the Liberals,
were dissatisfied with the succession and were reluctant to regard
Carol's renunciation as final. All parties, however, felt that in the
king's failing condition the Averescu cabinet was not sufficiently representative to govern alone. Brătianu sounded opposition leaders on
the possibilities of forming a national cabinet. General Averescu made
several unsuccessful efforts to achieve a coalition with the National
Peasants, perhaps in an effort to free himself from his dependence
upon the Liberals. Having failed to create a coalition he was obliged
to resign on June 3, 1927.

A new "impartial" cabinet under Prince Barbu Ştirbey (a relative
by marriage of the Brătianus and periodically proposed as the head
of a caretaker cabinet, the last time in 1945) came to office and included some Liberals and Dr. Lupu, who had split with the National
Peasants in February and formed an independent peasant group.
After negotiations with the National Peasants, three members of
Maniu's party joined the coalition. The principal object of this cabinet, which was in effect a temporary Liberal-National-Peasant coalition, was to preside over new and free elections. However, negotiations
between Maniu and Brătianu broke down. Maniu refused Brătianu's
proposal for a common list of candidates in the coming election with

21. The electoral abuses were brought up by opposition leaders in parliamentary
interpellations after the elections.

a majority of the seats going to the Liberals. The Liberals resigned from the Ştirbey cabinet on June 21, stating that it had failed in its mission.

On June 22 the king called Brătianu, who formed an all-Liberal government, with the addition of Dr. Lupu, Argetoianu, and Titulescu, and issued a manifesto: [22]

The mission of the Government headed by M. Barbu Ştirbey to achieve an understanding and collaboration between the various political parties has not succeeded, and because of the differences of views in the midst of the cabinet, the electoral campaign threatened to become the occasion of agitation favoring political passions and subversive currents. In these conditions, a government was required which could be upheld by a solidly organized and experienced party and could assume entire responsibility for the situation. His Majesty the King has entrusted us with this heavy responsibility. We desire the sincere application of the laws guaranteeing the liberty of elections. We will not permit the disturbance of order nor the violation of law, and will not tolerate anarchist tendencies. Closely united with our collaborators in the parties which assure us their co-operation we will carry out our program which the country knows well.

This manifesto is a nice epitome of the Liberals' politics. Presenting themselves as the solid defenders of the law and the constitution, they had actually achieved, with the cooperation of the king, a very neat coup. By breaking the Ştirbey coalition and relying on the king's mistrust of the opposition, Brătianu had driven the National Peasants back into the wilderness without the slightest popular justification. The references to "subversive currents" and "anarchist tendencies," while conjuring up the specter of communism, cannot be taken very seriously unless the whole mass of the peasantry was to be considered subversive. It is not surprising that the National Peasants should have seen all the complicated political maneuvers of those years, including the schisms in their own ranks, as Brătianu machinations.

The Liberals dropped their talk of a national cabinet, and conducted the elections of July 7, 1927, in the usual manner; they won 298 out of 387 seats in the chamber; Dr. Lupu was rewarded for his cooperation with 22 seats. The National Peasants managed to obtain 49; Averescu's People's party and Iorga's group failed to obtain even the minimum of 2 per cent of the votes. The political picture

22. *L'Économiste roumain* (Organ de l'Institut Économique Roumain et de l'Association des Banques Roumaines) (July 1, 1927), p. 171.

was reverting to a two-party system, in the Rumanian style, with the National Peasants the only significant opponents of the Liberals.

Two deaths, however, were to undermine the position of the Liberals. On July 20, 1927, King Ferdinand died; [23] he was succeeded by the five-year-old Michael under a regency comprising Ferdinand's second son Prince Nicholas, the Patriarch Miron Cristea, and the first president of the Court of Cassation, Buzdugan. All parties recognized the regency but Maniu immediately demanded the resignation of the Liberals and new elections. With the death of Ferdinand, the Carol issue again insinuated itself into the conflict between the National Peasants and the Liberals. The National Peasants maintained a somewhat equivocal attitude toward the regency and while not demanding Carol's return, gave no indication that they would not welcome it. Carol, on his part, was issuing ambiguous statements from abroad, saying that he was making no plans for return but that if the people called him he would not be deaf to their appeal. The government accused the National Peasants of duplicity and prohibited their political meetings. Maniu responded by a call for a popular movement to oust the Liberals by all legal parliamentary and extraparliamentary means. In October, 1927, Mihail Manoilescu, who had been associated with General Averescu's People's party and who was to blossom into a well-known political economist, was arrested by the government on the charge of carrying political letters from Carol to Rumanian opposition leaders. The government brought him to trial, but he was acquitted, much to the Liberals' discomfiture. During the trial the government quoted letters to show that Carol had abdicated of his own will; Manoilescu in his defense maintained that Ferdinand had wanted Carol to return but that efforts at reconciliation had been thwarted by the Brătianus.

On November 24, 1927, Ion I. C. Brătianu died. With his death, following close upon that of the king, the Liberals began to lose their grip, although they remained in power for another year. There was no change in the government; Vintilă Brătianu became head of the cabinet and leader of the party. Although he had been a conscientious minister and had determined the party's economic policy, he lacked the political stature of his elder brother. Feeling the insecurity of his position, he proposed collaboration with the National Peasants, on the basis of an equal division of cabinet posts and a common list in new elections with 55 per cent of the seats going to the Liberals.

23. For a resumé of events after Fedinand's death see "La Situation politique en Roumanie après la mort du roi Ferdinand I," *M.A.B.* (*Mezinárodní Agrárni Bureau*) *Bulletin du Bureau International Agraire,* No. 1 (Prague, 1928), pp. 55–69.

Maniu naturally refused the offer, and Vintilă Brătianu declared his intention to continue as head of the government.

In the winter and spring of 1927–28, the National Peasants extended their attacks on what they called the usurping government. Maniu embarrassed the government in its efforts to obtain a foreign stabilization loan by declaring on December 22, that his party disapproved of the new budget and that a government without the support of the nation was not in a position to receive foreign loans.[24] In January, 1928, the National Peasants sent representatives abroad, to Paris, London and Berlin, to persuade foreign opinion that the Liberals lacked national approval.

Large protest meetings were held throughout Rumania, climaxed by a massive peasant demonstration in Alba Iulia on May 6. This demonstration aroused great excitement and some apprehension, but it ended in a slightly ludicrous vein. Thousands of peasants came from all over Rumania, though principally from Transylvania, to attend a dramatic denunciation of the Liberals, but at the conclusion of the rally the leaders were at a loss as to what should be done next—a problem that always plagued the Peasant leaders. Some of the more ardent ones wanted to prepare a "March on Rome," and indeed a column of peasants did march off in the direction of Bucarest, but dispersed on the way. Other leaders favored a moderation in sharp contrast to the violence of the oratory, which had blasted the government as the "enemy of the people." Most humiliating, the National Peasants were forced to appeal to the government to provide rail transport to return the peasants to their homes. But despite this touch of *opéra bouffe*, the demonstration was an impressive display of the opposition's ability to call out the peasantry.

It is quite possible, however, that the government was less worried by the direct threat of these measures than by their effect in increasing the difficulty of obtaining a stabilization loan, the principal preoccupation of Vintilă Brătianu during his year in office and his principal excuse for remaining in power. In the summer of 1928 the loan threatened to be the rock which would wreck the government. In July Vintilă Brătianu convoked the chamber in extraordinary session to report on his negotiations and to get authorization to obtain an external loan of up to $250,000,000. The National Peasant depu-

24. It should be added, however, that Maniu had not blocked discussion or voting on the budget. On December 27 the National Peasant representatives Madgearu and Popovici, while repeating that the Liberal government did not have legal authority to contract foreign loan, stated that if it did succeed the National Peasants would not subsequently refuse to recognize the undertaking, but would respect engagements taken, however unjustifiably, in the name of the state.

ties boycotted the assembly, formed their own gathering, and resolved that laws passed by the Liberal chamber could not bind the Rumanian nation. Vintilă Brătianu tried to persuade the regency that he should remain in office until the loan negotiations were completed. Ultimately, his delays and in particular his request that even after the completion of the negotiations he be permitted to retain office to supervise the application of the loan brought him into conflict with the regents, who were anxious to calm the political situation. Overestimating his position, he resigned on November 3 and dropped the negotiations.

To his surprise his resignation was accepted. The regents consulted Maniu and Averescu on the formation of a coalition cabinet; Maniu would make no agreement except on the basis of new and free elections. The regents requested Titulescu to form a coalition cabinet; Titulescu failed. Finally, the regents were obliged on November 9 to call upon Maniu to form his own cabinet.

Thus ended the long regime of the Brătianus. The combination of two failures contributed to their defeat. Politically they failed to obtain the mass support of the peasants, necessary under universal suffrage, but were unwilling, or unable, to adopt measures to prevent the rise of an effective opposition. Economically, they were unable to restore either the national finances or the condition of agriculture. The stabilization loan and the bad harvest of 1928 directly contributed to their downfall, but the continuing economic uncertainty and instability of the postwar years always gave the opposition a long stick with which to belabor them.

Composition and Political Principles of the Liberals

Although the National Liberal party [25] was pleased to trace its origins to the group of young Rumanian intellectuals who had been inspired by the ideals of the French Revolution of 1848, the temper of the Brătianu party in the 1920's bore a far greater resemblance to the rigid and narrowly conceived liberalism of Guizot in the latter years of the July monarchy. In both cases there was the same curious combination of a not unimpressive austerity with the crassest manifestations of the spirit of "enrichissez-vous." The limitations of the Brătianus' conception of political liberty should be evident from

25. This was the party's official title. The word national has usually been omitted in this paper to avoid possible confusion with the term, National Peasant, which indicates the actual fusion of two distinct parties.

the preceding section; they consistently rigged elections, were masters at backstage maneuvers, exerted a decisive influence over King Ferdinand, and maintained the unholy reputation of the gendarmerie. In their economic policy they displayed few of the characteristics normally associated, at least in Anglo-Saxon countries, with classical economic liberalism. The state took the lead in economic activity through monopolies and subsidies, tariffs were highly protectionist, agriculture was subjected to export duties, and foreign capital was viewed with marked suspicion.

It is perhaps too easy to dismiss the liberalism of the Liberals as pure hypocrisy having no relation to their actual practices, or to conclude, as did Mihalache, that "the Liberal party has had the tactic of bringing to its bosom the most advanced elements and of uniting them with the most conservative and reactionary elements. For the advanced elements it has one task: to write principles into the program; for the reactionary elements it has another: not to carry them out!"[26] The divergence between creed and reality cannot be attributed solely to hypocrisy and double-dealing. The Brătianus, for all their highhanded and arbitrary ways, were not unprincipled, nor are the distortions of Rumanian liberalism simply a product of personal ambitions and selfishness.

Historically, the two factors which gave Rumanian liberalism its particular bent were nationalism and the absence of a middle class. From the very beginning the Liberals were ardent nationalists and desired above all to transform Rumania into an independent modern state. A liberal creed was attached to this nationalist aim largely because of the general association in the mid-nineteenth century of liberalism with the various European national liberation movements; the Rumanian principalities in 1850 were surrounded by three autocratic empires, and it was altogether natural that liberalism should have been regarded as a weapon in the movement for independence. At the same time, liberalism in the West was intimately related to the rise of the urban bourgeoisie. In Rumania, as this element was conspicuously absent, the state was the only organ which could assume the functions of this bourgeoisie. Hence from the very outset the Liberals relied upon the state as a principal medium for economic and political progress.

In its composition the Liberal party was based originally, as were all the early political formations, upon the landowning class, perhaps primarily upon the smaller landowners, who were in opposition to the great boyars but who were scarcely representatives of a bour-

26. Mihalache, *op. cit.*, p. 27.

geoisie. In the course of time it gained additional support from the growing professional and bureaucratic groups, which made their appearance with the development of the state. With their interest in commerce and finance the Liberals obtained control of the principal banking institutions, such as the National Bank, founded in 1880, and the Banca Românească, founded in 1911. These institutions, along with the possession of important administrative posts, came to be the real strongholds of the party. Because of their predominantly nationalist outlook and their ambition to modernize the Rumanian economy, the Liberals desired to create a strong national industry. Since a nascent industry was faced with strong foreign competition, the Liberals were high tariff advocates and disciples of Friedrich List. Moreover, although Rumania was sorely lacking in capital, mistrust of imperialism—which in any Balkan state was not altogether unfounded—led the Liberals to adopt a very grudging attitude toward foreign capital. By the beginning of the twentieth century the Liberals had already formulated the phrase which was to be associated with Vintilă Brătianu's economic policy: "prin noi înșine"—through ourselves.

While the development of Rumanian liberal principles does, then, find at least a partial explanation in the conditions of the country, it led to some very serious consequences. Since the state, which was controlled by a narrow oligarchy, was the principal and perhaps indispensable vehicle for economic progress, business and bureaucracy became identical. Aspirants to financial and to political success scrambled up the same ladder. Just as the state represented a concentration of political power in the hands of a restricted number, so Rumanian industry, instead of developing through the interplay of competitive producers, was created by fiat and state subsidy and was highly concentrated. These circumstances favored the worst forms of corruption. The size of the individual's income did not depend upon his productivity or even upon his economic acumen, but was more easily increased through influence, deals, and state-granted monopolies. At the same time, the total national income was so low that the vastly expanding bureaucracy which accompanied the growth of the state was inevitably underpaid and was driven to graft, bribes, and the concoction of new variations on the traditional methods of obtaining bakshish.

The main lines of the Liberal party's policy and outlook had been established before the First World War, and the Liberal regimes between 1922 and 1928 attempted to continue the party's traditions under the altered circumstances of the post-1918 world. In this they were faced with a dilemma, partly of their own making. In the narrow political life of the Old Kingdom, with its restricted franchise and small ruling class, the Liberals had been most successful in retaining power for the greater part of Rumania's independent existence; with the Conservatives as a foil they were even able to appear as the supporter of progressive forces, and did indeed attract a number of peasant leaders and socialists into their ranks.

With the agrarian reform, however, and the appearance of a new electorate under universal suffrage, their situation became less comfortable. It was not that they were driven to the Right—on the whole their attitude showed a marked consistency—but that their actual policy now appeared in more obvious contrast to their theoretical principles. After the agrarian reform they could no longer pose as opponents to the boyars; they became quite clearly the advocates of industry as opposed to agriculture. Since the great majority of the population were peasants, universal suffrage was bound to produce mass parties opposed to the financial and industrial domination of the Liberals, whose only defense was a perversion of the electoral process. Under these circumstances, it is rather surprising that the Liberals should have been the agents for the introduction of both the agrarian reform and universal suffrage. Two explanations may be offered. In the first place, the Liberals' initiative in these matters was by no means as great as they proclaimed it to be. They were intelligent enough to see which way the wind was blowing and realized that an attempt to block electoral and agrarian reform would merely produce a violent social upheaval. Their initiative was largely in adapting themselves to the course of events. At the same time, a closer examination of their action shows that they attempted to avoid the full implications of these reforms. Their dilatory tactics in the history of the agrarian reform have already been described. The same evasiveness is apparent in their electoral policy.

In 1913 Ion I. C. Brătianu did come out for electoral reform, but his intention seems to have been the unification of all electors in one college rather than three, not universal suffrage. The franchise apparently would have been limited to literates, which would have excluded the greater part of the peasantry. In 1914, according to Mihalache,[27] Constantin Brătianu, third brother of Ion I. C. Brătianu and leader of the Liberals in the last decade, declared universal suffrage to be an aberration. The 1917 amendment, passed under the pressure of social unrest, provided for "proportional" representation. The Constitution of 1923 omitted this term, and the electoral law

27. Mihalache, *op. cit.*, p. 28.

of 1926 introduced the system of the majority party premium. In these developments, as Mr. Mitrany has observed, one can detect a "subtle reactionary alchemy."

On the other hand, the Liberals' agrarian and electoral policy may not have been altogether opportunistic. There is ample reason to believe that they really regarded western European society as a model for Rumania. Many of them had been trained in Paris and in their personal lives they strove to be as Western as possible. Hence, they probably quite honestly felt that ultimately the western European peasant cultivator who enjoyed the franchise should find his replica in Rumania. Unfortunately, this goal had little to do with present Rumanian realities, and the Liberals were confronted with the alternative of Balkanizing their Western ideals or of being overthrown by them. They chose the former course.

The disparity between liberal theory and Liberal party practices in the post-1918 period appears clearly in a lecture on the "Liberal Doctrine" delivered in 1923 by I. G. Duca, who later became leader of the party on the death of Vintilă Brătianu.[28] After taking pains to refute the prevalent belief that between Rumanian parties there were only differences of persons and ambitions, not of conceptions and doctrines, Duca defined the Liberal credo in the following formula: "Progress in all forms but within the framework of the concept of individual property." Progress, however, could be realized only "through order, through democracy, through nationalism, and through social harmony." By order he meant the avoidance of anarchy, not the absence of change. He defined democracy as government of the people, by the people, and for the people, and in antithesis to demagogy. While opposing excessive or exclusive nationalism, he held that progress was possible only through the developments of national forces; economic nationalism expressed the instinct of self-preservation and was a means "to safeguard the material individuality of each nationality, to prevent its destruction by elements superior in strength or in organization." Collaboration with foreign powers or even with foreign capital was not excluded but it should be on terms which corresponded with national interests. He regarded social harmony as a necessary counterbalance to the doctrine of class struggle.

Duca then went on to show that liberalism was not a rigid doctrine, but had adapted itself to changing circumstances. It had abandoned the classical idea of property as sacred and inviolable and had accepted the principle of property as a social function, allowing for such measures as expropriation and the nationalization of the subsoil. In the field of political economy Rumanian liberalism had

28. I. G. Duca, "Doctrina Liberală," *Doctrinele partidelor politice,* pp. 103–110.

dropped Manchesterian laissez faire and had recognized the right of state intervention to protect the weak against the strong. "Interventionism has arisen from the complexity of modern economics not merely as a condition of progress but as a means of avoiding violent conflicts and anarchy." Finally, in the social realm, Rumanian liberalism had advanced beyond unlimited individualism to the recognition that the individual had responsibilities for the preservation of justice and general equilibrium.

Duca recognized the far-reaching implications of these modifications and granted that "To-day there exists an antinomy between the formulae of classical liberalism and those of modern liberalism. . . . Liberty is not a sufficiently broad or inclusive concept to embrace everything which the present liberal doctrine represents." But, he maintained, the Liberal party was right in keeping its name, as a symbol forever associated with the renaissance of the Old Kingdom and the creation of Greater Rumania.

The difficulties of Duca's exposition are obvious. In so far as he defined liberalism along recognizable and customary lines, it clearly did not describe the Rumanian Liberal party. In modifying the doctrine to explain the interventionist and "state socialist" policies of the party, he so altered it that there was little reason—beyond sentiment and patriotism—to label the result "liberal." Understandably, he did not become involved in the even more difficult task of providing a liberal explanation for the electoral practices of his party.[29]

The divergence between liberal theory and the realities of the administration was too great to be overlooked, but was usually explained on the grounds of expediency. For example, in 1924, I. N. Angelescu, general secretary of the Ministry of Industry and Commerce, justified state economic intervention as a temporary necessity:

As soon as the elements of the national wealth have developed, intervention of state economic policy is quite useless. National output would reach a maximum, and its utilization on the international market would be achieved in the best conditions without the state's intervention. Until then, however, the state's economic needs and far-reaching aims may be in contradiction to the momentary needs of economic freedom.[30]

29. Rumanian Liberals have frequently resorted to the theory, so ably developed by the Italian philosopher, Benedetto Croce, that liberalism is not really a party program but rather a regulative principle standing above parties, with the duty of assuring that political and social changes are made in conformity with the requirements of liberty. Whatever the virtues of this theory, it is obvious that the Rumanian Liberal party was scarcely in a position to be considered as a detached regulative principle.

30. I. N. Angelescu, "The Increase of Production and Its Influence on the National Currency of Roumania," *Correspondance économique roumaine,* published by the Rumanian Ministry of Industry and Commerce (January–February, 1924).

A more realistic defense of the role of the Liberal party as the leading exponent of the Rumanian bourgeoisie was provided by Stefan Zeletin.[31] Zeletin, however, did not approach the subject from the point of view of liberal principles but employed a quasi-Marxian analysis, though for purposes that were certainly not Marx's. He contended that Rumania was actually in the process of duplicating the course of capitalist development which had taken place in the western European states a century or more earlier. In his view capitalism passed through three stages, each with its own political and social system:

    a) commercial capitalism—mercantilism
    b) industrial capitalism—liberalism
    c) finance capitalism—imperialism.

Rumania was now in the mercantilist phase, which implied energetic state intervention in the economic life of the nation.[32] High protectionist tariffs were justified as proper mercantilist measures, as was the fight against foreign capital.

The leading force in Rumania's economic development, according to Zeletin, had been the smaller boyars who, in the nineteenth century, had entered commerce and finance and by the twentieth century had become a real bourgeois class. He identified the history of the Rumanian bourgeoisie with the history of the Liberal party, which was and remained the "classical party of liberalism." As for the unhappy condition of the peasants, Zeletin held that a period of peasant misery was to be expected as a necessary phase in the transition to capitalism; just as the expansion of the British economy at an earlier date had been accompanied by enclosures and the destruction of the yeomanry, so the backward mass of the Rumanian peasantry had to suffer in the rise of Rumanian capitalism. The peasant was destined to play a secondary role in social movements and none at all in politics. In short, Zeletin was a stout defender of the Rumanian bourgeoisie, whose standard-bearer was the Liberal party, as an indispensable and inevitable element not only of past but of future progress. He condemned the Socialists on the grounds that since Rumanian capitalism was still in the process of formation and had

---

31. Zeletin's two most important studies, which led to lively controversies in the 1920's, were *Burghezia română, origina și rolul ei istoric* (Bucarest, 1925), and *Neoliberalismul* (Bucarest, 1927). An extensive criticism was made by the Social Democrat Șerban Voinea in *Marxism oligarhic* (Bucarest, 1926). A brief appraisal of Zeletin along with other Rumanian political and economic writers is given in Ion Veverca's review article, "L'Évolution économique de la Roumanie, *Archives pour la science et la réforme sociales, 16,* Nos. 1–4 (Bucarest, 1943), 332–337.

32. Zeletin, *Burghezia română*, p. 19.

a revolutionary character, "a proletariat pursuing its own revolutionary goals is nonsense."

Although Zeletin's thesis, because of its callousness and low regard for the potentialities of the peasantry, could scarcely have been employed as a party doctrine, it was at least closer to the real situation than Duca's interpretation of Rumanian liberalism and did attempt to provide a justification—if only in terms of historical necessity—for the actual practices of the Liberals, the tariff policy, the economic nationalism, the supremacy of the financial oligarchy, the lack of interest in the peasants, and the hostility to radical or revolutionary politics. Nevertheless, Zeletin's defense of Rumanian liberalism, if it may be called such, will not bear critical examination. Apart from the arbitrary assumption that historical developments must follow a set course, his assertion that Rumania was retracing the path of the mercantilist states of the seventeenth and eighteenth centuries was based upon very questionable examples and forced parallels. The entire histories of eastern and western Europe display important social, political, and economic differences; the circumstances giving rise to mercantilism in the West were altogether different both internally and externally from those of nineteenth-century Rumania. The development of Rumanian capitalism had been continually and decisively affected by contemporary influences from the West. The curious formation of the Rumanian financial and industrial oligarchy was not a replica of the rise of the bourgeoisie in western Europe but was a particular product of Rumanian society, though similar in many respects to developments in other eastern European states. Nor is Zeletin's dismissal of the impoverishment of the peasantry as a universal necessity a tenable proposition; in some countries it did occur, but in others, such as central Germany, Bohemia, and Switzerland, industrialism developed along with a free and prosperous peasantry.

The position and activities of the Rumanian Liberals cannot satisfactorily be explained in terms of "liberal" principles, as Duca attempted to do, nor can the party be regarded simply as the sign of the rising bourgeoisie in the mercantilist phase, as Zeletin would contend. More than any other party the Liberals bear the mark of the intermingling of Western and traditional elements which so characterizes modern Rumania. The resultant anomaly led to numerous disheartening social and political consequences:

Unfortunately, our glorious urban institutions, for all their liberal-democratic techniques, are pure falsehoods. . . . We have introduced liberal commercial laws, but with anti-semitism at their base; we have introduced universal suffrage, but with ballot stuffing; we have ruined rural households in order to increase credit institutions, but we have not permitted free competition among these institutions, but have favored some—those belonging to us—and have attacked others—those belonging to our adversaries; we have encouraged national industry, but not for the benefit of the rural population, as would have been right, since they made the sacrifices, but for the benefit of politicians who are pensioners of this national industry; we have centralized the administration of the country, but not in the hands of a trained bureacracy but in the hands of the party and its partisans; in a word, we have aped the European bourgeoisie in form, but at bottom we have persisted in the sycophantic habits of the past. In this way we have transformed political life into a hopeless turmoil.[33]

Economic and Agrarian Policy

The 1911 program of the Rumanian Liberal party stated that "The agrarian question has undoubtedly been the chief preoccupation of the Liberal Government," but, significantly, went on to say, "A country in such geographic conditions and with its natural wealth cannot remain exclusively an agrarian country." [34] The second phrase was to be the dominant theme of the Liberals, and in the guidance of their actual conduct certainly overshadowed whatever agrarian preoccupations they may have had.

In November, 1921, just before its return to power, the party held a general congress and adopted a new program, suitable to the needs of Greater Rumania.[35] Like most political programs it attempted to promise all things to all people. The workers were to have an increased share in the benefits of industry. The agrarian question was seen as not merely one of property relations but of production. Better farming techniques were to be introduced, and the party undertook to encourage agricultural education, expand peasant credit, and organize the sale of agricultural products on a cooperative basis. Measures would be taken to enable the peasant to make use of forest land. As regards general economic policy:

The point of view of the National Liberal Party has long been known: the development of the wealth of the country, principally by labor, initiative, and Rumanian capital. This policy assured the economic inde-

---

33. C. Rădulescu-Motru, *Țărănismul, un suflet și o politică*, p. 43.
34. *Istoricul Partidului Național-Liberal*, pp. 196–199.
35. *Ibid.*, pp. 231–234.

pendence of Little Rumania; it will assure the economic independence of Greater Rumania. Such a policy does not exclude the collaboration of foreign capital, but it wishes to have relations of sincere collaboration with such capital, not relations that will degenerate into a monopoly, dangerous to the national sovereignty and leaving the Rumanian nation poor in one of the richest lands of Europe.

As in 1911, the 1921 program combined a professed interest in the agrarian sector with a determination to develop the wealth of the nation—i.e., to industrialize—primarily through local initiative and capital.

Facing this optimistic program was the bleak reality of Rumania, devastated by the war but with extensive new territories whose economies were as yet unintegrated. Because of the campaign against Bela Kun's Hungarian Soviet republic in 1919, the war had lasted a year longer than in the West. By 1921 some recovery had been made and the first postwar budget presented, but the principal work of recovery and unification still lay ahead. The Liberals attempted to achieve recovery and industrialization simultaneously; in this effort, which strained Rumania's limited economy, interest in agriculture occupied a second place.

1. UNIFICATION OF THE ECONOMY

Before the First World War, the Old Kingdom, Bessarabia, Bucovina, and Transylvania had belonged to entirely distinct economic organizations, and their amalgamation after the war involved not merely administrative and financial readjustments but a complete reorientation in transport, commerce, and communications. The process of reorganization required a number of years, and indeed was not really completed by the end of the interwar period. Western Transylvania and the Banat suffered from the disruption of their ties with the Hungarian plain, the more so as industry was moved toward eastern Transylvania for reasons of security. Bessarabia seems never to have recovered from the loss of the Russian market for its agricultural produce.

A number of steps toward unification had been made before the Liberals came to office. Administrative centralization began under General Averescu in 1920; the various agrarian reform laws had been coordinated in some measure. In 1920 Russian rubles and Austro-Hungarian crowns had been exchanged for lei. This process was carried forward under the Liberals. The law of February 23, 1923, unified the tax system for the whole of Rumania. Banks of the Old Kingdom, many of which were controlled by the Liberals, extended their influence into the new territories, either by absorbing local banks or by setting up branch offices.[36] The nationalization laws of 1924, which will be discussed presently, increased the participation of the Old Kingdom in the industrial life of the new provinces. These measures evoked threefold criticism: the provinces complained that they were being exploited to the benefit of the Old Kingdom; the minorities, especially the Hungarians, complained that they were suffering discrimination; the opposition parties charged the Liberals with using their official status and banking connections for the personal advantage of party members. Although it is next to impossible to find the core of truth in Rumanian financial scandals, there is little reason to doubt that the acts of unification and centralization were to the advantage of the Old Kingdom as against the provinces, of the Rumanians as against the minorities, and of the Liberal party as against all comers.

Transylvania with its relative wealth was the happy hunting ground for such activities (Bessarabia suffered wretchedly from the administrative centralization, but seems rather to have been a place of exile for unsuccessful administrators and political black sheep). National Bank credits were more generously supplied to Rumanian than to Magyar banks.[37] In 1929 the National Peasant economist, Virgil Madgearu, charged the Liberals with having introduced the law for the nationalization of methane gas for the purpose of gaining control over Transylvanian industries.[38] On the other hand, as Mr. C. A. Macartney has pointed out, the actual effect of "nationalization" upon the minority firms in Transylvania was less than might have been expected because of the generally lax way in which the measure was applied.[39] With respect to taxes there was a general belief among the Transylvanians that they were paying more than their

36. Alfred Bonafous, "Les grandes banques d'affaires de Roumanie," *Revue d'économie politique, 36* (Paris, 1922), 323–340.

37. C. A. Macartney, *Hungary and Her Successors*, p. 322.

38. G. C. Logio, *Rumania*, p. 125. According to Madgearu, an exclusive monopoly for the production of methane was given to a Liberal group, who supplied gas to industrialists at excessive prices, forcing them out of the market and leaving it free for rival firms belonging to Liberal confreres.

39. "The 'nationalization' of the minority firms has consisted in the practice of putting in a few Rumanian directors, who are given a packet of free shares or allowed to buy them at a nominal rate. After this, the average Rumanian director has been perfectly content to fill the role of guinea pig, his contribution to the business being to protect it against the Government. As most of these directors are Liberal politicians, they have usually been able to do so effectively. The activities of the 'Special Economic Commissions' have thus, paradoxically enough, been the strongest defence for the minority firms." Macartney, *op. cit.*, p. 324.

share, because of stricter tax collection, and were receiving less in the way of public benefits.

2. RECOVERY

In tackling the problem of economic recovery the Liberal Minister of Finance, Vintilă Brătianu, adopted a policy of stern but primitive retrenchment. A dogged and truculent nationalism was manifest in the futile effort to revalorize the leu, in the restrictive tariff schedules, and in the suspicious attitude toward the investment of foreign capital. While his policy did achieve some desirable financial housecleaning, it was a strait jacket on the Rumanian economy and signally failed in its major aims. The fault, perhaps, lay not so much with his ideas as such, which did show a sturdy desire that Rumania should stand on its own feet, as with the fact that his goals and technique were not in accord with the potentialities of the Rumanian economy and administration.

One of Vintilă Brătianu's paramount aims was a balanced budget, which he saw as the keystone to the country's economic well-being. Between 1919 and 1922 the budgets, even though they made no provision for servicing the national debts, showed deficits which were covered by new issues of paper currency. He set about to balance the budget by cutting expenses to the bone, by covering expenses solely from the normal resources of the state, and by giving the budget sufficient elasticity to meet the fluctuations of the currency. Beginning with the fiscal year 1922–23 the budget showed a constant surplus of revenues over expenditures. Later reports of the French technical adviser to the National Bank indicate, however, that the announced surpluses in this period were in fact either nonexistent or far smaller than would appear from the accounts.[40] He also succeeded in consolidating part of Rumania's considerable foreign indebtedness by means of a British loan and in arranging for regular means of payment of a portion of the nation's debts.[41] These measures were necessary in clearing up the complete economic chaos of the war years; they did not, however, succeed in really strengthening the economy.

40. According to the Royal Institute of International Affairs, *The Balkan States: I. Economic*, p. 48, somewhat the same thing occurred in all the Balkan states. After 1924 most of them showed a budgetary equilibrium that was, in fact, largely fictitious, partly because of doubtful accounting techniques, and the continued increase of expenditure even after the *de facto* stabilization of the currencies, indicating that the budget equilibrium was dependent upon continued rising prices.

41. V. V. Badulescu, "La Dette publique roumaine," *L'Économiste roumain*, 2, No. 4 (April, 1926), 111–114.

Vintilă Brătianu was particularly unsuccessful in his efforts to revalorize the leu, which had been one of the chief reasons for his budget policy. The currency had been badly hit by the war, by the unbalanced budgets which had led to state borrowing from the National Bank, and by the unfavorable balance of payments. In 1923, however, with the balanced budget and the funding of some of the foreign debts, the currency ceased to depreciate, although it remained very unsteady. His severe deflationist policy, which was to restore the leu to its prewar gold level in the course of ten or fifteen years, had a depressing effect upon production; the restriction of currency led to a stringency in credit and a great rise in the interest rate. The leu did not recover but wobbled in such a manner as to create an atmosphere of chronic uncertainty in trade and industry. As the years passed there was increasing clamor for a stable currency. Vintilă Brătianu was reluctant to seek the aid of foreign powers or the League of Nations in stabilizing the currency, largely, it appears, because of a fear of external interference and supervision over internal financial policy.[42] In 1927, however, the original plan of revalorization was abandoned, and the last hectic year of the Liberal regime was spent in attempting to secure a foreign loan to stabilize the currency. But by that time the internal political situation had placed Vintilă Brătianu in the center of a vicious circle: the political crisis impeded his foreign negotiations and his delay in obtaining the loan undermined his position in the country.

The same exaggerated and self-defeating rigidity is to be seen in the field of foreign commerce. Immediately after the war, when production was low and demand great, export trade was put under severe controls and restrictions, though imports were unrestricted. The resulting great excess of imports over exports was checked in 1921 by rising tariffs. After the Liberals came to power the import tariff became increasingly an instrument of industrial protection. Tariffs were raised in 1924 and again in 1926 and 1927. By the end of the Liberal regime, Rumania had one of the highest tariff systems in Europe. This policy was in accord with the whole tenor of Liberal thinking with its emphasis upon the protection of industry.

More surprising, however, was the policy on exports. After 1922 the initial system of export prohibitions and quotas was dropped but was replaced by high export duties. There were several reasons for these export restrictions and duties. They were designed in a period of shortage to keep down the internal cost of living as an anti-inflationary move. They facilitated the process of directing the trade of

42. *L'Économiste roumain, 3,* No. 9 (June 15, 1927), 164.

the new territories away from Austria, Hungary, and Russia and into the domestic market. Most important, perhaps, they came to be an important source of fiscal revenue. Since they were payable in gold or foreign currency, they supplied the government with funds for foreign debt payments.[43] Between 1923 and 1926 they yielded a greater revenue than the import duties; the government was naturally reluctant to part with them. They had, however, an altogether depressing effect upon Rumanian commerce and upon agriculture. Since exports were really the sole means by which Rumania could improve its adverse balance of payments, these duties, in their effect of reducing exports, appear to have very little justification.

Export duties were dropped in 1927, and Vintilă Brătianu announced, "The progressive reduction of these taxes until their final suppression forms, as you know, part of our governmental program." At this time he took the position that Rumania was at last ready to move on to a new stage of activity. "If up to the present I have been obliged to perform the work of a doctor in healing the wounds of the past, I hope to be able to resume in the future my profession as engineer—which is to create." [44] Whether or not one accepts his assertion that the Liberals had planned these changes all along, it must be admitted that the Liberals were remarkably adept at reversing themselves and then assuming credit for farsightedness.

To summarize, the Liberals' policy for recovery was only in part successful. Despite an almost puritanical view toward the economy and the desire to improve "through ourselves," their program had a way of destroying on the one hand what it attempted to create with the other. The Brătianus' injunction that Rumania get a firm grip on itself seemed likely to lead to self-strangulation.

3. INDUSTRIALIZATION AND EXPLOITATION OF RESOURCES

The Liberals not only tried to bring about economic recovery, they were also intent upon exploiting the natural resources of the country and creating a national industry, primarily by state encouragement. In 1927 Vintilă Brătianu defined the principal factors in the development of the nation's riches as "the state, professional chambers, official bodies, and private action, individually or in association." [45] A law for the encouragement of national industry, already passed in 1912, was extended to the whole of Rumania in 1921. Industries

43. Pasvolsky, *Economic Nationalism of the Danubian States*, p. 452.
44. Vintilă Brătianu, exposé de motifs for the 1928 budget, *L'Économiste roumain, 3*, No. 10 (December 1, 1927), 338.
45. *L'Économiste roumain, 3*, No. 4 (April 1, 1927), 83.

covered by this law were permitted to purchase public land at a discount, were exempted from duties on imported machinery, and received reduced transportation rates and cheap fuel. In 1923 the Liberals introduced a National Industrial Credit Association for the purpose of granting credit to manufacturers and of encouraging industrial development; the government owned 20 per cent of its stock, the National Bank 30 per cent, and private investors 50 per cent. Tariffs, as has been mentioned, were designed to protect industry from foreign competitors.

In their industrial activities the Liberals most clearly demonstrated their suspicion of foreign capital. This suspicion was nothing new. In the 1890's the Liberals, then in opposition, had led a successful campaign against granting concessions to the Standard Oil-Diskonto Gesellschaft consortium.[46] In the 1920's they maintained they were not hostile to foreign capital but would not be dominated by it. In 1923 Vintilă Brătianu protested to a foreign correspondent:

It would be madness to suppose that we can develop the country without the help of foreign capital. We need it in every form to develop mineral resources, water power, and industry. We also require things which must be paid for in foreign money. But we want this capital to operate within the lines of a general policy which is approved of by the state and which accords to the interests of the country. We do not want the type of investor who comes to exploit the country simply to make money, but one who has a feeling for our national evolution and keeps our interests at heart. We want to be treated as an adult and not as a minor.[47]

Nevertheless, the Brătianus were accused both by the opposition in Rumania and by foreign investors of being economic xenophobes. The accusations are based largely on a series of four "nationalization" laws passed in 1924: [48] a law for the commercial exploitation of state enterprises (June 6, 1924), laws on water power (June 23) and other sources of energy (July 1), and a mining law (July 3).

These laws, which covered a wide range of industrial activities— hydroelectric power, natural gas, petroleum, mines, railroads, river navigation, postal services, telephones and telegraphs, and government monopolies—had generally the same provisions. Invested foreign capital in the enterprises could not exceed 40 per cent; the remaining 60 per cent was to be covered by state and private Rumanian

46. C. G. Rommenhöller, *Gross-Rumänien* (Berlin, 1926), p. 434.
47. *Times* (London), May 19, 1923.
48. A French text of these four laws is given in *L'Économiste roumain,* Nos. 2–6 (1924).

capital. At least three-fourths of the personnel and two-thirds of the boards of directors were to be Rumanians. Since the subsoil had been nationalized under the constitution, all mines and oil wells were in the form of concessions which would ultimately revert without indemnity to the state, although existing enterprises were to be guaranteed their holdings for a period of fifty years. Because of its importance to the oil industry, the mining law created the greatest stir and the most complaint from foreign investors.

The Liberals' suspicion of foreign capital was not altogether groundless; pre-1914 foreign investments in the Balkans, while of vital importance to their development, were entangled in the play of power politics. In view of subsequent actions in other states and in Rumania itself, the 1924 laws must be considered as quite mild. But at the time they were regarded as inhospitable and evoked formal protests from abroad and lavish criticism at home. Essentially, however, the question was not whether the Liberals were justified in their suspicions nor whether the opposition was right in charging the Liberals with personal greed, but whether Rumania was in a position at that time to develop at the desired rate without the benefit of foreign capital. From the subsequent turn of events it would appear it was not. The limitation of foreign capital, together with the stringent monetary policy and the impediments to agriculture united in stifling the economy. When the People's party took office in 1926 it promised better relations with foreign capital, and when the Brătianus returned in 1927 their tone underwent a change. Foreign observers spoke of Vintilă Brătianu's more cooperative attitude, and *L'Économiste roumain*, his faithful echo, wrote hopefully of increased foreign interest in Rumanian enterprises.

4. AGRARIAN POLICY

The general economic program of the Liberals did not make for a constructive agrarian policy. Not only was agriculture relegated to second place in the attentions of the administration but several of the courses pursued were directly inimical to it. The encouragement of industry was at the expense of agriculture; the commercial and financial policy impeded the rehabilitation of farming after the war and the dislocations of the agrarian reform.

Of course, many of agriculture's woes were not the fault of the Liberal policy. As has been seen in the preceding chapter, the underlying sources of the agrarian problem are numerous and deep-rooted. Rumania, for all its natural resources, was a poor country and no government could have established a flourishing peasantry overnight.

Nevertheless it may be said that Liberal policy harmed rather than aided agriculture. The more important question, however, is whether the sacrifices exacted from agriculture were more than balanced by benefits to the whole of the economy. Final judgment of Liberal economic policy must rest on this question, which will be examined presently.

Liberal neglect of Rumanian agriculture was criticized by Constantin Garoflid, Minister of Agriculture in the Averescu cabinet of 1926: "It is not normal that our country should possess a *Crédit Industriel*, while agriculture is deprived of a financial institution when its needs are at their greatest." [49] The limited supplies of capital were directed by the government and the banks into industrial channels where they were promised better returns. Indeed, facilities for agricultural credit were less than before the First World War.[50] The absence of credit, only in part a consequence of policy, drove the peasants to the usurers and into chronic indebtedness. The handling of payments and compensation for land transferred in the agrarian reforms served to drain money from the agricultural sector of the economy. Peasants were urged to make full payment as rapidly as possible, while the funds received were not devoted to the amortization of the long-term bonds owing to the expropriated landowners but became a source of revenue for the state.[51]

A serious drag on agriculture was the tariff policy pursued by the Liberals. The import tariffs, especially the duties on agricultural implements and textiles, raised the operating costs of the peasant.[52] Even more crippling were the export duties which primarily affected agricultural products, the chief Rumanian export. On some occasions these duties equalled 50 per cent of the value of the product.[53] They were not only a heavy burden on agriculture but completely disorganized the grain trade. Since the smaller peasants were producing primarily for their own consumption, the export duties did not affect them directly, but as the tariffs were aimed at maintaining a low cost of living they affected those particular commodities which the small peasant did supply to the local market.

Against these disadvantages, the Liberal party offered very little

49. *L'Économiste roumain*, *2*, No. 5 (May, 1926), 160. During his short term in office Garoflid attempted to establish such an institution but was unable to put it into effect.

50. Mitrany, *The Land and the Peasant in Rumania*, p. 425.

51. *Ibid.*, p. 421.

52. The duty on ploughs was 20–30 per cent ad valorem, that on imported sacks was about 50 per cent.

53. Mitrany, *op. cit.*, p. 436.

in the way of concrete benefits. Liberal agrarian policy can be divided under two heads: measures taken in supplementing or amending the agrarian reforms and measures for the improvement of agriculture.

Of the land reforms, only that for Translyvania had provided for the expropriation of forest land. Article 132 of the 1923 Constitution approved the principle of expropriating forest land in the Old Kingdom, Bessarabia, and Bucovina for firewood and construction purposes. The law implementing this article was published on July 1, 1924. Where woodland was needed and was not available from state holdings, it could be expropriated from private owners leaving them a minimum of 100 hectares. Communal woodlands were to be created, the exploitation of which was to be under the control of the state.[54]

By the law of March 13, 1925, and the executive regulation of April 15, which abrogated Articles 120–124 of the 1921 law, the Liberals, to safeguard peasant holdings, considerably stiffened requirements for the sale and purchase of agricultural property. The state was given the right of preemption on lands received not only under the 1918–21 reforms but under earlier distributions of state domain. If this right were not exerted, purchases could be made only on the following conditions:

1. The purchaser was to be a Rumanian citizen, a cultivator of the land or a graduate of an agricultural school, and residing and working in the commune in which the holding was situated.

2. Holdings could be sold in minimum blocs of 2 hectares in the plains and 1 hectare in the hills.

3. Sales could be made only five years after their owner had received definite title to his property following full payment of its price.

4. The purchaser could not own more than 25 hectares of cultivated land, including the area to be purchased. Houses and gardens, up to one hectare, could not be mortgaged or sold; land up to 25 hectares could be mortgaged only to certain authorized institutions.

The detailed instructions in the accompanying administrative regulation made the act of sale quite complicated by requiring numerous forms, proofs of domicile, and evidence of proper ownership. While the Liberals did not make peasant land inalienable they did render the process of transfer slower and more difficult and extended the state's rights of preemption to a large proportion of peasant properties. This law was in harmony with the tight-laced spirit of the Liberals in 1924–25 and showed the same restrictive view of property as the mining law of 1924. Historically, the reversion toward inalien-

54. See Diaconescu, *Chestiunea ţărănească în România*, pp. 266–272, for analysis of the text of the law.

ability was an aftermath of nearly all the land reform measures. It is characteristic of the liberalism of the Liberal party that it should have feared—though perhaps correctly—the consequences of free and uninhibited sales of land.[55]

The Liberals, in the law of April 14, 1925, instituted chambers of agriculture, modeled on the chambers of commerce, and united in a Union of Chambers of Agriculture. At first sight these organs appeared to have very important functions: to be the official representatives of agricultural interests, to give advice on agricultural legislation, to supervise agricultural schools, to collaborate with the administration in the application of laws, to improve livestock, to aid in the advancement of agricultural techniques, to prepare statistics, and to organize fairs. They were also to elect members to the senate.

Unhappily, the chambers accomplished very little. Their budgets depended upon the Ministry of Agriculture, and they were not supplied with sufficient funds to carry out the work delegated to them.[56] They were not even representative of the whole of the peasantry. Each chamber was composed of 17 elected members and 11 appointed functionaries. But since only proprietors with a minimum of 3 hectares of arable land, or tenants with 10 hectares were permitted to vote for members, a large percentage of the poor peasants was not represented at all.[57] (In 1930, 52 per cent of the peasant farms were of less than 3 hectares.) Worst of all, the chambers, with their right to elect senators, became hopelessly entangled in politics. Under the law creating them, the government could dissolve the chambers for serious irregularities or bad faith in the accomplishment of their legal work or for activities against the interests of the state. Inevitably, the chambers were repeatedly dissolved on any pretext for the purpose of facilitating the election of senators.

In May, 1928, the Liberals passed a law for the classification of cereals, designed to improve the quality of grain destined for export and to reduce the number of middlemen between producer and foreign consumer. There had been frequent complaints of the inferior quality of exported Rumanian grain and the presence of an excessive amount

55. In 1911 the Liberal program has spoken of the desirability of creating a medium property by natural selection, that is, by the purchase and sale of land. The 1924 law certainly represents a retreat from that position. On the other hand, as will be seen below, the National Peasants revised the 1925 law, for the purpose of permitting "natural selection," but with unfortunate results for the poorer peasants.

56. F. E. Manoliou, *La Reconstruction économique et financière de la Roumanie et les partis politiques* (Paris, 1931), p. 159.

57. Filip Chefner, "Camerile agricole în România," *M.A.B.: Bulletin du Bureau International Agraire, 2* (1926), 36.

of impurities. An improvement was undoubtedly desirable. Yet the low quality of exported grain was but a symptom of the generally bad condition of agriculture. Attacking the problem at the level of exports was indicative of the Liberals' attitude. The opposition sharply criticized the law as missing the point: "We are not suffering from a commercial crisis," said Mihalache, "but from a crisis of production. The problem of production must be solved first." [58]

In July, 1928, shortly before the Liberals fell they passed a cooperative code which had little effect except to reorganize previous cooperative organizations and to increase the direct control of the state. On the whole, as has been mentioned, the cooperative movement was and remained weak and ineffectual. In 1923–24 the National Bank granted 600 millions of lei credit to the whole of the cooperative movement, whereas private bankers received 7,500 millions.

A "battle for production" was inaugurated in 1928 by the Minister of Agriculture, Argetoianu, and in March an agricultural congress voted a resolution which is striking in its complete emphasis upon technical improvements: better seeds, more rational crop rotation, more fertilizers, the expansion of experimental stations. The resolution opposed a further extension of the area under wheat and recommended an effort to raise the output per hectare. In no case, however, did it penetrate to the level of agrarian reforms, as defined in the preceding chapter, but was wholly occupied with desiderata, which were simple enough to call for but very difficult to achieve.

These final efforts of 1928 were, however, of little import, as they were in large part a belated effort to meet the challenge of the opposition which was on the point of coming to power.

It is not easy to judge the successes and failures of the Liberals' economic policy. It seemed easier immediately after their defeat to see their errors and particularly their shortcomings in the agrarian question. But with the failure of subsequent administrations to improve agriculture or to provide a stable economy the nature of the Liberal failure becomes less obvious. Moreover, many of the economic practices of the Brătianus, regarded as heretical at the time, have become generalized not only in the Balkans but throughout Europe; state-supported industrialization has become a commonplace and has received a substantial body of theoretical justification. Yet with all these added qualifications, it may be concluded that the Liberal policy failed.

58. Quoted in Mitrany, *op. cit.*, p. 452.

For all their opportunism, favoritism to party members, and questionable economic ethics the Liberals had an economic policy. It was not a "liberal" policy and it was not altogether self-consistent, but it was manifest in almost all the economic legislation passed between 1922 and 1928, in agriculture as well as in industry, finance, and commerce. It was based upon a strong nationalism and upon a greatly simplified view of the nature of economic progress. Failing to realize the double-edged nature of most economic decisions, the Liberals had a rather naive faith in the possibility of creating things by fiat. They spoke of Rumania's natural resources as though they were something to be garnered with a little diligent shoveling; they expected the currency to regain its prewar gold level by a mechanical correction of the budget and the balance of trade; in so far as they concerned themselves with agriculture they attempted improvements at the level of export trade or of Chambers of Agriculture. The same attitude was shown in their tendency to restrict movement: currency issues were held below the level necessary for normal business transactions; both imports and exports were inhibited; sales of agricultural land were impeded.

This Liberal attitude should not be confused with "planning." There is little evidence that the Liberals had a comprehensive view of the economy. Industry undoubtedly expanded at the expense of agriculture, yet the policy of export duties on agricultural produce would not indicate a consistent program of nourishing industry through the proceeds of agriculture.

The Liberals fell between two stools. They were unwilling, more for nationalist than for economic reasons, to accept the consequences of a free economy; they feared it would keep Rumania a weak agrarian state at the mercy of foreign capital and unable to provide the means for its own defense. But they were not fully aware of the far-reaching consequences of a directed policy of forced industrialization. In a country as poor and as small as Rumania, a successful policy of development "through ourselves"—and not merely a policy whereby a minority skims off the cream at the expense of the majority—would have involved a long-range program of organized forced savings quite beyond the powers of the Brătianu regime.

The Liberals' economic program had a decisive effect upon their political position. Under the best of circumstances, it would be difficult to persuade a peasant electorate that agriculture should pay for the advancement of industry. In Rumania, with a very primitive peasantry on the one hand and a not very public-minded group of industrialists on the other, it was impossible, especially when there

was a large and articulate Peasant party vociferously criticizing
"artificial industries." The Liberals, however, were unwilling to accept the logical consequences of this contradiction and make a clean
break with democratic procedures. They preferred to pervert them
and when, in 1928, that failed they fell from power. In the 1930's
there was to be less squeamishness in this matter.

VII

THE PEASANTIST PERIOD, 1928–30

Survey of Political Events

PERHAPS the most disheartening episode in Rumanian history between the wars was the failure of the National Peasant party during its brief term of office after the fall of the Liberals. The period between the formation of the Maniu government in November, 1928, and Maniu's resignation in October, 1930, is a watershed: 1928 was the culmination of a political struggle which had been going on since the end of the First World War; 1930 was the beginning of the long descent into the abyss of 1940 and 1941. The inability of the National Peasants either to relieve the agrarian question or to maintain their political power ended the prospect of a peasant democracy.

When the regents, on November 9, called upon Maniu to form his own government, the National Peasants came into office on a wave of national enthusiasm and optimism. There were widespread rejoicings over the "bloodless revolution"; not only peasants but even business circles and some Liberals were happy to escape from the confining atmosphere of the Brătianu regime. On November 11 Maniu formed an all National Peasant cabinet, including in its important posts: Vaida Voevod at the Interior, G. Mironescu, a wealthy Moldavian who had come from Take Ionescu's party, in the Foreign Office; Ion Mihalache at Agriculture; and Virgil Madgearu at Commerce and Industry. On the following day he announced that "Our first aim will be to give the principles of the Constitution their real meaning and impart a character of strict legality to the working of the administration." [1] He went on to say that he would not disrupt his predecessors' work in the negotiations for a stabilization loan, that he would organize agricultural credit, and give greater power to local institutions. Certain ministries were to be abolished, martial law and censorship to be suspended.

In these initial statements the general aims of the new government are apparent: the primary stress is upon restoring, or rather creating for the first time, a truly constitutional regime. Secondly, the aid of

1. *Times* (London), November 12, 1928.

foreign capital is to be sought to repair the national economy. Thirdly, if not as an afterthought at least not underlined, agriculture is to be assisted. Considering the battle against Liberal arbitrariness and the general clamor for a stable currency and foreign capital, such an order of emphasis is not surprising, but it does indicate that direct interest in the welfare of the peasantry was qualified by other, though not necessarily unrelated, considerations.

In the general elections of December 12 the National Peasants, allied with the German party and the Social Democrats, won an overwhelming victory in what is conceded to have been a free and fair election. They gained about 80 per cent of the votes and 348 seats in the chamber (333 seats to the National Peasants, 7 to the German party, and 8 to the Social Democrats). The Liberals obtained only 13 seats; the Averescu-Iorga coalition 5; the Magyars 16; Dr. Lupu's dissident peasants 5; the Peasant Labor party (a Communist organization) and Cuza's anti-Semitic Christian League failed to gain the necessary 2 per cent of the votes. Despite their criticism of the 1926 electoral law, the National Peasants did not repeal it when they came into office and, like the other parties, took advantage of the government premium.

The first major step was the stabilization of the leu. Vintilă Brătianu's foreign negotiations were resumed, and an agreement was reached in Paris on February 3, 1929.[2] A $72,000,000 loan for stabilization and railway construction was floated in Washington, London, and Paris; a further $30,000,000 was secured against a concession of the Rumanian match monopoly to a Swedish group. The security of the loan was based on the revenues of the Institute of State Monopolies, created for the purpose. Orders for railway equipment were to be made in the countries floating the loan. The French economist, Charles Rist, who had informed Maniu in December that the loan was dependent upon a reorganization of the treasury, went to Bucarest to supervise the loan and the operation of Rumanian finances. All these conditions were, of course, precisely what Vintilă Brătianu had hoped to avoid through his unsuccessful policy of revalorization. On February 8 the Rumanian assembly passed a law fixing the leu at 10 milligrams gold, 167.18 lei to the dollar.[3]

The government worked hard to attract foreign capital and to set

2. Largely for reasons of prestige, Brătianu, unlike the governments of the other Balkan states, had not gone to the League of Nations for the stabilization loan but had sought it through independent negotiations. Maniu felt obliged to continue this course, although it was reported that he could have obtained better terms through the League.

3. For a detailed account of the monetary reform, see Alexandre-Ionesco Ivanof, *La Réforme monétaire roumaine* (Paris, 1929).

internal finances in order. In March the 1924 mining law was revised to give more favorable treatment to foreign concessions. State expenditures were reduced through the elimination or consolidation of several ministries.[4]

For all their energetic beginning, before the National Peasants had been in power a year, the first flush of enthusiasm was beginning to fade. The badly defeated opposition undertook to rally its forces and started a press campaign of villification and sensational rumors. After the passage in July of the administrative reform bill, which attempted to reduce excessive centralization and place greater authority in the hands of local administrations, both the Liberals and General Averescu's party withdrew from the assembly. In the same month was uncovered an absurd fascist plot among army officers to overthrow the government. To defend the regime against these fascist currents, some of the party's younger followers set up their own paramilitary bodies.

At the same time that the Right was increasing its activities, the government came into conflict with the Left. Bessarabia was still a trouble zone; there were frequent reports of Soviet espionage teams crossing the Dniester. In February, 1929, A. Dobrogeanu-Gherea, son of the old Social Democratic leader and himself a former leader of the Rumanian Communists, was arrested and sentenced to eight years' imprisonment for secretly returning to Rumania from the U.S.S.R. In August a strike broke out among 3,800 coal miners in the Jiu Valley. Troops were called and when the strikers attempted to take over the electric plant of the Lupeni mines the troops fired, killing over a score of miners. The massacre in the Jiu Valley has often been cited as an example of the perfidy of the National Peasants, but it should be said that when the government investigated the event, it not only blamed the miners for having violated the law but also censored the mining companies for permitting the conditions which had led to the strike. It dismissed all the police and military officials connected with the affair.

A couple of months later an attempt was made on Vaida Voevod's life. In the investigation which followed, one suspect, who was later proved to have been innocent, was horribly beaten and crippled by the police. Again there was a public scandal and the government

4. The bewildering changes in the names and numbers of Rumanian ministries seem to be largely a result of the need to provide portfolios for persons or groups who have supported the administration. The Ministry of Fine Arts has been the favorite post to be granted as a political reward.

was charged with bad faith. The National Peasants reprimanded the offending officials and maintained that such police brutality was an evil inheritance which they were attempting to eradicate. Such incidents are of importance here only in showing the tenacity with which old habits persisted under the new order.

The failure of the economy to rally provided the really vulnerable point for opposition attacks. The stabilization of the currency had given rise to overly sanguine hopes that money would become plentiful—the Bucarest Jockey Club on the strength of it had doubled its bridge points—but much of the funds went to paying old debts. Crops had been bad in 1927 and 1928, and one of the first tasks of the Maniu government had been to send relief supplies to Bessarabia. The 1929 harvest was excellent, one of the best in the interwar years, but exports were not great, and world grain prices were already beginning the long descent which was to continue until 1934.

The death in October, 1929, of one of the regents, Buzdugan, produced a typical Rumanian crisis. The Liberals contended that the two other regents should select the third member. The National Peasant assembly, however, elected the new regent, Constantin Sarațeanu, thus laying the party open to the same criticism that it had made of the Liberals in the creation of the regency in the first place. Moreover, Maniu seems to have failed to inform some of the Peasant members of the person to be selected and rumors spread, assisted by wishful opposition thinking, that the Transylvanians were forming an inner cabinet in the government. The principal result of the regency affair, however, was to arouse general dissatisfaction over such an arrangement and to increase talk of Carol's return.

In 1930 the situation was even less favorable. Economic improvement failed to round the corner. The opposition press increased its polemics by publishing wild reports of Soviet mobilization on the frontier, Communist uprisings in Bessarabia, and the government's secret intention to devalue the leu. This technique, long familiar in Rumania, was designed to rattle the government into making a false step, and did succeed in driving it to pass a law establishing a prison sentence for persons found guilty of spreading tendentious rumors likely to damage the credit of the state. Under this law the government confiscated several newspapers.

The municipal elections of March, 1930, showed an increase in Liberal strength, as the National Peasants led only by two to one. In May by-elections government candidates were returned in five constituencies, but were defeated in Cernăuti by a Ukrainian Nationalist candidate and in Roman by a fascist. The Communist candidate in Timişoara polled over 25,000 votes. Here were the seeds of the political upheavals of the next decade.

At this point, when the National Peasants still commanded a strong majority but were suffering a perceptible loss of popularity and a slackening of impetus, Carol dramatically returned to Rumania on June 6, 1930. His return was not a surprise, as there had been rumors about it for weeks, so many in fact that the government had forbidden the mention of his name in the press. Maniu, after announcing that the government had sanctioned his return, resigned and was replaced by Mironescu, who annulled the act excluding Carol from the throne. He then resigned and a brief period of confusion ensued. The Liberal party split on the question; Vintilă Brătianu sharply opposed Carol's return and expelled a section of the party under Gheorghe Brătianu, the historian and adopted son of Ion I. C. Brătianu, who had come out for Carol. After two days, during which Marshal Presan attempted unsuccessfully to create a coalition cabinet, Maniu was recalled and formed a new National Peasant government, much the same as his first but with the addition of the economist Manoilescu, who had worked diligently for Carol's return.

The details of Carol's spectacular return are not altogether clear. Apparently the initiative had been his but Maniu had welcomed him.[5] As has already been noted, the National Peasants had never been satisfied with Carol's renunciation of the crown. The disadvantages inherent in the regency, which still had many years to go before Michael reached his majority; the hope of having a king on their side as Ferdinand had been on the Liberals'; the increasing difficulties of the party and the portents of waning popularity; and finally the obvious popular approval of Carol's return—all these combined to make the National Peasants accept the fatal step. At that the party

5. Ten years later Maniu wrote an article in the journal *Timpul* (September 14, 1940), describing his attitude toward Carol's return: "Ever since 1926 I was against Prince Carol's retirement and favored his return, not only in order to satisfy public opinion—which manifested this desire increasingly—but also to insure the continuity of the dynastic order and the normal government of the country. . . . Therefore, in my capacity as Prime Minister I favored the return of Prince Carol, but only under certain well-defined conditions which were to be put into force from the very beginning. However, after only a few weeks of his reign, I realized to my regret that these conditions were not being fulfilled. Thus, among other things the Coronation of King Carol II and of Queen Helen, arranged for the month of September 1930, was indefinitely postponed. Instead, and in defiance of Christian morals, he compromised his reign by leading a life against which I protested unceasingly for ten years. Having arrived at the conclusion that under these conditions I could no longer accept responsibility for Prince Carol's return and for his rule, I resigned, but maintained my attitude of energetic and continuous protest."

leaders were not in complete agreement. Some desired Carol's immediate proclamation as king, some were hostile to him, and others advocated his entering the regency. Maniu himself was opposed to proclaiming him king until Carol should leave Mme Lupescu and achieve a reconciliation with his wife. "But," he said later, "I could not force my views in face of public opinion." [6]

The newly constituted government was short-lived. When Maniu learned that Mme Lupescu had returned to Rumania contrary to what he believed to be Carol's agreement, he resigned in protest on October 6. A new National Peasant cabinet was formed under the wealthy but colorless Mironescu, without Maniu or Vaida Voevod. Although this cabinet remained in office until the following April, its dismissal was only a matter of time. Carol had announced his desire to create a coalition government, and as soon as the National Peasants had completed a new loan agreement they were removed from office. The second National Peasant government of 1932–33 will be discussed later in connection with the depression.

Maniu's resignation in October, 1930, was a significant event as it marked, when viewed in retrospect, the conclusion of Rumania's brief experiment with responsible government. In so far as his action was a protest against royal irresponsibility and bad faith, Maniu was remaining true, as he did always, to his conception of legality and constitutionality. But as a protest against the king's moral standards it was misdirected. "Bourgeois sexual morality," Mr. Hugh Seton-Watson has said, "is probably less esteemed in Rumania than anywhere else on the Continent. It was not the right issue on which to base the whole conflict between Democracy and Dictatorship." [7]

The episode is inexplicable without some insight into Maniu's personality, which, in its rather cold incorruptibility, was in the sharpest possible contrast to the laxness and opportunism of Rumanian public life. Born in Transylvania in 1873, Iuliu Maniu had studied law in Vienna. He had been attorney of the Uniate Metropolitanate of Blaj and professor of law at the Blaj Theological Academy. As deputy to the Hungarian parliament he had gained a reputation as a stubborn and doughty opponent of Hungarian policy in Transylvania. The clerical atmosphere of Blaj and the parliamentary atmosphere of the Budapest chamber had a lasting influence. Maniu

6. John Gunther, *Inside Europe* (London, 1936), pp. 367–369, includes an unpublished speech by Maniu which was to have been delivered in 1934 and which provides some additional details concerning the National Peasant leader's position on Carol's return.

7. Hugh Seton-Watson, *Eastern Europe between the Wars, 1918–1941* (2d ed., Cambridge University Press, 1946), p. 204.

was renowned as the man in permanent opposition and as one whose acts were always directed by what he considered to be the judgment of posterity. From the very beginning of postwar politics his strength of character gave him an influence which is otherwise difficult to explain. He has always been a source of tremendous admiration to his followers and of singular exasperation and hatred to his opponents.

Those traits, however, which contributed to Maniu's very considerable stature had two serious disadvantages. His personal probity not only led him into politically untenable positions, such as making a political issue of Mme Lupescu, but was far too elevated for his party to emulate. There was always a noticeable divergence between Maniu's precepts and the activities of rank and file of the party, and while Maniu cannot bear the responsibility for the foibles and shortcomings of his followers, it left him, as leader of the party, open to charges of hypocrisy. A more serious drawback was the negativeness and passivity, though not from weakness, of Maniu's attitude; he was always withdrawing, retiring, and resigning, frequently on occasions which demanded a more positive response. Characteristic of this attitude and showing both an admirable democratic belief in his compatriots, together with the absence of any constructive action, is a speech he delivered later, in February, 1932:

To-day the nation is deprived of its constitutional rights; we are on the threshold of bankruptcy, both economic and moral; we see anarchy enthroned in men's souls and hatred fomented in the provinces, and in the murmur of this growing dissolution one hardly hears the voice of the national conscience, one and undivided. . . . In such solemn moments you ask for my guidance. I shall offer you none. You have both intelligence and conscience. I pray you to revere the memory of the sufferings which brought about the consummation of the national unity.[8]

More, however, was involved in Maniu's resignation than personal differences between two individuals. In effect, the leader of a government which had come into power with a tremendous—and authentic—majority of votes surrendered its authority to a monarch who had assumed the crown only four months earlier. Admittedly, there was nothing unconstitutional in this, since the king had the right to appoint and dismiss ministers, but it did bring out the implicit contradictions in the Rumanian constitution between the powers of the monarch and representative government. More than that, it raises

8. Quoted in G. C. Logio, *Rumania*, pp. 59–60.

serious doubts as to the significance of representative government in a country such as Rumania.

The National Peasant defeat, for such it proved to be, is open to two interpretations. Either the party ineptly permitted itself to be eased out of office, thus failing to maintain its responsibilities as the representatives of the great majority of the electorate, or the true sources of power and influence in Rumania were not embodied in the electoral process which had so strongly shown its approval of the National Peasants. Both interpretations, of course, are largely true. The full significance of Maniu's resignation could not be apparent immediately, and it could well have been a tactic of *reculer pour mieux sauter* for which he was well known. Nor was Carol's ultimate overthrow of the parliamentary system necessarily implicit in his initial activities, although it was widely known that he favored a coalition cabinet under the parental eyes of the monarch and disliked the wrangling of politicians. Nevertheless, the surrender of delegated authority rather than resistance to Carol's arbitrary moves is the responsibility of the National Peasants and especially of Maniu.[9]

On the other hand it would be difficult to gauge the relative strength —if it had come to a clear-cut decision—of the National Peasants, for all their popular majority, and the king. The issue, if it had become such, would have been between the "constitutional" elements of Rumanian political life—i.e., the actual strength residing in a party honestly elected by a majority of politically illiterate voters —and the nonconstitutional or apolitical elements, i.e., the rallying power of the crown itself, the attitude of the army, and all the backstage, Byzantine aspects of Rumanian politics. Such an issue would have been in doubtful balance, and it is quite possible that the National Peasants could have won out only if they had undertaken a more dynamic course, including recourse to force. This in turn would have been a denial of Maniu's whole concept of constitutionality and legality, and might indeed have led to the dictatorial practices he had combated so long.

9. Admittedly, this is an oversimplification. There was a great difference, in degree if not in kind, between Carol's refusal to give up Mme Lupescu and his subsequent abrogation of the 1923 Constitution. Furthermore, since Maniu's views on the Lupescu issue were essentially ethical rather than political, it would have been difficult for him to have obtained the support of the government or the nation; under the circumstances resignation was his only move. This retirement, however, deprived Rumania of the one man who was in a position to stop Carol's political encroachments.

But even had it been a different issue Maniu's response by resignation was likely, as his whole political outlook came close to passive resistance.

Actually the question never presented itself in such a formal manner. Moreover, the most important factor which was to wreck the National Peasants was the onset of the great depression, which not only undermined the popularity of the party but destroyed its economic program and weakened its political defenses against the attacks of the opposition. When one regards the general collapse of parliamentary institutions—many of them far stronger than the fragile structure in Rumania—throughout central and eastern Europe during the depression years, it is quite obvious that the fall of the National Peasants was not solely the consequence of Maniu's personal differences with King Carol, although this dispute did provide the particular pattern in Rumania.

By the time of Maniu's resignation the world agrarian crisis had begun and was especially disastrous in Rumania which had not made a complete recovery from the First World War. The 1930 harvest was good but prices were ever lower. The stabilization of the leu failed to bring about the anticipated business revival. Ten years later Virgil Madgearu concluded,

To have obtained the favorable results which were expected from the stabilization of the leu it would have been necessary for this operation to have coincided with a period of international economic prosperity. In fact it was made too late, only eight months before the outbreak of the world crisis which was to produce general disequilibrium and disorganization of international economic life. Thus, the world economic crisis surprised Rumania in a moment of convalescence, achieved by artificial means, annihilated all the favorable results obtained in the course of 1929, and accentuated to the extreme the evils under which the national economy had suffered before the stabilization.[10]

With stabilization and the fall in world agricultural prices, the peasants who had borrowed during the period of inflation and rising prices found themselves with an overwhelming burden of indebtedness. A cry went up for the reduction of debts, a league against usury was formed, riots broke out in Moldavia and Bessarabia, accompanied by attacks on Jewish money lenders. Worse years were yet to come but this foretaste of depression was clearly involved in the decline of the National Peasants.

In addition to these two external factors—the arrival of Carol on the political scene and of the depression on the economic scene—the National Peasants were also laid low by internal weaknesses and contradictions. These derived a) from the dual origin of the party,

10. Virgil Madgearu, *Evoluţia economiei româneşti*, p. 309.

b) from certain shortcomings inherent in the peasantist philosophy, and c), as a result of a) and b), a watering down of this philosophy into a somewhat eclectic position which lacked the strength to oppose the onrush of the Rightist authoritarian doctrines of the Carolist era.

Origins and Composition of the National Peasant Party

The National Peasant party was created by the amalgamation of the Rumanian National party of Transylvania and the Peasant party of the Old Kingdom at a general congress of both parties held in October, 1926. Other political formations had had temporary affiliations (Iorga's National Democratic party) or had been absorbed (Take Ionescu's faction of the Conservatives and the Bessarabian Peasant party), but the strength of the party lay in these two organizations. The origins and composition of the National party and the Peasant party were quite different and explain some of the characteristics of the National Peasants' policy when in power.

The Peasant party of the Old Kingdom appeared during the troubled months after the First World War. Some of its leaders had been members of the ephemeral Party of Labor which arose during the constituent assembly of 1917 to vote against the terms of the agrarian reform amendment.[11] The principal figures of the Peasant party were Ion Mihalache, a schoolteacher of peasant origin and a man of considerable intelligence and integrity; Dr. Lupu, a country doctor with a long record of interest in peasant problems, but a rather erratic politician who veered from extreme radicalism to blatant opportunism; the Bessarabian writer and political philosopher, Constantin Stere, an intermittent member; and the economist Virgil Madgearu, its principal theorist on economic affairs. Although of this group, only Mihalache could be said to have been a peasant, the party in its first years was a radical agrarian movement, similar in its general lines and purposes to the other agrarian currents which appeared in the states of eastern Europe immediately after the First World War.

The Rumanian National party of Transylvania had its origins in

11. A group of progressive deputies broke away from the Liberal party to form a Labor group. They opposed the limitations of the agrarian reform and desired to extend expropriation to all properties over 100 hectares. The Party of Labor soon dissolved, however; some of the group went into General Averescu's People's League, others returned to the Liberal party, but the rest, including Dr. Lupu, helped to found the Peasant party.

the Hungarian parliament in the first years of the twentieth century as spokesman of the Transylvania Rumanians against the policy of the Magyars. By the time of the creation of Greater Rumania it had a long experience with parliamentary practice and had become the leading party in Transylvania. Its two outstanding leaders were Alexandru Vaida Voevod, an ardent Rumanian nationalist, and Iuliu Maniu. The National party was the defender of the Rumanian peasants against the Magyar overlords and advocated extensive agrarian reform, but it was more nationalist than peasantist in its outlook, and its leaders were from the middle class. It was a vertical rather than a horizontal organization and while it had great support among the Transylvanian peasants, it was also representative of the Rumanian intellectuals, professional men, and small tradesmen.

The difference in the two parties' origins was reflected in the attacks they directed against the Liberals, their common enemy. To the Peasant party the Liberals were the spokesmen of the ruling classes, the ciocoi, and the financial interests; to the National party the Liberals were the advocates of administrative centralism, of Old Kingdom primacy, of unconstitutional and arbitrary politics. While the National party and Peasant party were joined in the brief Vaida Voevod government of 1919–20, it would be a mistake to regard this coalition as an immediate prelude to fusion. After the fall of the Vaida government, the parties drifted apart and despite periodic reports of union did not unite until October, 1926, more than six years later. In the meantime the National party had absorbed Take Ionescu's Conservatives and had even merged for a time with Iorga's party, which temporarily included the sinister Argetoianu. In a lecture delivered in 1923 Mihai Popovici, one of the Transylvanians and later Minister of Finance in the National Peasant government, was quite critical of the Peasant party and denied that it could reconcile its individualist principles with its social radicalism.

In 1924 there was an attempt at fusion but it failed, according to Madgearu, because "certain intriguers in the Camerilla found favorable ground among certain formerly conservative elements in the National Party." [12] Actually, King Ferdinand himself seems to have opposed the union of the two parties.

On the advice of the King that the Rumanian National Party should unite with other parties, the fusion with the party of the late Take Ionescu and later with that of Iorga was carried through and only on

---

12. Virgil Madgearu, "Fuziunea Partidului Țărănesc cu Partidul Național," *M.A.B. Bulletin du Bureau International Agraire, 4* (1926), 6.

the wish of the King was the fusion with the Peasant Party frustrated after Maniu had succeeded in moving the Peasant Party to accept his ten-point program, by which he had rendered not only the crown but the country a great service, for the Peasant Party as a result gave up its idea of the class struggle and its republican sentiments.[13]

Ultimately the common interests of the two parties proved greater than their differences, but even after their amalgamation they were not altogether in harmony, as is shown in the case of Dr. Lupu's break from the National Peasants in February, 1927. According to Dr. Lupu, the National party had virtually the same social views as the Liberals, the 1926 electoral pact between the Peasants and the Transylvanians was only a "non-aggression pact between two political adversaries," the National party had absorbed reactionary elements and was too regional.[14] Madgearu, in rebuttal, accused Dr. Lupu of opportunism:

In reality, Dr. Lupu has broken from our party because he no longer believed possible the arrival of a constitutional democratic regime and because he found it necessary to employ opportunist tactics, to collaborate with no matter whom in no matter what fashion in order to participate in the government of the country . . . One can well understand the true character of Dr. Lupu's effort, which he represents as a reconstitution of the old Peasant Party. . . . If he succeeds he will give the Liberal Party the occasion of garnishing its future government with a "Peasant" appendix.[15]

Although Dr. Lupu's subsequent participation in the Liberal government smacked of opportunism,[16] his contention that the two parties did not represent the same social views was not unfounded.

After the National Peasants came to power, there was occasional friction between the Peasant and Transylvanian ministers, but largely through the personalities of Maniu and Mihalache the party remained united, and indeed the worst schism after the party's fall from power was not along these lines but occurred when Vaida Voevod's Ru-

13. V. V. Tilea, *Iuliu Maniu, der Mann und das Werk* (Hermannstadt, 1927), p. 24.
14. See the defense of Dr. Lupu's action in Petre P. Suciu, "La Scission dans le parti national paysan roumain," *M.A.B.: Bulletin du Bureau International Agraire, 2* (1927), 71–78.
15. V. N. Madgearu, "Essai d'une scission dans le parti national paysan roumain," *M.A.B.: Bulletin du Bureau International Agraire, 2* (1927), 69–70.
16. It is interesting to note that two decades later, in 1945, Dr. Lupu repeated the same move. He again left the National Peasant party (which he had rejoined in 1933) on the grounds that it was reactionary, formed a new peasant party, and collaborated with the Communists in the National Democratic Front.

manian nationalism led him to introduce an excessive chauvinism into the party's platform.

The principal effect of the dual origin was not, however, party instability but the ambiguity which it imparted to National Peasant policy. This effect should not be overemphasized because, as will be seen presently, the Peasant party's policy was by no means fixed and had undergone important modifications even before the amalgamation.

The Peasant Ideology

The political and economic principles of the National Peasant party displayed a number of inconsistencies, part of which stemmed from the dual origin of the party. A more fundamental difficulty, however, lay in the party's professed "peasantism" (*ţărănismul*). The Peasant party is usually regarded as the spiritual descendant of the populist (*poporanist*) movement which flourished in Rumania at the turn of the twentieth century and which was to some extent derived from the Russian *narodniki* of the latter years of the nineteenth century. Although this genealogy is not altogether incorrect it is quite misleading. Before the National Peasants had come to power and indeed before the two sections of the party had united, the populist doctrines had been significantly modified, and for a very good reason. In so far as a thoroughgoing and coherent populism was formulated, it proved incapable of facing contemporary problems; and conversely the working program developed by the Peasant party, not to speak of its actual practices, contained a number of extraneous elements, some of which were quite incompatible with a consistent populist outlook. This transformation is quite apparent in the development of the peasantist doctrine through such men as Constantin Stere, Ion Mihalache, and Virgil Madgearu.

A powerful current of rather diverse agrarian ideas, known broadly as populism, *narodnichestvo*, sprang up among Russian intellectuals in the second half of the nineteenth century, and was associated with the "going to the people" movement and the formation of the Land and Liberty party. Russia and Rumania, as has already been observed, had numerous social and economic similarities in the years before the First World War. Both were countries of large latifundiary estates, and of recently emancipated but land-hungry peasants who lived in a state of semiservitude. (The Rumanian term neoiobăgia, neoserfdom, finds a close parallel in the Russian *polukrepostnoe sostoyanie*, semibondage.[17] To be sure, the Russians were concerned with

---

17. Cf. Lancelot A. Owen, *The Russian Peasant Movement, 1906–1917* (London, 1937), p. 9.

certain problems that were less important in Rumania. The narodniki, for example, were involved in the conflict between Slavophiles
and Westerners; in Rumania nearly all writers looked to the West,
and the principal manifestation of an anti-Western feeling was the
Fichtean nationalism of some of the populists. In Russia the peasant
commune was more important than in Rumania and was the focal
point of the semisocialist ideas of the narodniki. Finally, Russia was
an autocracy and the narodniki tended to split on the question whether
to advocate revolution and violence or reform and propaganda; in
Rumania the weak international position of the new state, together
with the presence of a constitutional government, however unsatisfactory, served to dampen the revolutionary side of populism. Despite
these important differences, the agrarian problems in the two states
were much the same, as was the challenge of Western capitalism.

Although Russian populism had a number of strands, its principal
thesis, so far as it concerns this study, was that the future of Russia
lay in the peasantry, especially in the development of the communal
institutions; that Russia could not hope to industrialize because its
capitalism had arrived on the scene too late to capture the external
markets which were regarded as the necessary stimulus for further
advance. From this it was concluded that Russia should progress to
a sort of agrarian socialism by avoiding the path of industrial capitalism with its attendant social miseries and evils. To be sure, not all
populists accepted all these arguments, and in later years the Social
Revolutionaries, who were something of a hybrid, admitted the possibilities of industrialization but continued to deny that agriculture
was destined to follow the course of capitalist development.

A direct transfer of the ideas of the Russian narodniki into the
Rumanian poporanist movement is to be seen in the writings of Constantin Stere, although this Russian influence was by no means the
only source of Rumanian populism, which had an indigenous development for the same reasons that caused its rise in Russia.[18] Stere,

18. Rumanian populism was also a literary movement reflecting the growing national
consciousness and desire to create a national language and literature. H. Sanielevici,
in a series of articles collected as *Poporanismul reacţionar* (Bucarest, 1921), made a
highly critical survey of the literary and philosophical sides of populism. In his unfriendly opinion, it was an escapist and reactionary movement, displaying a medieval
turn of mind and an unwillingness to face reality. The socialist Dobrogeanu-Gherea,
while admiring certain sincere if misguided aspects of the populist position, regarded
it as a dangerous movement because it could be used by the ruling groups to conceal
the real misery in Rumania behind an idyllic mask. Populism could mean anything or
nothing: "The whole country is covered with populists and populism, civil and military populists, lay and clerical populists, men and women populists, liberal populism,
conservative populism, government populism, opposition populism, national populism,
anti-semitic populism, democratic populism, socialist populism, and populist populism
properly speaking." *Neoiobăgia,* p. 229.

however, was the most brilliant of the populist writers and through
his journal *Viața românească* exerted a far-reaching influence. He
was born in Bessarabia of a boyar family, had associated with the
narodniki, and had been banished to Siberia for his activities.[19] He
later came to Rumania where he joined the nascent socialist movement. In 1899 he broke with the socialists on the question of collaboration with the Liberals, and in 1900 led a group into the Liberal
camp.[20]

The best exposition of Stere's populist ideas was a series of articles,
entitled "Social Democracy or Populism," published in *Viața românească* shortly after the 1907 peasant uprising.[21] The articles were
primarily a polemic against the Social Democrats, but they provide
the main lines of Stere's thought. Stere denied the Marxist analysis
of the economic position of the peasant and held that the peasantry
was neither proletarian nor bourgeois but a distinct social category.
"The peasantry, as the undifferentiated base of society, constitutes
a separate social category, upon whose back are raised all other social classes, not excepting even the industrial proletariat." [22] In a
peasant society there could be no class struggle; since the elements
of production were not differentiated, there would be no classes. Consequently, the elements leading to class struggle had been introduced
via the superstructure of differentiated classes standing above the
peasantry. The only way to progress in a peasant society lay through
strengthening the peasant economically by means of cooperation and
by introducing a true "rural Rumanian democracy." [23]

With regard to industrialization, Stere started from the premise
that different countries could evolve in different manners, that the
"thorny road of capitalist industrialism" was not the only way. To
the question whether "industrialization after the European model"
was inevitable or even possible in Rumania," his response was negative. Industrialization could not develop without foreign markets, and

19. Trotsky and Rakovsky, *Ocherki politicheskoi Rumynii*, p. 123.
20. C. Titel Petrescu, *Socialismul în România*, pp. 150–151. The socialists of course
regarded Stere as a renegade. The problem which faced the Rumanian socialists was
that which faced socialists elsewhere, but worse. The party had spent years in the
wilderness with little prospect of achieving any effective power. Stere felt that since
there was no hope of a revolution, it was wise to collaborate with the more progressive
of the existing parties—the Liberals. For some years he was regarded as the unofficial
adviser of I. I. C. Brătianu.
21. The articles, "Socialdemocratism sau poporanism," appeared in six issues of
Viața românească: August, 1907, pp. 170–193; September, 1907, pp. 313–341; October
1907, pp. 15–48; November, 1907, pp. 173–208; January, 1908, pp. 49–75; and April
1908, pp. 59–80.
22. *Ibid.* (September, 1907), p. 338.
23. *Ibid.,* p. 341.

Rumania, a backward state, had small chance of capturing them from the great industrial powers.[24]

An economically backward country, by the very fact of its backwardness, inevitably finds itself in a state of painful inferiority. . . . For this reason, the simple fact that the industrial development of a country has been delayed itself serves as an impediment in the battle for markets.[25] . . . Thus, from theoretical deductions confirmed by the critiques of capitalism made by K. Marx himself, and from the sad experience of our industrial protectionism, we reach the conclusion that Rumania *cannot follow* the industrial development of Western Europe.[26]

Having denied the possibility of Rumanian industrialization, Stere proceeded to develop his own theory of progress, which was based upon a view of Rumanian society as a cultural and historical entity with its own "national genius." In this connection he was particularly incensed by the socialists who would insist that nothing good could arise in Rumania until after the triumph of socialism in the West. Stere's organic nationalism, while deploring "vulgar or ferocious" anti-Semitism, saw the Jews as alien elements and agents of "vagabond capital," who by their increasing numbers and wealth threatened to disrupt the inchoate cultural development of the Rumanian nation. He realized that the struggle for political democracy in Rumania could be achieved only through "determined, conscious and organized action—but this way is, unfortunately, still in large part closed to our peasantry." [27] He would therefore seek political support in the wealthier peasants, the village petty bourgeoisie, and the intelligentsia.

As to the economic goal, the conditions in Rumania demanded "the organization of the whole national economy on a peasantist foundation: a vigorous peasantry, master of the land on which it works, and for which—through the organization of a perfected system of co-operative societies—the advantages of small properties are united with all the technical advantages to-day available only to large property." [28] Stere did not deny the desirability of any industry whatsoever, but recommended a type of industrial organization which could make use of the peasants' free time in the winter months; in other

24. Although this argument closely resembles that of the narodniki, nowhere in these articles does Stere cite a Russian authority. Most of his arguments are culled from the German Social Democrats and from Marx and Engels themselves.
25. *Ibid.* (October, 1907), p. 36.
26. *Ibid.*
27. *Ibid.* (January, 1908), p. 59.
28. *Ibid.* (April, 1908), p. 59.

words, a form of peasant household industry designed to satisfy internal consumption.[29] He was opposed to the Liberals' effort to create a national industry by means of a protectionist tariff. Small urban industries should remain as crafts and serve as accessories to agriculture. Existing large industries, such as the petroleum industry, should be nationalized, not socialized, and become a state monopoly. In summary, he advocated:

A free peasantry master of its land, the development of crafts and small industries, with the aid of an intense cooperative movement in the villages and in the towns; state monopoly of large industry (with the exception of special cases which are able to develop on their own without prejudice to the economy): this is the formula for our economic and social progress, which the very conditions of our national life impose upon us.[30]

Although Stere's thesis is well argued, it presents serious difficulties. In the first place, his initial premise that the peasant is the "undifferentiated base of society" has altogether negative implications, since it is precisely by a "differentiation" of society, by surmounting the primordial peasant, that the dynamic process of economic advance has been achieved. Moreover, while he could point to the undoubted obstacles confronting Rumania in any attempt to emulate the West, the actual fact was that Rumania had long since been caught in the toils of the West; the cash nexus had even penetrated agriculture through the commerce in cereals and had, as has been seen, contributed to the serious plight of the peasantry. His ideal of a prosperous small peasant was based on the models of Denmark and Switzerland—favorite paradigms of the populists—the structure of whose markets and economies was altogether different from that of Rumania. His recommendation that industry should take the form of household crafts, to occupy the peasant during the winter months, has also had much popularity but is of limited value. The separation of cottage industry from agriculture has generally been the mark of advancing cultivation. Any industry run on such an intermittent basis would be forced to remain on a primitive and inefficient level. Moreover, the winter unemployment was in part a consequence of the extensive nature of Rumanian agriculture; a more labor-intensive form of peasant cultivations would diminish this seasonal difference. Above all, cottage industries have shown small powers of resistance

29. *Ibid.*, p. 60.
30. *Ibid.*, p. 68.

to the competition of machine-made goods.[31] Stere's theory really provides no adequate solution to the problem of improving the level of agriculture or the status of the peasant.

In addition to these shortcomings, Stere's populism contained certain very dangerous implications which were to be realized in the 1930's. Along with his desire for a rural democracy and a rustic economy, there is also the persistent note of organic nationalism, with its eloquent love of the "national genius" embodied in the Rumanian peasant, its fear of the alien cultural and economic intrusion of the Jew, its belief that Rumania had its own particular destiny to fulfill, and its desire to avoid the "Golgotha of capitalism." In Stere these elements appeared in a relatively moderate and balanced guise, but taken together and intensified they closely resemble the driving impulses of the Iron Guard.

The connection between certain aspects of populism and the Rumanian fascism of Codreanu is not accidental but is closely bound to the question of Rumania's relation to Western industrial society. Rumanians faced by the impact of the West with its power, high material level, and more articulate cultural development, have always been in peril of being driven to one of two emotional extremes: either abject imitation of the West or rejection. In general, imitation has prevailed, though frequently with quite un-Western consequences. In Stere, however, there is the element of rejection, although it is moderated by an effort at a rational analysis of the actual relations between Rumania and the industrial West. In the Iron Guard, on the other hand, the rational element is dissolved, leaving only the emotional reaction in a singularly malignant form. Therein lies the danger of this type of populism: in so far as it fails to provide a solution to Rumania's social and economic questions, it is apt to erupt into a wildly irrational and negative movement.

While these potentially dangerous qualities appear in Stere's work, it would be a mistake to read them into the future Peasant party. Indeed, as will be shown presently, the Peasant party, despite Stere's affiliation with it and despite the persistence of the populist ideology, did not pursue a populist course but followed a different line, which

31. The Peasant party economist, Madgearu, conceded that the populist writers were incorrect in their views on cottage industry (*op. cit.*, pp. 11–12). These arguments have nothing to do with the question of the value of decentralized industrialization based upon household units, since with the use of electric power such industries might be quite feasible. Cf. League of Nations, *Industrialization and Foreign Trade*, p. 50. But the introduction of such things as electric power presupposes a whole series of developments not included in the populist theory.

also led to difficulties but of another kind. An indication of this difference appears as early as 1920 when a Peasant party deputy said: "We are not against industry, and not against towns, and not against 'foreigners,' and we have nothing in common with the populism of *Viața românească*." [32]

In the remarkable parliamentary speeches of the Peasant leader Ion Mihalache in 1920 and 1921 one finds a quite different attitude from that expressed in Stere's writings. Mihalache was at once more authentically peasant and more pragmatic than Stere. In his attack on the existing order and the ruling class he showed the anger of the peasant against the boyars and a profound distrust in the willingness or ability of the old parties to defend him. He violently assailed the temptation of "social harmony"—"Social harmony is the seductive song by which the naïve are put to sleep; while they are sleeping the ruling class satisfies its own class interests"—and announced that the peasants must organize for their own defense. He thus granted the existence of social classes and of a class struggle. He did not, however, erect either the concept of classes or the class struggle into theoretical principles, but said they were merely names for what was obviously happening in Rumania:

"Class struggle," the parties of social harmony shout at us. "So be it," we reply if that is the only means by which the peasantry can guarantee the realization of its needs.

"You are not a class party. The peasantry is not a social class," the socialists shout at us. "So be it," we also answer the socialists; we are very little interested in the definition whether we are or are not a class party. [33]

Mihalache stated that the peasantry had a class attitude toward the large proprietors because its goal was the elimination of large estates and the establishment of the peasant as master of the land. He did not, however, regard the peasantry as the exclusive class. "The Peasant party is not opposed to the development of all other social classes; in contrast to the Socialist party which proposes to dissolve the bourgeoisie and replace it with a single social class, the Peasant party considers legitimate the existence of other social classes, industrialists, merchants, etc." [34] His concept of the function of the

32. Sanielevici, *op. cit.*, p. 432. The deputy, unnamed, was protesting against the anti-populist line of Sanielevici's periodical *Curentul Nou*.
33. Mihalache, *Partidul Tărănesc în politica țărei*, p. 32.
34. *Ibid.*, p. 39.

peasant lacked the overtones which are found in Stere and at the same time he did not endow the class struggle with an independent vitality as the mainspring of history.

He had a pragmatic view toward industry; while he opposed the control exerted by the Liberals over the nation's economy, he did not adopt Stere's view that Rumania must follow a different course of development from the West. He did not even deny the socialists' contention that in the long run increasing industrialization might introduce capitalist development into the countryside, but present politics could not wait for that eventuality:

It is possible that in the future it will be as you believe. I do not come with prejudices against socialism. It is possible that mechanization will make such great progress in agriculture that personal equipment, individual initiative, and the personality of the man will not be the essential factors in agricultural production they are to-day . . . and then it may occur that the notion of individual property will suffer a great blow and socialism will come to the peasantry. It is possible. But gentlemen, in politics we must base our actions not on what might happen in decades or in future centuries. A healthy policy is the management of current needs, of the real necessities of the existing society.[35]

This essentially practical tone ran through Mihalache's pronouncements, and his thesis was the simple and straightforward one that the great majority of the Rumanian peasants had been deprived of land and kept out of power by the greed and selfishness of the boyars. His aim was to correct that state of affairs by organizing the peasants to protect themselves (he admitted the assistance of intellectuals, but without the connotations of Stere's intelligentsia) by redistributing agricultural land, by establishing small peasant farms which he believed were more efficient than the large estates, and by increasing peasant cooperation. In pursuing this line he attacked the parties of "social harmony" for their hypocrisy and the socialists for their doctrinaire denial of the role of the peasantry. While a patriot and a monarchist, he displayed little of Stere's organic nationalism. The principal limitation to Mihalache's position was that he did confine himself largely to the immediate agrarian question, and did not really explore the connections between agriculture and the whole economic complex.

Turning to the Peasant party economist Virgil Madgearu, one

35. *Ibid.*, p. 35.

finds a broader if less intense view of the economic scene. By a series of articles in the early 1920's [36] Madgearu established himself as one of the leading spokesmen of the Peasant party, although unlike Mihalache there was little of the peasant about him. He had a Leipzig doctorate and was a professor at the Academy of Commercial Studies in Bucarest.

Madgearu, like Stere and Mihalache, argued that agricultural development, in contrast to the views of the Marxists, was from large holdings to small peasant properties, which could demonstrate a higher level of productivity. He also maintained that the peasantry constituted a separate social category; while granting that some peasants employed labor and others were virtually an agricultural proletariat, he denied that this proved a lack of homogeneity in the peasantry.[37] On the other hand, Madgearu's writings displayed a spirit quite different from Stere's. He saw that the populists had been wrong in their belief that agrarian countries would evolve without becoming involved in industrialism, since in fact capitalist industry in the form of factories, cartels, and trusts was developing by leaps and bounds in the agrarian states. The peasant *mystique* which appeared in Stere's populism was lacking in Madgearu. Indeed, Madgearu's "peasantism" was founded upon a set of ideas which were typically "liberal" in the Western sense of the word.

He granted the existence of the class struggle, but for him it was not a dynamic concept but a mere statement of fact. It was not the peasants who preached social discord but the false exponents of "political harmony," the old oligarchy, who had created the antagonisms[38]. He denied that Rumanian liberalism could develop an adequate peasant policy, but for the reason that real liberalism had perished. Contemporary Rumanian liberalism was founded on a financial oligarchy, financial trusts, and a despotic militaristic state. He opposed the industrial policy being followed in Rumania, not from the populist desire to avoid a "capitalist Golgotha," but because industrialization was not developing on the basis of free competition. "If peasantism does not have an inherent tendency against

36. Some of these include *Țărănismul* (Bucarest, n.d.), "Doctrina Țărănistă," in *Doctrinele partidelor politice, Revoluția agrară și evoluția clasei țărănești* (Bucarest, 1923), *Agrarianism—un discors parlamentar* (Bucarest, 1927).

37. *Doctrinele partidelor politice*, p. 72. However, in his last work written in 1940, Madgearu admitted that in Rumania there was a tendency toward a differentiation between the middle peasantry and the agricultural proletariat. *Evoluția economiei românești*, p. 34.

38. Madgearu, *Țărănismul*, p. ii. On several occasions he quoted with approval Guizot's remark, "The class struggle is not a hypothesis, not a theory, but purely and simply a reality."

industrial development, it is, on the other hand, against tariff protectionism, the creator of hot-house industries, trusts and cartels." [39] He denied any contradiction between agrarianism and industrialization; he admitted the necessity of developing Rumania's industries and natural resources but rejected those industries which required continued artificial support. Wherever public utilities or basic industries showed signs of becoming monopolies they should be regulated by the state.

In the political sphere, the peasant was important not because of any innate rustic virtues but because he represented the great majority of Rumanian citizens. He should not be deprived of his share in the government for any theoretical reason, whether coming from the Left or the Right. Socially the peasant was important because of his threefold role as producer, consumer, and citizen.

The peasant, having become a small proprietor of land, through allotment or purchase on his own, has an interest in earning from the cultivation of his lot the greatest product which can be obtained in the shortest time, to endow his holding with equipment and livestock, and to provide enough for himself and his family. This presupposes an organization of production which guarantees a maximum return and an organization of sales, which, by doing away with intermediaries, gives the villager the whole value of his produce. . . . The peasantry forms the most numerous strata of consumers. It is therefore directly interested in the industrial regime. Understanding the necessity of encouraging the progress of a national industry, it cannot admit a protection based on a prohibitive tariff system which artificially maintains certain industries that lack any favorable conditions for their development. . . . Finally, as citizen the peasant has an interest in living in a community of free men, who administer their interests through elected representatives. [40]

Madgearu's criticism of the Social Democrats, while to some extent based on their hostility or indifference to the peasantry, was along lines quite different from Stere's. He opposed Social Democracy primarily because in Rumania it was apt to produce extremist repercussions either to the Left or to the Right:

It is problematic whether a Social Democratic party could soon succeed in penetrating the peasant masses, not so much because the mentality of the latter, attached to the idea of private property, is closed to the socialist ideology, as because the economic influence of the parties of "social

39. *Doctrinele partidelor politice*, p. 85.
40. Madgearu, *Ţărănismul*, pp. 21–27.

harmony" over the villages, along with their means of propaganda, would be able to frustrate any serious action by the Social Democrats among the peasants. As long as the Social Democratic party was unsuccessful in attracting the peasant masses, it could only be a spectator, condemned to a passive role. In periods of burgeoning "ministerialism" in its ranks, it would be in the situation of seeing its leaders agreeing to collaborate in the governments of the bourgeois parties, of the capitalist oligarchy. This would lead to breaking the unity of the socialist movement and to strengthening the revolutionary syndicalist and communist currents, the adversaries of political democracy. A change in direction away from political democracy and toward a proletarian dictatorship would, however, give rise to reaction in the cadres of the parties of order and social harmony, a restriction of public liberties through a state of siege, courts martial and censorship, with the tendency to install a white dictatorship. Whoever has closely observed the course of events in recent years can foresee the fate of the Rumanian people if it were to be their lot to oscillate between the rule of the financial oligarchy in a democratic form and the same rule of the financial oligarchy installing a political dictatorship every time it appeared to be in danger of being ousted or destroyed by a dictatorship of the proletariat. Cannot the entry of peasantism into the political arena determine a new orientation to social evolution? [41]

In these prophetic words, Madgearu's criticism of the Social Democrats is seen to be altogether practical and was really meant as a plea for cooperation from the Social Democrats in defeating the financial oligarchy of the Liberals and in fending off Leftist excesses.

In his foreign economic policy, Madgearu displayed none of the populist mistrust of the West. He believed in freeing trade channels and giving a friendly reception to foreign capital, and he heartily opposed Vintilă Brătianu's economic xenophobia.

Clearly, the spirit prevailing in Madgearu's writings is quite unlike that of the earlier populists. Peasantism has become a radical democratic movement. In many respects Madgearu's position is a great advance over Stere's populism. It shows none of the irrational and primitive strains and is thoroughly aware of the twentieth century. It avoids integral nationalism and advocates international cooperation. Above all, it realizes that the peasant cannot remain isolated but is involved in the complex of the world economy. It was Madgearu's principal desire to keep the peasant from being exploited in this economy.

41. *Ibid.,* pp. 15–16.

But in thus escaping the limitations of populism Madgearu's peasantism contained its own weaknesses. In the first place, this rationalization of the peasantist philosophy, which gave it an almost middle-class flavor, was in danger ultimately of depriving it of its fighting strength. A more serious drawback, though Madgearu was scarcely at fault, was that the ideals and indeed the society on which Madgearu based his argument and which he was trying to translate into Rumanian terms were on the verge of suffering a terrible setback throughout Europe. A third and more specific danger was that the very broadening of Madgearu's concepts with their acceptance of a number of nonpeasant elements (especially the qualified support of industry and the interest in foreign capital) would, in the course of time, lead these elements to claim first attention.

An analogous shift in direction is observable in the series of Peasant party programs of 1921, 1922, 1924, and 1926, as may be illustrated by comparing the passages on agrarian affairs, industry, and foreign capital.[42] Rumanian political programs should not be taken very seriously as a guide to probable action, but as each of these was prepared while the party was in opposition they do at least show the Peasants' changing views on Rumanian economic policy.

The projected program of 1921 is quite radical in tone but vague and loosely formulated in its contents.[43] It affirms that the land must belong to those who cultivate it and that the state should have con-stitutional right to continue to purchase large and medium proper-ties and transfer them to the actual cultivators. Expropriation should follow the model of the Bessarabian agrarian reform (i.e., all prop-erties over 100 hectares) and be applied by bodies elected by the peasantry. Only the state should have the right to purchase land, peasant holdings should not be larger than a peasant family could cultivate with its own labor, and measures should be taken to prevent the reappearance of large properties.

The 1922 program is generally similar in tone. It omits the right of the state to purchase medium and large properties and merely

42. *Proectul de program al Partidului Țărănesc din România* (Bucarest, 1921); Partidul Țărănesc, *Programul și Statutele* (Bucarest, 1922); Partidul Țărănesc, *Programul General și Statutele* (Bucarest, 1925); Partidul Național-Țărănesc, *Principiile programul și statutul* (Bucarest, 1926). A projected program was voted by a congress of the party on November 20–21, 1921; a definitive program was passed in the general congress of Iași on November 26–28, 1922, and was modified by a congress in Bucarest on October 26–27, 1924. A new program was adopted in the congress of October 10, 1926, when the National and Peasant parties fused.

43. It contains a large number of Slavonic words, which were later replaced by more sedate words derived from French or Latin. The whole document bears the impression of Stere's influence.

says that the state should assist the process of evolution toward "properties of cultivation." It would extend expropriation to properties of over 100 hectares with the exception of model farms necessary for the improvement of small cultivation. (This qualification was omitted in 1921.) It is less explicit on restrictions on sale of land, but goes into greater detail on the question of communal pastures and forests, agricultural education, experimental stations, and credit.

The 1924 program omits reference to the land belonging to him who cultivates it, and stresses the need for correction of abuses of the agrarian reform. It would extend expropriation to properties over 100 hectares, unless they were organized farms with their own inventory and equipment, in which case they could be 250 hectares in regions with demands for land, and 500 hectares in regions where the need for land had been satisfied. It shows greater interest in rationalizing peasant holdings through establishing norms for the sale and purchase of land, preventing the fragmentation of property, and consolidating small properties.

The 1926 program—after the fusion of the National and Peasant parties—is substantially the same. It emphasizes the need for completing the land allotments and for raising the level of production. It makes one significant addition, however, in advocating freedom of purchase and sale of agricultural land—after a period of transition—to promote the "natural selection of serious cultivators."

The four programs show a consistent trend away from a radical agrarian policy advocating a leveling out of properties and determined to maintain family cultivated plots, to a more elastic concept with less emphasis upon land distribution than upon the improvement of production. The principal changes occurred before the union of the Peasant party with the Transylvanians.

The 1921 program takes a very narrow view of industry. "Agriculture cannot advance if it is not aided by the establishment of certain industries . . . but industry to be successful must be based only on those things which can be made from what is found in the country." It recommends cottage industries which could occupy the peasant after the completion of his work in the fields. It recognizes the need of a national industry and of tariffs, but the latter should not be excessive.

The 1922 program follows the same lines, but adds the need of state control over the exploitation of natural resources. It opposes the support of "artificial" industries, protection of monopolies which raise the cost of living, and state monopolies.

The 1924 program for industry is brief and presents fewer restrictions. It still favors small and cottage industries but approves the encouraging of large industries, especially those which use agricultural products.

The 1926 program is still briefer. However, in contrast to the 1924 program on the utilization of sources of energy, which stresses the need for public control, it "encourages private initiative and capital." This is a complete reversal of the 1922 program which criticized the "anarchic exploitation" of sources of energy for "private capitalist interests."

With respect to foreign capital, the preface to the 1921 program has some very unpleasant things to say about "capitalist imperialism which has achieved world domination." While it admits the value of foreign loans to repair the railway system, "we must have, however, great care when it is a question of taking loans from bankers of other countries. We must take the precautions of the mouse when it goes for food that it is not seized by the cat!"

The 1922 program omits the prefatory harangue against capitalist imperialism. It rejects foreign railway concessions but grants the need of foreign credit to repair transport and consolidate the national debt. The suspicious note is still present: while Rumania needs foreign credit, the party recognizes the tendency of the large capitalist states to exploit through concessions the riches of backward agrarian states such as Rumania. "We are fully aware of the great difficulties and dangers of the immediate future."

The 1924 program drops this attitude completely and has a special section on collaboration with foreign capital, the necessity of attracting it to repair the economy and to develop the natural riches of the country. It favors equal treatment to foreign and Rumanian capital, an attack on the policy of the Liberals.

The chapter on collaboration in the 1926 program is identical with that of 1924, except in its omission of the phrase, in speaking of attracting foreign capital, "in a form corresponding to the national economic interests." The phrase probably sounded too much like a Liberal party pronouncement.

From these examples it should be quite clear that the policy of the Peasant party underwent an important and perhaps fundamental evolution from its radical origins of 1921.[44] Moreover, the bulk of changes occurred before the fusion of 1926, a fact which would con-

44. Similar changes are observable in most sections of the programs. For example, the programs through 1924 demanded the dissolution of the security police and the rural gendarmes, and the inauguration of the eight-hour day. These points were dropped in the 1926 program.

firm the supposition that the principles of the Peasant party itself were unstable. The evolution traced here was to be carried even farther when the National Peasants came to power in 1928.

Economic and Agrarian Policy

A fair illustration of the economic interests of the National Peasant government is to be found in Virgil Madgearu's little book, *Rumania's New Economic Policy*, published in 1930. Of the 63 pages of text, 14 are devoted to agriculture, 22 to the exploitation of state enterprises and the reform of the mining law, ten to foreign trade policy, and eleven to the improvement of transport. The fact that the booklet was published in England and designed for foreign readers merely underlines the preoccupation with affairs other than agricultural. As has been seen, this broadening of interests was the result of the pressing demands of financial, monetary, and commercial matters in 1928–30, but also of the internal trend away from a purely agrarian outlook.

The most striking feature of the agrarian policy of the National Peasant government was the things it neglected to do or even to consider doing. While the party's attitude toward further redistribution of land had become increasingly moderate, nevertheless in 1926 the program of the united party called for expropriation of properties over 100 hectares. Not a step was taken toward carrying out this measure. To be sure, many reasons militated against such a move. Agriculture was still in the process of readjustment from the previous reforms. Expropriation would undoubtedly have caused a political furor since the mere passage of time was serving to consolidate the previous reform, with all its shortcomings and abuses. Moreover, since the 1917 act was entered in the constitution, it could be modified only by a constitutional amendment, which was forbidden under a regency. Quite obviously, however, the National Peasant party by 1928 was not the radical agrarian movement which had attempted to introduce the reform bill under the Vaida government of 1920.

A second omission was the failure to take any active steps toward the consolidation of peasant strips, a measure which was virtually a precondition for any effective improvement of agriculture. Again, this would have been unsettling and peasant support for this particular reform was by no means certain.

The only serious measure taken in connection with agricultural property relations was an act passed in 1929 which amended the Liberals' law of 1925 concerning the alienation of allotments obtained through the agrarian reforms.[45] The new law, which was designed to facilitate the transfer of land and to further a "process of selection among the peasant cultivators," abolished certain of the restrictions and delays imposed by the Liberals and greatly simplified the procedure of sale, although maintaining safeguards to keep land in the hands of actual cultivators and limiting purchases to Rumanian citizens having not over 25 hectares of land.

The idea that a "process of selection" would enable peasants with "superior competitive efficiency" to create prosperous holdings has had considerable popularity not only in Rumania but in other eastern European states.[46] For such a process to have beneficial consequences, however, it is necessary, first, that superior efficiency on tiny holdings will actually result in sufficient capital accumulation to buy out less efficient peasants, and, second, that the peasants displaced in the process have some alternative means of employment. Otherwise the poorer peasants would be reduced to a landless proletariat and the land taken over by the wealthier peasants. Such seems to have been the effect of the National Peasants' law, although it was not the sole cause; the survey of sixty Rumanian villages made in 1938 reported that the law of 1929 had intensified the differentiation in the peasantry by building up the category of middle peasants on the one hand and of increasing the agricultural proletariat on the other.[47] It was this law perhaps more than any other single act which gave

45. See above, p. 125.
46. Wilbert E. Moore, *Economic Demography of Eastern and Southern Europe,* p. 105, cites a Greek author (C. Evelpedis, *La Réforme agraire en Grèce,* Athens, 1926), as an advocate of this view. In Rumania the alienation of peasant property has had a tangled political history in which at one time or another almost all political parties have reversed their positions. Up to the 1918–21 reforms, official policy tended toward inalienability, whereas the older reformers, such as Dobrogeanu-Gherea and Garoflid, demanded alienation as a necessary step to creating an independent peasantry. The Liberals in 1911 came out for a "process of selection," but in 1925 they restricted the transfer of land. The Peasant party, on the contrary, in 1921 was for government control of all sales, whereas in 1929 it moved toward freer purchase. The Communists, it may be added, roundly condemned the National Peasants for their 1929 law, but Lenin, in his agrarian writings before the Russian revolution, was strongly for alienation. The Communist position is seen in Pătrăşcanu's interpretation of the 1929 law: "From the point of view of opening a way for capitalism in the villages and of differentiation within the rural strata, the measure represented an advance in comparison with the past. But what was the cost of this progress? The land of the poorest and economically most feeble layers of the peasants quickly became the principal object, the prey on which urban banking capital and the village bourgeoisie threw themselves." Lucreţiu Pătrăşcanu, *Sous trois dictatures* (Paris, 1946), p. 106.
47. *60 Sate româneşti,* II, 6. The depression doubtless intensified this effect. During the 1946 famine in Moldavia the same thing occurred: peasants who had obtained land under the 1945 reform began to sell to the larger peasants at such a rate that the government was obliged to pass a law nullifying these sales.

rise to the charge that the National Peasants really represented the richer peasants and the village bourgeoisie.[48]

A similar attitude appears in the other principal agrarian measures of the National Peasants; the law for the organization of cooperation, of March 28, 1929, and the law for the organization of rural mortgages and agricultural credit of July 29, 1929. These laws were acclaimed at the time as proof of the government's concern for the peasant, but they need not be considered in great detail here.[49] Laws for credit and cooperation are hardy perennials in Rumanian legislative history, but none of them appears to have accomplished much. These particular laws were quickly blighted by the onset of the depression.

The law for the organization of cooperation abrogated the act passed by the Liberal government in July, 1928, which the National Peasants thought gave the state too much control over the cooperative movement. The new code was designed to broaden the legal frame "to offer the cooperatives the freedom of movement which every economic enterprise needs if it is to develop in the present economic world." [50] Notwithstanding this effort to assure greater autonomy and independence, a foreign observer concluded in 1930 that even the new regime had not abandoned the idea that the cooperatives were a government maid of all work.[51] The real difficulty, as has been mentioned before, was that the poor peasant, that is, the average Rumanian, had very little to offer in a cooperative movement. Until the level of the peasantry was raised above the margin of subsistence, the cooperative movement was bound to be a name rather than a reality and to be altogether dependent upon the state for financial support and direction.

The law for the organization of rural mortgages and agricultural credit was intended to improve the channels supplying credit to agriculture, which had been seriously undernourished during the Liberal

48. This charge is given some weight when one considers Madgearu's remark, made in 1930: "With farms of medium size, limited to 25 hectares, the agricultural credit granted will be used in a more economical way and will bear fruit in a degree hitherto unknown in our agrarian organization." *Rumania's New Economic Policy*, p. 11. In a country where 75 per cent of all agricultural holdings were under 5 hectares, and 92 per cent under 10 hectares, reference to farms of medium size could have only an extremely limited application.

49. Analyses of the law for the organization of cooperatives may be found in Mitrany, *The Land and the Peasant in Rumania*, pp. 409–411, and in F. E. Manoliou, *La Réconstruction économique et financière de la Roumanie et les partis politiques*, pp. 236–237, and of the law for the reorganization of agricultural credit in Manoliou, pp. 239–243.

50. From the exposé de motifs, cited in Mitrany, *op. cit.*, p. 409.

51. "Rumania: The State as Co-operator," *Yearbook of Agricultural Co-operation, 1930*, pp. 404–428.

regime. New institutions were set up to provide credit suitable to agriculture's particular wants. It was hoped that these would stimulate the influx of foreign capital "to satisfy the needs of agricultural financing." [52] In its form the new law was better adjusted to the needs of agriculture, but the depression completely halted the desired flow of capital. It may be doubted if this law was of primary benefit to the poor peasant, who was of necessity a bad risk and whose impoverished condition prevented him from employing credit profitably.[53]

In addition to these financial measures, the National Peasants passed acts for the organization and reform of agricultural instruction intended to spread and popularize better agricultural techniques and to prevent trained agriculturalists from being completely absorbed by the bureaucracy; a law of July, 1929, for the reclamation of the inundated region of the Danube; measures for leasing agricultural machinery to cultivators and developing seed selection stations; and a law to promote systematic colonization in areas of sparse population. These measures, while desirable in themselves, could be of only marginal benefit.

Although the National Peasants' concern with agriculture is shown by the fact that the budget of the Ministry of Agriculture in 1929 was double that of any of the preceding postwar years,[54] the general results are somewhat flat and uninspiring. According to Madgearu ten years later, the National Peasants, because of the difficult circumstances under which they had received the stabilization loan and because of the increasingly unfavorable international economic situation, had been unable to carry out all their financial plans but had been forced to limit themselves to certain priority tasks: assuring the liquidity of the National Bank's portfolio, liquidating the state's floating debt, reconstructing the railways, and making certain productive investments. "The necessary means were lacking to create an agricultural mortgage bank." [55]

Doubtless, financial difficulties and the lack of capital were important obstacles, and the depression washed away what might have been promising beginnings toward improvement in agricultural finan-

52. Madgearu, *Rumania's New Economic Policy*, p. 9.

53. Manoliou, *op. cit.*, p. 242, was of the opinion that certain measures of inspection and control, included in the law to safeguard the credit societies, would have the effect of discouraging the small cultivator and diminishing his productive efforts.

54. According to Mitrany, *op. cit.*, p. 453, after the First World War the budget of the Ministry of Agriculture had not exceeded 33,500,000 gold lei until the advent of the National Peasants. In 1929 it reached the figure of 73,500,000 gold lei.

55. Madgearu, *Evoluția economiei românești*, p. 306.

cial organization. But the agrarian policy had other defects. In the first place, the National Peasants fell into the old Rumanian fallacy of counting too greatly upon an act of legislation to cure any problem.[56] Much more serious however was the fact that while the National Peasants had an agrarian policy it was scarcely a peasant policy. The measures actually taken were not of the kind that could greatly help the poor peasant. The modifications of the party programs between 1921 and 1926 foreshadowed this attitude, but even so the more far-reaching parts of the 1926 program were not carried out.

Measures intended to benefit agriculture were not, however, limited to agricultural legislation. The new tariff policy inaugurated by the National Peasants on August 1, 1929, was specifically designed to assist the farmer. The National Peasants had consistently attacked the Liberals' (and the People's party's) tariff policy, which was highly protectionist, raised the cost of agricultural equipment, and was "in its technical structure a feeble instrument of negotiation for securing markets for our export products." [57] The new tariff was, as Madgearu announced, based on the recommendations of the Geneva Conference of 1927. It created a more elastic customs system to permit commercial conventions with other states. Duties on goods were divided into two groups: 1) irreducible minimum duties for goods produced within the country and requiring protection; these could not be reduced through convention; 2) duties on all other articles, which could be reduced through mutual arrangement with other states. Even before signing any customs conventions the government reduced the duties on agricultural equipment.

In thus lowering the cost of imported agricultural equipment as well as in reducing tariffs on articles of mass consumption, the 1929 tariff undoubtedly benefited the peasant. As to the protection of industry, "it was in general calculated so as not to exceed the difference by which the conditions of local production were more difficult than conditions of foreign production, and only for branches of industry which had the possibility of sound development in the country." [58] The tariffs did not renounce industrial protection but tried

56. Note, for example, Madgearu's remark, "Up to 1929 agricultural instruction in Rumania was based on no uniform principle, nor was it adapted to the situation, since its organization was not based on legislation which could solve the problem as a whole." *Rumania's New Economic Policy*, p. 12. Clearly the real reasons for Rumania's lack of adequate agricultural education were not to be found in the absence of a uniform legal code.

57. Madgearu, *ibid.*, p. 39.

58. Madgearu, *Evoluția economiei romănești*, p. 221.

to protect only those industries showing "natural" promise of development and to promote the necessary rationalization of those industries which had been permitted to become inefficient behind the Liberal tariff.

Throughout Madgearu's exposition of the 1929 tariff there is an evident desire to increase international cooperation and trade, and an altogether friendly attitude toward the great capitalist powers— an attitude quite different from Vintilă Brătianu's cautious and rather grudging admission of the need for increased trade and foreign capital. This attitude is most clearly shown in the laws of 1929 modifying the Liberal acts of 1924 on mines and the commercialization of state-owned enterprises.[59] The National Peasants criticized the 1924 laws as chauvinistic and failing to promote the exploitation of natural resources. "The aggressive nationalist policy exemplified in the Mining Act of 1924, which did so much harm to the country, bringing it into a state of financial and economic disorganization, could not continue without grave consequences for our economic future. A policy of sincere co-operation with international capital is the only means of improving the situation." [60] The new laws threw open the doors to foreign capital. With the exception of requiring that 75 per cent of the personnel (both administrative and subordinate) be Rumanians, no restrictions were placed on the percentage of foreign capital in the companies or upon the nationality of directors and chief officials.

These laws were in marked contrast not only to the attitude of the Liberals but also to the policy recommended by Constantin Stere in 1921.[61] Stere, with his hostility to "vagabond capital" and the menace of imperialist great powers, opposed foreign capital investments in the Rumanian petroleum industry, since all profits passed beyond the frontiers. Nor was foreign capital concerned with satisfying the needs of the population but only with raking in a profit. He was, however, aware that without foreign capital the resources simply could not be developed. He disapproved of the Liberals' policy of "nationalizing" petroleum and creating concessions with a majority of Rumanian capital. Having no confidence in the Liberal plutocracy's willingness or ability to defend the nation's interests, Stere advocated state operation of the petroleum industry. Foreign capital

59. A detailed comparison of Liberal and National Peasant policy on this question, from a pro-Liberal position, is given by Alexandre G. Georgesco, *Le Régime juridique et financière des capitaux étrangers en Roumanie* (Paris, 1932).

60. Madgearu, *Rumania's New Economic Policy,* p. 30.

61. C. Stere, *Naționalizarea Industriei de Petrol: Cuvântare rostită în sedința Adunării deputaților din 28 Martie 1921* (Bucarest, 1921).

should be obtained not through investments but through loans undertaken by the state. In this way Rumania would have full control over
the allocation of capital and would not, except for the interest on
loans, see the profits from the oil industry go abroad. The petroleum
policy of the National Peasants, as formulated in 1929, was even
more removed from Stere's recommendations than from the Liberals'
policy. It was, however, perfectly consistent with their economic outlook during their term in office.

Rumanian transportation and communications had been in notoriously bad condition since the First World War, and the Liberals'
policy of retrenchment had been particularly damaging to the railway system. The 1929 stabilization loan allocated $34,000,000 for
railway expansion and $9,000,000 to pay off overdue railway debts.
By a law passed in July, 1929, the National Peasants transferred the
state railways to an autonomous public body, "to be administered
according to commercial principles." [62] They also undertook to repair and extend the highway network, and abolished the primitive
corvée which was still being used for road maintenance. In 1930 the
International Telephone and Telegraph Corporation received a concession for the construction of the Rumanian telephone network.

The stabilization loan required a reform of the National Bank and
of the state accounting system. In March, 1929, the government
passed a series of new statutes for the bank; the principal changes
were the abolition of the ceiling on the issue of currency, established
by the Liberals' in 1925, and the limitation of the influence of the
state in the appointment of directors. The bank was given somewhat
greater independence from state control and powers to maintain the
newly achieved stability of the currency. In July, 1929, the government passed a law reforming the state accounting system and the organization of the budget. There was no doubt that Rumanian state
finances needed reform and modernization. The accounting system
had been that of France of 1860, plus the accretion of a number of
purely Rumanian practices, with the result that the actual condition of government finances at any given time was never known with
any exactness. The new law, in reorganizing the preparation of the
budget, exerted more stringent control over the expenditures of various ministries. While this law was well intended, its actual results in
rationalizing Rumanian finance methods seem to have been very

62. Madgearu, *Rumania's New Economic Policy*, p. 50. The organization of Rumanian railways after 1918 had been altogether hectic. In 1925 the Liberals had given
some autonomy to the railways; this policy was reversed by the People's party in
February, 1927, and reestablished by the Liberals in August of that year.

slight. In 1929, 1930, and 1931 there was an increasing disparity between budget revenue forecasts and actual receipts.

Certain late measures of the National Peasants will be considered presently in connection with the depression. But from the above it should be evident that during their brief term in office they passed a great deal of legislation, generally consistent in aim, and definitely reversing the main lines of the Liberals' policy. The most important measures, however, were not in the field of agriculture.

A word might be said on the relation of the National Peasants to foreign agrarian movements. Throughout eastern Europe a strong agrarian current appeared after the First World War. More or less extensive land reforms took place in the belt of states between Soviet Russia and central Europe, and peasant parties of varying political shades made their appearance. In 1921, on the initiative of the Bulgarian Peasant Prime Minister, Alexander Stambuliski, and with the support of the Czech agrarian leaders, Antonin Švehla and Milan Hodža, was formed the International Bureau of Agriculture, known as the Green International. Initially the bureau, which established its headquarters in Prague, was an organization for cooperation among the agrarian parties of the Slavic states of eastern Europe. In 1923, Virgil Madgearu, in discussing the international policy of the Rumanian Peasant party, showed a lukewarm attitude toward the Green International. In his opinion, its purposes were not clearly defined and it displayed a tendency toward Pan-Slavism which would scarcely recommend it to the Rumanians. Above all, he felt that international peasant action had only limited value. "The nation is a decisive factor in determining social progress, since no political party can form itself on an international base. Internationals can be annexes to the development of political action; they cannot become supranational." [63]

The Green International broadened somewhat in the following years. In 1925 Hodža defined the scope of the movement: "We know that agrarian democracy . . . is the strong bond which will create of the peoples an international unity, a formal, organic and psychological unity against which all attacks, whether directed by the imperialist right or the bolshevist left will be shattered." [64] The bureau's secretary Karl Mečir pointed out that the peasantry by their very nature and strong local attachments were not to be organized into a rigid international. The purpose of the movement in his eyes was to

63. *Doctrinele partidelor politice*, p. 86.

64. Milan Hodža, "La Politique étrangère et l'organisation internationale des agriculteurs," *M.A.B.: Bulletin du Bureau International Agraire, 8–9* (1925), 22.

serve as a clearing house to establish common ties and to exchange information.[65] In its general lines it represented an attempt to defend the eastern European peasantry against the more highly organized forces of industrialism and the dynamic inroads of Soviet communism.

In 1926 and 1927 the Rumanian and Finnish Peasant parties joined the Green International. There were no real meetings until 1928, when the bureau was formally constituted. After that annual congresses were held until the movement was engulfed by the depression and the political storms of the 1930's. Eventually it came to include peasant parties from Czechoslovakia, Bulgaria, Yugoslavia, Rumania, Austria, Switzerland, Poland, France, the three Baltic states, and Finland. Although Mihalache had spoken of the rising peasant tide in eastern Europe, and Madgearu and Lupu contributed articles to the later issues of the bulletin of the Green International, it appears to have had no effect upon the course of internal Rumanian politics, and the Rumanians were among the less active members of the bureau.

A far more active, though in its aim unsuccessful, international effort was the agrarian bloc of eastern European states, in which Madgearu played a prominent part. This bloc had its origins in the growing agricultural crisis of 1930. The failure to obtain any favorable action at the first preliminary international conference for concerted economic action (held in Geneva, February 17 to March 24, 1930) led some of the agrarian states of eastern Europe, with the Little Entente at the core, to act together in defense of their interests. A series of conferences at Štrbske Pleso, Bucarest, and Warsaw during the summer of 1930 were attended by representatives from Bulgaria, Estonia, Hungary, Latvia, Poland, Czechoslovakia, Yugoslavia, and Rumania. The attempt was made to coordinte the economic policy of the members of the bloc and to obtain better commercial conditions from the industrial states. The failure of the bloc to achieve its aims belongs, however, in the more general framework of the depression.[66]

The economic, agrarian, and administrative policy of the National Peasants in 1929 and 1930 has definite homogeneity. A prevailing emphasis upon decentralization and autonomy appears in the administrative reform, in the laws for mines and state enterprises, in the reorganization of the cooperatives. An attempt to relax restric-

65. Karl Mečir, "Le Bureau International Agraire," *M.A.B.: Bulletin du Bureau International Agraire, 4* (1926), 26–29.
66. See below, pp. 184–185.

tions and to permit a natural circulation is seen in the abolition of the censorship and state of siege, in the 1929 tariff, in the law permitting the free sale and purchase of peasant property. A friendly attitude toward foreign capital appears in all the laws on trade and the exploitation of natural resources and in the important concessions granted to foreign firms. Finally, a concern for agriculture is shown not merely in the agrarian laws but in the tariff and financial policy. While many of these measures failed to produce the anticipated results, and some were applied inefficiently, still, taken together, they constitute a recognizable policy and one quite different from that pursued by the Liberals. The conflict between the National Peasants and the Liberals was not merely a struggle for office and a place at the feeding trough, although it is not difficult to cite instances where *mirosul fripturei* ("the fragrance of the roast joint") played an important part.

Two questions, however, must be answered. Was it a peasant program? Was it adequate to the economic needs of Rumania, and in particular did it provide a solution to the agrarian question?

From the preceding discussion of the development of the party's ideology, its modifications of program, and its actual policy there can be little doubt that the National Peasant government was not very "peasantist" either in its composition or in its activities. That is not to say that the National Peasants lacked an agrarian program or that they were indifferent to the peasant; certainly the party regarded itself as the spokesman of the peasantry. But in the course of the party's evolution, from its inception after the war to its arrival in power, a significant change had taken place. Perhaps it was mostly a change in emphasis. Initially as was so well shown in Mihalache's speeches, which are more representative than Stere's more sophisticated arguments, stress was upon the peasant and upon the measures which should be taken to improve his condition. When the party came to power, the chief concern was for greater political democracy and more economic liberty, from which the peasant was to benefit. To some extent this shift showed the influence of the Transylvanians with their middle-class and professional interests, but the Peasant party itself had gone a long way in this direction. Moreover, this change was quite natural, given the passage of time and the subsiding of social ferment. But if such a change was natural, it was also dangerous: in Rumania, if the peasant did not command first attention it was too easy for him not to be taken into consideration at all.

The most important reason for this change, and it has been a fatal defect of most peasant parties, is that a purely peasant movement is almost impossible to sustain both because of the nature of its support and the limitations of its program. Because of their relative physical isolation and simple, often primitive, way of life, the peasants are exceptionally difficult to organize politically. A peasantist philosophy has proved to be uncertain and ambiguous in its aims; it can provide mood and feeling, and is a natural inspiration to poster art, but it becomes confused on the more practical level and for a very fundamental reason. Those elements which are celebrated in the peasant—the primordial qualities, the roots planted deep in the earth—represent everything which the modern world is not. In so far as the peasant is defined in these terms, he provides no clue to the solution of the manifold problems confronting contemporary society.

Therefore one can either reject the peasant outright as an essentially neutral or negative factor, as was the tendency among the Liberals and the Social Democrats,[67] or attempt to broaden the peasant concept by adding, often quite eclectically, other principles. This, in fact, has happened to most peasant movements in practice. Various types of alliances can be made, sometimes with conservatism [68] or with socialism.[69] The actual course which the Rumanian peasant movement took was to absorb Western political and parliamentary democracy together with some of the forms of liberal capitalism—the "trust-busting" capitalism, which believes in free enterprise but favors state intervention to prevent the formation of trusts and monopolies. By this means the peasantry, comprising the greatest numbers of citizens, became identified with the majority will of political democracy, and the economic welfare of the peasant with the belief in economic advance through the free competition of an idealized capitalism.

Apart from internal reasons, such as the conflict with the Liberal

67. Thus, the super-Liberal Zeletin said: "The peasant is the very personification of the principle of inertia: he wishes to be just as his ancestors were. For him tradition is sacred. . . . Capitalism raises itself on the ruins of the agrarian classes, peasants and boyars." *Neoliberalismul,* pp. 16, 20. The Social Democrat Ilie Moscovici concluded that the peasant "cannot be a factor of progress as producer, cannot give new methods of production, cannot enrich society. The peasantry has no immediate interest in changing social forms; by its individual property, its isolated work, its narrow horizon, it forms a conservative element, almost the most conservative in contemporary society." "Lupta de clasă şi transformarea socială," *Doctrinele partidelor politice,* p. 302.

68. C. Rădulescu-Motru thought there was a natural alliance between the peasantry and the enlightened conservatives. He sought to develop this idea in his study, *Ţărănismul, un suflet şi o politică.*

69. In Rumania this effort took two forms: an internal alliance with the socialists, if the latter would drop their doctrinaire attitude toward the peasantry; or externally, seeing in the Western proletariat an ally in the common struggle against the domination of Western industrial capitalism.

party, certain external circumstances help to explain this particular development. In the years immediately after the First World War Germany was in eclipse, the Soviet Union was in the midst of a social experiment of which none of the Peasant leaders wanted any part, and the Western powers, particularly Great Britain and the United States, were clearly the dominant states. As a result one finds among the writings of the National Peasants a rather curious Anglo-Saxon overlay, both in political and economic affairs.

The National Peasants are not necessarily to be reproached for having thus donned a somewhat eclectic garment; the narrowness of pure peasantism rendered some such addition necessary, especially when the party came into office. But it may be doubted whether in fact this combination was able to help the peasantry. In the first place, one of the most profound evils in Rumanian society has been the abyss between the peasant and the governing and urban classes. Although Rumania was not a caste-bound society, but had a constant if not very voluminous movement up from the peasantry, the transition—symbolized by discarding the *opinci* (peasant footwear) for shoes and acquiring a knowledge of French—was very sharp, and the persons who had crossed the line were all too tempted to escape as far as possible from their peasant origins. Under these conditions the Peasant party's absorption of nonpeasant principles was the beginning of its actual alienation from the peasantry. Indeed, in the 1930's and 1940's the National Peasants, as a party, became increasingly removed from their rural origins.[70]

In the second place, it is doubtful whether free competition is unqualifiedly beneficial in Rumania's case. Internally, the policy of "natural selection" among the peasants had as its aim the creation of a prosperous middle peasantry. The drawbacks of this policy in a country of small holdings under 3 hectares with an increasing pressure of population have already been discussed. It might of course be maintained that such a process of selection—whatever its hardships on the submarginal cultivators—was a necessary step to creating a sound peasant economy. But for political if not for other reasons this created a serious contradiction between the National Peasant party's role as standard-bearer of the peasantry and the actual effects of

70. The National Peasants whom I met in 1944, in Bucarest or at their country estates, could hardly have been called representatives of the peasantry. Many of them were democrats politically (though some were not) but one had the feeling that they regarded the "good peasants" as something essentially *other*. They were mostly middle-class lawyers, doctors, engineers, and business men who regarded Mihalache's continued use of peasant clothes with gentle amusement as rather quaint.

such a policy upon a large percentage of the peasants.[71] Externally, the approach toward freer trade and the abandoning of industries unless they were capable of "natural" development (though Madgearu was not against protection of infant industries) had certain shortcomings. Recent economic analysis, admittedly still under debate, has considerably modified the definition of the natural development of industry through the idea of "social marginal net profit" and "external economies." [72] It has also raised doubts whether a small backward state should regard classical free trade as an ideal policy. Aside from the theoretical aspects of the question, it is obvious that the success of such a policy is dependent upon a congenial atmosphere in the realm of international trade and finance.

It was the unhappy fate of the National Peasants to have based their policy upon a world situation which was just on the brink of collapsing in the great depression and which, to date, shows little sign of returning to those conditions upon which their foreign commercial policy was founded.[73] Of course, the National Peasants can hardly be blamed for not foreseeing the consequences of the world collapse. Nevertheless the fact that they had thus committed themselves to a pattern which was to be shaken to the ground had fatal consequences for their internal position. They had abandoned the narrowness of the original radical peasantism of 1920–22 for a more promising set of ideas, and when these collapsed their economic program was bankrupt.

Similarly, in the political field they had rested their hopes upon political democracy—again by a somewhat too formal acceptance of Western principles. When Carol and the rising antiparliamentary movements began to come into action in 1930 and 1931, they were defenseless. In 1928 the National Peasants won much praise for the orderly behavior of their mass demonstration at Alba Iulia and their official disavowal of the one column of peasants which had halfheartedly started a march to Bucarest. This very spirit, which was

71. The Communists, of course, have seen in this contradiction a betrayal of the peasantry by a party which had come to represent the lower middle class and the wealthy peasants. Admitting the contradiction, this charge can be judged only in connection with the success of the Communists' efforts at a solution. See below, pp. 325–327.

72. Cf. P. N. Rosenstein-Rodan, "Problems of Industrialization of Eastern and South-Eastern Europe," The Economic Journal, 53 (1943), 202–211, and a criticism by Yuan-Li Wu, "A Note on the Post-War Industrialization of 'Backward' Countries and Centralist Planning," Economica, 12, New Ser. (1945), 172–178.

73. In 1930 Madgearu said: "A new economic ideology was spreading over Europe— the spirit of international economic co-operation, which asserted itself so impressively at the Geneva Economic Conference in May 1927. Rumania understood the spirit of Geneva . . . " Rumania's New Economic Policy, p. 39.

essential to their constitutional and legal principles, helped to cause their subsequent downfall. In abandoning, perhaps inevitably, the strong peasant fervor in favor of majority parliamentary support they failed to preserve their ultimate point of support.

The combination of their political and economic principles, which clearly had a mutual effect upon one another, thus led to their overthrow under the impact of the depression and in the particular circumstances of Maniu's quarrel with King Carol.

In comparing the Liberals and National Peasants, in many ways antithetical, one is struck by a curious parallel between them. Both were somehow out of phase with world developments. The Liberals embarked on a policy of economic nationalism and semiautarky during just the years Europe was making a last if unsuccessful effort to restore the old economic order. The National Peasants, when they came into office, attempted to reverse Rumanian policy at just the time when the European economy was moving into a new stage of economic nationalism. Both parties fell into contradictions arising from their Western preoccupations and the realities of the Rumanian situation. The Liberals in attempting to copy Western capitalism ceased to be "liberal" in the process; the Peasants in attempting to copy parliamentary democracy ceased to be "peasants." The Peasants' economic policy bore a far greater resemblance to traditional liberalism than did that of the Liberals, whereas the Liberals' economic policy—at least in its restrictions and hostility to Western capital—had points in common with the initial attitude of the Peasants.

The following decade was to witness an attempt to overcome these contradictions by carrying certain of the implications to an extreme degree. The Liberals' economic policy, if it was to be realized, implied a move toward corporatism and more state control: this was to be the line followed by the neoliberalism of the Carolist period. On the other hand, the failure of the National Peasants to safeguard the peasant was the cause, in part at least, of the upsurge of the Iron Guard. In both cases the parliamentary pattern was dropped.

VIII

THE CAROLIST PERIOD: DEPRESSION, 1930–33

ALTHOUGH the ten years between 1930 and 1940 were increasingly dominated by the figure of King Carol, and in that sense may be considered as a unit, three more or less distinct phases are observable: a period of confusion and transition from 1930 through 1933, a period of uneasy stability from 1934 to 1937, and a period of crisis from 1938 to 1940. These phases resulted from a complicated intermingling of economic, political, and international circumstances.

On the international level the decade witnessed the return of the most decisive of all factors in Rumanian history: the impact of great power interests, which had been relatively in abeyance during the first years after 1918 with the collapse of the German, Austro-Hungarian, and Russian empires. As has been seen above, Rumania has been fated throughout its history either to be within the orbit of a great power or caught in a conflict between two or more great powers. Its independence in the nineteenth century had been achieved through a temporary equilibrium of these foreign forces, and the creation of Greater Rumania was possible only because of the power vacuum in eastern Europe. The 1930's saw the revival of Soviet Russia and the hectic ascendency of the Third Reich. The predominance of German influence in the late 1930's and the special turn of events given by the German-Soviet pact of 1939 were of decisive importance in determining the course of Rumanian history.

Internal politics advanced in three stages: a time of political uncertainty accompanied by rapid changes in the government, the breakdown of the older parties, and the burgeoning of new movements; a period of apparent stability during the four years of the Tătărescu administration from the end of 1933 to the end of 1937; a period of royal dictatorship which began with Carol's dissolution of all political parties in 1938 and ended with his abdication and flight after the territorial losses of 1940.

Economically, the picture was one of continuous slump until 1934, and then a slow rally accelerating until the outbreak of war in 1939. Industry was the chief gainer; agriculture barely recovered from the losses of the depression. Economic policy underwent a tremendous change, in Rumania as elsewhere, from a paralyzed economic liberalism to increasing controls in commercial, financial, and industrial activity.

King Carol's own role in all these developments is rather elusive. In the intricate game of political maneuvering his shrewdness is seen in the fact that starting from a weak position he not only established himself but drove all other political groups into the wilderness or prison. But for all his adept political manipulations and his flamboyant propaganda there is something unsubstantial about his reign, and nothing seems less real than his dictatorship. While he was not, as king, the frothy playboy the international press had depicted, he did not, either in his ideas or actions, show himself to be a statesman of any magnitude. He had a strong bent for personal rule, to which he attached some rather inconsequential corporatist clichés and an exaltation of the "younger generation." He seems to have had no coherent set of economic ideas beyond a romantic notion of himself as the first peasant, the first laborer, and the first public servant of his realm. The real economic direction came not from Carol but from the increasingly powerful industrialists who came to the fore in the years after the depression.

Survey of Political Events

Between Maniu's resignation in October and the accession of the Liberals in November, 1933, Rumanian political and economic life was more than usually bewildering and confused. The depression was undoubtedly largely responsible for the feeling of panic and uncertainty apparent in the governments of these years. At the same time, the political events were not wholly a reflex of the immediate economic influence but had a certain logic of their own. Rumania's quasi-parliamentary party system was beginning to crumble, extraparliamentary groups were moving into the foreground, and Carol made his first if not successful effort to reorganize political life according to his own lights. These developments proceeded from sources deeper than the depression, though they were intensified by it; they were a part of that profound social crisis which has stricken most of the world in the last thirty years.

The National Peasant cabinet, reconstituted under Mironescu after Maniu's resignation, had a brief and unhappy career. Mironescu was an altogether colorless figure; the government during his term in office was halting and hesitant in its actions, and showed none of the enthusiasm of 1929. Carol was known to feel that the old parties—

and it is illustrative of the nature of Rumanian politics that the National Peasant party had by this time already become an "old" party —had outlived the impulses which had created them. He desired a rearrangement of the political mosaic to give due place to "younger" elements and believed that this required the installation of a disinterested government of "personalities." Besides the knowledge that Carol was counting their days, the National Peasants saw their once impressive popularity draining away, through the depression and their manifest failure to bring about the new Jerusalem.

In by-elections of January, 1931, the government lost a number of seats, and perhaps the only safe conclusion one can draw from Rumanian elections is that the loss of government-held seats means an undeniable fall in public confidence. The customary flurry of rumors presaged the government's overthrow, and indeed its negotiations for a second foreign loan were the condition for its remaining in power, as had been the case with Vintilă Brătianu's government three years before. On March 10 the loan agreement was signed in Paris, and on April 4 Mironescu resigned. Rumania's outstanding diplomat, Titulescu, was recalled from London—a standard procedure during the cabinet crises of these years—to form a coalition government. Both the National Peasants and the Liberals accepted on certain conditions but Iorga, significantly, voted against it and demanded a cabinet of personalities.

On April 18 Carol called upon Iorga, who, with Argetoianu as his capable hatchet man, formed a cabinet of at least some of the talents. Iorga, announcing his program to be hard work and economy, summoned and immediately dismissed the National Peasant chamber. New elections were held, but even with Argetoianu doing his efficient best at the Ministry of the Interior and with an electoral pact with the Liberals, the government bloc of National Union obtained only 48 per cent of votes. The National Peasants of course were forced down to 15 per cent, and Maniu announced his retirement from politics. The Communists' Workers and Peasant Union won five seats, their first representation in the chamber. Incidentally, none of their members was returned from Bessarabia, reputedly the seat of Rumanian communism; all five were from the industrial centers of Transylvania, the Banat, and Bucovina.

Carol's guiding hand is evident in the creation of the Iorga-Argetoianu government, and after its formation he announced his intentions to preside over cabinet meetings once a week. Nicolae Iorga, the internationally known and incredibly voluminous historian, had never commanded any following beyond a coterie of admirers. His individualism, or perhaps his vanity, had made him an uncertain political ally, and he took to himself the role of mentor and guardian of the Rumanian national consciousness. His efforts in politics, however, were far less impressive than his output as a historian.[1]

The government's term in office was not edifying.[2] As the economic situation deteriorated, the complete absence of any organized political support made itself felt when all the other parties began a violent press campaign; the Liberals belabored Argetoianu's financial policy as one of bankruptcy; the Transylvanian press threatened a demand for autonomy; the aging Marshal Averescu, bitterly disappointed by Carol's failure to select him as man of the hour, assailed both the government and the king. A crisis rose between Carol and the government over the salaries of state officials. The government, faced by a bad deficit and the failure to obtain an additional loan from France, was attempting to reduce official salaries. Carol opposed this and forced Iorga's resignation on June 6, 1932.

After an unsuccessful effort by Titulescu, the National Peasants, under Vaida Voevod, were recalled for their second term of office. In the elections of July they obtained only 45 per cent of the votes, a great decline from their 80 per cent of 1928, but sufficient to give them the premium. The Iron Guard and other fascist groups showed gains and won some additional seats, primarily in Bessarabia, the region of deepest discontent. An effort was made to bring Maniu out of retirement; he did resume leadership of the party but was unable to reach an understanding with Carol.

The program of the new National Peasant government was along the same lines as its predecessors and included the reintroduction of the administrative decentralization law, which had been revoked by the Iorga government; a modification of the electoral law, which all parties promised to change but which they somehow did not get around to when in power; and a reduction of taxes and expenditures. The party had an initial success in obtaining a Swiss loan of 50 million francs for the payment of back salaries of state officials. In October, however, Vaida Voevod resigned after a disagreement with the influential Titulescu on the question of Rumanian-Soviet nego-

1. For a recent tribute to Iorga, who was assassinated by the Iron Guard in 1940, see John Campbell, "Nicholas Iorga," *The Slavonic and East European Review, 26*, No. 66 (November, 1947), 44–59.

2. For a particularly jaundiced account of the Iorga-Argetoianu administration see G. C. Logio, *Rumania*, pp. 39–52. Logio, as a foreign business man, was especially bitter on the subject of Rumanian business ethics and heartily disliked Carol, "who promulgates rascally laws defrauding the unwary foreign investor and trader."

tiations,[3] and was replaced by Maniu, with Titulescu as Foreign Minister. On January 8, 1933, Maniu again broke with Carol, and on January 14 Vaida Voevod returned to head the government.[4]

By this time the National Peasants were badly disorganized. With Carol's assistance a definite split in the party leadership between Maniu and Vaida Voevod was developing and was to lead to a rupture in 1934. The government itself had not only lost its peasant enthusiasm but under Vaida Voevod's leadership was rapidly drifting into the political habits of the Liberals. On the first of February oil workers at Ploeşti struck over a wage decision, and a fight ensued between strikers and troops. At the same time in Bucarest some 7,000 workers in the state railway shops went on strike. The government hastily proclaimed martial law in Bucarest, Cernăuţi, Galaţi, Iaşi, Timişoara, Ploeşti, and the oil fields. The Communist party and its affiliates were again dissolved, the government passed laws against antisocial and antistate organizations, and over 200 Communists were arrested throughout Rumania. This brought a protest demonstration from the railway workers, troops were called out, and there was a vicious street fight.

To some extent this tension was a fatal by-product of the deepening depression, and the strikes, while obviously having their roots in the misery of the Rumanian industrial workers, were not confined solely to economic demands. Indeed, since the installation of the Groza regime, the Communists have played up the revolutionary elements of the railway strike and the guiding role of the Communist party in it. Even so, the government all too hastily resorted to the very measures for which it had so long taken the Liberals to task.

Moreover, while Vaida Voevod was thus combating labor unrest,

3. Rumania and Soviet Russia had not resumed diplomatic relations since the First World War because of their inability to reach any agreement on Bessarabia. In January, 1932, the Poles, with French urging, had signed a treaty of friendship and nonaggression with the U.S.S.R. Now Poland and France were pressing Rumania to do the same. Vaida Voevod, apparently without consulting Titulescu, had instructed the Rumanian representative in Warsaw to negotiate with Litvinov. Titulescu had heard of his move and had objected to the manner in which the negotiations were being conducted and especially to the possibility that Bessarabia might be recognized as a subject of dispute. In this disagreement Titulescu was sufficiently influential to squeeze out Vaida Voevod.

4. In this instance the specific difficulty arose over the dismissal of Colonel Marinescu, Prefect of Bucarest. Carol had been installing military officers in a number of civil posts. The National Peasant government undertook to replace them by civilians. Colonel Marinescu, in a circular letter, denied rumors that he was about to be removed and said that since he was appointed by the king, only the king could remove him. Mihalache, Minister of the Interior, then demanded his resignation, and failing to obtain it resigned himself. Maniu supported Mihalache and the cabinet resigned.

he was on good terms with the up-and-coming Iron Guard. Indeed, a year later he said, under oath, that as early as 1929, when he had been Minister of the Interior, he had been in touch with the Iron Guardists for the purpose of directing their youthful enthusiasm toward less extreme ends and "of drawing the attention of the organization to the necessity of combating Communism." [5] In 1934 Vaida Voevod, after failing to get the National Peasants to accept his "numerus Valachicus"—a device to oust non-Rumanian minorities, especially the Hungarians, from posts in the government and in "nationally important enterprises"—abandoned the party and formed his own hypernationalist, semifascist political group.[6]

In November, 1933, the Vaida government resigned, partly at least because of the king's dissatisfaction with its handling of the increasing fascist activity and its failure to prevent attacks directed against himself, Mme Lupescu, and his entourage.[7] After five years out of power the old Liberals, under Duca, came into office on November 14. Duca, who, like Vaida Voevod, stated that he had tried to "channelize" the energies of the Iron Guard, undertook to dissolve the movement on the eve of the new elections. On December 29 he was assassinated by three Iron Guardists at the Sinaia railway station. After several days' confusion, Gheorghe Tătărescu became head of the Liberal cabinet which was to remain in office until November, 1937.

During these three years of hectic political changes, five main developments are observable:

1) The growing influence of the king. While Carol was unsuccessful in establishing a government of personalities, he was making rapid progress in unraveling the old political fabric and undermining and splitting the leadership of the major parties. He was also increasing his extraparliamentary influence through his camerilla and through his appointees in administrative posts.

2) The increasing paralysis and confusion of the National Peasants. As has been seen already, their decline was more or less implicit in the situation as of 1930, and during the following years the

5. *Patria,* March 31, 1934, quoted in Pătrăşcanu, *Sous trois dictatures,* p. 76.

6. See C. A. Macartney's account of a conversation with Vaida Voevod on the "numerus Valachicus," *Hungary and Her Successors,* p. 326.

7. Although internally Rumanian politics were moving to the Right, the Vaida government did, in July, sign the London Convention defining aggression, to which the U.S.S.R. was also a signatory. This step, which marked a slight improvement in Rumanian-Soviet relations, was a part of the realignment of forces after the rise of Hitler.

leadership divided, many of the party's most capable men deserted, the party's popularity declined, and an increasing number of peasant supporters were attracted to the Iron Guard.

3) An apparent recovery of the Liberals. The Liberal party had been badly hit by their defeat in 1928 and the schism between Vintilă Brătianu and Gheorghe Brătianu, occasioned by Carol's return. With Vintilă Brătianu's death in 1930 the way was cleared for a gradual reconciliation with the king. The Young Liberals (Gheorghe Brătianu) failed to make any significant headway, and under Duca the old Liberals seemed to be heading for a comeback.

4) The flowering of fascism. The meteoric rise of the Iron Guard was the most spectacular event of those years, and trailing in its wake were a number of less fiery fascist, semifascist and anti-Semitic formations of unequal importance. In the party system they served to replace the older coteries, such as Iorga's and Averescu's parties, which were fading from the scene, but in fact they heralded the collapse of parliamentary government.

5) The total impotence of the Left-wing labor movements. They had never been strong in Rumania, but during these three years they were driven from the offensive, however weak, to the defensive. Popular discontent did not, after 1933, swell the ranks of the labor movements but strengthened the Iron Guard.

The Struggle against the Depression

During these years the economic situation steadily deteriorated. It was estimated that the nominal national income in lei dropped by about 45 per cent between 1929 and 1932.[8] While Rumania was able to maintain a positive balance of trade throughout the depression, the value of exports fell from 29 billion lei in 1929 to 14 billion in 1933 and 1934, even though the weight of exports increased from 7,000,000 metric tons to 8,000,000. Imports fell from 1,102,000 metric tons in 1929 to 467,000 in 1933 (450,000 in 1932). State revenues declined from 36 billion lei in 1929 to 18 billion in 1933.

The depression in Rumania had been initiated by the world agricultural crisis in 1929, which produced a tremendous fall in the price of agricultural products, particularly disastrous in the Balkan states because of their inability to compete with the great overseas producers. As industrial commodities fell neither so soon nor so far the resulting price scissors hurt the peasant as agricultural producer

8. Royal Institute of International Affairs, *South-Eastern Europe* (Oxford University Press, 1939), p. 127.

and Rumania as agricultural exporter. The average price per metric ton of Rumanian exports fell in 1934 by 62 per cent of its 1922–30 average, whereas the price of imports fell by only 33 per cent in 1936. Internally agricultural prices dropped to 44 per cent of the 1929 level, industrial prices to 62 per cent.[9] The situation was further aggravated by the inauguration at this time of an agrarian protectionist policy by the European industrial states. After 1928 Germany introduced high agricultural tariffs; Italian grain and flour duties reached prohibitive levels between 1929 and 1931; France imposed heavy tariffs on cereals.

In May, 1931, the failure of the Austrian Kredit-Anstalt unleashed the financial crisis which swept across Europe and ended the flow of foreign capital to Rumania. Inevitably, the fall in grain prices, the disappearance of foreign markets for agricultural produce, and the stoppage of foreign credit had a disastrous effect upon the Rumanian economy. State finances, never on a very steady foundation, and having just been reorganized in 1929, were hit by the decline in revenues (direct taxes dropped from 8.6 billion lei in 1930 to 3.4 in 1933), and there was a budget deficit each year between 1930 and 1934.[10]

One peculiarity should be observed in the Rumanian depression. In several respects Rumania was in a better position than the other Balkan states. Because of a series of good harvests in 1929, 1930, and 1931, and because of petroleum exports, it was able to maintain a considerably better balance of trade. Moreover, because of the acquisition of a good deal of foreign capital in the loans of 1929

9. Madgearu, *Evoluția economiei românești*, p. 80, and *Breviaire Statistique de la Roumanie* (Bucarest, 1940), p. 226:

	Wholesale agricultural prices	Industrial prices	Prices of industrial products required by agriculture
1929	100	100	100
1930	68.2	92.9	98
1931	50.8	72.0	86.6
1932	47.7	62.2	80.9
1933	44.9	62.2	81.1
1934	44.1	63.4	82.6
1935	48.4	75.2	90.2

10. As a matter of fact, a budgetary deficit in Rumania is a very relative term; many of the so-called budget surpluses of the 1920's were quite fictitious. See Ludovic Iavorschi, *L'Equilibre budgetaire en Roumanie de 1920 à 1932* (Paris, 1933). I doubt if the budget deficits can in any way be regarded as a planned attempt to counter the depression, since all the governments promised balanced budgets and the deficit appeared as the result of altogether undirected and uncontrolled expenditures through a number of channels.

and 1931, Rumania was somewhat less pressed financially than the other states, and was indeed the last of the Balkan countries to introduce foreign exchange controls and to declare a partial moratorium on foreign debts.[11]

Nevertheless, Rumania was the slowest to show signs of recovery, an indication that something in addition to the general causes for the depression was having an effect. Such was the opinion of the French foreign advisers to the Rumanian National Bank, MM. Rist and Auboin. According to Auboin, in his report of 1935, a distinction should be drawn between the causes of disequilibrium arising from the world crisis and those proper to Rumania itself. In his opinion the first were predominant between 1929 and 1932 in the fall in prices and the disruption of international credit. But local causes became manifest, especially after 1932, despite a certain easing of international conditions. The two principal evils, in his view, were the weaknesses in the whole Rumanian credit system and the unstable budget position, both of which had afflicted Rumania since the First World War. As a financial adviser he was particularly indignant that the Rumanian government should try to enjoy all the benefits and amenities of a modern state through its expenditures but should still rely upon primitive means of organizing state finances: "It is necessary to adopt and apply not merely the methods of expenditure but also the methods of receipt of modern states." [12]

The fall in prices and the reduction of credit presented the Rumanian peasant with a serious debt load which he was in no position to discharge. The advocates of small peasant agriculture have contended that one of the principal advantages of this form of cultivation was the peasant's resistance to crises through his ability to cut expenses, reduce his relations to the market, and live on his own. It is true that debts contracted for agricultural investment were quite small in Rumania as compared with other European states.[13] Never-

11. Rumania introduced exchange controls on February 27, 1932; Hungary, Czechoslovakia, Yugoslavia, Austria, Bulgaria, and Greece had introduced them between August and October, 1931. Rumania declared a partial moratorium in January, 1933; Greece, Bulgaria, and Yugoslavia had done so in 1932.

12. Roger Auboin, *Rapport annuel sur la situation financière et monétaire de la Roumanie* (Bucarest, 1935), p. 36. Auboin was primarily concerned with Rumania's ability to honor its foreign obligations, and hence stressed the need of tightening state finances and creating a sound budget, perhaps at the expense of local requirements. Nevertheless, his, and Rist's, reports are devastating in their picture of the irresponsibility of Rumanian financial administration, its slovenliness, and tendency to make increasingly complex and meaningless regulations.

13. Comparative figures in the International Institute of Agriculture's *Farm Accountancy Statistics for 1928-29* (Rome, 1932), show very little investment and very little debt for Rumanian farms as contrasted with those of other European states. These

theless the peasant did have a burden arising from purchases of land after the agrarian reform or from debts incurred for consumption, and it is necessary to emphasize that the size of the greater number of peasant holdings put their owners on the margin of subsistence. These debts had been contracted during years of rising prices and at a high rate of interest. When the depression came the debts, in many cases not used for productive purposes but merely to keep the peasant going, quite exceeded his capacity to pay. Thus, in 1931, the average indebtedness per hectare, in an investigation of 60,000 farms, was computed at 3,218 lei. Since for an indebtedness of 3,500 lei per hectare the interest averaged 700 lei per hectare, and the average gross income was 2,000 lei per hectare, 35 per cent of the gross income was absorbed by interest on debts.[14]

The figures for 1932 were even bleaker. In that year the number of debtors owning less than 10 hectares who applied for debt relief was 2,474,781 or 64 per cent of all small proprietors.[15] The total land owned by those peasants amounted to 5,696,000 hectares, or 60 per cent of the total of small properties. The total debt was 37.4 billion lei, 15,000 lei per debtor, or 6,585 lei per hectare. It may be concluded that the smaller peasants were the more involved in debt since by these figures the average size of properties under 10 hectares was 2.5 hectares, whereas the average size of the debtors' properties was 2.3 hectares. Of this debt 24.21 per cent was owed to popular banks and cooperatives, 43.58 per cent to private banks, 31.42 to private individuals, and 0.79 to other institutions. A League of Nations inquiry into agricultural credit in central and eastern Europe, made at about this time, found that in Rumania banks of agricultural credit charged 9–13 per cent; private banks 12–15 per cent plus a quarterly commission of 1–3 per cent; and private lenders from 12 to 22 per cent and even up to 30 per cent.[16]

---

figures mean nothing statistically, however, as they cover only 63 Rumanian farms having an average area of 30 hectares; 30 of them are forest-farming combinations with an average area of 50 hectares. This point is worth mentioning only because Frederick Hertz, in his study, *The Economic Problems of the Danubian States* (London, 1947), p. 111, takes these figures as representative and expresses his surprise that in the depression the Rumanian peasant should have been regarded as debt-ridden.

14. Nicolae Cornăţeanu, "Effects of the Agricultural Crisis on Peasant Farms in Rumania," *International Review of Agriculture, 22*, No. 7 (Rome, 1931), 211E. In 1928 the gross income had been 6,000–7,000 lei, which would make the interest charge only 10–11 per cent.

15. G. Costanzo, "Credit Conditions and the Indebtedness of Agriculture in Central and Eastern Europe," *International Review of Agriculture, 24* (1933), 238E; Madgearu, *op. cit.,* p. 83.

16. International Labor Organization, *Industrial and Labor Information, 41*, No. 1 (January 4, 1932), 22.

In addition to the debts of small farmers, 15 billion lei were owed by debtors owning over 10 hectares (who had applied for debt relief in 1932), making a total of 52.4 billion lei of agricultural debts.[17] Some 17,000 middle and large proprietors contrived to run up a debt 40 per cent as large as that of 2½ million peasants. The size of the debt apparently increased with the size of the property: 524 debtors (those owing 5,000,000 lei or more), with average properties of 200 hectares, owed over 40 per cent of the total debt of proprietors of over 10 hectares. Moreover, the average size of property of debtors owning more than 10 hectares was 53 hectares, whereas the average size of all properties over 10 hectares (according to Ministry of Finance figures which appear to be those used) was only 30 hectares.

It would thus seem that the weight of the debt load fell upon the extremely small and the large properties, whereas the middle peasantry was less affected. That is, the peasant owning about 10 hectares was in a relatively good position to weather the crisis, a fact of only limited relevance, however, to Rumania. The figures also show that Rumania's agricultural debt was of two essentially different types: debts of the small peasants who were unable to create or maintain a self-subsistent holding in the ten years after the agrarian reforms, and the debts of the larger properties, which were probably suffering directly from the fall in world grain prices which hit them as exporters.

As the finances of the state were badly weakened by the depression, its power of direct assistance to agriculture was limited. Since the peasants' plight was a result of their debts and low prices, the obvious tasks of the government in Rumania and elsewhere in the Balkans were to support the price of grain, to try to obtain more favorable export conditions, and to provide for a conversion or moratorium of agricultural debts. These remedies did not represent any particular program but were rather specific measures passed under an increasingly severe situation with growing indications of peasant unrest.

By the time of Maniu's resignation in October, 1930, the agricultural crisis had become acute and there was growing agitation for a reduction of debts. Three prominent economists, Madgearu, Manoilescu, and Argetoianu, each published a plan for a readjustment of agricultural indebtedness; in each plan the state was to assume responsibility for part of the burden. Nothing was done at this time.

17. Constanzo, *op. cit.,* p. 238E, taken from the Rumanian Ministry of Justice, *Conversiunea datorilor agricole* (Bucarest, 1932).

partly because the plans required large sums of liquid capital, which was not on hand.

The Mironescu National Peasant government attempted to improve the situation from the credit side. It undertook negotiations in Paris for an agricultural loan to provide for the establishment of an agricultural mortgage bank, a long-cherished aim of the National Peasants who hoped to facilitate thereby the transfer of agricultural debts into long-term obligations less onerous as to time of payment and rate of interest. Eventually agreement was reached on a second development loan, modeled after that of 1929, of 1.3 billion francs, of which 200 million was to go to the creation of the Agricultural Mortgage Institute and the remainder for railway, roads, and Treasury working capital. The loan met with much local criticism; there was general resentment at the continuation of foreign financial supervision which it entailed; the director of the National Bank fought the loan so stubbornly that the government was obliged to dismiss him; Titulescu and Argetoianu opposed the whole idea of borrowing foreign capital for a land bank at a time when such an institute could be only a palliative for the agricultural crisis. Indeed, the *Credit Agricol Ipoteca* was formed on the eve of the credit crisis which hit Europe in 1931.

In a final flurry of legislation, just before its fall, the Mironescu government passed two other measures designed to improve agricultural credit: a law to keep down the interest rate of agricultural credit institutions and a law against usury, prohibiting exaggerated rates of interest by private lenders. These laws, which were in the spirit of the National Peasant program, were altogether inadequate. The credit problem in Rumania was not to be solved by attempting to prohibit what was a secondary symptom. Like much Rumanian legislation, they were an effort to improve the weather by adjusting the dial on the barometer. Furthermore, they did not touch the question of the existing agricultural debt load which was becoming unsupportable.

In December, 1931, the chamber, with all major parties concurring, voted a moratorium for agricultural debts. From 1932 to 1934 appeared a series of laws for the relief of agricultural indebtedness. These laws, passed by successive governments in turn, were in part political measures and in part concessions progressively extorted by the deepening depression. As at the time of the land reforms of 1917–21, political competition plus popular pressure forced the parties toward more and more extensive measures. No party dared come out against debt relief when the more radical groups, including the irrepressible Dr. Lupu, were demanding a complete moratorium or a cancellation of debts. But if the necessity of relief was admitted, the methods were by no means agreed upon. Banks opposed debt cancellation as ruinous to future credit and as throwing a heavy burden on them. The state proposed relieving the banks of their losses, but this in turn evoked protests from foreign creditors who maintained that increasing the state's indebtedness contravened the loan agreements. The simple fact, of course, was that there was no solution that would hurt no one; against the damage to the credit structure had to be set the obvious inability of the peasant to pay his debts and the certain social dangers of undertaking foreclosures.

In April, 1932, the Iorga government passed a law by which debts of all properties under 10 hectares were reduced by half, the remainder to be paid over a period of thirty years at 4 per cent interest. Debts of properties over 10 hectares were to be diminished by the reduction of accumulated interest or by special legal procedure, if 60 per cent of the borrowed capital had been used for agricultural purposes. Although in 1930 Iorga had stated his opposition to assuming charge of the debts of the larger landowners,[18] the law framed by his government was immediately abused by the big owners, who employed it to slough off debts acquired, as it was said, on the green cloth rather than on the green fields.[19] The law also had the effect of increasing the demands of urban and other nonagricultural debtors.

In October, 1932, the Vaida Voevod government suspended this conversion law and introduced a system of moratoria. To prevent misuse the debtor had to prove that agriculture provided 60 per cent of his total income, that the money borrowed had been for agricultural purposes, and that the debt did not exceed 20,000 lei per hectare of arable land.

This measure, which was largely a delaying action, was supplemented by the law of April, 1933, which abrogated the act of 1932 and granted a five-year moratorium with a 1 per cent interest charge. If the creditor offered a 50 per cent reduction of the debt the moratorium ceased to apply. In this case the remaining 50 per cent was to be paid off in half-yearly installments. Holdings between 10 and

18. *Adeverul*, September 9, 1930, cited in G. C. Logio, *op. cit.*, p. 170.
19. According to Logio, *ibid.*, pp. 170–171, the larger landowners were the most insistent that agricultural debts should be converted and were intended to be the principal beneficiaries. In his opinion the controls exerted over the peasants who took advantage of the law—the prohibition of mortgages and the direction of cultivation—would further undermine their position.

50 hectares were also granted a five-year moratorium, with the possibility of the creditor offering a 33 per cent reduction in the debt. Holdings of over 50 hectares were granted a six-month moratorium and a possible reduction of 25 per cent of the debt. The debtor, if he wished, was permitted to abandon his holding, retaining one-fifth of it for himself, the remainder to go to meet his debts. The law was an improvement over its predecessor in scaling the provisions in accordance with the size of the holding.

A year later, in April, 1934, the Liberal government passed a new law whereby all agricultural debts without respect to size of property were reduced by 50 per cent, the residue to be paid in 34 half-yearly installments at 3 per cent interest. For payments in advance debtors were to receive a 6 per cent annual reduction on their debts. Debts paid off within two years were to benefit from a 70 per cent reduction of the total, those paid off in five years gained a 60 per cent reduction. While the creditor had a theoretical right to refuse conversion he was obliged to make a formal declaration of the fact and to accept a ten-year moratorium which could be prolonged for an additional five years. This law was more sweeping than its predecessors, especially in its pressure on the creditor, and it did provide the peasant with an incentive for a quick liquidation of his debt.

These laws, for all the political bickering which accompanied them, were a necessary consequence of the crisis and progressively extended the scope of conversion. They were negative measures, however; while they eased the peasants' debt load they in no way improved his basic situation or remedied the condition which had led to his plunging so hopelessly into debt.[20]

Besides reducing peasant debts, the governments of the depression years tried to maintain the price of grain and to secure favorable export markets. As with the other acts of those years, their efforts were hesitant and often inconsistent. During its period in office the Mironescu government had accelerated the National Peasant party's policy of removing the remaining export duties on agricultural products, and in April, 1931, it passed a law for the valorization of

20. Madgearu, while admitting that the Liberal law of 1934 had meant a benefit for all farmers, maintained that the peasant debtor was still in a sufficiently difficult position which excluded him from obtaining the credit necessary to rationalize his cultivation. According to his estimate, peasant credit available after the conversion was only one-seventh of what it had been before. He also pointed out that the peasants as shareholders in the cooperative banks lost 2¾ billion lei through the conversion. Op. cit., p. 84. This, however, would not hit the poorer peasant who never had the funds to invest in the first place.

farm products, aimed principally at maintaining the prices in the home market by the reduction of various charges and taxes. The Iorga government, however, at once superseded this measure by inaugurating in July, 1931, an export bounty of 10,000 lei for 10,000 kilograms of wheat and 16,000 lei for flour, the cost to be met by a bread tax. The government, however, discovered that it lacked the funds to carry out this measure and discontinued it in 1932. Moreover, it turned out to be largely for the benefit of the export houses rather than the producers and merely tempted Rumanian exporters to engage in wheat dumping. On the other hand the tax on bread, which was to pay the bounty, was borne largely by the peasant consumer.[21] In 1933 and 1934 a different method was tried; the last Vaida Voevod cabinet set up a State Cereal Commission by which the government appeared on the market as a consumer to support wheat prices.

Like debt conversion, the price-supporting measures, which were taken up by the various governments in turn, were not the result of any over-all plan but were simply steps to counteract the depression. In fact, in their effect they ran against all plans for agrarian improvement. The parties, in their programs and writings, had all agreed that the future of Rumanian agriculture lay in intensive farming and in persuading the peasant to abandon extensive cereal cultivation for which his small holding was obviously ill-suited. The bounties on wheat had precisely the opposite effect and led to an even greater emphasis upon cereal production. Between 1930 and 1935 the area under wheat showed a definite, if highly irregular, tendency to rise.

The governments also undertook to obtain more favorable foreign markets. The first effort, under the National Peasants, was by means of collaboration with the other eastern European states in an agrarian bloc. Through the series of conferences in 1930 the agrarian states attempted to create a program of common action to gain preferential treatment from the industrial states for their agricultural products. Although the agrarian bloc pleaded its case at various meetings of the League and at international conferences between 1930 and 1932, it failed to open markets for agriculture. Its requests were opposed by the maritime states and overseas grain producers as contrary to free trade and the most-favored-nation principle. Madgearu, one of the most eloquent spokesmen for the bloc, declared that the agrarian states did not demand permanent preferential treat-

21. Manoliou, *La Reconstruction économique et financière de la Roumanie et les partis politiques*, p. 284.

ment but merely assistance to recover from the depression.[22] The whole tenor of international trade policy at that time was against his recommendations, and nothing tangible was achieved. Nor did the various international efforts of 1931–33—the Tardieu Plan, the Stresa Conference, and the London Economic Conference—bring the southeastern European states any substantial benefits in relieving their foreign indebtedness, establishing common economic policy, or providing more favorable foreign markets.

With the failure of international attempts to obtain better markets for its agricultural produce, the Rumanian government was driven toward increasing restrictions and controls. Although Rumania under the Brătianus had pursued a policy of economic nationalism, and was to do so again in the latter half of the 1930's, the commercial and monetary controls imposed by the different cabinets between 1931 and 1933 did not, in their inception at least, appear to be the result of any comprehensive policy but were applied as emergency measures. Many of the steps were taken by Virgil Madgearu, who had been a bitter critic of the Liberals' policy and was later to attack the trend toward increasing protectionism; he repeatedly explained that he was being forced against his wishes into these restrictive measures.

In the spring of 1932 the government introduced foreign exchange controls to preserve the national currency in face of the deteriorating balance of payments and the threat of speculation. Import controls were imposed in December, 1932, and were, according to Madgearu, primarily designed to stimulate exports and only secondarily to restrict imports, although the association of the two was inevitable and followed from the exchange controls.[23] In the summer of 1933 Madgearu declared a moratorium on foreign debts [24] and in the autumn demanded their reduction. In defending these moves he stated that unless markets were opened to Rumanian products the government was left with no alternative but to restrict imports, control exchange, and freeze its foreign obligations. All these moves "served directly or indirectly as an instrument of agricultural protection." [25]

In the same years Rumania was making the first steps toward clear-

---

22. A. Bussot, "Le Bloc des états agricoles de l'Europe centrale et orientale et son programme," *Revue d'économie politique, 47* (Paris, 1933), 153.

23. Madgearu, *op. cit.,* p. 238.

24. Under this measure the equivalents of sums due abroad were deposited in lei in the National Bank; they could not be withdrawn from the country but could be invested in Rumania. Part of Rumania's subsequent industrialization was financed by these captive funds.

25. Madgearu, *op. cit.,* p. 247.

ing agreements and bilateral trade, again in the effort to find markets. In 1931 a trade convention was made with Germany which reduced its duties on Rumanian maize and barley; in 1932 agreements were reached with France for the export of maize and with Germany for meat.

All these steps, however, were defensive efforts to protect agriculture against the depression. It is less easy to find much evidence of attempts to get at the roots of the agrarian question. The different cabinets passed a variety of laws, some of them transparent vote-catchers, others old favorites which each new Rumanian government seemed to pass as a matter of routine. All the cabinets announced their goal of increasing the use of agricultural machinery: the Mironescu government passed an act reducing the import duties on agricultural equipment by two-thirds, the Iorga government in 1932 and the Liberals at the beginning of 1934 granted credits for the purchase of agricultural machinery. To judge from the figures on the consumption of agricultural equipment the results were very slight, at least until 1934 with the beginning of recovery.

The only apparent effort at overcoming the disadvantages inherent in Rumania's system of strip cultivation was a law for the establishment of agricultural associations passed by the Iorga cabinet in July, 1931. By this law cultivators whose separate properties formed an economic whole could combine to cultivate their land more rationally by the introduction of mechanical cultivation, use of fertilizers, selected seeds, and other technical improvements. Funds required by the associations for this purpose could be obtained through the cooperative and agricultural banks, the state to assume 6 per cent interest on the loans on the condition that the association follow a plan approved by the Ministry of Agriculture. Nothing seems to have come of this law, and a very similar semicollective state-sponsored proposal was attempted by the Antonescu regime a decade later.

In general, 1931–33 were years of steady retreat before the onslaught of the depression. In the course of this retreat a number of economic devices were developed, in Rumania as elsewhere, which were to take on increasing importance in the years to follow. To a considerable extent they had been introduced to protect agriculture but they were soon to find pleasanter and more lucrative employment.

IX

THE CAROLIST PERIOD: NEOLIBERALISM,
1934–37

Survey of Political Events

THE term neoliberalism, which may appear a gross misnomer for these singularly unliberal years, is descriptive of two facts: 1) The Liberal party returned to office and, what is more, remained there for the full term of four years, thus repeating its record as the only party under the 1923 Constitution to achieve such a feat of endurance. Nevertheless, the Liberal cabinet of the 1930's was not the same as the party of Ion I. C. and Vintilă Brătianu. Not only did King Carol really hold the leading strings of political power but within the Liberal party itself (not to speak of Gheorghe Brătianu's Young Liberals) there was a growing cleavage between Gheorghe Tătărescu, the head of the government, and Constantin Brătianu, the third of the elder Brătianu brothers, who was party chief. This split did not become open until later, but Tătărescu as a king's man was clearly moving away from the old lines of the Liberals. 2) The leading ideas of the administration at this time have a certain relation to the doctrine of so-called neoliberalism, which was advanced in the 1920's but which at that time was associated with Averescu's People's party.[1]

The years 1934 and 1935 were a kind of plateau in the troubled history of the 1930's. The depression leveled off and there was a slow move toward recovery. The political party system, while basically completely unstable, did at least pause from the rapid changes of government which had marked the years 1931–33. King Carol seemed less bent on securing a personal political dictatorship. Even on the international scene there was a temporary, if uneasy, breathing spell. The first impulse of fascism which had brought Hitler to power had not set all of east Europe tumbling as had been feared. Rumania reestablished diplomatic relations with the U.S.S.R.[2] The Lit-

1. The People's party was a melange of "regenerated" liberalism combined with an emphasis upon order and discipline, plus a great deal of crass opportunism.
2. Without, however, obtaining a clear statement of recognition of its possession of Bessarabia. For a discussion of this point see Philip E. Mosely, "Is Bessarabia Next?" *Foreign Affairs, 18,* No. 3 (New York, April, 1940), 557–562.

tle Entente remained, the Balkan Entente was formed, and people were heard to say that the Balkans were beginning to mature. It was only a lull before the storm but it was perceptible.

The political history of these years is relatively uneventful. In the elections of December 20, 1933, the Liberals obtained a handsome majority in the chamber. After Duca's assassination and the creation of a cabinet under Tătărescu, a period of comparative quiet ensued. That this period was not one of tranquillity is shown by the repeated prolongations of the state of martial law, which had been applied after Duca's death and remained in force throughout the Tătărescu administration. In reality an intense tug-of-war was going on between the king and Tătărescu on the one hand and the Iron Guard on the other. It was less a conflict than a competition to gain a monopoly on the increasingly nationalist and extremist atmosphere which was pervading Rumania.

The relations between the Carol regime and the Iron Guard were equivocal, to say the least. Duca, leader of the Liberals, was assassinated by the Iron Guard, and yet the efforts of his successor to control the movement were certainly not convincing.[3] The Guard was officially dissolved but it quickly reappeared in a new guise as the All for the Fatherland party and continued to flourish. Even one of the Liberal members of the cabinet, Iamandi, ascribed the growth of the Iron Guard to the fact that since 1929 successive governments, including the Liberals, had tolerated or halfheartedly encouraged it in the hopes that they could deflect it from its more violent aims and find in it allies for combating communism.

Tătărescu said in 1936 that there was an abyss between the Liberals and the extreme Right, both in methods and concepts, but added, rather obscurely, that only a policy of conciliation was possible in a country where one-third of the population was minorities.[4] He held that the Liberals were tolerant of all parties, if they obeyed the law, but could not permit movements favoring either a red or a white dictatorship. There was all the difference in the world, however, between the earnest and efficient manner in which the government pursued the Communist party,[5] and the obvious indulgence

3. In the trial of the assassins, for example, it was well known that the Guardist leader, Codreanu, was closely implicated in the murder but he was acquitted.

4. *Times* (London), April 24, 1936.

5. It was in 1936 that Ana Pauker, now Rumanian Foreign Minister, was sentenced to ten years' imprisonment, along with 18 associates, on the charge of propagating communism. She gained a good deal of publicity at this time because of public criticism of her treatment in prison and because of a newspaper dispute between *Dimineaţa* and *Universul* over her trial.

with which the Iron Guard and the other fascist formations were treated.

By the 1930's the Iron Guard had become the manifestation of a quite powerful current in Rumanian life, a current arising out of the strains and dislocations in the society and intensified by the depression. The government, instead of opposing the current, tried to become master of it, and during these years it took on many of the attitudes and paraphernalia of the extreme Right. Early in its term in office the cabinet pressed for powers to issue decree-laws during parliamentary recess, ostensibly to improve efficiency. In the same year, 1934, the government announced that supervision of telephone calls—wire tapping—was to be extended from international to local and interurban calls. Compulsory labor brigades were introduced in 1936. Carol, for his part, was more and more the flamboyant father of his people. To counter the Iron Guard youth formations he created in 1934 his own youth movement, *Straja Țării*. Carol's own activities may in part be ascribed to his willful and arbitrary character, his belief that the king should be more than a passive symbol, and his dislike and distrust of the Rumanian party system,[6] but the atmosphere of the time unquestionably nurtured these inclinations.

In 1936 the temporary calm showed signs of breaking and a new element, foreign relations, began to play its decisive role in determining Rumanian politics. It was only a relative change; Rumania has always been exceedingly sensitive to the reverberations of international events, and the rise of the extremist fascist parties in the 1930's was certainly associated with other similar movements elsewhere in Europe. Nevertheless, it may be said that up to 1936 the most important factors in the Rumanian political scene had been internal: the failure of the democratic parties to establish themselves, the long-standing social tensions and the chronic misery of the peasantry, and the personal influence of King Carol and his entourage. These internal forces continued to exert an important influence but the uneasy equilibrium of 1934 and 1935 was broken by the ascendancy of the European fascist states and the mounting international crisis leading to the Second World War.

Titulescu, the strong advocate of the League and of the Versailles system, and at that time advocate of Little Entente-Soviet collaboration, was removed from the Foreign Office in August, 1936. His fall

6. In 1937, in an interview with the journalist Wickham Steed, Carol said that in his own country political parties were sterile and their leaders fit only to criticize. It would be his business as king to discipline them and harness them to constructive work. Notes on the interview are quoted in Pavel Pavel, *Why Rumania Failed* (London, n.d.), p. 142.

appears to have been the consequence of personal differences but presaged a shift in Rumania's international orientation. As Rumania had been one of the principal gainers in the First World War, all the governments up to this time had a similar foreign policy, pro-French and against any treaty revision, which indeed was the only way Rumania could preserve its new territories from Hungarian, Bulgarian, and Soviet claims. When it became clear that the Western powers had lost the initiative, foreign policy became less simple. The extreme Right was vociferously pro-German. Carol personally would have preferred to stay clear of German influence, since only the Western attachment gave promise of guaranteeing all the territories acquired by the war. But if Britain and France weakened, he was inclined to improve his relations with Germany. Rumania's relations with the U.S.S.R. had improved somewhat in the 1930's, but it was a negative improvement—a hope of assurance against Soviet attack. The underlying hostility between the two powers was deep and so pervasive as scarcely to require any discussion. Thus in 1937 Carol stated to Wickham Steed that the chief difficulty of Rumania's position lay in the fact that "the immense weight of Russia was always bearing upon her and she had to withstand it as best she could. Russia was, so to speak, the hereditary enemy. As regards Hitler, he felt admiration for Hitler, whom he did not look upon as a sinister or dangerous man." [7]

From 1936 on, as a consequence of this shift in the international balance, the extreme Right became more and more blatant; anti-Semitic activities increased in extent and vileness; university students showed the advantages of their education by attacking Jewish shops; hostility and scorn for the decadent democracies became the vogue; defections from the old parties decreased their strength and added to the forces of the Right.

During this time the National Peasant party, as the principal nonfascist opposition to the government showed little strength or determination. Mihalache did attempt to reinvigorate the peasantist element in the party's ideology and formed a "peasant guard" to protect National Peasant meetings from fascist bullies. In May, 1936, there was a demonstration of some 80,000 peasants in Bucarest, directed against the Liberals, demanding better conditions for peasants and workers and decrying the tolerance shown to the fascists. These efforts, however, had no significant results.[8]

7. Quoted in Pavel Pavel, *op. cit.,* p. 139.
8. According to Pătrăşcanu (*Sous trois dictatures,* p. 114), the National Peasants had planned a large demonstration in November, 1935, but had canceled it upon Carol's promise that the Liberal government was about to fall and that they would succeed it.

In November, 1937, the Liberal government reached the end of its term and resigned. Carol requested Mihalache to form a new cabinet, on the unacceptable condition that he collaborate with Vaida Voevod. On his refusal, Tătărescu was recalled to form a cabinet and prepare for elections. He obtained Iorga's collaboration and made an electoral pact with Vaida Voevod's nationalist group. Then, to the general surprise, it was announced that Maniu and the Iron Guard leader Codreanu (and also Gheorghe Brătianu) had formed a non-aggression pact to insure free elections. This pact in recent years has been loosely used by the Communists to prove Maniu a pro-fascist. Such an interpretation obviously will not hold water, and there is no reason to doubt that his purpose in making the pact was as he defined it: to guarantee that Tătărescu could not employ the usual method of fixing the election. It was not a political agreement nor were joint lists established. It might also be added that the Rumanian Communist party gave its support to the National Peasants even after the pact with the Iron Guard.[9]

Nevertheless, the pact was a blunder. It was bound to have a demoralizing effect upon democratic elements struggling for survival to see an alliance between Maniu and the frank and open enemy of democratic and parliamentary institutions, especially since the National Peasant electoral campaign could not be directed against the Iron Guard. Codreanu certainly had much more to gain from such a pact in being able to associate his name with Maniu's. Above all it showed the National Peasants' own loss of confidence in themselves or their ideas, and was in the sharpest contrast to their refusals to make any deals on the road to power in 1927 and 1928. The defection of some of the outstanding leaders of the party in the following months was a further indication of the disruption of the party.

The pact was, however, successful in its immediate aim; by the balancing of forces which it achieved the elections were relatively free (though they elicited a low turnout of the electorate, a sign, perhaps, of the decline of parliamentarism).[10] For the first time in Rumanian history, and the last, a government in power failed to get the 40 per cent of the votes necessary for the premium. The government obtained 36 per cent, the National Peasants 21 per cent, the

9. *Ibid.,* p. 135.
10. Whereas in the 1928 elections 77.4 per cent of the registered voters actually voted, the percentage dropped off steadily in subsequent elections; in 1937 the figure was only 66 per cent. It is possible, and it has been suggested, that government pressure in 1937 kept people from the polls in some areas. A very interesting analysis of this election is given by C. Enescu, "Semnificația alegerilor din decemvrie 1937 în evoluția politică a neamului românesc," *Sociologie Românească, 2,* Nos. 11–12 (November-December, 1937), pp. 512–526.

Iron Guard 16 per cent, and the National Christian party (the fusion of Goga's and Cuza's nationalist, anti-Semitic parties) 9 per cent. Rumania's curious electoral system had broken down. The Liberals' failure was clearly a loss of confidence. The National Peasants or the Iron Guard seemed the most likely alternatives.

At this point, however, Carol moved in and on December 28, 1937, called upon the Transylvanian poet and lyrical fascist, Octavian Goga, to form a cabinet. Carol's own explanation of this surprising decision, which was in fact the immediate prelude to his personal dictatorship, was that he had no alternative. He could not bring back the Liberals; he did not want the Iron Guard in power, so his only move was to spike the guns of the extreme Right by putting in another but less dynamic Rightist party. There was, of course, another solution: to have called in the National Peasants, but the personal feud between Carol and Maniu precluded that course. There is no evidence, however, that Carol was at all reluctant to take power into his own hands.

Goga was installed with a rather heterogeneous cabinet including Gen. Ion Antonescu and three runaways from the National Peasants, chief of whom was Armand Calinescu. This government had a brief and hectic career, notable chiefly for arousing foreign protests because of its anti-Jewish activities but for little else. On February 10 Carol ended the farce, dismissed Goga, and set up a government of National Union under the Patriarch Miron Cristea, including an assortment of old worthies: Averescu, Vaida Voevod, General Vaitoianu, Mironescu, Iorga, Tătărescu, Argetoianu, Calinescu, and General Antonescu. It was a strange collection when one considers Carol's advocacy of the "younger generation." The period of explicit royal dictatorship had started.

Economic and Agrarian Policy

If the drift toward a royal dictatorship was induced by the victories of fascism throughout Europe and by the political conflict within Rumania itself, a third reason was the economic policy pursued after the depression. While much of the dictatorial paraphernalia of these years may be attributed to Carol's personal tastes or to the political desirability of making use of the nationalist and fascist sentiments of the times, a quite separate impulse toward an authoritarian, corporatist society was contained in the economic policy of neoliberalism.

Perhaps the clearest illustration of this impulse is to be found

in the writings and career of the economist-politician Mihail Manoilescu, a man who never achieved his political ambitions in Rumania
but whose unorthodox economic writings have attracted a fair amount
of international attention. Trained as an engineer, he became engaged in politics after the First World War as a member of General
Averescu's People's party. In 1927 he was arrested by the Liberal
government for his efforts to bring Carol back to Rumania; he was
later rewarded by being foisted on the Mironescu cabinet as Minister
of Industry and Commerce. Although he held a number of cabinet
posts in the governments of the 1930's, he did not fare as well under
Carol as he had hoped. He was, however, called to the foreign ministry in 1940, and had the unpleasant privilege of signing the Vienna
Decree by which Rumania lost Northern Transylvania.[11]

Manoilescu began his political career as a neoliberal and as an
opponent of the peasantism (ţărănismul) of the radically inclined
Peasant party of 1922.[12] At that time he announced democracy to
be his ideal and the essential truths of liberalism to be valid and time-
less. He criticized the peasantist doctrine, elaborated by Madgearu
and Stere, as anachronistic and self-contradictory. Since the land
reform had already been achieved, the Peasant party, born too late,
had lost its *raison d'être*. Like all opponents of the Peasants, he denied the homogeneity of the peasantry and its ability to act successfully as a class. He deplored the party's current emphasis upon class
struggle, as beyond the powers of the peasantry to master and as
dangerous to society. As for liberalism, he felt that its historical manifestations—as distinct from its essential principles—had been altogether too limited by an atomistic concept of society, by the passive
role assigned to the state, and by the narrow definition of private
property. Superficially, in his opposition to peasantism and his re-
formulation of liberalism, he was not far from the Liberal Duca.

But if one examines his neoliberalism of 1922 and 1923, certain
very important differences appear. In the first place, he openly attacked the Rumanian Liberal party and was thus not obliged, as
was Duca, to reconcile liberalism to the party of the Brătianus. Unlike
Duca, who pleaded for "social harmony," Manoilescu was for a "political equilibrium" of the various independent productive groups
which form society; he advocated vertical rather than horizontal
parties. The principal difference, however, lay in Manoilescu's em-

11. A brief biography is given in the bibliography of his works: Florin Em. Manoliou,
Bibliographie des travaux du Professeur Mihail Manoilesco (Bucarest, 1936).
12. His two principal studies in this connection are *Ţărănism şi democraţie* (Bucarest, 1922), and "Neoliberalismul," in *Doctrinele partidelor politice*, a lecture delivered
in February, 1923.

phasis upon economic productivity: "In order to live as a civilized state, Rumania requires the political and social form which will realize its energies to the maximum." [13] This emphasis had a decisive effect upon his whole line of thought. The peasant, because of his relatively low productivity, could not be the dominant factor in Rumanian social and economic life. On the contrary, Manoilescu defended the old Rumanian oligarchy which had been the necessary advance guard in the national awakening. Above all he saw society as a planned work of engineering. "To-morrow the principles of scientific organization will dominate the whole of society and will be applied to the entire system of national production as to a single enterprise." [14]

It was this ideal, and not any "regeneration of liberalism," which marked the real divergence of Manoilescu's neoliberalism from the views of the old Liberal party. This distinction is quite important. As has been seen, the Liberals had taken over nineteenth-century liberalism largely for nationalist reasons. In the course of applying it to Rumania, they had warped it beyond recognition, especially in regard to economic nationalism and state control. Nevertheless, it remained a derivative, if a perverted one, of the liberalism of the nineteenth century. As a result the Liberals were caught in a contradiction between their actual policy and their political philosophy, and it has been noted that the Liberal leaders justified their economic policy on grounds of temporary necessity or because of Rumania's backward condition. Even in their stress upon industry the old Liberals held a somewhat simple view of the exploitation of natural resources coupled with a nationalist desire to have a strong Rumania.[15]

In Manoilescu, on the other hand, economic productivity, that is, industrialization, was the focal point of his thought, and drove him entirely away from liberalism toward a doctrine of corporatism. Manoilescu's best known work, *The Theory of Protection and International Trade*,[16] shows a notable evolution from his articles of the

13. *Doctrinele partidelor politice,* p. 161.

14. *Țărănism și democrație,* p. 50.

15. In this connection it should be noted that Zeletin's neoliberal defense of Rumanian liberalism (see above p. 114) has a rather retrospective air, justifying Rumanian economic policy in terms of the earlier mercantilist behavior of the western European states. Zeletin also wrote a book on *Neoliberalismul,* but his point of view was quite different from Manoilescu's and really referred to the modifications of liberalism mentioned by Duca and appearing in the 1923 Constitution. Zeletin approached the subject in a quasi-Marxist fashion and regarded the development from liberalism to neoliberalism as one of historical necessity. Manoilescu, on the other hand, displays a marked voluntarism.

16. The book was first published in French, *Théorie du protectionnisme et de l'échange international* (Paris, 1929); an English translation appeared in 1931; a

early 1920's although many of the changes were implicit in the earlier writings. In 1923 he had wanted to reformulate liberalism to meet contemporary requirements. By 1930 he was attempting a total refutation of the classical theory of international trade as it had come down from Ricardo. The core of his new theory, which he reiterated incessantly, was that "the product of the labor of an industrial workman is almost always exchanged for the product of the labor of several agricultural workmen." [17] From this premise he concluded that international exchange was only to the benefit of the industrial country and furthered the economic domination of the European industrial states.

The economic domination of a country signifies the economic state which allows the produce of the labor of its workmen to be exchanged for the produce of a larger number of workmen of other countries. In the life of nations, as in the life of individuals, wealth never comes only from one's own labor. "Make others work for you" has always been the classical means of becoming wealthy.[18]

If an agricultural country is absolutely unable to produce industrial goods it is obliged to make this disadvantageous exchange, but if it can produce an industrial article—even at a permanently higher cost than a foreign industrial state—it should do so rather than import. Thus, even though it might require the labor of 300 Rumanian workmen to produce a quantity of cloth that could be produced by the labor of 100 British workmen, it would still be advantageous to do so, if, to import the cloth, Rumania was obliged to export a quantity of wheat which had required the labor of 500 workmen. With his theory of permanent protection, Manoilescu was quite critical of those protectionists, such as List, who had gone only halfway and rested their argument on the fostering of infant industries. He demanded protection, however, only for those industries whose "productivity surpasses the average productivity of the country." He opposed autarky, which he thought defensible only as a measure of preparedness for war, and did believe in an international division of labor, but one which was based upon specialization within different branches of the more productive industries.[19]

---

revised and expanded version later appeared in German, *Die nationalen Produktivkräfte und der Aussenhandel* (Berlin, 1937).

17. Manoilescu, *Theory of Protection*, p. vi.

18. *Ibid.*, p. vii.

19. It is unnecessary here to give an account of his quite lengthy effort to provide a mathematical refutation of the principles of free trade. His chief attack was upon

Regardless of the theoretical merits or fallacies in Manoilescu's analysis, it is obvious that he had made a clean break with economic liberalism. Moreover, he flatly denied the premise upon which the Peasantist economists had based their argument.

An agricultural country cannot raise itself by increasing slowly and uniformly the income of all its agricultural producers. Economic progress never spreads in a similar manner in all parts of a country. All the work of progress begins through a *center* or *nucleus of progress* and these nuclei are formed by the industries which represent a superior productivity.[20]

Far from admitting the Peasants' attack on "artificial industry," he held the artificiality of the support to be of no consequence so long as his rather loosely defined "productivity" increased.

The principal danger in Manoilescu's doctrine lay not in its stress upon industry nor in its denial of the ability of Rumanian agriculture to lift its own level of productivity. Industrialization in some form appears to be a necessary element in raising the miserable economic conditions of the peasant states of southeastern Europe, and it is quite unlikely that remedies sought in the agricultural sphere alone can produce an adequate alleviation. But in Rumania the critical question in many cases is not what is to be done but who is to do it.

In a country with such marked social and economic inequalities, with industry monopolized in the hands of a narrow, state-subsidized group, Manoilescu's doctrine of protectionism would have the fatal

---

the famous Ricardan cloth and wine example of comparative costs in the determination of exports. In my opinion he gains little in attempting to make a logically watertight demonstration, and indeed by trying to establish an absolute argument on the basis of a much oversimplified model he weakens the argument that in practice the operation of free trade has caused backward agricultural countries very serious difficulties. In particular he seems to underestimate the problems involved in the task of increasing the productivity and capital intensity per worker and assumes that protectionism alone is an adequate stimulus for the industrialization of a backward country. To be sure some of his contentions, such as the distinction between "national gain" and "individual profit," have been considerably elaborated in recent years, and the recognition of the extent of hidden unemployment in a peasant society has led to numerous recommendations that planned industrialization is the only remedy; but such recommendations (e.g., K. Mandelbaum's *The Industrialization of Backward Areas*) are based upon premises quite different from Manoilescu's. For a critical appraisal of Manoilescu's theory see J. B. Condliffe's review in *The Economic Journal, 43* (1933), 143–145, and Jacob Viner's review in the *Journal of Political Economy* (1932). M. Kalecki's review of the German edition of Manoilescu's work, in *The Economic Journal, 48* (1938), 708–711, is relatively favorable as regards Manoilescu's recognition of the plight of backward countries, though critical of his theoretical approach.

20. Manoilescu, *Theory of Protection,* p. 30, n. 1.

effect of increasing this inequality and extending the power of the industrial groups. Moreover, the policy of extending protection exclusively to industry and not to agriculture—whatever its intrinsic benefits for the national economy—would mean increased costs for the agricultural sector, uncertain markets, and, at best, a forced transfer of personnel from agriculture into industry. Furthermore, if over three-fourths of the electorate belongs to the peasantry, it is difficult to see how such a process could be achieved within the framework of a representative government.

Manoilescu's response, quite naturally, was to abandon liberal politics and take up corporatism on the Italian model. In the 1930's he wrote a number of articles on the "Century of Corporatism." In 1934, for example, he made a comparison of the liberal, the Communist, and the corporative societies.[21] Corporate society "is characterized by *organization*. It allows freedom of individual possession of the means of production. The corporative economy assumes that the maximum of social welfare is realized by the discipline of economic activities in harmony with the ends of the state. Its motto is: National interest; its representative type: the organizer." Employing a quasi-scientific jargon, Manoilescu defined "corporative space" as a

space where the egoistic impulses of the individual do not cease to exist and always represent active forces, but where, in addition to these forces [which are the sole qualities of a "liberal space"] there is a system of forces which direct individual actions toward a common goal created by the ends of the state. . . . Corporative space is a "magnetic field" dominated by national "lines of force" directed uniformly toward the ends assigned by the state.[22]

It is not necessary to take Manoilescu's utterances on this line very seriously or to inquire who was to determine these all-powerful state aims. He welcomed the coming of the royal dictatorship as the embodiment of the necessary revolution against outworn forms.[23] Apart from the vanity and opportunism which runs through his work, the significance of his writings lies:

1) in the evolution they display from the neoliberalism of the 1920's to the more thoroughgoing corporatism of the 1930's, and

21. *L'Espace corporatif* (Paris, 1934).
22. *Ibid.*, p. 6.
23. It is somewhat ironic that Manoilescu, who had boasted of his friendship with Mussolini and the Germans, should have been forced as Minister of Foreign Affairs to sign the Vienna Award in 1940, by which his fascist friends obliged Rumania to give up Northern Transylvania. The blow was so great that he collapsed at the conference table.

2) the distinctly undemocratic implications of this evolution in economic ideas, at least in their Rumanian context.

It would be absurd to suppose that the actual development of Rumanian economic policy was based upon any such theoretical considerations, but there is a reasonably close parallel between the progress of Manoilescu's ideas and the development of the economic and industrial policy of the Rumanian government from that of the old Liberals under Vintilă Brătianu to that of the Liberal government of the 1930's. Although the old Liberals had favored a program of industrialization with state support, it was handled primarily through the private banks, controlled by the Liberals, and was directed chiefly toward extracting natural resources and creating secondary industries. Moreover, the tight-fisted fiscal policy of Vintilă Brătianu had served as a check on economic activity.

After 1933 industrialization proceeded at a much more rapid tempo and in a somewhat different direction. The private banks after the depression played a less important part in financing industry; the principal initiative was by the National Bank or the state itself, both through state-owned corporations and through the growing importance of the state as consumer of industrial products. Expansion was most extensive in heavy industry; large cartels appeared and there was a notable concentration of industrial activity. Between 1933 and 1938 the number of "large" industrial concerns (i.e., with at least 20 workers and more than 10 horsepower) increased only from 3,487 to 3,767, whereas the installed horsepower increased from 529,965 to 746,789, and the employed personnel from 184,777 to 289,117.[24] The horsepower employed in capital goods industries increased from 287,266 in 1932 to 452,870 in 1937, as contrasted with a more modest increase from 237,442 to 289,666 in consumer goods industries. The output in quantity of capital goods had by 1937 increased by 57.4 per cent over the 1927 level, consumer goods by 45 per cent.[25] The production of steel, which had hit a high of 143,511 metric tons in 1928, and dropped to a low of 103,046 in 1932, rose from 144,766 tons in 1933 to 276,532 in 1938.[26] There was no doubt that the policy was directed toward heavy industry and was having results.

Two important reasons for this industrialization were, of course, the depression and the rearmament program. The collapse of the grain market and the spread of agrarian protectionism among the

24. Madgearu, *Evoluția economiei românești*, p. 149.
25. *Ibid.*, p. 160.
26. *Breviaire statistique de la Roumanie* (1940), p. 164.

industrial states naturally stimulated Rumania, as it did the other Balkan states, to create its own industries. The growing international tension in the 1930's led to a heavy demand for arms and munitions. In 1937 the president of the Rumanian union of metallurgical and mineral industries stated that the principal characteristic of the years of recovery had been the large industrial investments, especially for the purpose of creating a powerful armaments industry.[27]

But if the depression and the demand for armaments stimulated industrialization, they in turn assisted in the rise of very powerful industrial interests, which progressively dominated not only the economic but the political scene.[28] These years witnessed the rise of such industrial giants—giants at least in Rumania—as Max Auşnit and Nicolae Malaxa. These men represented a different type of influence from that of the Brătianus. The latter, through their position in the banks, had equated the Liberal party with a policy of industrial advance through the financial institutions, but they were primarily politicians. Auşnit and Malaxa, on the other hand, were primarily industrialists who were able political manipulators but whose field of action was outside the political arena. It might be added that King Carol himself, who operated "outside" politics, was by no means disinterested in industrialization and had a large personal stake in the new industries.[29]

Rumanian industries, and especially the new heavy industry, required both protection and capital. Industrial protection had marked the whole history of Rumanian tariff policy, and even the National Peasant tariff of 1929 did not renounce it. But the new devices, developed as defenses during the depression, became far more potent weapons than any which had existed heretofore. Indeed, they were far more effective in assisting industry than in fulfilling their ostensible function of safeguarding national finances and the currency.[30]

27. Quoted in Pătrăşcanu, *op. cit.*, p. 26.
28. An example is the Skoda scandal of 1935, in which a storm was raised over a contract for armaments made by the National Peasants with the Czech Skoda works in 1930. Although an effort was made to involve some National Peasant ministers in charges of graft, the real cause of the scandal appears to have been that the contract had been made "without regard for the law concerning national armament activity."
29. For obvious reasons it is difficult to ascertain the extent of Carol's industrial interests. According to Pătrăşcanu (*op. cit.*, p. 48), in published reports of enterprises in which he was a shareholder Carol held 30 to 35 per cent of the shares of the Malaxa works, and almost as much in several smaller industries. Four of the largest sugar mills were in his hands, as well as a beer factory. He had important shares in the gold mines and the telephone company and a large control of Banca de Credit Român.
30. Rumania's exchange position and the leu never achieved any stability despite the most elaborate series of measures. I would agree with Antonin Basch's conclusion (*The Danube Basin*, p. 143) that the signal failure of Rumania either to achieve cur-

To the protective tariffs, which were greatly increased in the 1930's, was added the system of import quotas and restrictions, plus a 12 per cent tax for all imports. Together these provided a high protective wall for the development of the national industry. Their effectiveness is shown by the fact that between 1933 and 1938 the percentage of imports of manufactured and semimanufactured goods dropped markedly, whereas that of machines and raw materials rose sharply.[31]

Protection alone, however, was not the only device employed to aid the expansion of industry; other forms of assistance included exemptions from taxation, state subsidies, special transport rates, the obligatory use of certain locally produced goods, and monopolies granted to industries considered nationally desirable.

Since the inflow of new foreign capital stopped during the depression, the supply of capital for industry had to come largely from internal sources. In part this was achieved through the tariffs, which diverted purchases toward local industry, and by the increasing state expenditures for armaments, which amounted to a tax on the public. In 1934 a 12 per cent tax on the construction of new buildings was imposed in an effort to divert investment toward industry and away from nonproductive expenditures. To a considerable extent the foreign funds frozen in Rumania at the time of the depression were subsequently employed in industrialization.[32]

The political implications of this economic policy—which was by no means a plan but rather the result of the depression and the deepening international tensions plus the steady pressure of interested industrial groups—were very similar to those observed above in the

---

rency stability or a price equilibrium, despite the relatively favorable balance of trade and rich resources, may be laid to bad management and political reasons, to which one could add that in many cases the measures taken were employed for purposes quite different from those for which they were presumably intended.

31. Madgearu, *op. cit.*, p. 252. Madgearu took a selected group of key imports and calculated their volume by percentage as follows:

	In per cent of total imports	
	1930	1938
Raw materials	5.86	12.82
Semifabricated	23.01	7.58
Machines	1.27	4.00
Manufactured goods	13.02	8.34

32. Oscar Jaszi, "The Economic Crisis in the Danubian States," *Social Research* (February, 1935), pp. 98–116, attributed a major role to captive capital in the creation of Rumanian industry. According to Madgearu (*op. cit.*, p. 353), foreign credit continued to serve those industries created by international capital, but in his opinion the most important source of industrial credit was the National Bank.

case of Manoilescu.[33] The trend toward heavy industry was a forced development, carried on by monopolies subsidized and protected by the state—probably the only way in which such industries could have been created in short order. It did not reflect a growing individual domestic demand, as the state was the principal consumer for the new products. The increased industrial production was largely balanced by continued low imports. Thus, over the eleven years from 1927 to 1938, industrial production rose from 59 to 69 billion lei, but total industrial consumption fell from 93 to 88 billion because of a fall in imports from 34 to 19 billion lei.[34]

On the short run at least, and relatively if not absolutely, this forced development was at the expense of agriculture. Funds which might have gone into agriculture went into industry; the peasant as a consumer was obliged to pay high prices for industrial products. The relation between agricultural prices and the price of industrial products necessary to agriculture, which had dropped from an index of 100 in 1929 to 53.4 in 1934, climbed only to 63.9 by 1937. Clearly such a policy was exposed to opposition from an electorate consisting largely of peasants—if the representative parliamentary system functioned. The economic policy of these years by its very nature implied an extension of control over political activity. The Tătărescu regime was the last effort to carry on politics in the traditional manner, through a quiet perversion of the constitutional system, but the growing differences between Tătărescu and the old guard of the

33. An excellent example of the political and social implications of this industrial drive is to be seen in a resolution of a congress of the Rumanian Federation of Manufacturers, held in Bucharest on February 3–6, 1936. The congress considered the industrialization of Rumania necessary not only for the development of the country's natural resources but to provide employment and meet the requirements of national defense and the balance of payments. It demanded a stable system favorable to the development of industry; privileges on tariffs and railway rates; legislation requiring public authorities to obtain all their supplies from Rumanian industry; statutory recognition of agreements between industrialists having the object of "improving production and sales by lawful means." In the field of social legislation the congress demanded that employers should be relieved of all charges which did not correspond "either to the workers' real needs or to the capacity of Rumanian industry." Specifically, it proposed that representation of employers and workers in social insurance schemes should be proportional to the amount shared in their support, the repeal of payments to employees for the first seven days' illness, and the repeal of the employers' civil liability to an insured worker in case of accident. The supervisory rights of the Chambers of Labor should be limited to small manufacturers and they should not be permitted to "tyrannize over employers in large-scale industry." Finally, it demanded that the Federation of Manufacturers be consulted on all laws and regulations affecting industrial life. ILO, *Industrial and Labor Information, 57,* No. 13 (March 30, 1936).

34. Madgearu, *op. cit.,* p. 257. There was, however, a rise in imports between 1934 and 1937 from 13 to 19 billion lei, corresponding to the general economic recovery.

Liberal party are indicative of the move toward a less inhibited industrial drive.

During the four years, then, between the depression and the inauguration of the Carolist dictatorship, it is possible to find inside Rumania, not to mention the external influences, three quite distinct factors making for the destruction of parliamentary government and the creation of an authoritarian regime:

1) Carol's own personality and his streamlined interpretation of the old-fashioned prerogatives of a monarch;

2) The unrest and growing extremism in broad sections of the population, which was finding a mouthpiece in the Iron Guard;

3) The economic policy of neoliberalism, which not only carried overtones of a more authoritarian state but through the centralization of economic power and control increased the possibilities of creating such a state.

While the general atmosphere of these years of neoliberalism resembled Manoilescu's teachings in its industrial protectionism, increasing economic nationalism, and growing corporatism, there was an important difference: contrary to Manoilescu's thesis, agricultural protection was maintained and extended. During the years 1935 to 1937 there was a complex system of minimum prices, state purchases, and export bounties for wheat. By the law of 1935 the government paid a minimum price of 35,000 lei for 10 metric tons of wheat weighing 75 kilograms per hectoliter. An export premium financed by a tax on milling, paid 10,000 lei per ten-ton truckload of wheat, and 12,000 lei per truckload of flour. This premium was dropped with the rise in agricultural prices but was reapplied in 1938. A Wheat Valorization Office was formed to supervise these payments and to improve the quality of wheat. Similar steps were taken for medicinal plants, textile plants, and wool.

In 1936 Rumania signed a series of wheat export agreements with Belgium, the Netherlands, Greece, Italy, Germany, the United Kingdom, and other states. Foreign trade in grains was also assisted by an extremely complicated system of taxing imports to pay for export bounties and permitting the exporter to keep a portion of the free exchange obtained by his exports. In general these measures, which were aimed at maintaining the commercial balance, had a beneficial effect in supporting the price of agricultural products and in increasing exports. Between 1934 and 1937 agricultural prices rose from 44.1 (1929 = 100) to 64.6; the value of agricultural production increased from 42 to 62 billion lei; the value of cereal exports rose from 2 to 10 billion lei (in quantity from one million to 2.2 million metric tons).

Two qualifications should be made however. The emphasis upon wheat exports and upon the improvement of quality was primarily for the benefit of the middle and large producer, though the maintenance of the price of grain did help agriculture as a whole. In the second place, as has been mentioned in connection with the depression, the premiums on wheat served to extend the area under wheat cultivation, in direct contradiction to the recommendations of agricultural experts, who continued to believe that "peasant agriculture should no longer limit itself, in imitation of the old system, to the culture of cereals; its success will come from a parallel development of the resources of the field and of livestock raising." [35] This contradiction, which shows the absence of any real coherence to the agrarian program of the Liberal government, had two obvious sources: wheat, for all its decline after the First World War, was important commercially and from the point of view of foreign commerce there was a strong incentive to support it. Moreover, the wheat growers were the larger farmers and were in a better position to make felt their wishes than were the small maize-producing peasants.

The government did, however, make certain efforts to increase the variety of agricultural production. The most elaborate was the creation, with the assistance of I. G. Farbenindustrie, of the "Soya" company, which was authorized to import soybeans, distribute them to cultivators, provide equipment, and purchase the entire crop for export to Germany. The area under this crop expanded rapidly, especially in Bessarabia: 1,465 hectares in 1934, 20,411 hectares in 1935, 58,037 hectares in 1936, and 102,000 hectares in 1937. The government through price guarantees and subsidies also furthered the cultivation of sugar beet, tobacco, rice, and textile plants.

These measures to diversify agriculture did not, despite all the publicity given to them, achieve very great importance. They were only a drop in the bucket compared with the vast area under peasant cereal cultivation, and their rate of expansion seemed unlikely to produce any general amelioration for a very long time. Moreover, the introduction of such industrial crops, whose main purpose— almost exclusively so in the case of soya—was for export, shows the persistent if natural effort to solve the agrarian question by a sort of legerdemain. The soybean had been an old favorite, and as early

---

35. G. Ionescu-Sişeşti and N. Cornăţeanu, *La Réforme agraire en Roumanie et ses conséquences*, p. 79.

as 1910 Dobrogeanu-Gherea had some harsh words to say of the men who thought it could magically solve the deep-rooted ills of Rumanian agriculture.[36]

The Tătărescu government, following precedent, also reorganized agricultural credit and the cooperative system, set up more experimental stations, and devoted funds to the raising of better livestock and the purchase of tractors, but those measures seem to have been only of marginal benefit.

The government did try in the law of March, 1937, for the encouragement of agriculture to grapple with the problem of land tenure. It regulated the transfer and mortgage of rural lands and undertook to enforce the indivisibility of property as a means of preventing the progressive subdivision of peasant holdings. The effort was unsuccessful. The two-hectare minimum, which in any case was too small for a self-subsistent holding, was not observed; the prohibition extended only to properties obtained from the state or with the state's assistance. An attempt was also made to promote the consolidation of peasant properties, but this met with too great opposition in the chamber and was dropped.[37] The government also exerted its right of preemption on sales of agricultural land for the purpose of providing land for the peasants but its achievements were insignificant. Between April 1, 1934, and August 1, 1938, of the 326,200 hectares put on sale the government used its right of preemption on only 12,250 hectares, 3.8 per cent of the total.[38]

In brief, if the position of agriculture was somewhat better in the years of the Tătărescu regime than in the depression it was largely a consequence of general economic recovery. Agriculture did benefit from the protective measures applied and extended by the government, although part of these benefits was lost by the continued depreciation of the leu, and some efforts were made to raise the level of agriculture and diversify production. Nevertheless, the government's chief interest was industry and commerce and the principal benefits to agriculture were those which corresponded to this interest. The desperate problem of the millions of small peasants owning less than 3 hectares, unable to support themselves and their families, dividing their land into smaller and smaller fragments, suffering from pellagra —this problem was scarcely touched.

It must be said, however, that in the 1930's there was a notable

36. C. Dobrogeanu-Gherea, *Neoiobăgia*, p. 254.
37. Valeriu Bulgariu, "Divizibilitatea proprietații țărănești," *Problema agrară* (Bucarest, 1946), pp. 77–97.
38. G. Ionescu-Sișești, "Le Nouvel Aspect du problème agraire en Roumanie," *Archives pour la science et la réforme sociales, 16,* Nos. 1–4 (1943), 264.

increase in scientific investigations of village life—sociological studies undertaken by Professor Gusti and his students, farm accountancy studies, examinations of rural health and diet—which brought into clear light the deplorable living conditions of the peasants. It was at this time too that the factor of overpopulation was brought into prominence, although as early as 1907 Constantin Garoflid had warned of its approach. Unfortunately, the real fact of overpopulation was too easily employed as a scapegoat, and one finds a growing tendency from the middle of the 1930's to place upon it all the responsibility for the plight of the peasant.

X

THE CAROLIST PERIOD: DICTATORSHIP, 1938–40

Survey of Political Events

WITH the advent of Carol's personal dictatorship, Rumania's parliamentary government came to an end. The particular party alignments of 1937 and the interplay of personal ambitions and conflicts may have determined the time and to some extent the form of the dictatorship, but the social and economic situation more than paved the way. The fact that Carol could reassert and indeed vastly expand the powers of the monarch on the ground of defending his people against the depredations of politicians illustrates the difficulty of creating a healthy representative regime in a country such as Rumania, where the bulk of the electorate are poverty-stricken peasants who have always been separated by a gulf from their rulers. The only constitutionally minded party which claimed to voice the sentiments of the peasantry, the National Peasant party, proved completely unable to master the situation. In the latter years of the 1930's it had only two alternatives if it was to regain its position: either to outplay the dictatorial movements in rough-and-tumble tactics, which its scruples forbade it from doing, or to recover the massive support which had carried it to power in 1928. It seemed incapable of achieving the latter and its 1937 campaign showed little of the zeal formerly displayed. Some of its most promising younger men, Calinescu, Ghelmegeanu, and Ralea, deserted to the king.

The Carol dictatorship was not merely a relapse into old practices; it was also an advance to a new authoritarian regime. In this it showed the political implications of a policy of forced industrialization in an agrarian society with great social and economic inequalities. If the relation between Carol's dictatorship and the expansion of heavy industry is not as inevitable as the Marxists would have it, it is, nonetheless, not difficult to see that such industrialization when directed from above by a handful of men would be conducive not merely to the perversion of democracy, as in the case of the old Liberals, but to its replacement by an explicit dictatorship. In this respect the advent of Carol's dictatorship is intimately bound to the agrarian problem, which in its broadest sense is the reverse side of the question of industrialization.

On the other hand, the tortuous history of Carol's last three years as king is of less interest here. Internally, it was the confused unraveling of the peculiar relations between Carol and the Iron Guard, a vicious if ambiguous struggle between two dictatorial movements. Externally, it was the attempt to ride out the rapidly mounting tempest of the Second World War. Carol, who had mastered the internal situation, was ultimately destroyed by outside events. So while the tumultuous events of the years 1938 to 1940 are of the greatest importance to Rumanian history in general, their relevance to the agrarian question is largely external. Unlike the fall of the Liberals in 1928, the collapse of the peasantist *esprit*, and the creation of a dictatorial regime, all of which are causally related to the agrarian question, Carol's fall was a political and diplomatic rather than an economic transition.

Immediately after removing the Goga cabinet and installing under martial law his new Government of National Union, Carol moved rapidly to create his new order. He abolished the 1923 Constitution and on February 20 promulgated a new corporatist constitution, subsequently ratified by a farcical popular referendum. The new constitution greatly augmented the king's powers, dwarfed the role of the legislative bodies, and did away with the party system. Ministers were selected by and responsible solely to the king and had to be of Rumanian nationality for at least three generations. The franchise was limited to citizens over thirty who practiced either agriculture or manual labor, industry or commerce, or intellectual activity; a corporatist concept of the voter replaced universal suffrage. The spirit of organic nationalism pervaded the whole document, stressed the responsibilities of the individual Rumanian to the nation, and circumscribed guarantees of civil rights and liberties. The economic and social outlook of the constitution is shown in Article 7, whereby no Rumanian could advocate by word or letter any changes in the form of the government (all constitutional amendments had to be initiated by the king), the division or distribution of property, exemption from taxes, or class hatred.

At the same time that Carol unseated the old parties by destroying their constitutional base, he attacked the Iron Guard, and in 1938 and 1939 directed an increasingly violent suppression of its formations. The Guard was outlawed, Codreanu was arrested, tried, and imprisoned. In November, 1938, he and thirteen of his followers were shot "while attempting to escape." In September, 1939, the Prime

Minister, Armand Calinescu, the strongest man in the Carol dictatorship and the executor of the campaign against the Guard, was assassinated. His death was followed by murderous mass reprisals against the Legionaries. Carol seemed to be thoroughly the master of his country.[1]

In place of the disbanded parties he concocted in December, 1938, a single body, the Front of National Rebirth. Through 1938 and 1939 he added the various regalia associated with a corporatist state, but there is little evidence that anyone took these trappings seriously. Administrative and political corruption, always healthy plants in Rumania, blossomed in full splendor in these years; public ethics hit a new low.

Meanwhile, however, the international situation was closing in and here Carol was caught, as it proved, in a hopeless dilemma. While throughout the 1930's the Rumanian state took on an increasing resemblance to the fascism of the Axis powers, and men of the extreme Right advocated a pro-Axis foreign policy, Rumania, with its interest in maintaining the Versailles system—the guarantor of its territorial integrity—could not be really happy in Axis company. Regardless of internal political developments, and Carol himself repeatedly stressed the difference between internal and external policy, Rumania had strong reason to rely on the Western powers. Germany, however, was clearly in the ascent and the Western powers were pursuing the policy of appeasement. With the collapse of Czechoslovakia after the Munich Conference the Little Entente broke down. In November, 1938, Carol visited both London and Berchtesgaden in an effort to maintain his balance.

The great blow to Rumania's position came with the Soviet-German pact of August, 1939, which forecast common action between the two

1. It is impossible to attempt here to clear up the obscurities in the struggle between Carol and the Iron Guard. Numerous interpretations have been made, of which two might be mentioned. The British correspondent, A. L. Easterman, in his book *King Carol, Hitler, and Lupescu* (London, 1942), was of the opinion that in assuming the dictatorship Carol was fighting fire with fire, that he was really anti-Guardist and anti-German. Under this interpretation he was attempting to preserve Rumania from German advances, and his fight against the Guardists, who are regarded as simple German tools, was a part of this national defense. A more complex interpretation is provided by the Rumanian Communist Lucreţiu Pătrăşcanu in *Sous trois dictatures*. Briefly, his thesis is that Carol had given secret support to the Guard on his road to the dictatorship, as a means of destroying the bourgeois-democratic parties, but had turned against it because of the potential social ferment it engendered and because the Guard was explicitly pro-Axis, whereas Carol was attempting to play a noncommittal game. Pătrăşcanu attributed the increasing violence of the measures employed by Carol against the Guard to the simple fact that having set up a dictatorship himself Carol had no weapon against another dictatorial movement except crude police repression.

great powers of eastern Europe, both of which were interested in revising the Versailles system. By the secret protocol of the Molotov-Ribbentrop agreement, the Reich recognized the Soviet Union's interest in Bessarabia.[2]

When war came, Rumania remained neutral, although the German control over the economy, which will be discussed presently, grew steadily. With the fall of France in the summer of 1940 and the disappearance of any hope of effective support from the West, Rumania was left with three unattractive alternatives: isolated neutrality, rapprochement with the U.S.S.R., or entering the German camp. Carol chose the latter course.[3] The corporate state was replaced by a totalitarian regime with the creation of the Party of the Nation, which included the Iron Guard and to which all government and business officials were obliged to belong. Horia Sima, the new leader of the Guard, came into the government.

After the Soviet ultimatum of June 26, resulting in the loss of Bessarabia and Northern Bucovina, Rumania renounced the Franco-British guarantees, and the active pro-Germans, Gigurtu and Manoilescu, were installed as Prime Minister and Minister of Foreign Affairs. The new direction was accompanied by zealous efforts to emulate the Axis powers through increased anti-Semitic and anti-British measures. The loss of Bessarabia and Northern Bucovina set loose other revisionist claims, and at the end of August, under German and Italian auspices, Rumania lost Southern Dobrogea to Bulgaria and Northern Transylvania to Hungary.

At this point Carol's policy of isolating and breaking up the political parties turned against him, and he found himself altogether without support in face of national indignation that a third of the nation's territory had been given up without a sign of resistance. As an eleventh hour prop for his regime he called in, on September 4, General Antonescu, who had been in disgrace for his association with the Guard. Antonescu forced Carol to renounce his dictatorial powers

2. Paragraph 3 of the Secret Additional Protocol to the Nonaggression Treaty of August 23, 1939, stated: "With regard to South-eastern Europe, attention is called by the Soviet side to its interest in Bessarabia. The German side declares its complete political disinterestedness in these areas." U.S. Department of State, *Nazi-Soviet Relations, 1939-1941* (Washington, 1948), p. 78.

3. According to ex-Foreign Minister Grigore Gafencu, Carol's decision was taken at a crown council meeting on May 29, 1940. *Prelude to the Russian Campaign*, trans. E. Fletcher-Allen (London, 1945), pp. 282-285. Such a decision is not surprising. Neutrality would have saved little except honor. The U.S.S.R. had been indicating, rather obliquely, the desirability of a revision in Bessarabia, and with the fall of France was determined to move quickly. The chances of a Rumanian-Soviet rapprochement were nil. On the other hand, German influence had increased steadily since the fall of Czechoslovakia.

and a couple of days later, with the agreement of Maniu and Constantin Brătianu, demanded his abdication. Carol fled the country, with Mme Lupescu and Colonel Urdareanu, the core of his camerilla. For Rumania, however, the absurd result was that popular indignation over the loss of Transylvania at the hands of the Axis merely placed in power an ardently pro-Axis government which immediately recognized the Vienna Decree.

Economic and Agrarian Policy

In the economic sphere the years of the Carolist dictatorship show four important characteristics:

1) a continued emphasis upon industrialization;

2) a reaction against small peasant agriculture and a growing agricultural paternalism;

3) increasing regimentation of the economy, both for economic planning and for military preparedness;

4) the growing dominance of Germany in Rumanian economic life.

The policy of industrialization which had got under way after the depression continued its course of expansion under the dictatorship, with the additional stimulus of the menace of war. After the outbreak of war the restriction of trade channels and raw material imports reduced industrial production somewhat. The loss of territory in 1940 produced, of course, a general dislocation of the economy. Industrial policy, however, was merely the culmination of the whole trend of the Carolist regime.

In the field of agrarian policy there was a noticeable reaction against small peasant holdings and renewed talk of creating a middle peasantry. As has been seen, the policy of all Rumanian governments on this question has been confused and contradictory. The National Peasants in 1929, by relaxing regulations for the transfer of peasant property, had hoped to create more prosperous and self-sustaining holdings, but their action had rather the effect of dispossessing the small peasant. On the other hand, the debt conversions of 1932–34 had the opposite effect and in a negative way were, as Garoflid called them, a new peasant resettlement in that they limited the effect of the economic crisis in weeding out the weaker peasants. The Tătărescu government had attempted to colonize relatively underpopulated areas with medium holdings and by the law of 1937 had tried, ineffectually, to check the subdivision of land.

Under the Carol dictatorship somewhat more extensive measures

were initiated, at least on paper. The 1938 Constitution, by prohibiting any public discussion of redistribution of property, showed
the regime's attitude toward further expropriation as a remedy to
the agrarian question. During the interwar years the governments
were accustomed to state that large estates had virtually disappeared
through the reforms of 1918–21, but after 1938 increased attention was paid to medium and large properties.[4] In the law of December 5, 1938 (amended January 7, 1939) the government established a Bank for the Industrialization and Valorization of Agricultural Products (BINAG), one of the recurrent efforts to provide
agricultural credit. It is to be noted, however, that by Article 6 of
this law the main credit functions of this bank applied only to farms
of over 5 hectares, thus overlooking the majority of the peasantry.[5]

The spirit of the regime is well shown in an article by the agricultural economist Valeriu Bulgariu,[6] who announced that King Carol,
"the first farmer in the land," had plans to change completely the
existing conditions in agriculture by a twofold effort to organize small
farming on rational lines and to encourage owners of medium-sized
estates to increase the area of their holdings.

When the great land division took place after the war, the agrarian reform went too far. . . . It assigned land to a very large number of
villagers, and as a result subsequent successive divisions had increased
the excessive subdivision of land. Reaction was necessary, and to-day
economists and sociologists are in favor of the concentration of scattered
property, a policy adopted by the government and all its agents.[7]

The desirability of concentrating peasant holdings was no new discovery, and Carol's regime for all its new direction was not a bit more
successful than previous regimes in doing anything about it. The
policy of creating larger holdings, also no novelty, was faced as always by the difficulty of creating them without dispossessing peasants
in the process. According to Bulgariu,

4. See, for example, Aureliu Lapedatu's article, "A Technical Study in Rumanian
Cereals," *Correspondance économique roumaine* (April–June, 1938), pp. 1–28, in which
the author discussed the manifest advantages of the large Rumanian farms in the use
of technical equipment for rational cultivation.

5. The same thing is to be seen in the case of the cooperatives. According to A. Galan,
"General Survey of the Co-operative Movement in Rumania," *Correspondance économique roumaine* (January–May, 1939), pp. 1–65, in 1939 one farmer in three was affiliated with one of the several agricultural cooperatives. Unquestionably the other
two-thirds included the poorer peasants.

6. Valeriu Bulgariu, "Agrarian Policy in Rumania," *The Banker, 49* (March, 1939),
344–348.

7. *Ibid.,* p. 346.

The government seeks to facilitate the forming of middle-sized estates of about 10 hectares in area, making them indivisible so that there can be no relapse into sub-dividing. The State has taken to itself the right of acquiring any land which is for sale. It gives preference in its purchase and distribution of land to farms adjoining it, in order that small properties may be enlarged and concentration attained even through private purchase.[8]

The execution of this policy was assigned to BINAG. If property purchased through BINAG could not be sold as a whole within two years, it could be sold in lots of not less than 15 hectares. Sales could be only to Rumanian subjects who undertook to cultivate the land themselves. Such properties could not be broken up and had to be transferred in their entirety. Moreover, such estates could be inherited only as a whole by a single heir. To some extent this law is similar to the German *Erbhofgesetz* of 1933, although it was not as restrictive since it did permit the sale of the land.[9] The aims of this measure were reasonable enough but it was of little use to the small peasant and certainly showed greater interest in the medium holder.

Along with the emphasis upon larger holdings was a rather superficial government paternalism for the peasant. Some of the activities were of value. The studies of village life continued and in several instances produced extremely useful collections of information for an understanding of the agrarian question. The emphasis upon a sociological interpretation of Rumanian peasant life was beneficial in focusing attention upon the realities in Rumania and getting away from the application of quite unsuitable Western political and economic concepts to the local situation. From the scholarly point of view this was all to the good. As a political phenomenon it had a certain danger. Looking at one's fellow countrymen as objects for sociological investigation does not overcome the social chasm between the rulers and the ruled, but may merely put it on a more enlightened basis. It is certainly preferable to dismissing the peasants as "animals who can speak," [10] but it still regards the peasant as object rather than subject.

Other manifestations of Carol's paternalism were of value only in providing employment for his publicity agents. The shabby quality of

8. *Ibid.*, p. 348.

9. For a discussion of the problem of succession to agricultural property and of recent European legislation in this regard, see M. Tcherkinsky, "The Evolution of the System of Succession to Landed Property in Europe," *International Review of Agriculture, 32,* No. 6 (June, 1941), 165E–196E.

10. I heard this definition defended in dead earnest by a landowner in Bucarest in the winter of 1944.

the social program of the regime appears in a speech delivered by Calinescu in January, 1939:

Gentlemen, it is enough to look at all that has been done to improve our workmen's conditions of living. The improvement of the work contract, pensions for old age, new buildings, the organization "Work and Joy." All these were designed to give a social significance to the present regime. . . . Thus a regime with authority was able to accomplish in the field of work problems things which nobody could accomplish in the demagogic regime of the democracies. . . . Also we must point out the activity of social order undertaken amidst the peasantry. Cultural hostels which are intended to develop the sense of solidarity in spiritual and educational matters among the peasants have already given the most wonderful results. And the Social Service, established last year, is the very greatest action that has ever been taken to raise the level of the peasants.[11]

The regime also tried its hand at planning. In the autumn of 1939 it undertook to organize agriculture to guarantee a sufficient output for military and civil requirements. The Minister of Agriculture was required to prepare an annual crop plan, to provide necessary seed, and to requisition labor for farms. More ambitious was a five-year plan drawn up in March, 1940, for the rationalization and intensification of agriculture. The work of the 1921 land reform, which had been dragging on for nearly twenty years, was to be completed. The area under wheat was to be reduced by 800,000 hectares, that under maize by 500,000 hectares. Output, however, was to be maintained by a higher yield. Fallow ground was to be diminished by 300,000 hectares. The surplus area was to be devoted to the cultivation of oil-producing, textile, industrial, and medicinal plants. Vegetable cultivation was to be encouraged with a view to improving peasant diet. The plan also included a program of technical improvements, dam construction, irrigation, and drainage projects. Agricultural laborers were to be given fair wages and assured a decent diet; the price scissors between agricultural and industrial products was to be closed. In all, the plan envisaged spending 600 million lei annually. One cannot say what the plan might have achieved had Carol not fallen and if Rumania had not lost a third of its territory and become involved in the war.

11. Armand Calinescu, *Roumania, the Country of National Renaissance and of Royal Revolution* (no pub., n.d.), a translation of a speech delivered in the Chamber of Deputies on January 28, 1939.

German-Rumanian Economic Relations

This plan, however, was but part of a larger scheme which concerned not only Rumania but the Third Reich. In the course of Nazi Germany's economic penetration of southeastern Europe in the 1930's,[12] Rumania was, initially at any rate, better able than the other states to maintain an independent position, partly because it had at least one important export, petroleum, which could be sold on the world market. In the mid-1930's the Rumanian government took definite steps to limit exports to Germany. As late as 1937 Germany's share in Rumania's foreign trade was no greater than it had been in 1929.[13] The German market was, however, important as a purchaser of Rumania's agricultural products. Thus, in 1937 Germany absorbed 61.2 per cent of Rumania's maize exports, 57.4 per cent of the barley, though only 8.3 per cent of the wheat.

Germany was not initially interested in Rumania's grain exports. Indeed the policy of protecting German cereal production, which had started before the Nazis, was not dropped until rather late, and Germany did not import large quantities of bread cereals until 1937.[14] It was, however, very much interested in obtaining fodder and oil plants; it was for this purpose that in 1934 I. G. Farbenindustrie had set up the Soya Company to foster soybean production in Rumania.

After 1937 the picture changed; the economic recession hurt Balkan exports and increased Balkan dependence upon the German market. The *Anschluss* in the spring of 1938 cast Germany's political shadow over all the Balkans, and a rash of German publications announced the Reich's destiny in *Südosteuropa*. German dominance was increased with the Munich decision and the failure of the Anglo-French economic drive in southeastern Europe to achieve any important countereffect. In Rumania the shift in the international political balance, more than purely economic penetration, led to

12. For an account of Germany's trade policy which brings out some of the benefits to the Balkan states see H. W. Arndt, *The Economic Lessons of the Nineteen-Thirties* (Oxford University Press, 1944), pp. 176–206; Antonin Basch, *The Danube Basin*, pp. 165–213, emphasizes the sinister aspects of the German advance.

13. Rumania's trade with Germany between 1929 and 1938 in per cent of total values was as follows:

	1929	1930	1931	1932	1933	1934	1935	1936	1937	1938 (including Austria)
Imports	24.1	25.1	29.1	23.6	18.6	15.5	23.8	36.1	28.9	36.8
Exports	27.6	18.8	11.5	12.5	10.6	16.6	16.7	17.8	19.2	26.5

(In 1937, Austria had provided 8.5 per cent of Rumania's imports and absorbed 6.8 per cent of its exports.)

14. Basch, *op. cit.*, p. 175.

Germany's growing economic influence. By 1938 Germany and Austria absorbed 26.5 per cent of Rumania's exports, but even in the German-Rumanian agreement of December, 1938, the Rumanians were able to block German efforts to increase substantially the clearing rate of the reichsmark.

A new stage was reached, however, in the German-Rumanian agreement of March 23, 1939, which really did tie Rumania's economy to that of Germany.[15] By this treaty, which was to run for five years, very close economic collaboration was envisaged, involving German assistance in the internal development of the Rumanian economy. The principal aim of this treaty, which emphasized the complementary nature of the two economies, was to expand and diversify Rumanian agricultural production. Germany was to assist in promoting the cultivation of agricultural products of interest to its economy, especially foodstuffs, oilseeds, and textile plants. New industries were to be established for processing agricultural products. Mixed Rumanian-German companies, in which Germany was to supply the machinery, were to exploit mineral and petroleum resources. The treaty also made provision for mutual collaboration in various industries, road, rail and water transport, and public enterprises. Rumanian and German banks were to collaborate on methods of financing the activities contemplated under the plan. Finally, the agreement provided that Germany would supply armaments and munitions to Rumania.[16]

In assessing the significance of this agreement, as well as Germany's increasing economic monopoly in the Balkans, it is necessary to distinguish between the actual effects under the international circumstances and its merits as a purely economic program. In actual fact, of course, Germany's economic activities in the Balkans proved to be part of its over-all task of preparing a war economy, and it could be maintained that to overlook the military premise behind Germany's actions is to miss the essential point. Certainly Germany's primary concern was to obtain in southeastern Europe a source of vegetable and mineral raw materials to assist in creating an economy secure from blockade. At the same time, Germany appears to have regarded

---

15. According to Grigore Gafencu, at that time Rumanian Foreign Minister, this economic agreement was designed to appease Hitler, who had displayed an ominous irritation over Carol's assault on the Iron Guard in the autumn of 1938. See his book, *Last Days of Europe* (New Haven, Yale University Press, 1948), pp. 23–25.

16. For a discussion of this agreement from the German side, cf. Anton Reithinger, "Grossdeutschland und Südosteuropa im Lichte der Statistik," *Allgemeines Statistisches Archiv, 29* (1939), 129–139, and German Institute for Business Research, "The German-Rumanian Trade Treaty," *Weekly Report*, Nos. 13–14 (April 6, 1939).

its activities in Rumania as primarily economic and not, directly at least, as an instrument for political penetration. The Germans did not feel they had Rumania sewed up diplomatically by this agreement.[17]

Although there was this hidden military menace in Germany's actions, Rumania did gain certain short-term advantages from its economic relations with the Third Reich. Contrary to numerous reports Germany was not merely draining Rumania in exchange for aspirins, harmonicas, and cameras. The relations with Germany, aside from the political danger, were certainly not without their disadvantages; there were all the limitations of being tied to a bilateralism with a much more powerful state, difficulties in obtaining certain commodities, and German reluctance to provide materials for secondary industries. In so far as it was possible Rumania struggled to keep the Reich from obtaining a too favorable rate of exchange and to retain as large a share as possible of its exports for the free world market. Nevertheless, Germany did offer a market for Rumanian agricultural products at prices which Rumania could not obtain elsewhere. In the absence of remunerative world prices and the failure of the other great powers to provide any assistance, Germany's policy, whatever its aim, was a benefit *faute de mieux*.[18] The benefits were not unconditional but the comparison should not be made with an ideal and stable system of free world trade, but with the collapsed and paralyzed situation of the 1930's.

As to setting up the German and Rumanian economies as complementary units in a system of regional trade, the most obvious danger was that Germany would in effect reduce Rumania to a colonial status, producing vegetable and mineral raw materials for the German in-

17. Thus Hitler in his letter to Mussolini of August 25, 1939, regarding the Soviet pact, indicated that because of this pact "Rumania is no longer in a situation to take part in a conflict against the Axis" (U.S. Department of State, *Nazi-Soviet Relations*, p. 81), a clear sign that the Axis leaders had serious doubts whether Rumania, even after the March economic agreement, was on their side. In the German diplomatic correspondence of 1940, the whole concern of the Germans appeared to be that Rumania, which was so important for its vegetable products and petroleum, should not become involved in military and political disturbances.

18. The conclusion of a study by the Royal Institute of International Affairs, *South-Eastern Europe, a Political and Economic Survey*, p. 198, stated: "At any rate up till the spring of 1939, the countries of South-Eastern Europe on balance have gained in a material sense and in the short run, by the increase in German purchases. Germany has helped to raise their export prices and to increase their national incomes, and she has not so far taken advantage of her bargaining position to turn the terms of trade in her favor, so that their 'real' incomes have been raised. On the other hand, one of Germany's objects may be to associate the economic systems of these countries so closely with her own as to make it difficult for them to sever their connections in time of war."

dustrial economy. Indeed, German economists commenting upon the 1939 agreement argued that Rumania should not undertake a further drive toward industrialization until the state of economic advance called for in the agreement was reached. In fact they claimed that under exchange control the industry of southeastern Europe had developed to such an extent that it had reached the saturation point and that control of investment was necessary.[19]

The agreement did, however, provide for the creation of industries preparing foodstuffs and raw materials for export and also for the development of railways and the armamants industries. That is, the Germans favored industries "organically" connected with Rumania's natural resources but were opposed to the expansion of secondary industry.

It is not necessary to point out the obvious advantage to Germany of this policy nor to go into the array of arguments which Hitler's economists employed to carry their point. But from the Rumanian side one very curious paradox arises, precisely the kind of paradox which runs throughout the history of Rumanian economic policy. The German policy, as shown in the March, 1939, agreement, resembled in many respects that of the National Peasant party and was in definite opposition to the industrial policy of the pro-Axis Manoilescu and of the Carolist regime. This opposition appears quite explicitly in an article by Ernst Wagemann, director of the German Institute for Business Research.

Wagemann, one of the most ardent advocates of Germany's destiny in the Balkans, was quite critical of Manoilescu's economic theory, though not on traditional grounds of free trade.[20] He regarded Manoilescu's policy as doubtful in practice because of the lack of consumer purchasing power in Rumania. Moreover, Manoilescu's emphasis upon increasing labor productivity would intensify rather than improve the problem of surplus population. "For the more labor-productive an industry is, the more capital and the fewer workers it needs . . . The solution of the overpopulation problem is to be sought least of all in the development of highly technical and strictly rationalized or, as Manoilescu says, 'labor productive' industries." [21] Wagemann recommended intensification and diversifica-

19. German Institute for Business Research, *Weekly Report,* Nos. 13–14 (April 6, 1939), p. 42.

20. Ernst Wagemann, "The Pressure of Population as an Economic Force," German Institute for Business Research, *Weekly Report,* Nos. 25/26 and 27/28 (June 29–July 14, 1939). This article is a translation from Wagemann's book, *Der neue Balkan; altes Land, junge Wirtschaft* (Hamburg, 1939).

21. *Ibid.,* Nos. 25/26, p. 3.

tion of agriculture, which would increase yield, diminish surplus population, and, incidentally, supply Germany with agricultural products. As for industry,

in the Balkan countries the point has not yet been reached where industrial plants can be developed with the resources available within the country. . . . Industrialization must be limited at first to those industries which make use of domestic raw material. Germany, the most important trade partner, can in the long run deliver industrial products, but not raw materials such as cotton. If industrialization includes the first processing of agricultural products and the smelting of mining products, the export is assured.[22]

While Madgearu's appraisal in 1940 of the 1939 agreement may have been cautiously phrased for political reasons, it probably reflects his views. His chief reservations concerned the manner in which the agreement might be carried out but not the principles of the agreement. He was worried lest wheat, which did not receive preference in the agreement, might suffer during the period of reorganization, although he was always in favor of reducing the production of cereals in Rumanian agriculture. More particularly, he was afraid that the system of assuring prices and markets for the peasants cultivating the new specialized crops might—if the peasants were unable to defend themselves through cooperative organization—be to their ultimate disadvantage, since the purchasing societies, which had a monopoly, could dictate prices. Here, of course, he showed a quite realistic awareness of the way in which the best laid plans were usually carried out in Rumania. He also expressed some concern lest the mixed German-Rumanian companies transfer all the benefits to Germany, the stronger partner. Finally, he was not pleased with Ger-

---

22. *Ibid.*, Nos. 25/26, p. 3, and Nos. 27/28, p. 3. There are several flaws in Wagemann's line of argument. His criticism of Manoilescu's theory in terms of the overpopulation question, or of unemployment, is not relevant to Manoilescu's thesis. Moreover, as Wilbert Moore (*Economic Demography of Eastern and Southern Europe,* p. 115–118) points out, diversification of agriculture also requires increased capital and an improved market structure. While Wagemann attacks Manoilescu's industrialization as failing to solve the overpopulation problem, Moore quite correctly shows that Wagemann's program for increasing agricultural output would scarcely compensate for the growth of population. Wagemann estimated that agricultural production in the Balkans could increase by 50 per cent in the course of a generation. Moore, however, shows that with Rumania's rate of population growth the per capita production in Rumania, using as a base European per capita production, 1931–35 = 100, would rise only from 48 to 55, hardly enough to justify Wagemann's rosy predictions. Moore's conclusion is, I believe, justified: "Wagemann's 'analysis' . . . follows from the official policy and not from a scientific appraisal of the facts."

many's increasing monopoly over Rumanian trade and hoped to keep the door open for other markets.[23]

Apart from these important qualifications, however, he expressed his approval of Germany's program for Rumania, the intensification of agriculture, the creation of agricultural industries, and the establishment of mixed companies for mining and petroleum. In general, he seems to have regarded Rumania's increasing economic ties with Germany as largely in the nature of things and only secondarily as a result of policy: "This situation is not so much the result of a crystallization of policy as a change in the structure of the Rumanian economy, which gradually with the advance of the process of industrialization diminished the degree of complementarity with a series of countries and increased it with regard to one alone—Germany." [24]

Although it may seem surprising that the German policy embodied in the agreement of March, 1939, should have more in common with the economic aims of a National Peasant than with a pro-Axis corporatist, the reason is obvious. The National Peasants, believing in economic interdependence and the international division of labor, disapproved of fostering Rumanian industry at the expense of agriculture.[25] Germany, for its own reasons, desired the Balkans to increase their agricultural production and to stay away from secondary industries. On the other hand, Manoilescu's industrial ambitions were unwelcome to the Germans because of their similarity to German aims, a case of like poles repelling. This antagonism arising out of an attempt at similarity is a characteristic of Rumanian history. The earlier effort of the Liberals to emulate the West had led to the economic xenophobia of the Brătianus.

The success of the German-Rumanian agreement could have been measured only after a number of years of peaceful development; it may be doubted whether the results anticipated could have been achieved in the five years of the agreement. But such a peaceful period was not to be granted. In the year after the inauguration of the five-year plan Rumania had lost one third of its territory, Carol had fled the country, and Marshal Antonescu had joined Hitler's war against the Soviet Union. The territorial losses alone severely disorganized the economic program. By the loss of Bessarabia, Northern Bucovina, Northern Transylvania, and Southern Dobrogea Rumania was deprived of 34 per cent of its total area, 37 per cent of the arable land,

23. Madgearu, *Evoluţia economiei româneşti*, pp. 372–374.
24. *Ibid.*, p. 301.
25. For somewhat analogous reasons, at the time of the First World War several Rumanian populists had been pro-German because they saw Germany as the industrial complement to Rumania's agrarian society.

44 per cent of the forest land, 27 per cent of the orchards, and 37 per cent of the vineyards. Of the area devoted to wheat (as of 1939) it lost 37 per cent, to maize 30 per cent, to sunflower 75 per cent, to hemp 43 per cent, and 86 per cent of the area devoted to soya. The regions, chiefly Bessarabia, in which the new industrial crops had been most intensively cultivated were lost. Finally, the whole economy was put on a war footing, first for Germany and then for Rumania itself.

Notwithstanding all Carol's laws and decrees, no real solutions were found to the agrarian question. It is illuminating to look through the volumes of the *Enciclopedia României*, published in the last years of Carol's reign as a monument to the Rumanian rebirth. Amid all the fanfare of Rumania's marvelous progress and glowing future, the articles on agriculture and land tenure strike a discordant and often deeply pessimistic note.

To be sure, the trend in the 1930's was toward increasing industrialization as the solution to Rumania's economic difficulties, and in the long run, had the war not intervened, this might have brought beneficial results even to agriculture. As it was, however, much of the industrialization was achieved at the expense of agriculture, and for all its expansion it was neither bringing agriculture any great technical improvements nor beginning to absorb the excess agricultural population. The five-year plan and the laws to rationalize land tenure and consolidate holdings might have provided a healthier foundation for agriculture had they been carried out conscientiously, but there is little evidence that they meant anything more than many previous legislative acts which clutter the Rumanian statute books. It is doubtful whether the peasant would have benefited greatly from a plan ordained by divine providence if it had been left to the Carol administration to execute it. With all its attacks on "outworn" parties and its praise for the younger generation, the Carol dictatorship lacked the stature to be a modernizing dictatorship along the lines of Kemal Ataturk's regime. The new German orientation might have benefited Rumanian agriculture, but given the power relations it is more likely that Rumania would have become the object of an efficient colonial policy.

Among the social studies undertaken in the period of Carol's dictatorship there was one which makes a fitting conclusion to the Carolist period, and indeed illustrates the failure to master the agrarian question during the interwar years. In the summer and autumn of 1939 a Rumanian research team made a field study of the *plasă* (an administrative unit in a judeţ) Dâmbovnicul, in the south of the

judeţ of Argeş.[26] This plasă was selected and is of interest for a
number of reasons. It lay midway between the Carpathians and the
Danube Valley and was in the heart of Wallachia. Having closer
communications than many regions with roads leading to the capital,
it had long been under the commercial influences which have so profoundly affected Rumanian society; it was not a primitive untouched
district but was showing the full effect of what the investigators
called "Americanization." Its population was almost entirely Rumanian and almost entirely devoted to agriculture. It lay near Răteşti,
the family estate of the Brătianus, and Topoloveni, Mihalache's
town, and had consequently received a good deal of attention from
the parties in their political campaigns. Hence, Dâmbovnicul, if not
the average Rumanian plasă, was an excellent representative of an
agricultural community of the Old Kingdom and displayed the principal problems peculiar to Rumania.

What were the conditions in this community in the summer of
1939? Over nine-tenths of the population was engaged in agriculture; in the remaining tenth there were more public officials than
merchants, tradesmen, or artisans. Of the 9,400 heads of families,
about two-thirds (6,681) were cultivators on their own land or estate
owners; 772 worked the land in dijma, that is, under the old crop-
sharing tenure; 571 were agricultural day laborers, 144 were farm
hands, and only 30 were tenants. About 87 per cent of the land was
agricultural; forests which had once been extensive had by this time
been reduced below the local needs for firewood and timber. Wheat,
maize, and oats occupied almost three-fourths of the arable land.

The density of agricultural population was somewhat below the
average for Rumania, but there were just under 70 inhabitants dependent upon agriculture per square kilometer of agricultural land.
Evidence of overpopulation was seen in the use of practically all the
land for cereals, the small size of exploitations, and in the search for
auxiliary sources of income. About 23 per cent of the families had less
than one hectare of land, and 56 per cent less than 3 hectares. These
small holdings were further subdivided into numerous strips; the
properties between one and three hectares, for example, were composed on the average of 6 plots of .3 hectares each. For the level of
cultivation in this region, 4–5 hectares were the minimum adequate
to feed a family of 4–5 members, but only 22 per cent of the properties were over 5 hectares. Competition for land was intense, the
terms for land worked in dijma were becoming increasingly severe,

26. Mihai Pop and A. Golopenţia, *Dâmbovnicul, o plasă din sudul Judeţului Argeş*
(Bucarest, 1942).

and the investigators found many of the old labor contracts and obligations associated with pre-1914 Rumania.

Unable to support themselves in the community, many peasants were seeking temporary work in nearby market towns, and a number traveled as far as Bucarest, a distance of about 70 kilometers. The exodus in most cases was not permanent, and the peasants after earning some money returned to Dâmbovnicul. This movement to the city was a reflection of the new conditions, which were also seen in the houses and garments of the peasants: houses were no longer built to last generations as was the case in the more isolated districts to the north; the national costume was relegated to Sundays. Birth and death rates were high and the natural increase outran the emigration away from the plasă. The standard of living was very low; many families were undernourished.

A definite differentiation in the peasantry was developing. A few peasants—mostly those who had inherited medium properties—were enlarging their holdings; a few new peasant estates of over 100 hectares had been created. The poorer peasants, including many who had been allotted land, were losing their holdings. Investigations into debts and credit showed that even after the conversion of 1934 about half the households were in debt. Credit provided by the cooperative banks went almost entirely to the larger peasants; in one commune holdings of up to 5 hectares received only 7.9 per cent of the loans. The special political interest shown by the parties in the judeţ of Argeş seemed to have brought no benefits beyond permitting local party stalwarts to obtain extra funds to purchase land from peasants who were in debt or in need of money.

Such, then, was the land of happy peasants with their colorful folkways so picturesquely displayed in the travel literature of the Carolist era.

XI

THE FASCIST PERIOD, 1940–44

Rumanian Fascism

THE term fascist period, here used to cover the years of the Iron Guard and Antonescu dictatorships is not altogether satisfactory except in the general sense of describing a dictatorial regime in military alliance with Hitler Germany. The government of Marshal Antonescu, especially after his victory over the Iron Guard in January, 1941, was really a military dictatorship, in many respects like the numerous other military dictatorships in Balkan history, although it took over many of the trappings and practices of fascism. The word fascism itself has been given any number of meanings and nuances. To some it is the death rattle of monopoly capitalism; to others, anti-Semitism and racial glorification; to others, a form of national chauvinism; and to others merely a synonym for dictatorship plus hooliganism. It would be fruitless here to attempt an exact definition of fascism, especially for Rumania where, at one time or another, practically every party has had the word "fascist" hyphenated to it by its opponents.

For all the vagueness of the term there was in Rumania a political current, appearing in a relatively unadulterated form in the Iron Guard and as a more or less important element in other political formations, which is quite recognizable and for which fascism is as good a name as any. Perhaps it can best be approached negatively, for ultimately it was a negative spirit. In the preceding sections the effort has been made to extract the positive content of several political currents and to examine their significance in terms of the problems of Rumanian society. It has been seen that the agrarian question was a perennial and chronic affliction deeply rooted in Rumanian society and to a very considerable extent the product of Rumania's contacts with Western industrial society. Along with the various attempts to find a positive solution—however inadequate or misdirected they may have been—there was also an impulse to a negative response. Indeed it is possible to say that fascism represents an irrational reaction against an unsolved problem in the body politic or, more precisely, in the context of an industrial or industrializing economy. It is something like a cancerous growth in an organism which arises from some chronic irritation, takes on a life of its own, displays great dynamism for a time, and ultimately is destructive of the body which produced it. If such an analogy be fair, it is necessary not to confuse an analysis of the unsolved problem with a justification of the fascist response, or to regard fascism as an inexplicable evil possessing the body of an innocent.

In its resort to the nonrational, fascism makes an appeal to the spontaneous, the organic, the primitive, and the mythical, to the instinctive rather than the logical aspects of human and social experience. From these it gains its emotional force and appeal. At the same time, the appeal to the natural and the traditional is itself an artificial and somewhat self-conscious act; the effort to reinvoke the spontaneous is itself not a wholly spontaneous act. Thus, fascism does not originate in the lowest and most backward strata of society but is usually in its initial stages an intellectual movement. In its origins at least it is not the creation of a nation or a social group which is at the bottom of the heap, but rather appears among those nations, social groups, or individuals which have advanced to the extent of being aware of their position and at the same time of being resentful and frustrated.

Conditions favorable to the various manifestations of fascism were certainly not lacking in Rumania. The struggle to achieve an independent national existence, the prolonged insecurity as a small state, the effort not only to escape the shadow of the great powers but to maintain a position in the scrambling of the Balkan states—all these led to an intense political nationalism which easily boiled over into chauvinism. The ethnic confusion of southeastern Europe and especially Rumania's sense of isolation in the "great sea of Slavs" produced a strong ethnic nationalism. Anti-Semitism had been endemic in Rumania since its appearance as an independent state; the Congress of Berlin had obliged the new Rumanian government to amend the constitution to grant Jews citizenship. The Jewish problem in Rumania was not a simple one. Especially in Moldavia there had been a rapid influx of Jews, largely from Russian Poland, in the nineteenth century; the population of the urban centers was largely Jewish; most of the commercial activities were carried on by the Jews. This situation, combined with Rumanian nationalism and the desire for self-assertion, produced the perfect atmosphere for anti-Semitism. The national literary movement at the end of the nineteenth century had a strong anti-Semitic tone. Professor Cuza, the Rumanians liked to say, was preaching the gospel of anti-Semitism while Hitler was still an infant.

But if nationalism and anti-Semitism are the constant handmaids of fascism, they do not wholly describe it. The element in fascism giving it its significance to the twentieth century is its response to the challenge of industrialism. It is for this reason that of the various political currents of pre-1914 Rumania populism had the closest affinity to some of the later manifestations of Rumanian fascism.[1] The populist response to this challenge, for all the specific rational arguments it may have advanced regarding the economic advantages of peasant farming, was fundamentally negative in its idealization of the unspoiled peasant and in its hostility to industry and the capitalist Golgotha. To these it added a strong cultural nationalism, a tendency to anti-Semitism, and that special characteristic of later fascism, a hatred of Marxism. To be sure, fascism is not generally anti-industrial. The tensions of contemporary industrial society impinge in different ways on different countries. But in the case of Rumania, with its particular position vis-à-vis industrial society, the fascist response in its most characteristic form involved this negation and an exaltation of the peasant.

During the interwar period Rumanian fascism developed in two phases. A number of fascist groups appeared immediately after the First World War, principally among students and the military, as a part of the general social turmoil brought about by the war. At that time fascism developed its leadership but did not become a mass movement. A second phase appeared with the depression; fascism broadened its influence and in the course of the 1930's increasingly dominated the political horizon. It took innumerable forms in Rumania: as an element in a larger political party, as a conscious imitation of foreign fascism, or as an authentic Rumanian fascist movement. In the first case, various manifestations of fascism, such as extreme chauvinism or anti-Semitism, appeared as a tendency in one of the established parties and often led to a schism. The defections of Octavian Goga and later of Vaida Voevod from the National Peasants may be taken as examples. In those cases where it took the form of an imitation of foreign fascism it was merely following the Rumanian practice of borrowing from the more developed European states.

An interesting example of borrowed fascism was the short-lived Fascia Națională Română, which began as a student organization

1. See above, p. 147.

in Bucarest in 1923 and was later absorbed by Cuza's League of
Christian Defense. This movement, which was never of any importance, was explicitly modeled on Italian fascism.[2] Its program had
all the formulae of early fascism, but smelled of the candle and was a
rather unimaginative academic exercise. A rabid anti-Semitism was
the core of the program, which included detailed plans of the best
ways to rid Rumania of the Jews. The Fascia was to be highly nationalistic, anticapitalist, antisocialist, anti-Communist, and anti-
parliamentarian.

But after a parade of these sentiments, with appropriate quotations from Mussolini, Barrès, and Maurras, and the promise of a
two-year dictatorship to eradicate rotten politicians, the actual economic program was reminiscent of populism. Rumania should be an
exclusively agricultural country; industrial states were less happy
and had social upheavals. Agrarian reform should limit property to
100 hectares and land should belong only to those who cultivated it.
Proposed agricultural improvements included the familiar clichés,
model farms, cooperation, more machinery, more fertilizer, and better seed. Industry should not be protected; cottage crafts should be
fostered. The commercial policy was quite simple: no imports without twice as many exports; this it was felt would assure a safe balance of trade. The program was clearly intended to appeal to peasants, workmen, and, above all, to the army, but in general it gives the
impression of being the outpouring of a rather vicious schoolboy,
which in all probability it was.[3]

Of far greater importance than this jejune attempt at fascism was
the Iron Guard, or, more properly, the Legion of the Archangel Michael, which, while it had a number of similar traits and copied certain Italian and German features, was an authentic Rumanian fascist movement. Its founder Corneliu Zelea Codreanu was born in
Iași in 1899.[4] Physically he was extremely impressive, tall, very handsome, with powerful and compelling features. He had received a good
deal of military training in his youth and had absorbed the nationalist
doctrines of Cuza and Iorga. In the spring of 1919 he began his career

2. Titus P. Vifor, *Doctrina fascismului român, și anteproectul de program* (Bucarest, 1924).
3. The only really original proposal was that the clubhouses of the disbanded political parties should be converted into state-supervised brothels.
4. There was a great controversy whether Codreanu was really a Rumanian or not.
His opponents pointed out that his mother was of German origin and his father had
changed his name from Zelinski to Zelea in 1902. Codreanu's supporters maintained
that the name Zelinski had been forced upon his forebears because they had lived
in southern Galicia under the Austrians, and pointed out that both sides of the family
had belonged to the Orthodox Church, a sign of their Rumanian nationality.

by organizing a group of companions in the Moldavian border town of Huşi to fight the Communists. In the same year he entered the law faculty at the University of Iaşi, where his principal activity was fomenting student riots against Jews and Communists. Codreanu was not of peasant origin; his father was a teacher, an active politician, and colleague of Professor Cuza. Codreanu not only studied at Iaşi but in 1922 attended lectures at the University of Berlin and later studied law at Grenoble.

In 1923 Professor Cuza founded his anti-Semitic party, the League of National Christian Defense; Codreanu became one of the party organizers. He was soon imprisoned for preparing a list of prominent politicians and Jewish leaders to be liquidated. While in prison he conceived the idea of the Legion of the Archangel Michael, taking the name from a statue of the saint in the prison chapel at Văcăreşti. Initially the Legion was a youth movement attached to the League of Christian Defense. Codreanu first gained national recognition in October, 1924, when he shot the police chief of Iaşi who had tried to break up his anti-Semitic activities. He was acquitted in a much-publicized trial which only augmented his popularity in anti-Semitic circles.

After 1924 Codreanu broke with Cuza. He always recognized his debt to the older man's teachings but felt that Cuza was tied to parliamentary politics and failed to see the need of a more dynamic policy. After a stay in France he founded, in 1927, an independent Legion of the Archangel Michael. In 1930 he created the Iron Guard as a combat unit to fight communism. In effect it was identical with the Legion, although intended to be its military branch and to include other groups desiring to enter the crusade.

When Vaida Voevod was Minister of the Interior in the National Peasant government he gave Codreanu a measure of unofficial support and even granted him permission to take a column of Guardists across the Prut to preach the archangelic gospel in darkest Bessarabia.[5] Mihalache, who replaced Vaida Voevod in 1930, took a sterner attitude and on January 11, 1931, attempted to dissolve the Legion and the Iron Guard. By this time the movement was gaining a strong mass following. In August, 1931, Codreanu won a seat in the chamber. The Liberal leader Duca again dissolved the Guard in 1933, for which he was assassinated, with Codreanu's knowledge and approval. In November, 1934, the movement assumed a new label, the All for the Fatherland party (Totul pentru Ţara), under the nominal leadership of General Cantacuzino. The Legion continued to grow in

5. Klaus Charle, *Die eiserne Garde* (Berlin; Vienna, 1939), p. 23.

strength and by the time of the 1937 elections it appeared to be the outstanding force in Rumanian politics.

With Carol's sudden counterattack in 1938 it collapsed in surprising fashion. On February 21, 1938, Codreanu disbanded the movement to avoid, he said, unnecessary loss of blood. This may have been a purely tactical retreat, but it was certainly an anticlimax to the blood and thunder of Legionary oratory. The following day he sent a letter to all the old ministers who participated in Carol's coup, protesting against the dictatorship, which he saw as a dead form, and complaining that the older generation had betrayed its own ideals of legality. In the spring he was arrested, on a charge of libel against Iorga, condemned, and imprisoned. In November, 1938, he was shot by the Siguranța "while attempting to escape."

What was the Legionary movement? In some respects it was a copy of Italian fascism and German national-socialism, with its colored shirts, Roman salutes, paramilitary formations, and cult of a leader—*Capitanul*. Its anticommunism, anti-Semitism, and antiparliamentarianism, however, were home-grown. Codreanu used to say that he had adopted these principles before he had ever heard of Hitler, and that indeed when he had been in Berlin in 1922 he was able to show the light to several Germans who later became prominent Nazis. Codreanu's anti-Semitism had something of the frenzied quality one finds in the authentic Nazi—he professed to be physically stricken at the sight of Jews. His anticommunism was in part a corollary to his anti-Semitism, in that he considered communism a vehicle of international Jewish machinations.

The anticommunism of the Legion cannot, however, be explained wholly in terms of anti-Semitism. To some extent at least it was a reaction against what might be called the outrageous logicality of Marxism. Like fascism, Marxism was a response to the tensions of contemporary society but in its critique it attacked not only bourgeois society but also all the popular coexisting romantic and traditional attachments: its internationalism outraged national sensibilities; its dialectical materialism robbed the world of its myths and its homely beliefs. Fascism was based precisely upon these nonrational but deep sentiments. Hence, despite their mutual assault upon bourgeois society and their similarity in tactics there was a mortal enmity between the two movements.

In these qualities, however, the Iron Guard was merely the Rumanian manifestation of a European phenomenon. It had, in addition, certain more specifically Rumanian features. While the Nazis and the Italian Fascists were not on good terms with the churches, the Legion of the Archangel Michael was avowedly an Orthodox Christian movement and was fully aware of its distinctiveness in this respect. Guardist meetings were preceded by a religious service. The employment of religious symbolism and mysticism was not merely a tactical device of the Legion but was an integral part of its ideology. This religious element was undoubtedly of importance in the diffusion and quality of the Iron Guard's influence in Rumania, especially among the peasantry.

A second quality of the Guard was its cult of the primitive; not, however, the German primitivism of an ancient golden age in the *Urwald* but the primitivism of contemporary Rumanian peasant life. Reacting against the frustrations and anomalies of Rumanian society the Guard invoked the unspoiled soul of the peasant, sometimes even to the extent of glorifying his illiteracy. Such a reaction is not difficult to understand. Anyone who has visited Bucarest and seen the pseudo-French culture of the wealthy, the overeager imitations in art, architecture, and thought, and then contrasted them with the attractive side of Rumanian peasant life, the strange but moving music, the magnificent taste and sensibility of peasant handwork and folk ballads, is strongly tempted to condemn the former and wish wistfully that something authentic and real could develop from this peasant culture. At best there is something touching in this attempt to restore a national integrity permitting the flowering of native potentialities in place of a bastard culture, derivative, and without life of its own.[6]

Unfortunately this problem cannot be solved by simply eradicating foreign influences and reverting to the simplicity of the peasant: "Those who have a Fall behind them can never become innocent again." [7] Rumanian folk culture, if left to itself for an indefinite period of time, might have evolved its own advanced cultural forms but it was not. The Rumanian peasant today adds a sheet iron roof to his picturesque hut, tops his traditional costume with a battered felt hat, and pins up a cheap photograph with his icons and wood

6. In this connection it is of interest to note that in his analysis of the 1937 elections, C. Enescu observed that the purely anti-Semitic vote (i.e., in the districts with a large Jewish population) tended to go to the Cuza-Goga party rather than to the Iron Guard, which seemed to gain its votes from a more general dissatisfaction with the whole of Rumanian public life. *Sociologie Românească, 2,* Nos. 11–12 (November–December, 1937), p. 523.

7. Alfred Weber, *Farewell to European History,* trans. R. F. C. Hull (London, 1947), p. 198.

carvings without the slightest feeling of incongruity. An attempt to take away the sheet iron, the manufactured hat, the photograph, and all which they imply would be a retrograde step.

A third, and less attractive, characteristic of the Legionary movement was a marked morbidity and cult of death. To some extent this derived from the Christian belief that death must precede resurrection. It was also an aspect of the idea of sacrifice and self-abnegation to be found in other fascist movements. It stimulated the "heroic assassination" and the "death squads" and contributed to the series of political murders which convulsed the 1930's.

According to the Legionary code the unit was not the individual but the "nest," a collectivity that included not only living Legionaries but ancestors and those yet unborn. This spirit led to the Legionary practice of continually exhuming and exalting dead comrades. The code included also the less distinctive commandments of loyalty, comradeship, obedience, discipline, work, and honor.

Such were the emotional drives of the Iron Guard. It is not surprising that the program of such a movement should have been vague. In fact, the Legion was against programs. "The country is going to ruin," said Codreanu, "not for lack of programs but for lack of men." [8] All the old parties had a superfluity of programs which had achieved nothing. Before a program could be meaningful, it was necessary to develop the new man, free from the corruption of the past. "Today the Rumanian people do not need a great politician, as is erroneously believed. The Rumanian people today need a great teacher and leader, who will overcome the powers of darkness and destroy the brood of Hell." [9] In their slogans the Legionaries used such phrases as *Omul și pogonul* (the man and the pogon) and *Hectarul și sufletul* (the hectare and the soul) but these should be understood not as an agrarian program but rather as a symbol of the peasant's deep ties with mother earth.

In 1937 Codreanu did create the Battalion of Legionary Commerce, the purpose of which was to replace the Jews in trade and to prove that Rumanians, too, could be good merchants. Restaurants and shops were set up which were to be the core of a new economic spirit. In Italy, fascism had formed an alliance with corporatism, and in Rumania a similar mingling took place in some of the fascist currents. But it is interesting to note that Codreanu did not take up corporatism. In spite of the fact that Manoilescu was a good friend of the Legion and had been elected to the senate on its list, his efforts

8. Codreanu, *Eiserne Garde* (Berlin, 1939), p. 273.
9. *Ibid.*, p. 275.

to incorporate his economic doctrines had little effect. Moța, one of Codreanu's lieutenants and theoretician for the movement—his initial scholarly contribution had been the translation of the Protocols of the Elders of Zion into Rumanian—had written that corporatism was "entirely colorless from a folk point of view." [10] Corporatism should not come before the basic reform, the creation of the new man, since it would only solidify the existing corruptions in society. It should come afterward if at all.

This distrust of corporatism is not without importance, for it reinforces the supposition that in the 1930's the corporatist current, which so characterizes the latter half of Carol's reign, was in its origins quite different from Guardist fascism, although both were antiparliamentary and in many cases made political alliances. Corporatism was a consequence of an economic outlook, the Guard was an emotional and evangelical reaction against the existing order.

In its initial stages the Iron Guard found its principal support in student circles and in discontented elements on the fringes of society. In the 1930's it became a mass movement, as is shown—in rough approximation at least—by comparing its popular vote of 30,783 (1.2 per cent) in 1931 with the 478,378 (16.5 per cent) votes it received in 1937.[11] It obtained a following in the peasantry and in urban middle class and working circles. Its most active members were the social misfits, unemployed intellectuals, dismissed civil servants, a number of the members of the old boyar families, plus an assortment of plain toughs and hooligans. The Communists, in attempting to relate this movement to the class struggle, have held that the active support for the Iron Guard came from the interstitial groups, the declassés—the broken aristocracy, the petty bourgeoisie, and the *Lumpenproletariat*.[12] While it is not to be denied that the Iron Guard would have a special appeal to the dispossessed and uprooted, the terms "petty bourgeois" and Lumpenproletariat are notoriously evasive and too easily become catchalls for phenomena not fitting into the Marxist scheme. A somewhat simpler approach would be to see Rumanian society as a whole suffering from general dislocation and the fascist current as a reaction to that dislocation, taking on greater intensity in those parts of society most seriously affected. This would account

10. Charle, *op. cit.*, p. 93.
11. In the same interval Cuza's League, initially the larger, rose only from 113,863 to 281,107, an accurate reflection of greater effectiveness of the Iron Guard's dynamism.
12. Cf. Lucrețiu Pătrășcanu, *Problemele de bază ale României* (3d ed., Bucarest, 1946), pp. 259–262. While his argument contains a good deal of truth it suffers from the necessity he feels to prove that the proletariat proper and the peasantry proper could not be activists in a fascist movement.

for the peculiar venom of the declassés as contrasted with the less
fanatical support of the impoverished which arose more specifically
from the depression.

It is difficult to obtain reliable evidence concerning the calculated
support given to the Iron Guard by interested groups, but there are
numerous indications that government ministers in the 1930's, such
as Vaida Voevod and Tătărescu, did support the Legion unofficially
and did not greatly hamper its activities. Undoubtedly in the vast
underworld of Rumanian police life, Siguranța officials found it a
useful organization for combating Left-wing labor movements. Perhaps one should not place too great stress upon such Machiavellian
motives. It is tempting to see in ministers, police chiefs, and mysteri-
ous financial interests absolutely cold and calculating individuals
who were not in the slightest affected by the atmosphere of their sur-
roundings. But after all both Vaida Voevod and Duca had said that
apart from the battle against communism they had hoped to harness
what they felt was constructive in the Iron Guard and divert it to less
violent activities. It would seem reasonable to assume that they, too,
were moved by some of the same sentiments which impelled the Guardists.

As to foreign support, there is no question that Hitler regarded
Codreanu as his ally, and for good reason. In November, 1937, for
example, Codreanu made his celebrated electoral declaration that he
was against the Western democracies, against the Little Entente and
the Balkan Entente, against the League of Nations, against bolshevism, and in favor of the Rome-Berlin Axis: "Forty-eight hours after
our victory we shall have an alliance with Germany and Italy." There
is also evidence that in later years, at least, the Germans gave financial support to the Iron Guard, although some of the proofs produced
by the Carol dictatorship are suspect. It would be wrong to conclude,
however, that the Iron Guard was nothing more than a German fifth
column. It was a very significant aspect of Rumanian social and political life.

Rumanian writers of various political beliefs have sought, understandably enough, to prove—by calling the Legion a tool either of
the Germans, or of intriguing police chiefs and politicians, or of a
class—that it did not represent the Rumanian people. Granted that
the Rumanian people are not by nature fascist beasts, nevertheless
the Iron Guard cannot be written off as a superficial phenomenon. In
its way it was the nemesis of all the false constitutionalism and pseudo-
democracy which have been observed in the course of recent Rumanian
history.

Yet the Iron Guard collapsed, not without some horrible spasms and death throes, but collapsed whenever a strong hand was raised against it. When Carol attacked it in 1938, despite the lash-back in the assassination of Calinescu, he had it under control. In 1940 he was overthrown by it only because his regime had been completely discredited. In January, 1941, the Guard was to show its ineffectiveness against Antonescu's army.

This strange weakness lay not in the fact that the Iron Guard was an artificial body, completely unrepresentative, but because it was all too indigenous. Its effectiveness seemed to be inversely related to its nearness to power. In opposition and under Carolist persecution, it seemed powerful and menacing; martyrdom became it well. When it came close to power it showed itself inept and maladroit. In the face of real problems, whether of government or of maintaining power, its aura vanished and its new men proved to be nothing but pillagers and thugs with no idea how to master a country, much less run it. The very negativeness of the Iron Guard, which gives it its particular interest, was its own undoing.

The Dictatorships

The Iron Guard enjoyed a brief period of triumph from September, 1940, to January, 1941, during which time it shared power with Gen. Ion Antonescu in a "National-Legionary State." Carol fell because the Germans lacked confidence in him but also because all political groups, including the National Peasants and the old Liberals, detested his regime which had discarded political freedom for the presumed interests of the nation and then had failed to make a move in its defense. At the last hour he had summoned Antonescu, a talented and forceful officer, but a man whose stern ambition both Carol and the Guardists failed to appreciate. After Carol's abdication and Michael's accession to the throne, Maniu and Constantin Brătianu supported Antonescu in the hope and on the condition that he would reestablish a constitutional regime. Such a hope had no chance of realization. Although Antonescu had been known as pro-French in the 1930's, he had by this time made his peace with Hitler and was thoroughly committed to a pro-Nazi policy.[13] He had long been criti-

13. It is evident, however, from the recently published memoirs of the former chief interpreter in the German Foreign Office that Antonescu's attitude was not one of obsequious servility. He vehemently criticized the Vienna Award to Hitler's face and expressed his desire to win back Northern Transylvania by force of arms. Apparently his outspoken attitude, which enabled him to match the Führer's harangues ("Er monologisierte genau wie dieser") plus his enthusiastic hatred of the Slavs and willing-

cal of traditional Rumanian politics and for several years had been in touch with the extremists advocating a "regeneration" of public life.[14] Moreover, while the Iron Guard had been harried under Carol, had lost its top level of leaders as well as much of its popular support, it still had its fighting cadres who felt that their day had come. The army, the only effective opposing force, was at this time badly demoralized by its inaction during the loss of Bessarabia and Transylvania.

In the cabinet formed on September 15 Antonescu was head of the state; Horia Sima, leader of the Guard, was Deputy Prime Minister; five other ministers were members of the Guard and the rest personal friends of Antonescu. The Guard was declared the sole legal party, responsible for the moral and material uplift of the Rumanian people. While Antonescu had been on good terms with Codreanu for several years and was at this time wearing the Legionary green shirt, tension quickly developed between him and his unruly allies. As a military man he wanted to reestablish law and order, whereas the Guard was champing for its revolution. Within the Guard itself were a number of factions, moderate and extreme, which were disputing Codreanu's mantle.

The pentup violence of the Guard, which had not found satisfaction at the time of Carol's abdication and had not been diverted into other channels, finally broke loose at the end of November, apparently with Horia Sima's approval but without Antonescu's knowledge. The Legionaries incited bloody Jewish pogroms and attempted to wipe out the politicians and civil servants of the previous regime. The army prevented the successful completion of this undertaking, but the Guard did succeed in killing the historian Iorga, the economist Virgil Madgearu, and in massacring sixty-four political prisoners in the Jilava Prison, most of whom had been Carol's agents and police chiefs instrumental in repressing the Legion.

By this time, however, German influence had become decisive. In October, 1940, German troops came into Rumania, ostensibly to reorganize the army; a German economic mission arrived to coordinate the Rumanian economy with the German war machine. The Third Reich's greatest interest was in increasing Rumania's output, and

---

ness to fight the Russians, won Hitler's confidence and trust to a surprising degree See Dr. Paul Schmidt, *Statist auf diplomatischer Bühne, 1923–45; Erlebnisse de Chefdolmetschers im Auswärtigen Amt mit den Staatsmännern Europas* (Bonn Athenäum-Verlag, 1949), pp. 511–512, 538, 548–549, 574.

14. Harald Laeuen, *Marschall Antonescu* (Essen, 1943), p. 27.

for this it required a degree of stability, not the hectic atmosphere created by Guardist terror squads. Consequently, when Antonescu in December began to take measures to bring the Guard to heel, he had German support, although the Legionaries refused to believe that the Germans would desert their most ardent allies. Antonescu proceeded to disarm their formations and to strengthen the army. Seeing their position undermined, the Guard on January 21, 1941, attempted to revolt. They were suppressed by the army after three days of savage fighting in which they outdid themselves in committing bestial atrocities. On January 27 Antonescu formed a new cabinet composed almost entirely of military officers. The Iron Guard was dissolved, the Legionary state abolished, and a firm military dictatorship under the *Conducator* came into being. Thus fell one of the first fascist movements in Europe and, ironically enough, at just the time Nazi Germany achieved complete predominance in Rumania.

Under the Antonescu dictatorship political life ceased altogether; the army and the Germans were in complete control. A couple of plebiscites provided the necessary stamp of legality and the government, with very few changes, remained in power for the next three years. In June, 1941, Antonescu joined Hitler in the war against the Soviet Union. Maniu and Constantin Brătianu supported the war until the recovery of Bessarabia and Bucovina, though they protested against the dictatorship. After Rumanian troops crossed the Dniester, they dispatched notes of protest to Antonescu demanding Rumania's withdrawal from the war. But by this time he was too deeply involved in the German adventure. In October, 1941, he annexed Transnistria, that part of the Ukraine lying between the Dniester and Bug rivers and including Odessa. Rumanian troops went on and on until they reached Stalingrad. Then began the slow retreat.

Well before his overthrow Antonescu, now a Marshal, realized that the war was lost but was unwilling to take the steps to extricate Rumania, although he permitted envoys of the political parties to establish contact with the Allies. In the absence of effective opposition he was able to maintain power until the Russians, who had been checked in northern Moldavia in the spring of 1944, resumed their offensive in the late summer. With the imminent threat of Rumania becoming a battlefield and being further devastated by increasing American bombing raids, King Michael seized the initiative, arrested him, and sought an armistice.

The Agrarian Question

The agrarian policy of the Iron Guard may be dismissed briefly. The Legionaries prided themselves on having no formal program and they were in power only five months. During its years of growth the Iron Guard had gained extensive influence among the peasants because of its range of emotional appeals and even more because of its extravagant if nebulous promises to provide land. As has been said, however, the slogan, omul și pogonul was less a directive—which would have been absurd, since a pogon equals half a hectare—than an emotional rally. For example, one of the Legionary writers, A. Balota, said that there should be a return to the village, not "to seek under false democratic pretexts social justice for the worker on the land, but to achieve ethnic justice for the peasant." [15]

The activities of the Guard during its five months in office appear to have been little more than pillage and extortion. Some of the actions purported to be in the Robin Hood tradition of taking from the rich to give to the poor, but the taking was far more evident than the giving. The Guard was active in the villages; there were incessant, parades, processions and ceremonies but no constructive action. The only important land measure was a decree converting Jewish-held rural property into state property, in exchange for "interest-bearing securities." Land thus obtained was to be used to provide for refugees from Bessarabia, Transylvania, and Bucovina. The abysmal failure of the Guard, for all its *élan* and promises, to achieve anything for the peasant increased the skepticism among the peasants, if such was possible, that anything good could come from the powers above. [16] The importance of the Iron Guard to the agrarian question does not lie in anything which it achieved, for it achieved nothing, but in evidence it affords of the dead rot in Rumanian society.

Although Antonescu frequently expressed his love for the Ru-

15. A. Balota, *Satul izvor de viața romănească,* quoted in Pătrăşcanu, *op. cit.,* p. 255.

16. In this connection I recall a conversation with a group of peasants in the village of Hangu in the Moldavian Carpathians in January, 1945. Like most mountain villagers they were desperately land hungry, and were particularly resentful that several thousand hectares of land, mostly forest, belonged to one large landowner. At that time they were curious to learn more about the activities of Petru Groza's Ploughmen's Front, whose organizers had not yet reached them. They were of course interested in the prospects of having more land but stated they were very skeptical of such promises. A number of the men in the village had joined the Iron Guard in the hopes of obtaining land; they had not received any land but had been imprisoned when the Guard was suppressed.

manian peasant,[17] under his dictatorship the overriding concerns were mobilizing agriculture for the war, compensating for the lost territories (though part of these were regained after 1941), and maintaining production against the drain on manpower and the requisitioning of equipment and livestock for military purposes. The majority of acts were specific war measures: price controls, export controls, laws against agricultural sabotage and speculation, control of livestock, state requisitioning of cereals, crop planning, and the mobilization of agricultural labor. Most of the measures had been initiated in Carol's reign under the trade agreement with Germany and the five-year plan for agriculture, but the war intensified them and put them on a directly military footing. By necessity there was an increase in the mobilization of agricultural labor. Field commandos and labor gangs were sent about the country under the supervision of gendarmes and rural agents of the Ministry of Agriculture.

An attempt was made to compensate for the shortage of manpower and livestock by increasing agricultural equipment, largely through import from Germany. If the figures are to be trusted imports in 1941 and 1942 were quite extensive: [18]

	1941	1942
Tractors with ploughs	1,000	2,814
Animal-drawn ploughs	20,000	40,000
Sowing drills	4,000	1,400
Harvesters	2,000	2,230
Hoes	10,000	30,000
Harrows	4,000	9,200
Threshers	200	250

By a law of June 22, 1942, for the organization of agricultural associations, the government attempted to overcome the disadvantages of small strip farming by means reminiscent of the Iorga law of 1931. By this act a group of at least fifteen cultivators residing in the same commune could constitute an agricultural association, authorized to purchase farm machinery, seeds, fertilizers, etc., sell produce in common, purchase or lease land, and obtain credit. The association was not an independent body however. It was to be man-

17. According to an admiring German biography, Antonescu first attracted attention during the 1907 uprising when, as a young lieutenant, he succeeded, without firing a shot, in persuading a crowd of rebellious peasants to disband.

18. Brief accounts of the measures undertaken up to 1943 are given by N. D. Cornǎțeanu, "International Chronicle of Agriculture: Rumania," *International Review of Agriculture, 32* (Rome, July–August, 1941), 247E–254E; and *34* (April, 1943), 156E–164E.

aged by five trustees; the Ministry of Agriculture was to supervise its business transactions, and technical and administrative control lay in the hands of the chief of the agricultural district. Members were obliged to conform to the requirements of the government crop plan. It was reported in 1944 that about 200 such associations had been established.[19]

This law did not really represent anything new in Rumania but was merely one of the various measures which had been applied from time to time to overcome the agrarian impasse. It represents, however, a somewhat different approach from that emphasized by either the National Peasants or the Carolist dictatorship. The National Peasants had placed greatest stress upon credit, cooperatives, and diversification of production, with a view to creating the small peasant on the Western model. The Carolist regime, in its activities of 1938 and 1939, was aiming at consolidation and the creation of middle properties. The law of 1942 was an attempt to improve the situation on the basis of existing circumstances, of utilizing in the most efficient way possible the uneconomic system of land holdings. To be sure, all the approaches overlapped somewhat, but in a way the 1942 act was a bridge to the agricultural policy of the post-1945 government.

The Germans, for their own reasons, were anxious to develop Rumanian agriculture as part of the economy of the new order, although their estimate of what could be achieved in Rumanian agriculture was relatively modest. A wartime analysis by some German experts [20] presented a very dismal picture of Rumanian farming as of 1940. According to their report the principal difficulties lay in the low yield resulting from the small size of the majority of the holdings (they noted that most of the large properties were cultivated in metayage) and in the inadequacy of the transport system, both the general network and the village roads. They doubted whether agriculture itself

19. Otto von Franges, "Agricultural Labour Communities in South Eastern Europe," *International Review of Agriculture, 35* (January–February, 1944), 22E–32E. Von Franges was heartily in favor of these associations, of which similar types had been established in Bulgaria and Yugoslavia. In his opinion they corresponded to traditional labor associations of the Balkan peasants and showed an admirable balance between individualism and collectivism, between control and liberty. He sharply contrasted these associations with agricultural cooperatives. The latter, while having a useful function, were obliged to neglect the poorer peasant. The associations, he felt, were the only possible compensation for the fragmentation of peasant properties and the only means of obtaining a decent improvement of productivity until the slow process of consolidation could take place.

20. H. L. Fensch and O. Thiel, *Rumänien, Untersuchung über die Betriebs- und Ernährungswirtschaftlichen Verhältnisse der Landwirtschaft.* (I have seen only a manuscript Rumanian translation of this study.)

was in any position to remedy either of these defects. They had hopes, however, that measures—such as those taken in 1942—of compensating for inefficient small holdings by means of common use of machines, purchase of seed, and organization of sale could bring some improvements. They believed that under existing circumstances it would be possible to increase agricultural production by 25 per cent over ten years and that some 40 per cent of the surplus of cereals and vegetables would be available for export to Germany.

The actual course of Rumanian agriculture during the war showed no such progress. The area devoted to cereals fell appreciably between 1940 and 1943 because of the labor shortage, the decline in livestock and equipment, and the price controls which held cereal prices well below industrial prices.[21] Yields fell off in the principal grains, maize and wheat. The total production of cereals dropped from a 1935–39 average of 75.7 million quintals (for the area as of January, 1941) to 61–64 million (38 million in 1942 following an exceptionally severe winter).[22] Because of war needs the area devoted to industrial and food crops increased, in most cases as the result of government support and crop plans. It was still very small, however, compared with that under cereals. In livestock the greatest reduction, as was to be expected, was in horses; cattle increased somewhat; sheep, goats, and pigs remained about the same.

The number of draft animals declined by one-third, though the most serious fall was between 1943 and the beginning of 1945; that is, at the time of the final military collapse when both German and Soviet troops were on Rumanian soil. There was a notable increase in the number of tractors (from 4,170 in 1940 to 8,340 in 1943 and 8,178 in 1945), although in the opinion of the Central Institute of Statistics it did not compensate for the decline in draft animals which were the only feasible form of traction on the small strip farms.[23]

21. Area devoted to cereals, 48 județe (area as of January, 1941):

	Millions of hectares
1935–39	7.4
1940	6.8
1941	6.6
1942	6.4
1943	6.6

Source: Institutul Central de Statistică, *Statistica agricolă a României în 1941–1944* (Bucarest, 1947), p. xiii.

22. According to the Central Institute of Statistics, *ibid.*, p. xv, the recorded figures for production may have been well below the actual production because of extensive and often irregular army requisitioning; the wheat crop may have been underestimated by 20 per cent, the maize crop by 10 per cent.

23. Institutul Central de Statistică, *Statistica agricolă a României, Vol. V, Inventarul agricol în Anul 1945* (Bucarest, 1947), p. 14.

The inventory of other agricultural equipment was more or less stable or showed a slight decline.

For all the controls and economic collaboration with Germany the Antonescu dictatorship appears to have accomplished nothing for Rumanian agriculture. The relative improvement, at least in terms of total production, which had appeared after the depression was broken by the war. The position of peasant agriculture was clearly deteriorating, and the industrial boom, arising mainly from war demands, was not an adequate compensation.

Although pessimistic voices could be heard in the Carolist dictatorship, the official attitude was optimistic. During the war years, however, there was increasing concern over the manifest failure of Rumanian agriculture to show any improvement. The agricultural census, taken in the spring of 1941, provided ample evidence of the unsatisfactory situation of the peasant. The veteran agricultural economist, Ionescu-Sișești, who had been writing confident articles throughout the interwar period, was quite gloomy in 1943.

It was anticipated that such a gigantic transformation of property [the 1918–21 reforms] would keep the peasant class in a state of equilibrium for a long time and that the country would benefit from a long period of prosperity because of the distribution of land to the peasants. Unhappily this hope has not been completely realized. Today, when all the claims of the peasants appear satisfied, and there is nothing left to distribute—since a minimum of large and medium property is indispensible —a new peasantry is appearing which threatens to take on a grave character if measures are not adopted in time. The very rapid growth of the population and the advanced fragmentation of properties are engendering this crisis.[24]

His recommendations, however, were largely a recapitulation of the various measures which had been legislated, if not applied with any consequence, in the 1930's: exerting the state's right of pre-emption, preventing subdivision of properties below a certain minimum, encouraging consolidation, and creating larger colonization holdings. If such steps were taken, he said, "the peasantry will be divided into two categories: on the one hand, peasant proprietors with holdings of an adequate size, on the other, a class of agricultural workers living on the product of their labor on the farms of others.[25] Ionescu-Sișești's hopes were not to be realized. Within a year and a

24. G. Ionescu-Sișești, "Le Nouvel Aspect du problème agraire en Roumanie," *Archives pour la science et la réforme sociales, 16,* Nos. 1–4 (1943), 263.
25. *Ibid.,* p. 267.

half the Communist party was in power and the last thing it wanted was such a "Stolypinist" situation in the countryside.

From the point of view of dramatic unity, the Antonescu dictatorship would make a convenient terminal point for recent Rumanian history, as the last act of a rake's progress. With a state encompassing virtually all Rumanians, a new constitution, and an extensive land reform, Rumania had entered the interwar period full, it seemed, of high promise. The promise had not been fulfilled, democracy did not flourish, the peasantry remained poor but prolific. The constitutional regime was replaced by a royal dictatorship and then by the *Walpurgisnacht* of the Iron Guard. Finally, Rumania was swept into the war to join Hitler's crusade. History, however, is no respecter of dramatic unity but persists in its devious course.

XII

THE COMMUNIST PERIOD: THE ADVENT TO POWER, 1944–45

ON August 23, 1944, King Michael, with the cooperation of a four-party bloc comprising the National Peasants, the Liberals, the Socialists, and the Communists overthrew Marshal Antonescu through a skillful palace coup d'état. On September 12 Rumania signed an armistice with the Allies. Six months later, on March 6, 1945, the Groza government, nominally a coalition but dominated by the Communist party, came into office and has remained in power since that date.

The sudden flowering of the Rumanian Communist party, the result of external rather than internal influences, marks a definite break in the continuity of Rumanian politics. Communism was not totally lacking a past in Rumania, and the Communist program had a relevance to Rumanian problems, but without the direct and active intervention of the Soviet Union the Groza government would not have obtained office. To be sure, the Conservative Marghiloman cabinet of 1918 was the direct consequence of Germany's military successes on the Eastern Front; the return of Brătianu in the same year was made possible by the Allied victory. The fall of Vintilă Brătianu and the success of the National Peasants in 1928 were to some extent connected with Rumania's foreign financial relations. Above all, Carol's fall and the Iron Guard and Antonescu dictatorships were certainly conditioned by the Nazi hegemony over southeastern Europe. Rumania has always been affected in its internal politics by direct or indirect foreign influences. Nevertheless, there is a difference.

All the preceding political changes hitherto considered were effected by parties or groups, which, if they were not popular, were at least associated with important Rumanian institutions. Thus the Liberals, the extent of whose popular support was doubtful, formed the oldest party in Rumania and were in control of the nation's banking and financial apparatus. Carol made use of the institution of the monarchy and its tradition of royal paternalism. Antonescu relied upon the army. The National Peasants, less well connected with the institutional framework, one of their weaknesses, were, in their period of growth, the representatives of a broad mass movement in the peasantry. As for the Iron Guard, while its rise was in part fostered by sympathetic politicians and its temporary success after Carol's fall was with the approval of the Germans, it was in its insane way the culmination of a widespread indigenous fascist impulse which had been building up in the interwar years.

The Rumanian Communists, on the other hand, while not altogether without support, enjoyed neither wide popularity (party membership in 1944 was approximately 1,000) nor control of the instruments of power, and they could not, in 1945 at least, have gained the latter without the aid of the Soviet Union. Admittedly, the previous political movements had by 1945 become rather threadbare, either through internal disintegration, senility, or public failure, and one might argue that a break with the past was salutary. But that the Communists were to create the new dispensation was in no way a Rumanian decision. Whatever the merits or shortcomings of communism as such, the Groza government was a Soviet creation. The implications of this fact will be considered shortly.

History of Marxist Parties in Rumania

In the first half of the nineteenth century there were slight signs of pre-Marxist socialism in the Rumanian principalities.[1] Some of Fourier's and Louis Blanc's ideas had been picked up by Rumanian students in Paris, and indeed a short-lived phalanstery was formed at Scaeni near Ploești. Marxist socialism, however, came to Rumania by way of Russia. In the 1870's Iași, capital of Moldavia, was a meeting place and haven for Russian revolutionaries. In 1879 the first Rumanian socialist newspaper, *Basarabia*, was published; its editorials were along Bakuninist-anarchist lines, with a strange flavor of anti-Semitism. In 1881 the first small socialist group in Iași was disbanded by the Rumanian authorities upon the demand of the Russian government.

Between 1887 and 1897 the socialist movement in Rumania revived and developed. Like many currents of foreign thought, Marxism in Rumania was something of a fad. All manner of people employed the terminology. Its political content was loosely defined and combined with anarchist and populist ideas. The intellectual leader of Rumanian socialism was the Russian emigré Constantin Dobrogeanu-

---

1. For a brief account of the socialist movement in Rumania, cf. N. Ghiulea, "Labour Organizations in Rumania," *International Labour Review, 9,* No. 1 (January, 1924), 31–49. C. Titel Petrescu has a lengthy but scrappily organized account in *Socialismul in România.* Trotsky was in Bucarest in 1913; his articles on the Rumanian socialist movement are collected in *Ocherki politicheskoi Rumynii.*

Gherea, whose stream of articles defining Marxism and applying it to Rumania had a lasting influence not only upon Rumanian socialism but upon Rumanian thought in general. In 1884 a socialist study group appeared in Bucarest, and in the following year a newspaper, *Rights of Man*. In 1890 a socialist club began to enter candidates in local and national elections. In 1893 was founded the Rumanian Social Democratic party with a program based upon that of the German Social Democrats. Rumania was recognized as a backward country which could not take the initiative in the socialist movement. The work of the Rumanian socialists was to be preparatory, their tactics moderate and legal. The demands of the program were universal suffrage, administrative decentralization, abolition of the standing army, separation of church and state, equal conditions for women, secularization of schools, equal application of laws, the right of association, limitation of the royal prerogative, a progressive income tax, and an eight-hour day. The program was explicitly antirevolutionary. The new party attempted to organize workers in the few industrial centers of the country, Bucarest, Galați, Brăila, and Ploești, and to anchor the socialist movement to the nascent trade unions. It also tried in 1897 to spread socialism in the villages, but this effort was immediately suppressed by the Conservative government. For the most part, however, in this period the socialist movement was confined to intellectuals, who had made a good deal of progress toward formulating a program which they felt suitable to Rumania's special needs.

Between 1898 and 1900 the socialists hit a crisis. A section of the party, weary of the political wilderness and seeing no future in isolation, were tempted by the devil, collaboration. In 1899, under their influence, the party changed its name from Social Democrat to National Democrat on the grounds that Rumania was not ripe for socialism. In 1900 Constantin Stere, later the populist leader, split the party by taking a group into the Liberal camp. By the turn of the century the first effort at creating a socialist party had collapsed in confusion and disagreement.

The Russian revolution of 1905 and the significant increase in urban and labor population led to a second revival of socialism. In this phase the party found a broader base of support; it had more contact with the working class and the trade unions, and a talented leader in Christian Rakovsky, a doctor of Bulgarian-Dobrogean origin with international socialist connections. The tactics of the party were still reformist. While labor groups in a few towns sided with the peasants in the 1907 uprising, the Social Democratic party took an altogether negative view and admonished the peasants to retire, as they were only playing into the hands of their adversaries. Nevertheless, in the repression that followed, the Liberal government suppressed the Social Democratic party and expelled Rakovsky from the country as an undesirable alien. He was later readmitted by the Conservative government.

The Rumanian Social Democrats campaigned against the Balkan wars, against Rumania's participation, and against the annexation of the Dobrogean quadrilateral. They came out for a federative republic of all the Balkan states, including Turkey. When the First World War came they maintained their antiwar stand and demanded Balkan neutrality. An inter-Balkan socialist conference held in Bucarest in July, 1915, issued a resolution favoring the German antiwar Socialists, Liebknecht and Luxemburg, and the Russian Left-wing socialists; opposing class collaboration and "social patriotism"; and criticizing the passivity of the Bureau of the Second International. On June 15, 1916, just before Rumania's entry into the war, the workers of Galaţi demonstrated against Rumanian participation. After Rumania entered the war, the Social Democrats remained opposed but ineffective. Party papers were confiscated, meetings disbanded, and Rakovsky arrested and imprisoned.

A new phase appeared with the outbreak of the 1917 revolution in Russia. On the first of May Russian troops liberated Rakovsky from the prison at Iaşi, and during the period of complete confusion on the Eastern Front in 1917 and 1918 the Rumanian socialist movement more or less merged with the Russian revolution. Rakovsky himself took an increasingly important part in the Russian revolution, becoming president of the Ukrainian Sovnarkom in 1919. Rumanian Social Democrats, under Mihai Gheorghiu Bujor, formed a Rumanian revolutionary battalion with its headquarters in Odessa. Inside Rumania itself, however, the socialists were repressed, both in Iaşi, held by the Rumanian government, and in Bucarest, occupied by the Germans.

At the end of the war, in the autumn of 1918, the social situation in Rumania was unsettled, and three years later Rakovsky observed, oversanguinely, that "the prospects of a revolutionary movement were excellent, the position of the administration was critical." [2] Within the country new radical parties sprang up, expressing the widespread dislike of Ion I. C. Brătianu, who was considered responsible for Rumania's involvement in a ruinous war. Externally revolutions were stirring in Austria, Hungary, and Germany. On the other

2. Trotsky and Rakovsky, *op. cit.,* p. 138.

hand, the steps taken toward agrarian reform in 1917 and 1918 provided a safety valve for peasant unrest. Rumania was among the victorious powers and Brătianu was soon to fight for its territorial rewards. The Bessarabian issue was already introducing a national element into the relations with Bolshevik Russia. At the same time Brătianu took firm measures against signs of social upheaval.

On December 13, 1918, the government harshly repressed a labor manifestation at the National Theater in Bucarest.[3] Social tension continued through 1919 and 1920 and reached a final climax in the abortive general strike of October 20–28, 1920. The strike was set off by the restrictive measures of the Averescu government, which had been called in as a party of discipline and order. The general council of the Social Democratic party and leaders of the labor syndicates had presented the government with demands to respect the right of association, to recognize work councils in industrial establishments, to remove troops from all factories, and to abolish the state of siege and censorship. The government responded by arresting the socialist and labor leaders, including the deputies to the chamber. The general strike which followed was precipitated by an independent strike of the workers in the railway shops, always the most militant section of Rumanian labor. The strike lasted only seven days and the government had little trouble in breaking it.

After the failure of the general strike the Rumanian socialist movement split, the more radical section forming the Communist party and the moderates the Social Democratic party. Before 1914 the Rumanian socialists had followed the moderate policy of the Second International and were perhaps even more moderate because of Rumania's situation as a backward agrarian state. The war, however, had the effect of associating the party with the more radical section of the international socialist movement. This trend to the Left was not for doctrinal reasons; the Rumanian socialists had not taken a Leninist position. Rather it was because the big Social Democratic parties in the West, in France and Germany, had become involved in the war and because the Russian Marxists, with whom the Rumanian socialist leaders had close personal contacts, were becoming the standard-bearers of militant socialism. Moreover, the antiwar stand of the Rumanian socialists had put them into conflict with the authorities and driven many of them into illegal activity. Finally, the Russian revolution itself produced a wave of enthusiasm which quite

3. According to the socialist leader Moscovici, the demonstration had no revolutionary intent, had occurred more or less by accident, and the socialist leaders had not known of it in advance. Petrescu, *op. cit.*, p. 318.

overpowered any doubts about the "ripeness" of east European countries for the socialist revolution. Thus, such men as Rakovsky and Al. Dobrogeanu-Gherea (the son of the socialist leader), who had been reformists before the war, joined the Communist camp.[4]

According to Rakovsky, the program of the party congress of April, 1919, accepted the basic theses of the Third International, but this trend was opposed by the Social Democratic leaders of Bucovina and Transylvania who were closer to the traditions of Austrian and Hungarian Social Democracy.[5] In 1920 a group of Rumanian delegates was sent to Moscow—solely as observers according to the socialist Petrescu—to examine the situation in Russia and to inform themselves on the principles of the Comintern. This group returned in January, 1921, and it transpired that they had affiliated the Rumanian party with the Third International. A general council met in February, at which the Communists gained control (according to Petrescu, the socialist leaders were in prison as a result of the general strike) and called a general congress for May, 1921. The government now stepped in and arrested for high treason all the delegates to the congress who voted for affiliation, some 70 in number.

After 1921 the Social Democrats and the Communists went their separate ways. In 1922 the Communists attempted to establish a united front in the trade union movement but were defeated. At a general council, the trade unions maintained their political independence; trade union members could belong to any party but party activity within the unions was to be prohibited. In 1925 the General Council of Trade Unions affiliated with the Amsterdam International Federation. The Communists in retaliation set up a "United" Trade Union General Council which never achieved a substantial following but which rendered any trade union activity liable to government repression.

The history of Rumanian Social Democracy between the wars is not inspiring, and the party never achieved a large following. It based itself upon the trade unions, a rather narrow foundation for a political party in Rumania. Moreover, it was never quite clear what the relations between socialism and the trade unions should be. Most of the Social Democratic leaders were trade union officials but in many cases they favored complete separation of political and union activities. There is little evidence that the Socialists had any success

---

4. This enthusiastic and nondoctrinal support of revolution was of course the cause of later friction when the Third International undertook to impose the Leninist outlook on the member parties.

5. Trotsky and Rakovsky, *op. cit.,* p. 140.

in improving labor conditions, partly because of their anxiety lest
their actions be considered subversive.[6] The Rumanian trade union
movement remained weak,[7] legislation passed to assist labor was not
applied, and the representatives of industry were successful in im-
peding labor reforms on the grounds of national interest.[8]

As a political party the Social Democrats had a fundamental handicap. In their interpretation of Marxism they believed that Rumania
had not yet reached the stage where it could embark upon or even directly prepare for the socialist revolution. The hopes of the party
lay not in Rumania itself but in the advanced states of the West. One
of the party leaders, Ilie Moscovici, said in 1923: "Lacking the objective factors—the concentration of capital, sufficient development
of industry, and a large proletarian mass—and not having the subjective factors—education and a class conscious proletariat—Rumania suffers all the contradictions of the capitalist regime without
having the necessary factors for social transformation." [9] Such a
passive outlook, which was admittedly depending upon developments
beyond Rumania to realize its ideals, was scarcely likely to win an
enthusiastic following. The Social Democrats considered it their
principal function to remove the obstacles set by the oligarchy to
the free industrial and capitalist development of Rumania, to lift
the cultural level of the masses, to bring democracy to Rumania, and
to foster international cooperation of labor.

Because of their weak position the Socialists wobbled between maintaining doctrinal purity and collaborating with other parties. They

6. For example, M. Flueraş, in 1926, felt it necessary to explain rather apologetically
that the great interest shown by the workers in labor legislation should not be interpreted as a revolutionary tendency. ILO, *Industrial and Labor Information, 17,*
No. 7 (February 15, 1926), 231.

7. Trade union membership increased only from 25,000 in 1919 to 42,000 in 1929.
Transylvania and the Banat had, in 1929, 25,000 members, the Old Kingdom only 11,000,
Bucovina, 6,000, and Bessarabia, 790. *Ibid., 33,* No. 8 (February 24, 1930), 265.

8. In 1934 the Rumanian Association of Chambers of Commerce and Industry submitted a memorandum to the Ministry of Labor which said, among other things, "The
improvement of the living conditions of workers can only be gradually achieved. Any
defiance of this rule must be detrimental to the national economy in that it would
bring about both a weakening of the credit of the state and an increase in unemployment, thus leading to a worsening of social conditions. The present limits of economic
possibility can only be exceeded by means of an increase of production brought about
through the formation of new capital and through an increase in the productive capacity of labor on a sound economic basis." *Ibid., 49,* No. 11 (March 12, 1934), 352. To a
degree, of course, this statement was perfectly true. On the other hand, the constant
reports of employers' infringements of labor laws, such as the weekly rest act, leave
no doubt that their actions were hardly determined by any such general considerations.
Cf. *Ibid., 52,* No. 11 (December 10, 1934), 325, report by the Rumanian Chamber of
Labor on the application of labor laws.

9. "Lupta de clasă şi transformarea socială," *Doctrinele partidelor politice,* p. 302.

worked with the National Peasants in the 1926 communal elections in an effort to oust the Liberals, and again in the general elections of 1928 which established the Maniu government. A dissenting splinter group broke away to form an Independent Socialist party, somewhat to the Left of the Social Democrats and advocating collaboration with "legal" Communists. Collaboration between the National Peasants and the Social Democrats ceased shortly after the former came to power. The Socialists charged the Maniu government with betraying the working class; at a party congress held in 1930 collaboration was condemned and the party reaffirmed its independence and single-minded loyalty to the workers.

In the years leading up to the Carolist dictatorship the Social Democrats were altogether ineffective and powerless. They drafted numerous resolutions against fascism and in favor of democracy, but were in no position to do anything about either. In 1935 and 1936, when courted by the Communists, who had adopted the Popular Front, they replied that they were unwilling to sign any agreement with the various Communist-front organizations and that common action was possible only if the Communists came into the open and renounced their illegal activities. In the 1937 elections they refused to have anything to do with the National Peasants because of the pact with Codreanu, and succeeded only in reuniting with the Independent Socialists, an achievement of little consequence.

After the overthrow of the parliamentary regime in 1938, the Social Democrats folded up. The collaborationist spirit again made its appearance. The party reexamined its theoretical principles and altered its definition of the state, which was no longer seen as a class instrument but as "an instrument useful and necessary to all." [10] Two of the Social Democratic leaders, Flueraș and Mirescu, entered the labor commission of the Goga-Cuza government. When Carol replaced the trade unions by corporatist bodies, the General Confederation of Labor was absorbed into the Front of National Rebirth, and one of the Socialist leaders, Grigorovici, became an undersecretary in the Ministry of Labor under the dictatorship.[11]

If the Social Democrats found agrarian Rumania an unpromising

10. This change was expressed in an article by Lotar Rădăceanu in *Gândul Vremii* (March–June, 1938), cited in Pătrășcanu, *Problemele de bază*, p. 269. Pătrășcanu was very critical of the theoretical position adopted by Rădăceanu and stated that it cleared the way to accepting the Carolist dictatorship. Still, such facility has its advantages. Rădăceanu is now in the Groza government whereas Pătrășcanu was discharged from the Ministry of Justice and ousted from the Communist party.

11. Titel Petrescu, while admitting a good deal of opportunism in these actions, defends them as necessary to preserve what rights still remained to labor.

environment for their moderate Marxism and their reliance upon the urban working class, the Communists encountered far more serious obstacles. In Rumania the question of communism was completely entangled in the issue of Soviet-Rumanian relations. More than in most European countries communism and high treason were regarded as completely synonymous terms. This national conflict, which the Rumanian Communists could not begin to overcome, dogged their efforts from the start. Rumania's relations with Russia had never been very good; tsarist Russia may have acted as protector of the Balkan Christians, but its own interests in the Black Sea littoral had always been a source of anxiety to the Rumanian principalities. The dispute over Bessarabia, beginning in 1812 and heightened by the territorial transfers of 1856 and 1878, was a constant source of irritation. Because of the Rumanian occupation of Bessarabia in 1918, the Soviet Union and Rumania did not resume full diplomatic relations until 1934.

In addition to this territorial dispute, the Communists faced another difficulty. The Third International was founded in the hope and expectation that the disasters and havoc of the First World War would create sufficient social upheaval to bring about the proletarian revolution. But as has been seen, while revolution threatened to gain the upper hand in many eastern European states, Rumania stood fast and indeed sent troops to put down Bela Kun's Soviet regime in Hungary. As a result Rumania, perhaps more than any state of eastern Europe, regarded itself as the bulwark against bolshevism, both against Soviet territorial advance and against the Communist revolutionary doctrine. All sides were in agreement on the point. Rumanian authors repeatedly referred to the agrarian reform as the most effective protection against communism. At the League of Nations and other international meetings, Rumania exerted a good deal of diplomatic pressure on the grounds of its importance as an outpost against the Soviet Union. For their part the Russians saw in Rumania one of the key points of the *cordon sanitaire*, an advance base for the malevolent capitalist states.

Where were the Communists to find their support in such a country? They sought it among the proletariat, the small peasants, and the national minorities. The proletariat, as the Social Democrats discovered, was too small to be effective, although the Communists did obtain their few nuclei in the industrial centers. As for the small peasants, the Communists, unlike the Social Democrats, tried hard to penetrate the countryside but the land reforms had weakened its revolutionary potentialities. Besides, the Peasant party was much more likely to obtain the support of the peasantry, and did. The

Communists did have some success with the minorities (the present leaders of Rumanian communism, Pauker, Luca, and Bodnaraș are all from the ethnic minorities), but any success in this direction would only intensify the feeling that they were an antinational and treasonous party.

Finally, the Communists were handicapped by the fact that almost from the outset they were an illegal party and with but occasional relaxations remained so throughout the interwar period. Although most of the Rumanian governments were not averse to having the Communists as a whipping boy, the Communists brought a good deal of their difficulties on their own heads by their tactics, which were devious, disingenuous, and unsuccessful. In 1921 Rakovsky remarked with some bitterness that General Averescu was arresting not only the "illegal" party workers but those working "lawfully." [12] In a similar spirit a Communist pamphlet of 1925, describing the uprising at Tatar Bunar in Bessarabia, castigated the cordon sanitaire and the provocative accusations that the Soviet Union was stirring up trouble, but went on to say, "Not only the free booters of Bucarest, but the capitalists of the whole world are trembling before the convulsions of the proletarian giant. They fear that the red wave rolling out of the East will burst the Dniester dam and flood onward to the coast of the Atlantic Ocean." [13] Although this dual policy of pursuing both legal and illegal activities received a brilliant defense and elaboration in Lenin's pamphlet, *Left-Wing Communism, an Infantile Disorder*, it has probably, in the long run, done the Communists far more harm than good. It may be, as Lenin said, that a good warrior should know all his weapons, legal as well as illegal, parliamentary as well as revolutionary, but such a military plan of campaign should have remained a highly classified document, not a broadside, and was bound to lose effectiveness with repetition. As soon as the enemy became aware of this tactic the Communists were left open to the charge of bad faith no matter what course they followed. In the case of Rumania, of course, they had very little opportunity for any legal activity in their own name, but their efforts to achieve fronts of one complexion or another in the 1920's and 1930's were all unsuccessful.

The Rumanian Communist party got off to an unfortunate start. The arrest in 1921 of the delegates who had voted for affiliation with the Third International deprived it of many of its leaders. Among

12. Ch. Rakovsky, "The Communist Movement in Roumania," *The Communist International*, No. 13 (n.d.), pp. 112–114.

13. *Bessarabia . . . The Roumanian Hell,* published in English by the British Section of the International Class War Prisoners Aid (London, n.d.), p. 13.

the active members who took their place was Ana Pauker, a young Jewish schoolteacher from Moldavia who had joined an illegal group in the Social Democratic party in 1918. She had married Marcel Pauker, son of a leading Rumanian publisher.[14] Elected to the Central Committee she became one of the party's most determined fighters. In 1924 when the party was definitely outlawed, she was arrested, but was subsequently released and left the country.

The directives of the Comintern did not facilitate the work of the Rumanian Communists. For example, the resolution on the national question, passed by the Fifth World Congress of the Communist International, stated that under the Versailles system a number of small imperialist states had been created in eastern Europe to fight the proletarian revolution.[15] The states had been formed by the annexation of large territories with foreign populations.

At the same time the struggle of the oppressed peoples against national oppression has become a struggle against the power of the imperialistic bourgeoisie who were victorious in the world war, since the strengthening of the new imperialist powers means the strengthening of the forces of world imperialism. The importance of the struggle against national oppression is still further augmented by the fact that the nationalities oppressed by Poland, Czechoslovakia, Yugoslavia, Rumania, and Greece, in their social composition are largely peasants, and the struggle for their national liberation is at the same time the struggle of the peasant masses against foreign landlords and capitalists.

Under these conditions, the resolution declared, the general formula, "The right of every nation to self-determination even to the extent of separation," should be rendered more specific: "The political separation of oppressed peoples from Poland, Rumania, Czechoslovakia, Yugoslavia, and Greece." The resolution noted with disapproval that certain Communist parties were falling into deviations on this question, that their slogans were not directed against the states founded on national oppression but toward partial reform and autonomy within existing boundaries.

The resolution was even more specific on the Ukrainian question, an evident example of the overlapping of Soviet and Comintern aims. The congress declared that the Ukrainian national problems in Po-

14. C. G. Costa-Foru, *Aus den Folterkammern Rumäniens,* p. 21; C. Bobrovskaya, "Two Bolshevik Heroines," *The Communist International, 14,* No. 3 (1937), 958–960.

15. "Resolution of V. World Congress of Comintern on National Question in Central Europe and Balkans," *The Communist International,* New Ser., No. 7 (December, 1924–January, 1925), pp. 93–99.

land, Rumania, and Czechoslovakia formed one Ukrainian problem demanding a common solution for all three countries. In this case it opposed slogans of autonomy for Carpathian Russia, the western Ukraine, Bessarabia, and Bucovina because they were directed toward forming a coalition with the wealthy strata of the Ukrainian peasantry. The congress, therefore, considered it necessary "for the Communist Parties of Poland, Czechoslovakia, and Rumania to launch the general slogan of separation of the Ukrainian lands from Poland, Czechoslovakia, and Rumania, and their union with the Soviet Ukraine and through it with the U.S.S.R." As for Transylvania and Dobrogea, the congress merely recommended that these areas be separated from Rumania and made independent regions.

Much of the nationalities program of the congress was admirable, its opposition to the hypernationalism of the Balkan states, its championing of national equality and cultural and educational rights for minorities. But these reform measures were clearly of less importance than the demand for separation. It is difficult to see how a party advocating the loss of Transylvania, Dobrogea, Bessarabia, and Bucovina was going to gain much popularity in Rumania, especially when the majority of the population in these areas (with the exception of Bucovina) and much the greatest number of peasants were Rumanians. With such instructions the Rumanian Communist party was never able to shake off the imputation of being an antinational party.

In addition to handing out such uncomfortable assignments, the Comintern heckled the Rumanian Communists for lapsing into any number of deviations. Because the party had been forced underground, it had been unable to conduct the necessary educational campaign to bolshevize itself, with the result that there were deplorable signs of "ultra-left and right liquidatorial tendencies." [16] The Sixth Plenum of the Executive Committee of the Comintern in 1926 felt called upon to rebuke the Rumanian Communists and directed them to correct their errors. Specifically the party was to issue a journal, fight the Right-wing deviations, and "struggle against even the smallest sectional manifestations."

At this time the party was troubled by two questions, the trade union issue and a united front against the Liberals. With regard to the "unitary" trade unions and their relations to the Amsterdam Union, the Central Committee of the Rumanian Communist party issued the following orders:

16. Al. Badulescu, in a review of the Rumanian party organ *Lupta de Clasă*, *The Communist International*, *4*, No. 15 (October 15, 1927), 311–312.

The duty of mobilizing the working class masses to insure the legality of the unitary trade unions is a primary one for us Communists. Although the unitary trade unions are not by any means a Communist organization and still less a Communist Party organization, as the Social Democrats and the bourgeoisie together maintain, they are the one legal organization based on the class struggle, and it is the duty of the Communists to use all their influence in the unitary and reformist trade unions, in the workshops and factories, for rousing the worker to fight for the legality of the unitary trade unions.

With this approach it is not surprising that the Social Democrats should have complained that wherever the Communists showed an interest in trade union matters, it was disastrous to the unions.

The Sixth Plenum criticized the Rumanian Communist party for its tactical errors in the 1926 communal elections when the party had preached the tactics of the united front of the working class with all opposition bourgeois parties against the Liberal oligarchy. This policy was considered to involve a serious misreading of the Rumanian situation. The error—it was an error in 1926 at any rate—lay in failing to realize that the Liberals were the most highly developed section of the Rumanian bourgeoisie, and that no real anti-Liberal bloc on the side of the opposition parties (i.e., the National Peasants) was possible. The effort to create such a bloc was a serious error, since it "obscures the class-consciousness of the working class, it gives rise to illusions which prevent the crystallization of the one social force which is actually capable of putting an end to the dictatorship of the Liberals: the united front of the proletariat with the broad masses of the peasantry, liberated from the guardianship of the opposition bourgeoisie." In effect this meant that the Communists were not to work with the National Peasants in ousting the Liberals but were rather to attract the peasants away from them.

In terms of the Rumanian situation this tactical directive of the Comintern was absolutely hopeless, although in a negative way it was correct in forecasting the difficulties in ousting the Liberals from their entrenched positions in the Rumanian economy. It must also be admitted that the Communists foresaw the dangers of Carol's return. "The 'Persecution and Exile of Prince Carol,' " said *Lupta de Clasă*, the party organ, "utilized politically by the opposition bourgeoisie can win over petty-bourgeois sections and create the illusion among many workers that a Rumanian 'Mussolini' regime would be in a position to change the miserable conditions of the masses. That Prince Carol is closely associated with the fascist organizations in Rumania is an open secret."

As might be expected, the victory of the National Peasants in 1928 caused no rejoicing among the Communists. In later years they wrote of the National Peasants as having come in on a wave of popular protest against the Liberals; but the Communists themselves were hostile to the National Peasants before 1928 and fought with them throughout their term in office. Under the National Peasants Bessarabia remained a center of discontent and international friction; Vaida Voevod courted the Iron Guard as allies against the Communists.

To some extent at least this conflict arose from the fact that the National Peasants came to office at just the time the Comintern went off on an ultra-Left tangent, denouncing socialists as social-fascists, and appeared firmly convinced that the Western powers were preparing an immediate assault upon the Soviet Union.[17] During this period Rumania was considered to have a foremost place in the anti-Soviet plans of the Western imperialists. All the energies of the National Peasants were described as being employed against the U.S.S.R., and even the feeble Rumanian Social Democrats were called warmongers.[18]

The Comintern again felt called upon to rebuke the Rumanian comrades. "In spite of the most savage terror, the Communist Party lives and becomes stronger. The only obstacle in the path to the growth of its influence over the proletariat and the toiling masses lies in the *slow* surmounting of *right opportunist* conceptions in some sections of its work, particularly in the field of the peasant movement." [19] The error here was the old heresy of regarding the peasantry as a social unit and failing to split the poor peasants from the kulaks. Counting on the depression to produce a revolutionary situation—although the swing to the Left had preceded the depression—the Comintern apparently had hopes of bringing social issues to the boil. "The increasing upsurge of the class struggle creates a basis on which the Communist Party could win the trust of the toiling masses, establish its hegemony. . . . With a correct policy the Communist Party can become a factor for the acceleration of the approach of a revolutionary situation." [20]

In retrospect this ultra-Left tactic of the early 1930's must be regarded as a disaster which wrought a great deal of damage. The

17. Of course these suspicions were fed by such events as Maniu's reported request in 1930 that the British survey the Black Sea coast with a view to constructing a strong naval base near Constanța. Pavel Pavel, *Why Rumania Failed*, p. 240.
18. T. Marin, "The Role of Rumania in Intervention against the U.S.S.R.," *The Communist International*, 7, No. 10 (May 15, 1931), 300.
19. *Ibid.*, p. 302.
20. *Ibid.*, p. 303.

veering from Right to Left in the Comintern in the 1920's had brought no results but had merely caused the local parties to be regarded as altogether untrustworthy and treacherous political allies. The tactics in 1930 of smearing all non-Communist groups as fascist certainly did nothing to prevent the rise of fascism. It is hard to say how important this was in Rumania. The Rumanian Communist party was clearly on the fringes of politics and failed to make any appreciable headway. By its irresponsible behavior, however, it enabled the parties of the Right to use the Communist label as a means of discrediting all working class activity.

The last effort of the Rumanian Communists to pursue a revolutionary line was the Grivița railway strike of 1933, in which many of the later Communist leaders—Gheorghiu-Dej, Vasile Luca, and Pătrășcanu—were involved and arrested. This strike, which began with economic demands, quickly assumed a political character. Vaida Voevod's National Peasant government violently suppressed it. After that, as Pătrășcanu said, the radicalization of the masses served to fortify the Iron Guard and the labor movement was put on the defensive.

The rise of Hitler and the realization that the fascist onslaught was not necessarily the immediate prelude to the Communist revolution was belatedly met by a shift in the party line, officially inaugurated at the Seventh World Congress of the Communist International held in the summer of 1935. Gheorghe Dimitrov, in the leading speeches, criticized the previous practice of calling Social Democrats social-fascists and came out for a popular front of democratic forces against fascism. Reflecting this change was an article by one of the Rumanian Communist leaders, Boris Stefanov.[21] "We are basing ourselves," he said, "upon the undoubted fact that the overwhelming majority of the working population of Rumania and even a considerable section of the bourgeoisie are opposed to fascism." What was required was a concentration of democratic forces, including the bourgeois parties, in an anti-fascist Popular Front. The Social Democrats were requested not to remain aloof and even the National Peasants received moderate praise: "The National Tsaranist (Peasant) Party is one of the biggest mass democratic forces in Rumania. Despite all the waverings and reactionary tendencies of some of its leaders, despite its great sins in the past in its relation to the Ru-

---

21. Boris Stefanov, "The Concentration of Democratic Forces in Rumania," *The Communist International, 14,* No. 3 (1937), 943. Stefanov, in 1920, had been one of the members of the general council of the Socialist party who signed the ultimatum for the general strike.

manian people, the National Peasant Party is nevertheless today one of the most important anti-Fascist forces." Stefanov undertook to refute criticisms that the Communist party was undemocratic, illegal, and antinational. As to the charge that it put forward irredentist slogans aimed at separating the new provinces from Rumania he replied that while the Communist party was against national oppression and for national self-determination it was the sworn enemy of the fascists who were trying to utilize the national issue to tear away Transylvania and Dobrogea and subject them to the fascist yoke. Significantly, even in this reconciliatory mood there was no mention of Bessarabia.

This change of tactics had no important results in the course of Rumanian politics. The Social Democrats remained suspicious and aloof. A Democratic Union was set up in the last years of the Tătărescu cabinet for the purpose of achieving a broad coalition against the extreme Right but, as Pătrășcanu said, while it was a legal movement it worked "in the ideological cadres of the Communist Party." [22] The Tătărescu government dealt severely with the Communists. In November, 1934, the party, with all its affiliates, was again dissolved; although it had never been reinstated after 1924 its front, the Workers and Peasants bloc, had participated in elections in the early 1930's. In 1936 was held the much publicized trial of nineteen Communists, including Ana Pauker who received a sentence of ten years' imprisonment.

At the time of the 1937 elections the Communists again attempted to create a Popular Front. This effort was foiled by the Maniu-Codreanu pact and by the Social Democrats' refusal to cooperate with either the National Peasants or the Communists. The Communists eventually threw their modicum of support to the National Peasants, a move which was later regarded as a mistake.[23] In retrospect it is indeed lamentable that some sort of Popular Front was not created in 1937, the last relatively free election which Rumania was to enjoy, but certainly the Communists by their previous activity had contributed to rendering such a front impossible and must share the responsibility for the breakdown of Rumanian parliamentary government.

Shortly after the German-Soviet pact, in December, 1939, Boris Stefanov, the same who had ardently supported the Popular Front

22. Pătrășcanu, *Sous trois dictatures,* p. 110.
23. According to Pătrășcanu, the Communists should have forced collaboration upon the Social Democrats, who, in his view, could not easily have refused; if the Social Democratic leaders had later tried to break away, they could have been unmasked. *Ibid.,* p. 134.

and had denied that the Communist party was antinational, wrote an article in *The Communist International* attacking British and French capital and its attempt to drag Rumania into the imperialist war, insisting that Rumania's interests demanded a treaty of mutual assistance with the Soviet Union (presumably modeled after the Soviet treaties with the Baltic states which involved the establishment of Russian bases and armed forces in these countries) and directing the Rumanian Communists to work for the right of self-determination in the annexed provinces (Bessarabia, Bucovina, Transylvania, and Dobrogea), even if this meant their political separation from Rumania. Although the Soviet Foreign Office publicly denied that Stefanov represented the views of the Soviet government, the article provides some evidence that the Russian interest in Rumania at this time was not limited solely to the recovery of Bessarabia. When this province and Northern Bucovina were taken over in the summer of 1940, the Rumanian Communists naturally defended the action and placed the blame on Carol for his bellicose declaration in the spring that he would fight for these areas. One other event, of importance for the future, occurred in 1940: Ana Pauker, who had been in a Rumanian prison since 1936, was exchanged for two members of the Rumanian parliament who had been picked up in Bessarabia when the Russians moved in.

After Hitler's declaration of war on the Soviet Union, the Rumanian Communists again shifted their tactics and called for resistance to the German aggression, but unlike the Communists in Bulgaria, Greece, and Yugoslavia they seem to have achieved very little in the way of partisan activity or sabotage.[24]

The Formation of the Groza Government

In 1944 a four-party bloc headed by Iuliu Maniu for the National Peasants, Constantin Brătianu for the Liberals, C. Titel Petrescu for the Social Democrats, and Lucretiu Pătrășcanu for the Communists collaborated with King Michael and his intimate advisers in preparing for the coup d'état of August 23 which ousted Marshal Antonescu, expelled the Germans from Bucharest, and brought Rumania to the side of the Allies. Negotiations for a Rumanian capitulation had been carried on sporadically in various neutral capitals since 1943, generally in Maniu's name, and in some cases with the knowledge of Marshal Antonescu and his Foreign Minister Mihai An-

24. In 1944 there was a good deal of vague talk about their deeds of derring-do, but I could never obtain any specific examples.

tonescu. These negotiations were not successful and were impeded principally by the Rumanians' understandable if unrealistic reluctance to face the fact that they must surrender to the Soviet Union and the Red Army. Their repeated requests for an Anglo-American landing in the Balkans or for some type of Western protection against the foe to the East had no possibility of success, given the strategic and political arrangements arrived at by the Big Three, and could only serve to intensify the suspicions of the Russians, who were in an increasingly powerful position as their forces drove westward into Europe. The coup finally came after a Soviet offensive broke the German lines in northern Moldavia in the summer of 1944. Following the coup a provisional government was formed under General Sanatescu; the four party chiefs were ministers but most of the cabinet posts went to army officers, in the expectation, apparently, that the first days of the government would be far more seriously threatened by conflict with the Germans than proved to be the case.

By the terms of the armistice signed in Moscow on September 12 Rumania was to join the Allies against Germany, supply twelve infantry divisions, intern German and Hungarian forces, and provide free passage for Soviet troops. It was obliged to face three economic obligations: provide for the Allied Command in Rumania, pay to the U.S.S.R. reparations of $300,000,000 over six years, and restore all loot taken by Rumanian troops from the Soviet Union during the war. The 1940 Soviet-Rumanian frontier was reestablished, but the Vienna Award giving northern Transylvania to Hungary was nullified. All persons arrested for favoring the United Nations or for racial reasons were to be released; war criminals were to be arrested; and fascist and Hitlerite formations disbanded. The application of the armistice was to be supervised by an Allied Control Commission operating under the Allied (Soviet) High Command. The term in parenthesis was clearly the ultimate authority.

With the arrival of the Russians the Rumanian Communist party took on new life and a new leadership in Ana Pauker, Vasile Luca, and Emil Bodnaraş, all of whom had learned their communism the hard way and had spent many years in the Soviet Union.[25] In Rumania as in the other eastern European states a distinction may be made between the purely local Communists, many of whose connections had been primarily with Western Communist parties, and the Moscow-trained group. The difference is somewhat difficult to define, since

25. In the beginning none of the three assumed official posts; Ana Pauker was occupied with high policy, Luca, among other things, edited the party organ *Scânteia* (*The Spark*), and Bodnaraş appears to have been busy preparing his armed squads.

all were Leninists, all disapproved of Social Democratic reformist policies, and all believed in party discipline. Yet there was a difference, which may be illustrated by an example. Communists who had participated in the coup of August 23, were pleased that Rumania had switched sides so facilely and that the country had been spared the devastation of an invasion. Among the people coming from the East, however, there was some disappointment that the state structure had remained intact and they rather regretted that the issue had not been settled by force of arms, which would have cleared the way for immediate Communist reconstruction. This difference in view led to a number of arguments as to whether communism could be created on a rubble heap, an important issue, of course, in the interpretation of Marxism. Those who approached the subject theoretically held to the belief that communism should cap the existing economic structure. The Russian experience, however, seemed to create a different emphasis: once one had achieved power and cleared the political air, communism could proceed to work constructively on the most unpromising type of terrain.

The four-party bloc soon showed signs of strain. Early in October the National Democratic Front was launched, comprising the Communist party, the Social Democratic party, the Ploughmen's Front, the Union of Patriots, as well as representatives of the newly revived trade unions. The Union of Patriots was a rather amorphous body, often called the vestibule to the Communist party, with the apparent purpose of attracting to the National Democratic Front nonproletarian elements, professional men, and intellectuals; it never achieved any particular importance.

The Ploughmen's Front, however, deserves some mention. It was originally founded at Deva in Transylvania in 1933. Its leader was the rather eccentric but prosperous landowner and industrialist, Petru Groza, who had been a minister in Marshal Averescu's People's party cabinets of 1920 and 1926. Initially it seems to have been a straightforward radical peasant movement, rather in the spirit of Mihalache's peasantism of 1920, born in protest against the agricultural debt load resulting from the depression and against the failure of the National Peasants to fulfill their role as spokesmen for the poor cultivator. Its 1933 program was largely a series of peasant demands; three-fourths of the amount of debts to be cancelled, the remaining fourth to be paid over a more or less extended period of time, depending upon the size of the debtor's property; monetary reform to provide more money; reforms in the civil service to prevent nepotism and the holding of multiple posts; the extension of expropriation to properties over 100 hectares as well as expropriation of forest land; abolition of special privileges to industry, monopolies and cartels; reduction of the cost of the products of state monopolies; abolition of metayage, payment in kind, and labor dues; increased mechanization of agriculture; and a truly democratic regime.[26]

During the period of the attempted Popular Front it collaborated with the Communist party affiliates and strongly opposed the tendency of the peasants to join the Iron Guard.[27] During the 1930's it did not achieve any widespread following except in Transylvania, but during the months immediately after August 23 it made rapid strides throughout Rumania, an expansion that was not altogether artificial but did represent an appeal to peasant dissatisfaction. By 1944, however, it had fallen under the direction of the Communists, who were unquestionably the guiding force in the National Democratic Front, and its later function was largely as the rural arm of the Communist party.

An important feature in the political situation in the months after the armistice was the fact that while the Rumanian state structure in the central Bucarest administration had remained intact, the countryside was politically almost a *tabula rasa*. The six years of dictatorships plus the war had broken up local party organizations and their connections with the party leadership. To a considerable degree the political leaders in Bucarest were generals without armies.[28] This exceptional concentration of all political life in the capital, although there has always been a great deal of centralization, gave a certain advantage to the parties of the Left which could rally the workers in the industrial sections of the capital for demonstrations and processions.

After a three weeks' political crisis, on November 5 a more "politi-

---

26. For a history of the Ploughmen's Front, cf. Gheorghe Micle, *Răscoala pământului; istoria luptelor politice ale țăranimii române 1933–1945* (Bucarest, 1945).

27. In 1937, Romulus Zăroni, who was briefly Minister of Agriculture in the Groza government, wrote a simple but very clear and effective pamphlet explaining why the hard-pressed Rumanian peasant should not be tempted by the antidemocratic reaction of the fascists: *De ce nu trebue să fie plugarul român fascist* (Cluj, n.d.).

28. During December, 1944, and January, 1945, I made fairly extensive field trips through Transylvania, Moldavia, and southern Bucovina. The farther I went from Bucarest the less organized were the local branches of the historical parties. In many cases the local Liberal and National Peasant leader had received no word whatsoever from his party's headquarters. The most impressive movement was the rapid expansion of the Ploughmen's Front which was extending its branches up into northern Moldavia and west to Timișoara. At the same time, in villages not far from Deva, its point of origin, there were many peasants who had never heard of the organization. It was my impression that, at that time at least, the growth of the Ploughmen's Front was by no means merely an invention of the National Democratic Front propagandists.

cal" coalition government was set up, again under General Sanatescu, with ministerial seats going to members of each of the four parties of the democratic bloc. This ministry was short-lived partly because of the vehement objections of the National Democratic Front to the National Peasant Minister of the Interior, N. Penescu. The case of Penescu is a perfect example of the curious political situation at this time. There is no question that the reason why the Communist-inspired National Democratic Front attacked Penescu was because it wanted control of that important ministry for itself. The directness with which Communist parties have gone after the ministry of the interior in all the eastern European states is well known. At the same time, Penescu was in fact violently anti-Soviet and anti-Communist and had indeed organized a section in his ministry to keep watch on the Communist party. That is to say, the Communists would have been quite justified in suspecting Penescu of hostile intentions, but that was not the reason they wanted him removed. In fact, the arguments they employed in the press were altogether disingenuous.

On December 2 the Sanatescu cabinet was replaced by a new government under General Radescu, who had gained a reputation for speaking bluntly to the Germans and being put in a concentration camp. The cabinet was about the same; Radescu took over the Ministry of the Interior, with the Communist Teohari Georgescu as Undersecretary. Petru Groza was Vice-Premier. For a time it appeared as though this ministry would be stable.

In January, 1945, however, two of the leading Rumanian Communists, Ana Pauker and Gheorghiu-Dej, went to Moscow. From all evidence it appears that they were given permission, or were instructed, to carry on their campaign. Shortly after their return, the National Democratic Front announced a bid for power on the basis of its program. By this program Rumania was to make a maximum war effort and to strengthen and democratize the army. There was to be an elimination of fascists, arrest and trial of war criminals, and honest fulfillment of the armistice terms. Above all, an agrarian reform was to be carried through. The Front announced that if it came to office Northern Transylvania would be handed over to Rumania. In February the crisis steadily mounted, with violent press polemics and periodic criticisms from the Soviet radio at the laxness with which the Radescu government was carrying out the armistice conditions. At first the attack was directed against the National Peasants and the Liberals, but when General Radescu rather untactfully indicated his displeasure with the agitation and demands, the Front turned against him. The National Peasant and Liberal papers were suppressed, in one case by a Soviet order, in the other by a strike of the printers' union. Teohari Georgescu refused to take orders from Radescu and demanded that the officials in the Ministry of Interior pay no attention to the general.

The crisis reached a climax on February 24 when, at the conclusion of a large National Democratic Front demonstration, the crowd moved into the palace square and headed toward the Ministry of the Interior. Shots were fired, several people were killed, and that night in a rash— and final—broadcast General Radescu roundly abused the Communist leaders Pauker and Luca, and called on the army to stand by him.[29] Certainly Radescu was a greatly provoked man but owing his appointment to an agreement of the four parties he was not in a position to take an independent stand when this coalition broke down under the Communist attack. Moreover, by his rather intemperate language and appeal to the army he left himself open to damaging attacks from the National Democratic Front and the Russians.

The Soviet Union, in the person of Deputy Commissar Andrei Vyshinsky, now stepped in and demanded General Radescu's immediate resignation. After some hesitation King Michael agreed and started consultations for a new cabinet; again Vyshinsky intervened and demanded that a National Democratic Front government under Petru Groza be installed.[30] Meanwhile the Soviet command had taken the necessary precautions. There was at that time only one Rumanian force capable of resisting the National Democratic Front's armed formations—the army. The Russians ordered the Rumanian units stationed in and near Bucarest to be sent to the front, and the capital was denuded of troops. The following weekend witnessed another mass demonstration which was clearly in a position to take over the government forcibly if need be. In the midst of the demonstration it was announced that the king had accepted the Groza government. On March 6, 1945, it was installed, as a coalition of the groups making up the National Democratic Front, and also including an insignificant

29. This riot is to me a particularly discouraging example of the difficulty of writing history *wie es eigentlich gewesen*. This incident, as it later proved, was the event which led to the overthrow of the Radescu government and the installation of the Groza cabinet. I had watched the procession and was in the crowd no more than fifty feet from the first shots. Yet at that time and since I have been unable to discover precisely what happened. I do know that the government had kept Rumanian troops off the street that day to avoid inciting trouble. The crowd did move toward the Ministry of the Interior building, although it showed little signs of direction. The first shots were fired from a small piece and from somewhere in the crowd, but by whom and for what purpose I do not know, although there has been no lack of stories and explanations.

30. An account of Vyshinsky's actions, taken from official American sources, is given in James F. Byrnes, *Speaking Frankly* (New York; London, 1947), pp. 50–55.

dissident National Peasant party and a Liberal fraction under the opportunist Gheorghe Tătărescu, whose government in 1936 had sentenced Ana Pauker to ten years' imprisonment.

Why did the Groza government come to power? This question is difficult to answer, even though many of the facts are reasonably well established, because it involves the intentions behind the foreign policy of the Soviet Union. In the first place, the Groza regime was directly and positively installed by the Soviet Union, in an explicit manner by Vyshinsky, but even before that by the Soviet decision to break up the Radescu government through the National Democratic Front. Although there is no convincing evidence that the National Democratic Front possessed broad popular support, it was not without effective strength in Bucarest. Before it came to office it was able to assemble large crowds of demonstrators, which were really quite impressive despite the tendency of Tass and the Communist press greatly to inflate their numbers. Moreover, it had special squads of armed guards, which had obtained weapons in preparation for the August 23 coup and had subsequently refused to relinquish them, much to the dismay of the National Peasants and Liberals. Nevertheless, they could not have stood up against the Rumanian army had General Radescu been given the opportunity to employ it. In no sense, however, did the National Democratic Front represent the will of the people, although it must be said that at the time there was a general political vacuum in Rumania. It is doubtful whether the historical parties represented the will of the people except in the purely negative sense of being anti-Russian.

In the second place, the U.S.S.R. did not overthrow the Radescu government because the Rumanians were sabotaging the armistice agreement, or to guarantee the lines of communication to the Hungarian front, or because the Radescu government could not maintain order. If the latter was true it was because Radescu had been deprived of the means. This is not to say that the Rumanians of the historical parties were behaving in a manner satisfactory to the Russians. Hatred of Russia among these parties was bitter and profound. There was a constant hope that somehow the Western powers would come to their rescue. Well before the end of the war, and indeed immediately after the armistice, many nonfascist Rumanians expressed the belief that a conflict betwen the Soviet Union and the Western powers was the only hope for Rumania. Nor were the Rumanians altogether reasonable in their fulfillment of the armistice conditions. There were numerous cases where they tried to squirm out of a delivery by means of elaborate legal technicalities in a manner inevitably highly exasperating to the Soviet authorities. In a word, many Rumanians did not realize the implications of the new situation and were doing everything in their power to avoid the consequences of their military defeat. Undoubtedly this attitude was well known to the Russians; it would have been difficult to have missed it.

Nevertheless, as far as may be judged from the evidence available, conditions in Rumania and the behavior of non-Communist Rumanian politicians were not a primary factor in determining Russian action; Soviet initiative in installing the National Democratic Front government did not arise from Soviet-Rumanian relations but was an aspect of Soviet policy regarding the pattern of the postwar world and Russia's relations with the Western powers, Great Britain, and the United States. It might be well here to review briefly some of the information which has come to light on Rumania's place internationally in the last part of the Second World War. The Soviet Union was certainly interested in preserving its gains made in eastern Europe before Hitler's attack, and as early as 1941 was pressing the British and American governments, without success, for an agreement on post-war territorial boundaries. Soviet frontiers with Rumania were to be those of 1940, i.e., Bessarabia and northern Bucovina being rein-corporated in the Soviet Union. In addition, the Soviet regime desired special facilities for bases in Rumania.[31] On April 2, 1944, however, as Soviet troops advanced into northern Rumania, Molotov gave a reassuring announcement: "The Soviet government declares that it does not pursue the aim of conquering any part of Rumanian territory or of changing the existing social order in Rumania."

In May, 1944, the British government proposed to Russia a division of areas of predominant interest, whereby, "in the main, Rumanian affairs should be the concern of the Soviet Government and the Greek affairs the concern of United Kingdom. This British-Russian understanding would apply only to war conditions and would not affect the rights and responsibilities which each of the three great powers would have to exercise at the peace settlement." [32] On the condition that it be limited to three months' trial and definitely did not establish postwar spheres of influence, President Roosevelt gave

31. Cordell Hull, *The Memoirs of Cordell Hull* (2 vols., New York, 1948), II, 1167. In connection with the request for bases in Rumania, one might note that in 1943 the Soviet Ambassador to Great Britain, Maisky, stated that the U.S.S.R. probably would not oppose a Balkan federation, provided it excluded Rumania, another indication, perhaps, of a special status for Rumania in Soviet plans. Robert E. Sherwood, *Roosevelt and Hopkins, an Intimate History* (New York, 1948), p. 714.
32. Hull, *op. cit.*, II, 1451–1455. Roosevelt's approval was given without Hull's knowledge and against his wishes.

American approval to the proposal. It is evident that Churchill's move was an attempt to regain the position lost when his plan for an Anglo-American invasion of the Balkans was overruled in 1943; he was clearly interested in securing Greece for Britain's Mediterranean sphere.

When Churchill and Eden visited Moscow in October, 1944, this arrangement was extended even further in establishing the degrees of influence the two powers should enjoy in the various Balkan states. According to former Secretary of State Byrnes, "We knew they had reached the informal understanding that, if the British found it necessary to take military action to quell internal disorders in Greece, the Soviets would not interfere. In return, the British would recognize the right of the Soviets to take the lead in maintaining order in Rumania." [33] The result undoubtedly was, as Hull points out, that "the Russians took it for granted that by the agreement of June 1944, Britain and the United States had assigned them a certain portion of the Balkans, including Rumania and Bulgaria, as their sphere of influence." [34] Hull was correct in his starting assumption that an agreement ostensibly limited to military affairs could too easily lead to political arrangements of a lasting nature. On the other hand, his opposition to spheres of influence and independent political action by one or two of the great powers does not seem to have been wholly consistent, nor would it have been convincing to the Russians, given the evident political action of the United States and Great Britain in Italy where the Russians had very little voice, though Hull maintains they were kept informed. In brief, by the end of 1944 not only did the Russians have considerable reason to believe that Rumania was in their sphere, but Anglo-American political as well as military action in Italy provided them with a precedent for independent action. The first power to make use of the October agreement was Great Britain in its intervention against ELAS during the Greek crisis of December, 1944.[35] Russia, at this time, kept to the bargain; the Soviet press and radio gave no sign of support for the Left-wing Greek partisans.

Such was the state of affairs when, in January, 1945, Russia appears to have given the green light to the Rumanian Communists.

33. Byrnes, op. cit., p. 53.

34. Hull, op. cit., II, 1458. Sherwood states, however, that Roosevelt sent a cable to Stalin indicating that the United States regarded the Churchill-Stalin conversations as "preliminary" and not committing the American government. Sherwood, op. cit., p. 834.

35. For recent accounts, from different points of view, of the background to the British intervention in Greece, see L. S. Stavrianos, "The Immediate Origin of the Battle of Athens," and W. H. McNeill, "The Outbreak of Fighting in Athens, December 1944," both in The American Slavic and East European Review, 8, No. 4 (December, 1949).

Between this decision, however, and the installation of the Groza cabinet in March the Yalta Conference took place. Although Stalin at Yalta made several pointed remarks to the effect that he "had no intention of criticizing British actions in Greece, nor . . . any intention of interfering in that country," [36] the agreement signed by the Big Three made no mention of spheres of interest. On the contrary, the declaration regarding liberated areas in Europe seemed wholly in accord with American interests and was, with slight modifications, the same as Roosevelt's proposed text:

The Premier of the Union of Soviet Socialist Republics, the Prime Minister of the United Kingdom, and the President of the United States of America . . . jointly declare their mutual agreement to concert during the temporary period of instability in liberated Europe the policies of their three governments in assisting the peoples liberated from the domination of Nazi Germany and the peoples of the former Axis satellite states of Europe to solve by democratic means their pressing political and economic problems. . . . The three governments will jointly assist the people in any European liberated state or former Axis satellite state in Europe where in their judgment conditions require: (a) to establish conditions of internal peace; (b) to carry out emergency measures for the relief of distressed people; (c) to form interim governmental authorities broadly representative of all democratic elements in the population and pledged to the earliest possible establishment through free elections of governments responsive to the will of the people; and (d) to facilitate where necessary the holding of such elections. . . .

When, in the opinion of the three governments, conditions in any European liberated state or any former Axis satellite state in Europe make such action necessary, they will immediately consult together on the measures necessary to discharge the joint responsibilities set forth in this declaration.

There is no question that the Soviet action in Rumania at the end of February was scarcely in accord with this declaration. As Byrnes later said, "From the close of the Yalta Conference to the present day it [the declaration on liberated Europe] has been a source of conflict between the Soviet Union and ourselves. But it is the basis on which we have shown the world that Russian actions in eastern Europe have been in violation of Russia's pledged word." [37] Unfortunately, there seems to have been no explicit discussion at Yalta of

36. Edward R. Stettinius, Jr., *Roosevelt and the Russians: The Yalta Conference* (New York, 1949), pp. 217–218, 244.
37. Byrnes, *op. cit.*, p. 34.

the possibilities of a contradiction between this declaration, which is not altogether unambiguous, and the British-Soviet division of spheres of influence.[38]

During the Rumanian crisis the Russian head of the Allied Control Commission refused to consult with the American and British representatives. Molotov informed Ambassador Harriman that "the Radescu Government was unable to maintain order and fulfill the armistice terms and that the Allied Control Council would take the necessary measures and keep the Allies informed," [39] but presumably after the decisive steps had been taken. Later, in September, 1945, Molotov admitted to Byrnes that Vyshinsky had "helped in the formation of the government," but said that the U.S.S.R. had acted because "there was very serious danger of disorder and civil war." [40] If there was danger of civil war it was only because the Soviet Union had urged the Rumanian Communists to action.

Thus the initial American protests and inquiries had no effect in checking the Russian action and the administration was unwilling to press the issue at this time, partly because the war was still being fought. It refused, however, to recognize the Groza government. The British, while also deploring the Soviet move, were in no position to make a vigorous objection. As Churchill explained in a message to Roosevelt on March 8, 1945:

We have been hampered in our protest against these developments by the fact that, in order to have the freedom to save Greece, Eden and I at Moscow in October recognized that Russia should have a largely preponderant voice in Rumania and Bulgaria, while we took the lead in Greece. Stalin adhered very strictly to this understanding during the thirty days fighting against the Communists and ELAS in the city of Athens, in spite of the fact that all this was most disagreeable to him and to those around him.[41]

It is reasonable to assume, then, that to the Soviet government the division of southeastern Europe into spheres of influence meant that it was to act in accordance with its interests in Rumania as Great

38. Stalin, in proposing an amendment to the declaration on liberated Europe— "support will be given to the political leaders of these countries who have taken an active part in the struggle against the German invaders"—remarked that Churchill need have no anxiety that this proposal applied to Greece, a fairly clear indication that he would consider the division into spheres of influence the basic agreement.

39. Byrnes, *op. cit.,* p. 50.

40. *Ibid.,* p. 52.

41. Quoted in a statement by James F. Byrnes, *New York Times,* October 18, 1947.

Britain had in Greece. Consequently, when challenged for having contravened the Yalta agreement—a challenge which might well have been received with some surprise and irritation—it responded either by warping the meaning of the declaration, by maintaining that subsequent investigation of the Groza regime required the united approval of all three powers, or by relying on the overriding priority of military requirements and the ultimate authority of the Allied (Soviet) High Command. It is difficult to see just how Stalin could have accepted the Yalta declaration without mental reservations. Apart from his doubtful record as an advocate of self-government and free elections, there was the undoubted basic dilemma that a popularly elected government would in all probability be anti-Soviet.[42]

Why did the Soviet government act at this particular time? It is possible that a connection exists between the British measures in Greece and Vyshinsky's work in Bucarest. But beyond this the underlying reason, apparently, was the assumption that the war in the Pacific would be more protracted than it proved to be, and hence that the Western Allies would be unable or reluctant to oppose this Soviet move to secure its position in a state which, after all, had been an Axis satellite and was certainly of great strategic importance to the U.S.S.R.[43]

This answer, however, leads to the further question whether the installation of the National Democratic Front government was primarily a security measure to protect Soviet interests in a vital strategic area or represented the first step of a premeditated campaign to communize all eastern Europe. There is, perhaps, no need to develop the arguments for the latter view; subsequent events themselves seem to support it. Even the Communists today hold to that interpretation.[44] There is no evidence, despite the upsurge of Russian nationalism during the war, that the Communists ever renounced their ultimate hopes of a world revolution and a worldwide union of Soviet

42. The same dilemma appeared, of course, in the Polish question. Harry Hopkins, in his last visit to Moscow, stated that the United States would accept any government in Poland which was desired by the Polish people and was at the same time friendly to the Soviet Union. I have yet to find satisfactory evidence that the expression of the popular will, in such a country as Rumania or Poland, would have any likelihood of bringing about a regime friendly to the U.S.S.R. This is not to say that the widespread antipathy may not have had political and historical justification, but merely that the formula of free elections and friendly government involved a contradiction.

43. This, at least, was the most satisfactory explanation I was able to obtain while in Rumania.

44. See below, p. 313.

republics. Certainly the Soviet political record leaves little doubt that agreements with bourgeois states were to be regarded solely as measures of expediency, not as means of reconciling the antagonisms of the two systems, which by definition were irreconcilable.[45]

Nevertheless, there is some evidence that developments were not all planned in advance in accordance with a secret blueprint, some indication of indecision in the Soviet leadership. In 1944 Ambassador Harriman suggested that elements in the Russian government close to Stalin opposed too close collaboration with the West, but that Stalin liked to have two strings to his bow.[46] Later, in April, 1945, Harriman cabled that he detected three parallel lines of Soviet foreign policy: 1) collaboration with the United States and the United Kingdom in a world organization; 2) creation of a security ring through domination of the border countries; 3) penetration of other countries through their Communist parties.[47] Since it is obvious, and should have been obvious to the Russians, that simultaneous pursuit of all three lines was impossible Stalin may have felt there were alternate paths to follow, that the course had not been set.

Two additional possibilities suggest themselves in this regard: The first is that initially the united front governments of the liberated states of eastern Europe were regarded not—as they later came to be—as mere springboards for exclusive Communist domination but as providing a modus vivendi for the states which had united in fighting Nazi Germany. The second is that the Russians may have regarded Rumania as occupying a special status and that actions taken there did not necessarily apply to the rest of Europe.

With regard to the first possibility, Isaac Deutscher, in his recent biography of Stalin, has suggested that the concept of a people's democracy—a much milder affair in theory than what the Communists had been trained to expect—as distinct from the Soviet system was taken seriously for a time after the war by Soviet political theorists;

45. An even more explicit indication, if it is authentic, of a long-held plan to use united front governments after the war as the first step to achieving a Communist revolution is to be found in a recent biography of Tito, in what purports to be a secret Comintern directive of May 9, 1941, stating that "The Communist world revolution must be presented as a series of measures to achieve 'true democracy.'" The steps to be followed look very much like those which have been taken in eastern Europe since 1945: establishment of a broad coalition government, then its progressive liquidation through arrests, trials in people's courts, etc. Stephen Clissold, *Whirlwind, an Account of Marshal Tito's Rise to Power* (New York, 1949), pp. 238–241. The author informs me that the directive came from the archives of the wartime pro-German Serbian police. Despite its apparent authentication by subsequent events, certain passages in it do not, in my opinion, ring true.

46. Hull, *op. cit.*, II, 1460.

47. Stettinius, *op. cit.*, p. 315.

Stalin may have felt such a form of government would "help him to preserve the condominium of the Big Three." [48]

In 1945 one does find such statements as Stalin's to Harry Hopkins "that Poland would live under the parliamentary system which is like Czechoslovakia, Belgium, and Holland, and that any talk of an intention to Sovietize Poland was stupid . . . the Soviet system was not exportable—it must develop from within on the basis of a set of conditions which were not present in Poland." [49] Now one may regard this statement as a triumph of mendacity or see certain sinister implications in the last phrase, but still there is an impression, for the short run at least, of Stalin's pursuing a noncommunizing line. Moreover, certain events in 1945 are rather difficult to explain on the premise of a fixed intention to sovietize eastern Europe. Why was Hungary permitted to have free elections in 1945, elections which brought in an anti-Communist majority? Even in Rumania, the Soviet presentation to King Michael of its highest award, the Order of Victory, would seem an unnecessarily extravagant gesture if he was to be dethroned at an early date. The inclusion in the Groza government of such a questionable person as Tătărescu, who was not really needed for his technical competence, whom the local Rumanian Communists regarded with great distaste, and whose presence certainly did not greatly reassure business circles, is perhaps best, if rather weirdly, explained by the Soviet determination to have a "bourgeois" politician in the new coalition.[50]

While it is true that Hungary, for a time at least, was permitted to enjoy the fruits of a free election, that Czechoslovakia preserved a relatively independent internal status until 1948, and that Finland, though at one time associated with Hitler, is still free of Communist control, there is little evidence that Rumania would ever have been permitted such freedom, or such a long leash. There is the possibility, suggested above, that Soviet interests in Rumania were more extensive than elsewhere. Historically, tsarist Russia frequently dis-

48. I. Deutscher, *Stalin, a Political Biography* (Oxford University Press, 1949), pp. 542–543.

49. Sherwood, *op. cit.,* p. 900.

50. I cannot prove this statement but it was the only plausible explanation I could obtain from some Rumanian Communists who were most embarrassed by Tătărescu's presence in the government. Deutscher, who is bothered by the same problem, cites several other actions which are hard to explain if Stalin had a definite and coherent plan to communize eastern Europe, e.g., Stalin's excessive concern with the Russian-Polish and Polish-German frontiers and the obviously damaging effect to the Communist cause of the reparations burdens placed on the defeated states. Deutscher's conclusion is that Stalin had no master plan but a number of extremely self-contradictory intentions. Deutscher, *op. cit.,* pp. 536–537.

played ambitions in Moldavia, the path of approach to Constantinople and the Straits; recent Soviet writings on Bessarabia interpret the "liberation" of that province from the Turks in 1812 as a half-completed freeing of the Moldavian people, frustrated by Napoleon's invasion. As has been noted above [51] the Soviet government in a few chance remarks showed a special concern over Rumania during the war. Since 1947, with the reinforcing of the iron curtain, Rumania appears to have become the most tightly sealed and impenetrable of all the Soviet satellites. Moreover, of all the nations of eastern Europe, Rumania offered perhaps the least promise of voluntary cooperation with the Soviet regime: there were the unresolved territorial conflicts, the absence of any Pan-Slav feeling, and a miserably weak Communist party. Hence even if one assumes, hypothetically, no fixed intention from the beginning to sovietize eastern Europe but only a desire to secure friendly governments and strategic security, Russian action in Rumania was likely to be heavy-handed and arbitrary.

These possibilities are suggested very tentatively; their further implications will be treated briefly in the first section of Chapter XIV. One observation, however, may be made at this point. The two interpretations, a) that the Russians had a blueprint for all of eastern Europe, or b) that there was no such plan but that their actions arose from the play of events, especially from the deterioration of international relations following the war, are not in their practical consequences as far apart as they might seem. In the first place, the term blueprint is misleading in giving an impression of a predetermined course of action. Communist strategy is more likely to be along the lines of a chess game: the very notion of the plan involves the consideration of alternative lines of action, depending in part upon the opponent's response. This Leninist flexibility, which is rather ponderous and mechanical in the Soviet regime's hands, often is forgotten after the fact by the Communists' own proclivity to see all developments as inevitable and foreordained by Stalin's wisdom. Perhaps the only constants are the ultimate goal of world communism and a deep sense of ill-will and hostility toward the Western bourgeois states.

Secondly, even if one assumes the Soviet intention to follow limited objectives, their application in practice immediately encounters some very thorny difficulties. Thus, the Soviet Union wanted friendly states on its western frontiers, since these states in the past had been avenues of invasion. Well enough, but such a state as Rumania has

51. See above, p. 265.

historically been not only an avenue of invasion into Russia but also a Russian avenue for expansion. As so often is the case in the world of power relations, the Russian attempt to secure what it regarded as its defensive requirements was at the same time a threat to the western European states, not to mention the border states obliged to be friendly. The Soviet demand for security carried with it potentially aggressive implications.

Further, even if one supposes that the united front governments were not meant to be merely flimsy covers for a Communist dictatorship, what did they mean, how were they to develop? Surely not toward bourgeois parliamentarianism, to the Russians a retrograde step. The concept of a united front, in the absence of a pressing fascist threat, was purely formal, and as soon as the Communists attempted to give it some content it became suspiciously, if inevitably, like a false façade. Similarly, with respect to elections, a single prearranged list of candidates would be the only means of maintaining the front; otherwise the Communists would feel obliged to rig the ballots to prevent a return to the old rut of bourgeois politics.

Finally, at the end of the war the Big Three coalition was bound to loosen, as coalitions always do when the common enemy has been defeated. But any increase in disputes, when viewed through Marxist-Leninist spectacles, was certainly to be interpreted as a sign of renewed bourgeois perfidy. Hence, it would require relatively little actual friction for the Russians to draw, or anticipate, the most damaging conclusions, which would in turn exacerbate relations and lead to a rapid deterioration of great power cooperation. For all these reasons it appears that the only difference between the two interpretations mentioned above is that if the Russians had from the outset a fixed determination to communize eastern Europe, by force if need be, there was no chance of an amicable settlement with the United States and Great Britain; if they did not have such a plan, there was only a very slight chance.

XIII

THE COMMUNIST PERIOD: THE 1945 AGRARIAN
REFORM

Marxism and the Agrarian Question

AGRICULTURE has caused much confusion and controversy among Marxists. As Lenin said, "The peasant question in modern capitalist states most frequently gives rise to perplexity and vacillation among Marxists and to most of the attacks on Marxism by bourgeois (professorial) political economy." [1] Marx's primary political and economic interest was in the development of capitalist industrial society and in the rise of the proletariat which was to inherit that society. Agriculture did not hold the key to the future, and in so far as it was involved in capitalist relations it would follow the main lines of capitalist development. In particular, he believed that the small independent peasant property could not survive in a capitalist society, for a number of reasons:

Destruction of rural house industries, which form its normal supplement, as a result of the development of great industries; a gradual deterioration and exhaustion of the soil subjected to this cultivation; usurpation, on the part of the great landlords, of the community lands, which form everywhere the second supplement of small peasants' properties and alone enable them to keep cattle; competition, either of plantation systems or of great agricultural enterprises carried out on a capitalist scale. Improvements of agriculture, which on the one hand bring about a fall in the prices of the products of the soil, and on the other require greater investments and more diversified material conditions of production, also contribute towards this end, as they did in England during the first half of the 18th Century. [2]

As can be seen, Marx used a profusion of reasons to demonstrate the necessary demise of peasant agriculture. In the first place, he

1. V. I. Lenin, "Small Production in Agriculture," *Selected Works,* XII (London, 1939), 288.
2. Karl Marx, *Capital: a Critique of Political Economy, Vol. III, The Process of Capitalist Production as a Whole,* ed. Frederick Engels, English trans. Ernest Untermann (Chicago, 1909), p. 938.

saw the transformation of small peasants into wage laborers and the expulsion of the agricultural population from the land as an integral part of the genesis of capitalism.[3] In the second place, he regarded the peasant farm as economically unsound and retrograde because of the high expenditure of money capital for purchase of land. "Small property in land creates a class of barbarians standing half way out-side of society, a class suffering all the tortures and all miseries of civilized countries in addition to the crudeness of primitive forms of society." [4] In this case peasant farming is seen not as a historical form being eliminated but as a degraded type of economic activity. Finally, peasant agriculture is technologically unable to survive: "In the sphere of agriculture, modern industry has a more revolutionary effect than elsewhere, for this reason, that it annihilates the peasant, that bulwark of the old society, and replaces him by the wage la-borer." [5] Here again the peasant is eliminated, though not at the time of the genesis of capitalism but in the course of the expansion of in-dustry. The variety of Marx's attacks upon peasant agriculture was to cause his followers confusion.

In the course of the development of the Marxist movement this analysis of peasant agriculture presented two disadvantages. First, it was not a doctrine that would win adherents among the peasantry but, if anything, would alienate them. Hence in countries with an important agricultural population it was a serious political handicap. Second, a more disturbing difficulty was that farm statistics from a number of countries in the latter years of the nineteenth century seemed to controvert Marx's conclusions; agriculture was not sharing in the anticipated concentration of capitalist development. Peasant farms were not being eliminated by large capitalist farms, but rather the peasant seemed to be gaining at the expense of the large farmers. These difficulties contributed to a crisis in the socialist movement in the last years of the century, especially in Germany where a strong revisionist movement appeared, which, among other things, denied that the process of concentration was bound to take place in agri-culture as in industry. Eduard Bernstein and Eduard David cham-pioned the view that peasant agriculture was proving its ability to survive. Karl Kautsky supported Marxist orthodoxy and while ad-mitting that the number of small farms was growing, contended that concentration was nevertheless taking place through the media of

3. *Ibid.*, I, English trans. Samuel Moore and Edward Aveling (London, 1887), pp. 740–758.
4. *Ibid.*, III, 946.
5. *Ibid.*, I, 513.

mortgaging, indebtedness, and leasing; that ultimately and in general large-scale agriculture would prove its advantages.[6]

The revisionist controversy had important repercussions in radical circles of eastern Europe, where agriculture was the principal occupation. The populists profited from the crisis and took over a number of the revisionist tenets. Most of the socialist writers in Rumania, as well as in Russia, were influenced by this controversy. In particular, Dobrogeanu-Gherea in Rumania and Lenin in Russia worked out their agrarian theories more or less in the context of this issue.

Much the most important Rumanian Marxist theorist was C. Dobrogeanu-Gherea (1855–1920).[7] Born of a Jewish family in Russia, Dobrogeanu-Gherea had been a member of Russian populist and socialist circles and had started his career as a revolutionary. He had come first to Rumania in 1875 to organize the underground transmittal of letters and books to Russia. He had been arrested by the Russian police and, after a period of Siberian exile and European travel, returned to Rumania where he settled permanently. He quickly mastered the Rumanian language and became not only a leader of the socialist movement but an important literary critic.

Gherea's outstanding contribution was the quite remarkable study *Neoiobăgia* (1910)—*Neoserfdom*—which undertook to apply Marxism to the special conditions of backward countries. His basic thesis was that the impact of capitalism upon a backward agrarian society, such as Rumania, produced a hybrid, in which there was a monstrous mingling of old and new. He called this result neoserfdom, which he characterized as:

Relations of production in good part servile and feudal; a condition of liberal-bourgeois laws, created in illusions and lies, and leaving the peasant to the discretion of the master; a tutelary legislation which decrees the inalienability of peasant land and regulates the relations between master and worker; finally, inadequate land for the so-called small peasant proprietor for cultivation and for maintaining his family, a fact which obliges him to become a vassal of the large proprietor.[8]

He undoubtedly tried to explain too many phenomena by the formula of neoiobăgia, but he had a profound insight into the corrosive

6. An account of this controversy, from the revisionist point of view, is given in the second edition of Eduard David, *Sozialismus und Landwirtschaft* (Leipzig, 1922) pp. 1–37.

7. Biographical sketches of Dobrogeanu-Gherea are given by Trotsky, *Ocherki politicheskoi rumynii*, pp. 69–78, and by Titel Petrescu, *Socialismul în România*, pp 340–348.

8. Dobrogeanu-Gherea, *Neoiobăgia*, p. 373.

effects of Western capitalism upon traditional social forms. As a socialist he believed that this process was inevitable:

Countries remaining behind enter into the orbit of advanced capitalist
countries; they move in the orbit of these countries; and their whole
life, development, and social activity are determined by the life and
activity of the advanced countries, by the historical epoch in which we
live, the epoch of bourgeois capitalism. And this determination of the
life and social activity of backward countries by advanced countries
is itself a necessary condition for their existence.[9]

He was therefore totally opposed to those populists who sought to
avoid the capitalist industrial path. "A country eminently agricultural," he said, "is a country eminently poor and socially and economically backward." [10] He believed that Rumania must enter the
procession, move toward increasing industrialization, break the feudal
bonds, and convert the liberal formulae into a reality.

He did not take sides on the David-Kautsky dispute over the future of large and small agricultural properties, but he pointed out
that this argument was not relevant to Rumania, since the miserable
half-serf was not a peasant proprietor in any meaningful sense, and
the latifundiary estate owner was not a large-scale farmer. Under
conditions of neoserfdom the latifundia tended to increase at the expense of the defenseless peasant; this was not because it possessed
any inherent competitive superiority but because of the abnormal system of social and property relations obtaining in Rumania.[11]

In the field of agrarian reform Gherea's whole stress was upon
clearing the way for the free development of capitalist relations and
getting rid of the feudal residues. He was not particularly in favor
of wholesale expropriation and redistribution of land, as the repeated
distributions of land without further reforms had merely prolonged
and extended the misery. He was most interested in abolishing feudal
relations and giving the peasant an opportunity to become a small
cultivator, which he believed to be a more advanced and efficient form
of cultivation than the latifundia. With the abolition of the feudal
servitudes, now disguised in contractual form, the large estate owners
would be driven to become modern capitalist farmers, and in all probability would also be forced to sell a good deal of their land to the
peasants. If this natural pressure toward sale of estate land proved

9. *Ibid.*, p. 35.
10. *Ibid.*, p. 482.
11. *Ibid.*, p. 248.

to be insufficient, then he would recommend forced sale or expropriation.

He admitted that this process would create an agricultural proletariat, but he held that a free proletariat was still in a better position than the semiservile peasant attached to his inadequate morsel of land. Moreover, once the proletariat became a distinct group it could be organized and protected by appropriate legislation. He granted that the reforms he recommended would not solve all problems overnight, that the contradictions inherent in capitalism would of course remain but these were, in his opinion, preferable to the existing anomalous situation. In response to the charge that in effect he was working for capitalism rather than socialism, he replied that a Marxist did not invent social forms but analyzed them.

By and large Gherea's social policy was quite moderate: the establishment of small farms which could become independent peasant properties and open the door to the development of capitalism. Nor did he think that too much could be achieved in the agricultural field alone: "This solution of the agrarian problem not only does not resolve the social questions of the country, but does not totally resolve even the problem of peasant misery." [12] Such a resolution could come about only through a rise in national productivity. Finally, it should be noted that he regarded the peasant revolt of 1907 as a negative event and as a disaster. "In the event of the success of a *jacquerie*, the result would be profoundly bourgeois, reactionary and anti-social-democratic, not revolutionary." [13] For this reason he was quite skeptical about the advisability of undertaking socialist agitation in the countryside. At the 1896 socialist congress, in which the question of rural propaganda was raised, Gherea said: "If it is easy to rouse the villages and create a socialist movement among the peasantry, I do not believe that it is so easy to dominate and master a powerful movement which would break out in consequence of propaganda in the village. Let us not by imprudent propaganda provoke a danger as great for the peasants as for the Socialist Party." [14]

In terms of Marxist thinking Dobrogeanu-Gherea made a significant contribution in his extraordinarily acute analysis of the conditions of the states on the fringes of the capitalist world and of the curious developments to which they were subjected. The principal difficulty of his view, however, was that as the basis of a party pro-

12. *Ibid.*, p. 430.
13. *Ibid.*, p. 185.
14. Quoted in Şerban Voinea's article, "Socialismul," in *Enciclopedia României* III, 288.

gram it would not really satisfy any social group. Although his attitude toward the peasants and toward peasant agriculture was not hostile, he was firmly opposed to the ideal of peasant society. Hence the Social Democrats were vulnerable to the attacks of the populists, who delighted, moreover, in ridiculing their revolutionary ideology and their modest liberal-bourgeois program. On the other hand the bourgeoisie would obviously find far more congenial companionship in the Liberal party.

The 1892 program of the Rumanian Social Democrats, which Dobrogeanu-Gherea helped to draft, showed the influence of his ideas on the agrarian question, although it was somewhat more radical. The principal emphasis was upon abolishing feudal residues and promoting a freer economy. It did, however, recommend gradual state purchase of private landed properties as well as public holdings, to create an inalienable domain to be leased out to cultivators, especially to syndicates of agricultural workers. (In *Neoiobăgia*, Gherea had mentioned this possibility but felt that until the existing structure of the Rumanian state was changed such a measure might do more harm than good.) The 1919 program of the Social Democrats continued to show his influence. Speaking of the semiservile peasant, it denied that the simple process of expropriation and resettlement would resolve the social question in the agricultural sector.

In the interwar years, the new generation of socialists—such men as Șerban Voinea, C. Titel Petrescu, and Lotar Rădăceanu—showed themselves to be strongly under the influence of Dobrogeanu-Gherea's ideas in their interpretation of Marxism as applied to Rumania. For example, Voinea felt that the principal task of Rumanian Social Democracy was to bring about bourgeois-capitalist development, since the revolution could be achieved only in the ripe conditions prevailing in the West.[15] He did feel that some revision of Marx was necessary in regard to the role of the peasants and their importance as a political force. The postwar agrarian movements in eastern Europe and the retreat to the New Economic Policy in Soviet Russia had, in his opinion, shown that it was dangerous for the peasants to develop an antiproletarian sentiment. So he was concerned with the method of finding village allies for the workers. While the peasants could not achieve the next level of society, socialism, this long-range problem should not interfere with present possibilities of cooperation with the peasant parties. "If with respect to the future profound theoretical differences divide us from the peasants, in regard to im-

---

15. See his study, *Marxism oligarhic*, an attack upon the Marxist-Liberal theories of Stefan Zeletin.

mediate political practices we find ourselves in full agreement. Both political organizations seek the removal of the oligarchic system of government." [16]

In the last analysis, however, Dobrogeanu-Gherea's interpretation of Marxism was unable to provide Rumanian Social Democracy with an adequate program for the agrarian question. The reasons for his failure are quite important. As has been seen, he made an important advance upon earlier Marxism in his efforts to make socialism relevant to the backward agrarian nations, in his realization of the importance of the agrarian question to the Marxist, and in his interpretation of the impact of capitalism upon a backward society. His analysis, however, did not go far enough. For if he saw that capitalism had produced the hybrid, neoiobăgia, yet he believed that the removal of the feudal relations—dijma, labor contracts, exceptional legislation, inalienability, etc.—would suffice to put Rumania on the right track. For that reason he was not interested in more specific remedies for agriculture, such as the various palliatives of the populists, or even in the redistribution of land, since this measure without the removal of the semiservile relations would be self-defeating. He was quite correct in his predictions that the Rumanian legislative mania, formal universal suffrage, and agrarian reform conforming to the old practice of handing out land would produce no lasting remedies for the ills of Rumanian society. Unfortunately he saw the feudal-capitalist combination as a mechanical mixture whereas, to pursue the metaphor, it more nearly resembled a chemical solution. The interaction of capitalist and traditional elements was producing a society, and however unpleasant some of its manifestations may have been, its creation was not a reversible process.

The insufficiency of this conception became evident as time passed. The Rumania of the interwar years presented just as many anomalies as it had in 1910, which is why Dobrogeanu-Gherea still makes very relevant reading. But the term neoserfdom no longer described it. Although semiservile elements still persisted in the countryside, they were not the outstanding characteristic. Yet Gherea's followers, such as Voinea and Rădăceanu, Rumanian Social Democratic theorists of the 1920's and 1930's, still contended that the country must be rid of the oligarchy as the first step toward healthy capitalism, ignoring the fact that the only type of bourgeoisie likely to arise in Rumanian society was an oligarchic one. In short, Gherea is responsible for the Social Democrats' unrealistic assumption that the peculiar form of oligarchic, bureaucratic capitalism which dominated Rumania was

16. *Ibid.*, p. 246.

an accidental feature on the body politic, to be removed like a wart.[17]

Just as the Rumanian Social Democrats hoped somehow to bring about a nonoligarchic capitalism, so, under Dobrogeanu-Gherea's influence, they wished to have a nonservile peasantry. In this, however, they were by no means consistent but fluctuated between admitting the desirability of small peasant farming and taking the more orthodox line on the advantages of large-scale cultivation. The land reforms of 1918–1921, while not at all to their liking, had the negative result of making the servile elements in Rumanian agriculture seem less important and of increasing doubts as to the likelihood of a prosperous small peasantry of the Western type. As a consequence, the Social Democrats failed to achieve any coherent agrarian program. Throughout the interwar period, at party congresses and in articles, they kept futilely insisting that the agrarian problem was very important and that the party must formulate its attitude on the subject, but they never overcame their dilemma. For a time they solved the problem by evading it, through seeking short-term political allies in the Peasant party, which presumably would be responsible for agrarian policy in the period of small peasant cultivation. A constructive alliance of the Peasant party and the Social Democrats would doubtless have been beneficial to Rumania but it was prevented both by the growing social conservatism of the National Peasants and by the Socialists' fluctuations between collaboration and doctrinal purity.

It is in the light of the uncertainties and contradictions of Social Democratic agrarian policy that Lenin's dynamic interpretation of Marxism is seen in all its originality and paradoxicality. As with many aspects of Lenin's thought, it is difficult to tie his agrarian policy to a consistent pattern or to say whether in apparent shifts he was changing his mind or, with his extraordinary subtlety, he was merely bringing forth a new response to a new "objective situation."

As a starting point it is instructive to compare Lenin's and Dobrogeanu-Gherea's views on the agrarian question. Both men pro-

---

17. The Communist Lucreţiu Pătrăşcanu (*Problemele de bază*, pp. 264–278) vigorously attacked the Social Democrats for their attempt to distinguish the Rumanian oligarchy from the bourgeoisie, and pointed out how it led to a tendency to collaborate with Carol's enlightened despotism as an antioligarchic force. Pătrăşcanu, of course, was intent on proving that capitalism is the real villain of the piece and that its more unpleasant manifestations in Rumania merely reflect the ugly qualities of capitalism in the last stage of monopoly and imperialism. There is, to be sure, something to be said for the opinion that Rumania in attempting to industrialize and compete with the highly developed capitalist states was obliged to take over an advanced form of capitalism. But in my opinion Pătrăşcanu was altogether incorrect in regarding the differences between Rumanian and Western capitalism as only superficial, a view which can be maintained only if Western capitalism is seen in the totally baleful light of the Communist interpretation.

duced their agrarian studies at about the same time, both were concerned with the need of relating Marxism to backward agricultural states, and both were writing under the influence of the revisionist crisis. Gherea had left the question of large versus small properties open, whereas Lenin stoutly defended Kautsky's orthodoxy, a fact of considerable importance later on. In several respects both men saw the problem in the same light: they realized that the dispute in the West between large and small properties was not the principal issue in Rumania and Russia, since the real difference lay between semiservile peasant cultivators and feudal estates; they regarded the small peasant holding as an advance upon the feudal latifundia. Both were enemies of the populist ideal of a peasant society. Both were against restrictive agricultural legislation and enforced inalienability of peasant property and desired the free development of capitalist relations in the countryside. Moreover, both men, initially at least, were opposed to the wholesale expropriation and redistribution of land, and were suspicious of nationalization of land because of the reactionary character of the existing state.

But with all these similarities, which set both men apart from the German Social Democrats and from the populists, there was a very important difference in outlook and center of interest. For Gherea the ultimate goal was the arrival of a socialist society; for Lenin, the revolution was the driving force of all his thoughts. Thus Gherea favored the development of capitalism in the villages, with all its attendant miseries and conflicts, because he thought it an advance upon existing semifeudal conditions. Lenin, on the other hand, urged the spread of capitalism in the village precisely because it would intensify the class struggle. "In this case," he said in 1902,

we want to support small property not against capitalism but against feudalism; in this case by supporting the small peasantry we give a tremendous impetus to the development of the class struggle. Indeed, on the one hand, we, by this, make a *last* attempt to fan the embers of the class ("estate") enmity of the peasants towards the feudal landlords. On the other hand, we pave the way to the development of the bourgeois antagonism of classes in the countryside, because that antagonism is still masked by what is supposed to be the common and equal oppression of all the peasants by the survivals of serfdom.[18]

Their attitudes toward the upheavals of 1905 and 1907 were altogether different. Gherea saw the 1907 peasant uprising as a tragedy,

18. Lenin, "The Agrarian Program of Russian Social-Democracy," *Selected Works* II, 312.

whose roots lay deep in the conflicts of Rumanian society; he hoped by his policy to rid Rumania of such dreadful and essentially negative jacqueries. Lenin, on the other hand, while aware of retrograde elements in a peasant revolt, recognized it as a powerful tool for advancing the cause of revolution.

It has been said that as a result of the 1905 revolution Lenin altered his attitude toward the small peasants; realizing their political importance, he abandoned the traditional views of Marxism.[19] This is not altogether correct, for in Lenin's writings well before the 1905 revolution one finds an intense awareness of the importance of the peasant in Russia. Moreover, he avoided the Kautsky-revisionist dispute by his threefold distinction between feudal estate, peasant property, and large capitalist farm, and based his opening tactics upon the conflict between the first two. Thus, in 1902:

Speaking generally, it is not the business of the Social Democrats to develop, encourage, fortify, still less multiply small-scale farming or small property. But the point is that we are not faced with a "general" but with an *exceptional* case of small-scale farming, and this exceptional character is clearly expressed in the preamble to our agrarian program: "The abolition of the survivals of serfdom and the free development of the class struggle in the countryside." Speaking *generally* the encouragement of small property is reactionary, because it is directed against large-scale *capitalist* economy and, consequently, retards the social revolution and obscures and glosses over the class struggle. But in this case we want to support small property not against capitalism but against feudalism.[20]

Or even earlier, in 1901:

We have seen that in the modern Russian countryside two kinds of class antagonism exist side by side: first, the struggle between the rural workers and the rural employers; and second, between the peasantry as a whole and the landlord class as a whole. The first antagonism is developing and becoming more acute; the second is gradually diminishing. The first is still wholly in the future; the second to a considerable degree already belongs to the past. And yet in spite of this, it is the second antagonism that has the most vital and most practical significance for the Russian Social Democrats at the present time.[21]

19. For example, F. Borkenau (*The Communist International*, p. 52) stated that Lenin before 1905, in supporting Kautsky, felt that it was impossible to win over the peasantry, but that after 1905 in considering the lessons of the revolution he saw the necessity of obtaining the support of the small peasants.

20. Lenin, *Selected Works*, II, 312

21. Lenin, "The Workers' Party and the Peasantry," *Selected Works*, II, 237.

itical switch,. as a result of the 1905 revolution, on the question of redistribution of land and nationalization. Before the 1905 revolution he stated that while he favored restoring to the peasants some land which had been cut off from them at the time of the emancipation, he was opposed to the wholesale redistribution of land, which had been urged by a section of the narodniki, the so-called Black Redistributionists, since it would have the reactionary effect of generalizing and perpetuating small-scale peasant production. As for nationalization, he said that ultimately he would favor it, but that it was premature in Russia and would only lead to state socialism.[22] By 1908 Lenin came to favor nationalization, not as a step toward socialism, but as part of the fight against the feudal relationships: [23]

The abolition of private property in land does not by any means change the bourgeois foundations of commercial and capitalist agriculture. There is nothing more erroneous than the opinion that the nationalization of the land has something in common with socialism, or even with the equal right to the use of land. Socialism, as is well known, means the abolition of commodity production. Nationalization, however, means converting the land into the property of the state, and such a conversion does not in the least affect private enterprise on the land. Whether the land is private property or whether it is in the "possession" of the whole country, of the whole nation, makes no difference in so far as the economic system on the land is concerned, nor does it make any difference whatever to the (capitalist) economic system of the rich muzhik whether he buys land in perpetuity, rents land from the landlord or state, or whether he "gathers up" allotment land abandoned by bankrupt peasants. If exchange remains, it is ridiculous to talk of socialism. . . . The economic significance of nationalization does not by any means lie where it is very often sought for. It does not lie in the fight against bourgeois relationships (as Marx long ago pointed out, nationalization is one of the most consistent bourgeois measures), but in the fight against feudal relationships.

He was still reluctant to accept wholesale redistribution of land, although he realized that a revolutionary movement would bring it to the fore: [24]

Concerning the attitude the workers' party should take towards the possible demand of the new farmers for the division of the land, a definite

22. *Ibid.*, II, 318–319.
23. Lenin, "The Agrarian Question in Russia at the End of the Nineteenth Century," *ibid.*, I, 208–209.
24. Lenin, "The Agrarian Program of Social Democracy," *ibid.*, XII, 334.

reply can be given. The proletariat can and must support the militant bourgeoisie when it is waging a genuinely revolutionary struggle against feudalism. But it is not the business of the proletariat to support the bourgeoisie when it is calming down. If it is certain that a victorious bourgeois revolution is impossible in Russia without the nationalization of the land, then it is still more certain that the subsequent turn to the division of the land is impossible without a certain amount of "restoration," without the peasantry (or, as it would be more true to say from the point of view of the presumed relationships: farmers) turning toward counter-revolution. The proletariat will defend revolutionary traditions against all such strivings and will not further the latter.

When the 1917 revolution came, however, Lenin was fully aware of the power of the desire for more land, even though as a socialist he opposed the extension of small private holdings. In his reply to Kautsky's criticisms, he said: [25]

Kautsky will never be able to refute the view that equal land tenure has a progressive and revolutionary significance in the bourgeois-democratic revolution. Such a revolution cannot go beyond this. On reaching this limit, it clearly, quickly, and easily reveals to the masses the inadequacy of bourgeois-democratic solutions and the necessity of proceeding beyond their limits, of passing on to socialism. Having overthrown tsarism and landlordism, the peasantry dreamed of equal land tenure, and no power on earth could have prevented the peasantry, who had been freed from landlordism and from the bourgeois parliamentary republican state, from realizing this dream. The proletarians said to the peasants: We shall help you to reach "ideal" capitalism, for equal land tenure is the idealization of capitalism from the point of view of the small producer. At the same time we will prove to you its inadequacy and the necessity of passing to the social cultivation of the land.

These two measures, nationalization and equal land tenure, were both regarded by Lenin primarily as tactical and political rather than as economic measures. The first was useful as a sweeping revolutionary step which wiped out feudal landholding. It was also desirable as the "agrarian system which is most flexible from the point of view of the transition to socialism." [26] Equal land tenure, however, was regarded as purely a necessary measure to gain the support of the peasantry. "When adopting the Land Socialization Act—the 'spirit' of which is equal land tenure—the Bolsheviks most explicitly and definitely declared: this is not our idea, we do not agree with this slo-

25. Lenin, "The Proletarian Revolution and the Renegade Kautsky," *Selected Works*, VII, 201.
26. *Ibid.*, VII, 205.

gan, but we think it our duty to pass it because it is demanded by the overwhelming majority of the peasants." [27]

Thus Lenin did in fact accept the narodniki goal of land distribution, a decision which undoubtedly was a factor in bringing the Bolsheviks to power. But when he explains this action in Marxist terms, one has the impression that something very odd has happened to the doctrine of Karl Marx. For example, in 1919 he said,

The proletariat after having defeated the bourgeoisie must unswervingly conduct its policy towards the peasantry along the following fundamental lines: the proletariat must separate, demarcate the peasant toiler from the peasant owner, the peasant worker from the peasant huckster, the peasant who labours from the peasant who profiteers. In this demarcation lies the *whole essence* of socialism.[28]

While the selection of random quotations may not do Lenin justice, it is interesting that whatever the circumstances Lenin should have seen in the demarcation of the peasant toiler from the peasant owner the "essence" of socialism. One cannot avoid feeling that there is a considerable distance between this view and Marx's critique of the peasant economy.

Tactically, of course, this emphasis derives from Lenin's basic plan of campaign for the proletariat:

First, with the "whole" of the peasantry against the monarchy, the landlords, the medieval regime (and to that extent the revolution remains bourgeois, bourgeois-democratic). Then with the poorest peasants, with the semi-proletarians, with all the exploited, against capitalism, including the rural rich, the kulaks, the profiteers, and to that extent the revolution becomes a socialist one.[29]

Briefly, then, Lenin saw the peasant question primarily in terms of its role in bringing about the Russian revolution. The question whether the Russian revolution was the one Marx had in mind has been endlessly disputed by the Social Democrats and the Communists. But whether one regards the bolshevist revolution as a betrayal or as a perfect manifestation of "Marxism in the era of imperialism," it is obvious that a profound change has occurred. Moreover, by his stress upon the peasantry Lenin was able to give a dynamics to the socialist movement in eastern Europe which not only was more power-

27. *Ibid.,* VII, 200.
28. Lenin, "Economics and Politics in the Era of the Dictatorship of the Proletariat," *ibid.,* VIII, 9.
29. *Ibid.,* VII, 191.

ful than what the Social Democrats had to offer but involved a much more realistic appraisal of the actual forces at work in a peasant society under the impact of capitalism.

It has been necessary to spend this time on Lenin because of the decisive influence of his ideas on the Communist parties in the interwar period. The agrarian policy of the Rumanian Communist party attempted to be a faithful reflection of the directives of the Comintern, although it often lapsed into deviations. In particular, the agrarian policy of the Rumanian Communists was dictated by considerations of political power rather than of economic reform.

The Comintern took a good deal of interest in the peasant question as a fruitful field for revolutionary opportunities. In 1923 a Red Peasants International was formed in Moscow in an effort to rally the peasantry to the Communist ideal and to combat the influence of the peasant parties uniting in the Green (Prague) International. The Red Peasants International, however, had very little success in any of its efforts, and in going through its reports one finds very little mention of Rumanian participation.

Unfortunately for the Communists, the Rumanian land reform, while in many respects ill-considered as an economic measure, did at least have the effect of making their task very difficult. For the extensive redistribution of land, whatever its shortcomings, robbed the slogan, land to the peasant, of much of its potency. Throughout the interwar period the Rumanian Communists seem to have been uncertain whether they should continue to attack the landlords with the whole of the peasantry, or the kulaks with the poor peasants. Actually they succeeded in doing very little with either.

In 1924, the Presidium of the International Peasant Council in Moscow sent out an appeal to the Rumanian peasants, first telling them that Bessarabia should be allowed to settle its own destiny, and then saying that the land reform was not being carried out. At that time it called for: immediate expropriation and uncompensated confiscation of all boyar property; no land to anyone unless he worked it himself; livestock and inventory for the poor peasant masses; no payment of taxes for armaments; no money for speculation; factories to the workers; and all power to the workers and peasants in alliance with the Soviet Union.[30] This, of course, was not an agrarian program but a call to revolution, and a rather poorly timed one at that.

While the Communists hated the Liberals they were not at all pleased with the National Peasants, who at best were regarded as

30. *Die Bauerninternationale* (Erstes Heft, Berlin, 1924), pp. 176–178.

representatives of the rich peasantry and the petty bourgeoisie and at worst as merely another section of international finance capital. They were particularly critical of the law facilitating the alienation and sale of peasant land as a means of undermining the poor peasant, even though Lenin before the revolution repeatedly supported this measure as a splendid device to extend capitalism into the village. The fall of the National Peasants was greeted as a just punishment.

The period of ultra-Left tactics was reflected in the agrarian program of the Communist parties. In 1931, for example, the Comintern rebuked the Rumanian party for its Right opportunist conceptions in the field of the peasant movement. The Rumanian party paper had stated that to attract the peasants to the defense of the Soviet Union and against the impending imperialist war it was necessary to penetrate the village: "At the present moment the peasant is the victim of the terrible economic and political crisis . . . The question of usury, taxation, and the acceleration of the process of differentiation and the proletarization of the village must all be discounted by our party in its work of winning over the peasant masses." [31] The authors of the article had clearly fallen into the Right opportunist conception of the peasantry as a class as a whole. The Comintern severely pointed out that the Rumanian Communist party could scarcely base itself on the kulaks in the struggle against intervention. The party was therefore to address itself to the middle and poor strata of the village with a challenge and a slogan. The principal slogan, however, which the Comintern had to offer, was a campaign against the lies about "Soviet Dumping"—a slogan that must have brought great joy indeed to the hard-pressed Rumanian peasant. It is plain that here the agrarian program of the Rumanian Communist party had little to do with Rumanian agriculture or even with Rumanian revolution but was an instrument for the defense of the U.S.S.R.

Although Lenin had announced that in the eventual progress from individual to socialized agriculture the small peasant should be persuaded, not dragooned, there was little evidence of this attitude in Stalin's exposition in 1929 of the reasons for proceeding with the collectivization of Russian agriculture.[32] He stressed the impossibility

31. Quoted in T. Marin, "The Role of Rumania in Intervention against the U.S.S.R.," *The Communist International, 8,* No. 10 (May 15, 1931), 302.

32. Cf. Stalin's speech of December 27, 1929, on the question of agrarian policy in the U.S.S.R., in *Voprosy Leninizma* (11th ed., Moscow, 1945), pp. 275–294. The accepted slogan on the peasant question was reliance on the poor peasants, in alliance with the middle peasants (generally, those who did not employ labor), and in continuous battle with the rich peasants or kulaki. This meant that while the kulak class was openly recognized as an enemy, the middle and poor peasants were not to be antagonized or forced into collective agriculture. Stalin later reiterated this point in his

of part of the Soviet economy being frozen in private cultivation while socialized industry was expanding: "Either one way or the other: either back—to capitalism—or forward—to socialism. There is no third way nor can there be." [33] He again attacked the old revisionist view of the persistence of the small peasant, and held that the peasant should be liberated from his slavish attachment to his little plot of land. Fortunately, he said, this slavish attachment did not exist in Russia because there was no private ownership in land—hence the importance of nationalization at the time of the revolution.

The Soviet move to collectivized farming was not, however, followed by any shift in the agrarian line of the Comintern. In 1931, Kolarov, speaking of the tasks of the Communist parties in agrarian countries, emphasized organizing and leading the strikes of agricultural workers, supporting the revolutionary struggle of the toiling peasant, understanding the differentiation in the countryside and especially the role of the middle peasantry, who must be neutralized or attracted.

The Communist Parties must make the question of the basic slogan in the village—viz., land for the toiling peasant and agricultural worker without purchase—completely clear, contrasting it with the collective agrarian policy of the landowners and the bourgeoisie. This slogan must be set up particularly against the bourgeois land reforms, connecting it with the struggle of the proletariat for power, for the Workers' and Peasants' Government. The *collectivization* of agriculture cannot take the place of the struggle for land without compensation in capitalist countries. Collectivization must come on a plane with the exposition of the lies and slanders concerning the U.S.S.R., contrasting the success of agriculture in the U.S.S.R. on the basis of its socialist reconstruction to the agrarian crisis of capitalist countries.[34]

Throughout these years the Communists both in Rumania and in Moscow were intent on proving both that the land reform had not rid Rumania of all boyar estates and that a differentiation was developing in the village between the agricultural proletariat and the wealth-

---

article "Dizzy with Success" in 1930, when he complained that the enthusiasm of some of the comrades had led them to use pressure on the middle and poor peasants. Nevertheless, one finds very little of this cautious tone in the above-mentioned speech, except for the conviction that somehow the nationalization of land a decade earlier had rid the peasant of his attachment to the land. As the turmoils of the years of collectivization showed, this was simply not the case.

33. *Ibid.,* p. 778.

34. V. Kolarov, "The World Agrarian Crisis and the Peasant Movement," *The Communist International, 8,* No. 9 (May 1, 1931), 270.

ier peasants. As a matter of fact, both these contentions were true
to a certain degree, as has been seen above in Chapter 3. But the Communists greatly exaggerated the extent both of large estates and of
differentiation, and their statistical efforts to prove their point were
either inaccurate or patently false.[35]

The adoption of the Popular Front in 1935 led to a corresponding
modification in the Communist agrarian policy. While ultimate aims
of socialism were not renounced, a distinction was drawn between
socialist reforms and reforms designed to restore democracy. The
militant revolutionary note of the early pronouncements was dropped.
The new policy appears in Lucrețiu Pătrășcanu's study of the basic
problems of Rumania, *Problemele de bază ale României*, written during the war but showing the influence of the Popular Front tactic.
Pătrășcanu was no proletarian but the son of a socialist intellectual
and himself a lawyer. He was not Moscow-trained, and while his writings were based upon Lenin, they have a certain Western outlook.
He led the Rumanian Communist party in 1944, was Minister of Justice in the coalition governments and in the Groza cabinet until the
beginning of 1948. His influence in the party diminished steadily
after the return of the comrades who had been in Moscow, and he
was eventually discharged from his position because he had become
"the exponent of bourgeois ideology and detached himself from the
masses and from the ideology and principles of the working class."

Much of Pătrășcanu's analysis of the Rumanian agrarian problem
is sound and illuminating, although on many points of fact he obviously relied on the information compiled by the National Peasant
economist Virgil Madgearu. He was fully aware, of course, of the
unhealthy state of Rumanian agriculture, the persistence of extensive cereal cultivation and low level of productivity, the failure of the
1918–1921 land reforms to establish a prosperous peasantry, the
persistence of metayage and other semiservitudes, the proletarization
of the poorer peasantry, and the inability of a great number of Rumanian peasants to support themselves on their meager holdings. In
trying, however, to adapt this promising material to perfect Marxist-
Leninist categories he overtaxed the evidence; he exaggerated the
failure of the 1918–1921 reforms to equalize land holdings, he probably gave too much importance to the differentiation between the
poor and the rich peasants, and in attempting to demonstrate the

35. Two such examples are S. Timov, "Wird Rumänien agrarsiert oder industrialisiert?" *Agrarprobleme,* International Agrarinstitut Moskau, Band 2, Heft 2 (1929),
pp. 310–346; and Tatarow, "Die Agrarkrise in Rumänien," *Agrarprobleme,* Band 4,
Heft 2 (1931), pp. 44–80.

prevalence of agricultural laborers he definitely mishandled his statistics.[36]

Pătrășcanu was at his best in showing that the optimistic statements of official Rumanian spokesmen during the interwar years were altogether unjustified, and at his worst in reducing the agrarian question to an oversimplified formula. He was too intent upon proving that all difficulties could be laid at the door of Rumanian capitalism, with the support of the moribund but sinister boyar class. There is of course a certain amount of truth in this contention, but it served to distort his analysis. For example, "overpopulation" as a cause of economic misery was obviously unwelcome to him since it put the blame outside the realm of political economy and made it an act of God. He was correct in maintaining that Rumanian officialdom had all too eagerly seized upon overpopulation in recent years as a perfect scapegoat for the prolonged failure to improve agriculture, but it cannot be written off as an unimportant factor. Pătrășcanu, however, felt obliged to attack it and devoted considerable attention to destroying the "myth" of overpopulation. He distinguished, quite properly, between absolute or biological overpopulation and an overpopulation resulting from economic circumstances. In his view there were three principal causes of this relative, or economic, overpopulation:

1) the existence of large properties, whereby 25,000 families held a quarter of the arable land, thus depriving hundreds of peasants of the possibility of creating a holding (according to the 1930 census 25,000 exploitations of over 50 hectares occupied only 18.8 per cent of the arable surface);

2) under semiservile conditions labor was intensively exploited; consequently one man was driven to accomplish the work on a piece of land which normally would provide a living for three;

3) the extensive use of women and children in place of men on boyar estates produced the appearance of overpopulation.

While these conditions, all of which he associated with the existence of large properties, doubtless had some effect—especially the first—they were certainly not the major reasons for Rumanian agrar-

---

36. Virgil Madgearu (*Evoluția economiei românești*, p. 358), making use of some calculations of the agrarian economist Roman Cresin, stated that while small cultivators under 5 hectares had an excess of labor power, middle and large properties required additional labor, evaluated at 190 million days a year. Of this, 40 per cent (around 371,300) was undertaken by paid agricultural laborers, and 60 per cent represented supplementary work performed by the families of small proprietors. Pătrășcanu, however (*op. cit.*, p. 85), took this figure of 40 per cent of paid agricultural laborers, equated it with the fact that 40 per cent of the arable land in Rumania in 1930 was in holdings over 10 hectares, and gave the quite unjustified impression that in effect agricultural laborers were responsible for the cultivation of all land over 10 hectares.

ian overpopulation after 1921. Moreover, he granted that Rumanian strip cultivation and dwarf holdings led to overpopulation because of their economic inefficiency but he went on to say :

The solution of this aspect of the Rumanian agrarian question cannot be achieved in the framework of small properties, nor in the framework of private property in land. It cannot find a solution either in individual or isolated fashion, but involves structural transformations which concern the whole of Rumanian society, hence far past the restricted limits of the agricultural sector properly speaking.[37]

In a word, for all his criticism of the "myth" of overpopulation Pătrăşcanu really provided no convincing evidence that it was not a real problem, nor could he. This point is important, because the propaganda for the subsequent 1945 agrarian reform was obviously based on similar premises.

In his proposal of remedies, he limited himself to immediate reforms, which were not socialist but which were intended to rid Rumania of fascism and restore a constitutional bourgeois society. For agriculture he advocated the complete expropriation of large properties over 50 hectares, the abolition of servile labor relations, the resettlement of landless peasants and peasants with insufficient land; distribution to the peasants of livestock and equipment obtained from the expropriated estates; cancellation of peasant debts to the banks and to the state. Other economic measures included the nationalization of the Rumanian Bank and the consolidation of the banking structure; state control over cartels and the nationalization of certain combines; an eight-hour day for labor, minimum wages, social security, and protective legislation. For a Communist it was certainly a minimum program.

In explaining this program, Pătrăşcanu relied upon the ideas of Lenin of 1900. The whole of the peasantry—while carrying within itself the latent conflict between poor peasant and the kulak—was the adversary of large property, although for a number of different reasons. In some European states peasant solidarity was no longer possible, but in Rumania there still remained a substantial antiboyar spirit common to poor and rich peasant alike.

The Agrarian Reform of 1945

Rumanian agriculture was disorganized after the defeat of 1944, although as always the very backwardness of peasant farming reduced the shock. The war had depleted stocks of grain, draft animals,

37. Pătrăşcanu, *op. cit.*, p. 105.

and equipment. There had been fighting during the spring and summer over a wide strip of Moldavia, and less extended fighting was going on in Transylvania. The German army had retreated, the Red Army had marched through the country. There had been a considerable dislocation of population, and many landowners had fled from their estates in Moldavia and Bucovina.

Despite these unsettled conditions there was initially very little peasant action. There were cases of peasants taking land, primarily from absentee owners or those who had fled the Russian advance. But as late as January, 1945, at Botoşani in northern Moldavia—a region bordering the Soviet Union and which had been under Soviet control since the preceding spring—an agreement was reached, with the approval of the local Soviet commander, whereby landowners who had left their estates could return to them, provided they agreed to operate them personally and not as absentees.[38]

When the National Democratic Front began its drive to power in February, 1945, the calm was broken. In September, 1944, the Rumanian Communist party had put forward a demand, incorporated in the program of the National Democratic Front, for the expropriation of land over 50 hectares. Even before Groza and the Communists came into office peasant committees in the villages began taking over large estates. While this display of zeal, in most instances initiated by local organs of the Ploughmen's Front, was authentic in the sense that it corresponded to the primordial land hunger of the Rumanian peasant, it in no way reflected a revolutionary situation. The peasants in the winter of 1944 were not in a gay frame of mind; they were poor, heartily sick of the war which had cost many of them their sons, not to speak of their horses, cattle, and equipment. They were tired of troops—German, Russian, and Rumanian—marching by and requisitioning. They did not like the old order, they hated the local gendarmes but they were not in a revolutionary frame of mind. They welcomed land but they were not in a rick-burning mood.[39] The premature seizures of land before any law had been passed were merely part of the mock revolution the National Democratic Front was undertaking.

One of the first acts of the Groza government after its tumultuous rise to power was to promulgate a decree-law, on March 22, 1945, for a land reform.[40] According to Article 1 of this law, "Agrarian reform

38. This may seem surprising, but I saw the agreement in the prefecture at Botoşani.
39. Such at least was my impression after traveling though some 30 judeţe in December and January, 1944–45.
40. A text of the law is given in a pamphlet published by the Rumanian Ministry of Information, *La Réforme agraire en Roumanie* (Bucarest, November, 1946).

is a national, economic, and social necessity for our country. Rumanian agriculture should be based upon sound and productive farms, which are the private property of those who cultivate them."

The stated purposes of the reform were:

a) the enlargement of the cultivable area of existing peasant farms which were less than 5 hectares;

b) the creation of vegetable gardens in the environs of cities, for workers, civil servants, and artisans;

c) the creation of new individual private farms for agricultural laborers without land;

d) the use of certain land for model farms and experimental stations, to be administered by the state.

The following land was to be expropriated:

a) all properties belonging to German citizens and to Rumanian citizens of German ethnic origin who had collaborated with Hitler Germany;

b) the properties of war criminals and those responsible for the "disaster of the country";

c) properties of those who had fled to countries with which Rumania was at war and of those fleeing after August 23, 1944;

d) the land of absenteeists (excluding persons on official business abroad, or absent by necessity, or workers who had gone abroad and who had less than 10 hectares);

e) properties of those who during the last seven years had not cultivated the land themselves (excepting those with less than 10 hectares);

f) properties of those who had volunteered to fight against the United Nations;

g) mortmain lands;

h) lands of private owners in excess of 50 hectares, including arable, orchards, meadows, ponds, marshes, and inundated land. The proprietor was permitted to select which 50 hectares he was to retain but it had to be in one place. Multiple properties and properties of husband and wife were considered as one.

All tractors, threshing machines, sowing machines, and combines found on expropriated land were to pass to the state for the creation of agricultural machine stations. Other equipment and livestock was to go to the state for redistribution to the peasants. Expropriation of inventory and livestock was to be in proportion to the amount of the proprietor's land expropriated.

The law exempted from expropriation rice fields, church and monastic properties, crown lands, and lands belonging to certain specified cultural and philanthropic institutions, urban communes, and co-operatives.

The mayor of each commune was directed to call a general assembly of all peasants having less than 5 hectares. This assembly was to elect a local committee of 7–15 members. These committees, whose actions were to be coordinated by a district committee operating with the Ministry of Agriculture, were to draw up lists of land to be expropriated and of peasants who were entitled to receive land.

Priority in the distribution of land was as follows:

a) cultivators mobilized in the anti-Hitler war;

b) widows, orphans, and invalids of this war;

c) widows, orphans, and invalids of any war;

d) landless peasants;

e) agricultural laborers and peasants who had worked on the land expropriated;

f) peasants with less than 5 hectares.

A necessary condition for all categories, however, was that the recipient lack 5 hectares of land.

Expropriation was without compensation. The price of the new lots was to be equal to the annual average harvest of one hectare, that is, 1,000 kilograms of wheat or 1,200 kilograms of maize. The new proprietors were to pay immediately in money or in kind 10 per cent of the purchase price, the remainder to be paid in ten years for peasants with little land and in twenty years for landless peasants. Landless peasants could obtain a three years' moratorium on the payment of their first installment.

Holdings created under this law could not be divided, sold, leased or mortgaged, either in whole or in part, except in certain special cases, with the authorization of the Ministry of Agriculture. The new land was received without obligations.

Lands expropriated and divided before the promulgation of this law were to be made to conform with its provisions.

By a subsequent administrative regulation certain large properties could be exempted from expropriation, if they were well-organized enterprises, suitable to serve as model farms under the direction of the Ministry of Agriculture; even these farms, however, were not to exceed 150 hectares.

For a number of reasons it is difficult to ascertain the results of the law in terms of the redistribution of land. Expropriation began before the law was promulgated, and although the irregularities in its application were not as great as some of the dispossessed landowners made out, there was a good deal of uncontrolled seizure and redistribution. A reform carried out so brusquely and through the agency of local peasant committees was bound to be a hectic procedure and not likely to be very accurately recorded. As has been mentioned already the statistics on the 1918–21 reform, even those presented officially, were far from accurate, and there is no reason to believe that the figures on the 1945 reform are a bit more reliable. Indeed, it is quite obvious that some of the figures were rigged for political purposes.

As of January, 1947, according to official announcement, 1,443,911 hectares had been expropriated under the 1945 reform from 143, 219 proprietors; 1,057,674 hectares had been distributed to the peasants and 387,565 hectares held as state reserve. Of the 1,114,888 peasants having claims, 796,129 had received land.[41] The average area expropriated was only 10 hectares. Of the number of peasants having claims 72 per cent received land. The average amount received per peasant was about 1.3 hectares. In magnitude this reform—if the figures are at all comparable—by no means equaled the 1918–21 reforms. For roughly the equivalent area (i.e., minus Bessarabia, though including Northern Bucovina and Southern Dobrogea), the first reform had expropriated 4,312,911 hectares, 2,824,962 hectares had been distributed to 1,036,367 peasants, an average of 2.7 hectares' per peasant.

The regional results of the 1945 reform correspond to the nature of the terrain, with the notable exception of Transylvania. In the mountainous overpopulated areas the average allotment was very small: 0.6 hectares in the Moldavian Carpathians, 0.7 hectares in the Wallachian Carpathians, and 0.5 hectares in Bucovina. In Dobrogea, which was relatively sparsely settled, the peasants received an average of almost 3 hectares. An interesting feature of the reform is that while in most of the regions the average area of land expropriated was relatively large (over 130 hectares in the Moldavian Plain, 111 hectares in the Danube Plain, 57 hectares in Dobrogea, and 58 hectares in Bucovina) the average area expropriated was only 5.5 hectares in the Transylvanian Plateau and 5 hectares in the Tisa Plain. Of the total number of expropriations over nine-tenths were in Transylvania, although the area expropriated in that province was only about one-half the total. Clearly this meant the expropriation of numerous properties well under 50 hectares and presumably reflects the forced reduction of the German communities in Transylvania.[42]

41. Institutul Central de Statistică, *Communicări statistice, Nr. 17, 15 martie 1947* (Bucarest, 1947), p. 9.
42. The extensive German settlements in Transylvania, many of which had been there

In January, 1948, the Statistical Institute of the new Rumanian People's Republic undertook an agrarian census to ascertain the distribution of land after the 1945 reform. Unfortunately, this census does not permit satisfactory comparison with that of 1941. It presents a table, comparing the number of agricultural exploitations in the various categories of size for 1941 and 1948, which shows, as might be expected, a decrease in the number of dwarf holdings under ½ hectare and of large holdings over 20 hectares, and a marked increase in the number of exploitations between 1 and 5 hectares. However, since the amount of area occupied by these categories of exploitations is not given and it is unclear whether the same types of land (especially forests and pastures) are included in both cases, the comparison is not very illuminating and may be misleading.[43] It was obvious, however, that the land reform of 1945 did not, as it could not, create a nation of prosperous small-holders. Indeed, the conclusion reached as to the size of Rumanian exploitations has a very familiar ring: "If 3 hectares represents in general the minimum lot necessary to sustain by farming a household of 4 persons, then more than half of the agricultural exploitations of Rumania fall short of this level and are obliged to have recourse to outside income." [44] To be sure, this sour note was not the one prevailing in 1945 and 1946, when the reform was being pushed through, but anticipated the new agrarian line taken up in 1948.

In judging the 1945 land reform, it is necessary to realize, however, that it was not a Rumanian reform but had its sources in the Soviet Union, and that its immediate aims were political not economic.

---

for hundreds of years, were greatly reduced by the wholesale transfer of nearly the entire able-bodied population to the Soviet Union in the winter of 1944–45. Undoubtedly a high percentage of the Germans had been actively pro-Nazi, but the Soviet order paid no attention to any such criteria.

43. Number of agricultural exploitations (excluding Northern Transylvania):

Size of exploitation		1948		1941	
		Number	Per cent	Number	Per cent
Total		2,596,900	100.0	2,303,472	100.0
0–½	hectare	190,169	7.3	277,500	12.0
½–1	"	246,016	9.5	213,088	9.3
1–3	"	933,383	35.9	760,700	33.0
3–5	"	604,540	23.3	441,213	19.2
5–10	"	462,607	17.8	449,716	19.5
10–20	"	122,262	4.7	116,537	5.1
20–50	"	26,607	1.0	27,845	1.2
Over 50	"	11,316	0.4	16,873	0.7

A. Golopenția and P. Onica, *Recensământul agricol din Republica Populară Română, 25 Ianuarie 1948. Rezultate provizorii*, Institutul Central de Statistică (Bucarest, 1948). For further details of the 1948 census see the Appendix. It appears that a good deal more land was included in this census than in 1941.

44. *Ibid.*, p. 18.

Although it was represented as the manifestation of the wishes of the broad masses of the Rumanian peasantry, it seems evident that the main outlines of the law were not drafted in Rumania at all but in Moscow. A comparison of the texts of the Rumanian land reform law with those for the provincial administrations of the Soviet Zone of Germany, passed in the summer of 1945, reveals striking parallels. With the exception of the size of property subject to expropriation (in Germany properties over 100 hectares were to be expropriated), the laws were altogether similar and in certain sections employed identical phrases.[45] Whatever the merits or faults of the reform, it was not a local measure but part of a more general agrarian policy being prepared for a much larger area.

In its general lines and intentions the agrarian reform clearly derives from Lenin's interpretation of class relations in a predominantly agrarian society: the need of eradicating the feudal remnants and of gaining the support of the peasantry by fulfilling its desires for land. In its specific context it was an important part of the National Democratic Front's attempt to obtain mass support in its political campaign. As a means of obtaining positive popularity among the peasants it may be doubted whether it was a great success, and there is no satisfactory evidence that it won the Groza government an enthusiastic peasant following. In the first place, it was physically impossible to grant the Rumanian peasant sufficient land to make him a satisfied and prosperous cultivator. Moreover, the peasants have always felt that the land was theirs and they have never shown themselves particularly grateful to those who parceled it out. On the other hand, the Communists' interest in winning over the peasantry should not be understood as merely a desire to gain popularity. The whole purpose of Lenin's peasant policy was to "neutralize" the peasantry at critical junctures in the party's progress so as to make sure it did not become actively hostile. As such a guarantee it was, perhaps, more successful.

The importance of the agrarian reform in eradicating feudal residues was indirect rather than direct. The Communists undoubtedly

45. Cf. *Frankfurter Zeitung*, September 12, 1945, which gives an account of the German laws. Both reforms started with the same formula that agrarian reform was a national, economic, and social necessity. In both laws local committees of poor peasants were to prepare the land lists, peasants with less than 5 hectares were entitled to land, payment could be in money or kind, with a 10 per cent payment the first year, although poor peasants could obtain a three-year moratorium. The price of the lots was the equivalent of one year's produce. New properties could not be sold, mortgaged, leased, or broken up. Farm machinery was to be placed in a common pool. These similarities are obviously no coincidence, and it is certainly unlikely that the German provincial administrations should have copied the Rumanian land reform independently.

exaggerated the economic importance of the boyars and the extent of their holdings. Nevertheless, a certain boyar spirit still prevailed in Rumania and the fact of land ownership continued to be a mark of prestige.[46] The agrarian reform, in this respect, was probably effective in removing one of the symbols, if not the real source of strength, of Rumania's traditional ruling group.

As an equalitarian measure the land reform undoubtedly has an emotional appeal. When one has followed the history of the agrarian question in Rumania and the way in which the landed interests held out against the peasants until forced to grudging compromises; when one has seen the peasant humbly removing his *căciulă* as the landowner passed, and has perceived the chasm between the peasant and his rulers, one is moved by a feeling that retributive justice has been done. Retributive justice, however, does not reconstruct a society, solve economic problems, or even guarantee that the peasant will not be burdened with a new master.

The immediate economic effects of the reform were unfavorable but should not be exaggerated. The law was applied in the midst of spring planting, and the carefully planned spontaneity of its execution undoubtedly caused a decline in production. Some well-organized large properties were broken up in the process, but on the whole the output of Rumanian large properties had not been very impressive and much of the land was let out. Their function as guides to improved cultivation could certainly be taken over by model farms.

In its professed aim of creating a prosperous peasant agriculture, the agrarian reform alone could have only marginal value, although it undoubtedly provided a temporary relief for a number of peasants. It did not solve the problems of overpopulation, low productivity, strip farming, and the progressive fragmentation of properties. Although the new allotments were not to be broken up, the reform did, by creating new small holdings, increase the area where fragmentation had been most destructive in the past. Essentially the agrarian reform was only the last step of a process which had been going on in Rumania since 1864—the gradual reduction of estate land and its conversion into peasant holdings. Unfortunately the process had been so slow that it could never be more than a palliative. As the final stage in this conversion the 1945 reform was of much less importance than its predecessor. It should not, however, be considered as merely a last step; for the Communists it was clearly a first step.

46. Moore, *Economic Demography of Eastern and Southern Europe,* p. 137, comments on the persistence of land ownership as a source of prestige and social position in these countries, and on the tendency of the successful tradesman or politician to acquire an estate.

XIV

THE COMMUNIST PERIOD: SINCE 1945

Political Developments

WITH the exception of a brief interlude after the Moscow Conference of December, 1945, the evolution of the Groza regime has been steadily toward exclusive political domination by the Communist party, increasing state direction of the economy, and complete absorption of Rumania within the Soviet sphere of control. Several stages are apparent: March-December, 1945, when the Groza government was holding on, with Soviet support, against the nonrecognition of the United States and Great Britain, and the opposition of King Michael and the National Peasant and Liberal parties; January-November, 1946, a period of uneasy and abortive compromise which broke down completely with the holding of national elections; December, 1946–December, 1947, a year spent in liquidating all political opposition and expelling the king; from 1948 on, the consolidation of the Rumanian People's Republic, the inauguration of economic plans, and a turn to collectivization in agriculture.

It is difficult to determine precisely the degree to which this progress was inherent in the Rumanian situation, and to what extent it merely mirrored the intensification of the cold war between the Soviet Union and the West. It was clear at the outset that having come to power through the will of the Russians, lacking extensive popular support, encountering widespread anti-Communist and anti-Soviet sentiment in the other political parties, and confronted by a difficult economic condition which was bound to be bad in the years immediately following the war, the Groza government if it was to maintain itself had every prospect of becoming increasingly dictatorial. At the same time, the phases of increasing severity and political *Gleichschaltung* not only paralleled similar trends in other eastern European states but are closely related to the growing animosity between the Great Powers, an animosity to which the eastern European issue greatly and at points decisively contributed.

At the Potsdam Conference, July 17–August 2, 1945, the American delegation presented its contention that the Yalta Declaration had not been carried out in Rumania and Bulgaria. The immediate Soviet response was, significantly, to condemn the political situation in Greece.[1] There followed lengthy and inconclusive debates in which Stalin at one point stated the problem clearly: "A freely elected government in any of these countries would be anti-Soviet, and that we cannot allow." [2] The Potsdam communiqué showed the failure to reach any real understanding:

The three Governments have also charged the Council of Foreign Ministers with the task of preparing peace treaties for Bulgaria, Finland, Hungary and Rumania. The conclusion of peace treaties with recognized democratic governments in these states will also enable the three Governments to support applications from them for membership of the United Nations. The three Governments agree to examine each separately in the near future, in the light of the conditions then prevailing, the establishment of diplomatic relations with Finland, Rumania, Bulgaria and Hungary to the extent possible prior to the conclusion of peace treaties with those countries.

The only concrete gains were declarations that the press would enjoy full freedom to report from these countries and that the work of the Allied Control Commissions would be improved through regular conferences, three-power consultation, and the free movement of the American and British representatives.

The Potsdam Conference did have certain immediate consequences in the Balkans, however. In Bulgaria the elections, which showed every prospect of being rigged, were postponed for a few months. In Rumania King Michael, on the strength of the Potsdam declaration, asked for the resignation of the Groza government as the apparent prerequisite to a peace treaty, and requested the assistance of the three powers in forming a cabinet acceptable to the United States and Great Britain. It was naturally, if incorrectly, assumed by the Russians and the Rumanian Communists that Michael's action was the result of a deep-laid American plan; their reaction was truculent and negative.[3] Groza refused to resign and took a trip to Moscow,

1. Byrnes, *Speaking Frankly,* p. 73.
2. Philip E. Mosely, *Face to Face with Russia,* Foreign Policy Association, Headline Series, No. 70 (July–August, 1948), p. 23.
3. Rumanians of various political views at first absolutely refused to believe that there was no American scheme behind King Michael's action, but if persuaded such was the case they showed great alarm at the thought of an undirected situation getting out of hand. As far as I know, American action in Rumania did not extend beyond informing King Michael that the Groza regime was unacceptable, a fact generally known, and indicating approval of measures taken to broaden it. The United States did not have, perhaps unfortunately, a positive, thought-out plan of action.

where he received full support. An anomalous situation resulted, in which the king declined to sign decrees and the government continued to carry on its business and even attempted to deny the existence of the rupture. There were, however, fleeting and perhaps illusory intimations in September and October of milder behavior and limited political objectives on the part of the regime. Minister of the Interior Georgescu indicated that political prisoners would be liberated; Prime Minister Groza stated that "his government did not intend to apply either collectivization of land or nationalization of banks or industry." Even Ana Pauker declared to an American correspondent that the Rumanian Communist party wanted unity to exist between the people, the government, and the king.[4]

The Rumanian impasse continued to disturb international negotiations. At the unsuccessful London conference, September 11–October 3, 1945, Molotov charged Byrnes with desiring a government in Rumania unfriendly to the Soviet Union and was apparently baffled by the American attitude, as he was reported to have said he wished he could discover what Byrnes wanted so they could negotiate.[5] Byrnes continued to maintain that the present government was not representative and refused, correctly, to accept Molotov's contention that it enjoyed "the support of the overwhelming majority of the population." On the other hand, while Byrnes, in a radio address on October 31, stressed the importance of the Russians having friendly states as neighbors and declared that "America will never join any groups in those countries in hostile intrigues against the Soviet Union," he seems not to have faced the fact that in pressing for free elections the United States was in effect supporting groups hostile to the U.S.S.R.

In Rumania open violence broke out on November 8, when a crowd celebrating King Michael's birthday was dispersed from the palace square by truckloads of Communist workers and fired upon by the Russian-trained Tudor Vladimirescu Division. Although the Groza government made a number of arrests and charged the historical parties with fomenting the outbreak, there is little question that the violence was introduced by the regime and its organized squads. It

4. See her interview with Sam Brewer, *New York Times,* October 19, 1945. In the course of this interview, however, she made two dots on a piece of paper and said: "We are realists . . . this dot is where we are and that one is Communism. When we come to an obstacle on the straight line between them we go around it, but we come back to our original line. We had to deviate to win the war. Now we must deviate to conquer present problems. But Communism is always our ultimate goal." A clear-enough sign, if that were needed, that the Communist party was not renouncing its ends, but not really a forecast of the policy to be followed.

5. Byrnes, *op. cit.,* p. 100.

would be rather naive, however, to assume that the crowd had gathered merely to felicitate the king; it was a political challenge, in a pattern familiar to Rumania and resorted to when the parliamentary structure collapsed.

The Moscow Conference, December 16–December 26, 1945, gave renewed hopes for continued allied cooperation and for an end to the political stalemate in Rumania. According to its final communiqué, King Michael was to be advised that one National Peasant and one Liberal should be included in the government, provided they were "truly representative members" of the parties, "suitable," and would "work loyally with the government." This reorganized cabinet should declare that free and unfettered elections would be held as soon as possible, elections in which all democratic and antifascist parties could take part; it should give assurances concerning freedom of the press, speech, religion, and association. Deputy Foreign Minister Vyshinsky and the American and British ambassadors to the Soviet Union, Harriman and Clark Kerr, were to form a commission to consult with King Michael and the Groza government on the execution of these tasks. As soon as these conditions had been fulfilled and the required assurances received, the United States and Great Britain would recognize the Rumanian government.

Although this formula had the approval of the three powers, it had little chance of success. From the point of view of the Western powers and the Rumanian opposition, the presence of two members in the cabinet could not be regarded as an adequate concession, so all hopes were necessarily placed upon the forthcoming elections, but it was quite clear by this time that a free and unfettered election was something which the Soviet Union would not permit. At no time could the historical parties of Rumania be regarded as positively friendly to Russia; by 1946, with the experience of the past fifteen months behind them, their hostility was profound.[6] Moreover, since American and British recognition would be given before the actual holding of elections, there was no obvious means of assuring their honesty, nor could there have been unless the Western powers had been willing to force a general showdown with the Soviet Union.

After a delay in which the terms "representative" and "suitable" occasioned some dispute, Mihai Romniceanu, Liberal, and Emil Hațieganu, National Peasant, entered the government. Both agreed

6. For example, in October, 1945, Maniu stated in a declaration that the "present government is a Quisling government imposed by Russia . . . the Soviet government is doing everything possible to keep Groza and Tătărescu in power." This statement was true, of course, but it is difficult to imagine that the Soviet Union would have permitted the exponent of such a view to come to effective power in Rumania.

to "work loyally" but held that their responsibility extended only to seeing that the Moscow agreement was carried out. Although they could scarcely be expected to assume responsibility for the cabinet's other actions, it was clear that no real coalition had been achieved. Groza, on his part, agreed to hold elections "as soon as possible" and to guarantee political rights. On February 4, 1946, the United States and Great Britain, with the explicit understanding that the Groza regime would fulfill the Moscow provisions, recognized the government.

For a time the political atmosphere relaxed somewhat, the opposition parties became active, set up newspapers, and planned their political campaigns. This promising situation did not last long. Soon the government resumed press censorship, political discrimination, arrests, and the terrorizing of anti-Communist politicians. In the spring and summer as violence increased the United States and Great Britain repeatedly protested against the delay in having the elections which they expected to be held in April or May.

The government, however, required time to undermine the strength of the National Peasants and to line up their own forces.[7] In March the Social Democratic party divided on the issue of running a common electoral list with the Communists. Titel Petrescu, leader of the party, was ousted and attempted to set up an Independent Socialist party. The indecision which had haunted the Social Democrats since their inception was now approaching its final and pathetic consequences. Petrescu, who was obviously uncomfortable after March, 1945, had compromised his own position by supporting the Communist drive to power; his belated break merely split the party, and the Left-wingers, opportunists, and Communist agents moved into the government fold. In April Tătărescu's Dissident Liberal party agreed to entering a common list with the Communist-dominated bloc. In July the regime issued two decrees, one abolishing the senate and establishing a unicameral legislature, the second creating a new electoral law which extended the franchise to include women but contained certain provisions facilitating the perversion of the electoral process.

The government finally held elections on November 19, 1946, and in all the unedifying history of Rumanian ballots these more than

7. A vivid eyewitness account of the election campaign is given by Reuben H. Markham, *Rumania under the Soviet Yoke* (Boston, 1949). Markham, who was expelled from Rumania by the Soviet Control Commission for too close association with the National Peasants and for speaking on their behalf, makes no pretense at being a dispassionate observer, but his account of Communist electioneering tactics appears to be substantially correct.

held their own. The patently false vote received by the government bloc. (the Communists, purged Social Democrats, Tătărescu Liberals, Ploughmen's Front, and National People's party, successor to the Union of Patriots) of 4,766,000, as against 880,000 for the National Peasants and 289,000 for the Liberals, was obtained through a crass combination of preelection press censorship and radio discrimination, terrorism and murder, falsification of electoral registers, multiple voting, and unabashed manipulation of the results.

There is little point in debating whether this election was more or less corrupt and unfree than its predecessors. If, as has generally been the case in Rumania, the perversion of elections is in inverse proportion to the government party's popular support, the Groza regime was clearly obliged to resort to extreme measures in rigging the election if it was to remain in power. But while it is true that a prevailing low standard of electoral ethics had been established by the Liberals in the 1920's and by the more outrageous plebiscites of Carol and Antonescu in the 1930's and 1940's, one should not resort to the rather shabby consolation that "Rumanians do not know the meaning of honest elections." The Communists knew; they had spent the preceding two decades criticizing electoral terrorism. The question is rather whether elections should ever have been regarded as a constructive solution under the prevailing circumstances.

The elections of November, 1946, mark the end of the Allied effort to resolve the Rumanian controversy. Wherein does the responsibility lie? There can be no doubt that the Groza regime and the Russians have the responsibility of breaking an international commitment. The Moscow decision was not faithfully observed in any meaningful interpretation of its terms. This responsibility is not lessened by reference to semantic difficulties, to the assumption that rigged elections aimed at simulating unanimous popular support represent true democracy to the Eastern soul, or that the opposition parties really were regarded as "fascist" by the Communists and hence not within the terms of the Moscow agreement. There may be semantic barriers between East and West but it is a dangerous delusion to take these as examples. The matter was much more simply one of taking the necessary steps to maintain and secure power. If that is the case, why did the Russians and the Rumanian Communists agree to a decision committing them to elections? Perhaps a partial answer is that it would be politically embarrassing to have to admit publicly the truth, that the "overwhelming majority" of the Rumanians really preferred not to have Russia as a neighbor, deeply mistrusted the Soviet regime and any party directed by it.

The United States and Great Britain share two responsibilities, one moral and one political. While they did not violate the Moscow agreement, they incurred a certain obligation toward those Rumanians who, wisely or unwisely, came to believe that the Anglo-American stand gave them some hope of resisting and combating the Communist party and Soviet pressure. As Arnold J. Toynbee observed in connection with an earlier but analogous situation, the Western powers, by encouraging the local opponents of the Russians "to look to them for a guidance and a protection which they had no intention of giving at any sacrifice to themselves . . . deterred them from coming to terms before it was too late . . . and merely exposed them to reprisals as satellites of . . . Russia's most dangerous enemies." [8]

The other element of Anglo-American responsibility concerns what might be called injustice in Thomas Hobbes's nonmoral but severely logical sense—involvement in a political contradiction. As has been mentioned, at no time did the Western powers really meet the fact that their expressed twin desires to have a Rumanian government friendly to the U.S.S.R. and one representing the majority of the inhabitants were, in all likelihood, incompatible. Stalin obviously required a friendly government and apparently believed he had received Allied agreement through his arrangement with Churchill. In 1945, when the question came to the surface, the United States, rather hesitantly backed by Great Britain, felt obliged to stand out for a truly representative government obtained through the holding of elections.

Now if the United States really desired to maintain amicable relations with the Soviet Union on the Balkan question, it should not have pressed so persistently for the one act which would certainly and predictably arouse either open Soviet hostility or, as happened, a dishonest and hence unsatisfactory response. On the other hand, if it is true that the Soviet regime by its very nature was impossible to get on with, that it would demand, as Byrnes said later, not friendly but subservient governments, that the anti-Communist politicians in Rumania were justified in their abiding mistrust of the neighbor to the East, then the alternatives left to the Western powers were either to give up, as not worth the cost, the attempt to influence events in the area, or to take the measures necessary to achieve their effective

8. Toynbee was speaking of the disaster which overcame the Transcaucasian republics after the First World War. *Survey of International Affairs, 1920–1923* (Oxford University Press, 1925), pp. 373–374. Of course, it might be contended that it was just a matter of time in any case before the political opposition, active or passive, was knocked down. But this possibility, which if strong was not a certainty, does not absolve the Western powers from a definite responsibility.

control over the situation. Admittedly the postwar attitude to be adopted by the Soviet Union was by no means clearly foreseen in 1944–1945, and as suggested above it may not have been altogether fixed, but if, as it appeared in 1950, any effort at American-Soviet agreement in eastern Europe involved fitting a square peg in a round hole there was not, during the period of uncertainty, even an effort to shave off some of the sharper edges of the peg.

In any event, whatever slight chances there might have been of resolving the Rumanian political crisis, through international agreement and peaceful internal adjustment, had disappeared by the time the elections were held. The National Peasants and Liberals naturally refused to accept the results, and their delegates did not occupy their seats in the parliament. In a formal communiqué of November 25, 1946, Maniu and Brătianu, after enumerating the electoral outrages, concluded: "Our parties consider that they can no longer authorize their representatives to continue to collaborate with the present government, the perpetrator of fraudulent and blood stained elections, with which they can have no solidarity whatsoever." [9] The United States and Great Britain did not accept the elections as representing the opinion of the Rumanian people or as complying with the assurances given by the Groza government.

The peace treaty with Rumania, which had been drafted by the Council of Foreign Ministers in the course of 1946 and was finally signed on February 10, 1947, did not materially alter the situation. Although Article 3 obliged Rumania to secure for all persons "the enjoyment of human rights and of the fundamental freedoms, including freedom of expression, of press, of publication, of religious worship, of political opinion, and of public meeting," it was in nowise observed.[10]

9. See the annex to the booklet published by the Rumanian National Committee, *Suppression of Human Rights in Rumania* (Washington, D.C., September, 1949), a hostile but heavily documented indictment of the Groza regime.
10. Some of the main points of the treaty, which in general followed the lines of the 1944 armistice, were: frontiers to be as of January 1, 1941, except for the Hungarian frontier which remained as of January 1, 1938; the obligation to repeal and henceforth not to pass any measures discriminating against persons for sympathizing with the United Nations; dissolving and not permitting in the future any organization of a fascist type or other organization conducting propaganda hostile to the Soviet Union or other United Nations; limitation of the army to 120,000 persons; reparations in kind to the U.S.S.R. to the amount of $300,000,000, payable in eight years from September, 1944; guarantee of economic and property rights of United Nations nationals; German assets in Rumania to go to the Soviet Union; free commercial navigation on the Danube for all states; Allied forces to be withdrawn from the country within ninety days of the treaty's coming into force, except for the Soviet right to retain forces necessary to maintain the line of communication with the Soviet Zone in Austria.

The Groza regime, bolstered by the simulacrum of popular support gained in the elections and faced by an opposition unwilling to accept an unwarranted minority position in parliament, undertook in 1947 to wipe out all unfriendly or doubtful political organizations. In the spring it unleashed a new wave of arrests of opposition leaders, arrests made suddenly, at night, and with no explanation. The Communist Minister of Justice, Pătrășcanu, expressed his belief that an uprising was being plotted but said "there was no evidence on hand fixing the responsibility upon former Premier Iuliu Maniu as leader of preparations for a revolution." [11] In July a number of National Peasant leaders, including Mihalache, were caught in an attempt to flee the country; the government arrested Maniu and the top party leadership and outlawed the party, an action which apparently evoked no popular response one way or the other.

Amid much publicity the regime, in November, tried Maniu and his followers, primarily on the charge of conspiring with "Anglo-American imperialism"; as the Communist paper, Scânteia, remarked, the United States was really the "twentieth defendant." Some damaging evidence was produced at the trial; observers seem generally to agree that certain members of the National Peasant party were shown to have been in contact with American intelligence officers to discuss means of overthrowing the regime.[12] Maniu, the principal defendant, while perfectly frank in his opinion of the government's illegitimacy and admitting attempting to smuggle National Peasants out of the country for the purpose of organizing resistance abroad, maintained that his opposition was within the framework of international agreements concerning Rumania, agreements which the government had flagrantly violated. But since the regime had effectively blocked any possibility of parliamentary opposition, underground planning—whether actually envisaging violence or not—was the only alternative to complete passivity.

The trial itself was conducted in a manner unhappily too familiar these days; the judge, Colonel Petrescu, was reportedly the director general of all prisons and concentration camps under the Antonescu dictatorship. Maniu and Mihalache were sentenced to terms of life imprisonment, the other leaders to terms ranging from one to twenty-five years. Whatever weight one may attach to the demands of *raison*

11. See his interview with W. H. Lawrence, *New York Times,* June 25, 1947.

12. As a matter of fact, as early as the spring of 1945 a number of Rumanians, some of whom had close connections with the Liberal and National Peasant parties, were developing underground plans for ousting the Groza government and sought to enlist American support. The charges of plots against the regime were not pure concoctions, whatever the purpose of the trial may have been.

d'état—and it is obvious that Maniu and Mihalache did represent a threat to the Groza government—it is absurd to regard in any manner their sentences as an act of justice.

While the Maniu trial was in progress, the controlled press raised a clamor against Tătărescu and pointed out, quite correctly, that many anti-Groza elements were being sheltered in the Ministry of Foreign Affairs and the diplomatic service. Tătărescu's position had been weakening for some time. In June, 1947, he had circulated a memorandum which contained a fifteen-point proposal for changing internal and external policy: he assailed the government's economic policy, expressed alarm over the country's low economic output, which was still at only 48 per cent of the 1938 level, requested better treatment of foreign capital and less stifling state intervention, and criticized the number of preventive arrests and the poor prison conditions. The Communists were naturally displeased by this note which clearly exceeded the conventions of "criticism and self-criticism." Rumors circulated of Tătărescu's resignation, and in September he was obliged to dismiss several hundred employees in the Foreign Office. On November 5 the parliament passed a vote of no confidence in him; the following day he and the other Dissident Liberal cabinet members were removed from their posts, to be replaced by Ana Pauker at the Foreign Office and Vasile Luca at the Ministry of Finance. (In December Bodnaraş took over the Ministry of War. The real rulers of the country were at last assuming governmental positions.)

Thus ended the political career of an able if unscrupulous man, who had first attracted attention in the early 1920's for his efficient action against the Communists and who had threaded a devious course through Carol's reign. Though disliked and mistrusted by all political groups, he seems to have had a rather Talleyrandian interest in the welfare of Rumania as he saw it.

Plans for the merger of the Social Democratic and Communist parties were announced in the autumn of 1947, though this amalgamation, which was in effect the complete absorption of the Social Democrats within a Leninist-Stalinist organization and ideology, was not completed until the following spring. It seems to have met with the sincere if ineffectual opposition of most of the socialists, some of whom joined Titel Petrescu's Independent Socialist party.[13] The Petrescu faction, however, was subject to increasing attack and

13. For an account of this last, faltering episode in the career of the Social Democratic party, see Valentin Thoma, "Wie es zur Liquidierung des rumänischen Sozialismus kam," *Die Zukunft* (July, 1949).

charged with illegally distributing political leaflets; on May 6, 1948, Petrescu was arrested and kept in prison without trial.

On December 30, 1947, King Michael, an anomalous monarch in a universe of burgeoning people's democracies, was suddenly and rather unexpectedly forced to abdicate. At the time he said his abdication was voluntary but subsequently, after his departure from Rumania, announced that it had been made under duress and he could not regard it as binding. Government propaganda became increasingly unfriendly to the king and listed with great relish the castles, forest land, and industrial shares that reverted to the nation. Following the overthrow of the monarchy the government at once announced the creation of the Rumanian People's Republic (Republica Populară Română) and prepared the draft of a new constitution.

Having thus eliminated the monarchy and all overt political opposition, the Communists then turned to the task of removing disaffected or doubtful elements in their own ranks. In the autumn of 1947 Gheorghiu-Dej, commenting on the rapid growth of the Rumanian Communist party to 710,000 members, had criticized the "low political and ideological level of our cadres and the presence of chauvinism among party members." In the course of a three-day congress of Communists and Social Democrats, assembled in February, 1948, to ratify their unification in a United Workers party, Minister of the Interior Teohari Georgescu launched an attack on the Communist Minister of Justice Pătrășcanu, whom he charged with falling under bourgeois influence and overestimating the forces of the enemy, the Western powers. Pătrășcanu was removed from his post and from the Central Committee of the party; later reports have suggested his being a likely candidate for a purge trial such as the other people's democracies have enjoyed.

There had been friction between Pătrășcanu, a local Communist, and the "Muscovites," Pauker and Luca, since before the installation of the Groza regime. They found him too nationalistic and he was undoubtedly alarmed by the heavy, mechanically brutal tactics of the new order, its complete disregard of the nation's sensitivities, and its absolute subservience to Soviet state demands. Without question, many of the same elements which created Titoism and similar national heresies in the Communist camp were present in the Rumanian party, but because of the basic weakness of the Communist movement in Rumania and the ineluctable dependence upon the Soviet Union they never had a chance of obtaining control.

In February, 1948, the Communists concocted a new Democratic Popular Front, comprising the United Workers party; the Ploughmen's Front, which had absorbed the dissident National Peasants to become a united peasant party; the National Popular party, which dissolved itself a year later on the grounds that the intellectuals and representatives of the middle class supporting this artificial organization should henceforth work within the cadres of the "mass parties"; and the Hungarian Popular party, controlled by the Communists but presumably designed to represent the Hungarian minority. On March 28 this bloc conducted and won elections, against a wholly spurious opposition, for a new assembly to vote on the constitution.

The Constitution of 1948 closely resembled the 1947 Constitution of the Bulgarian People's Republic and was clearly derived from and inspired by the Soviet Constitution of 1936. Apart from the fact that the latter is concerned with the union of a number of constituent republics, the principal differences reflect the transitional character of the so-called popular democracy. The People's Republic is defined as arising from the struggle against fascism, reaction, and imperialism rather than from the overthrow of landlords and capitalists. Private property is still recognized as one form of ownership of the means of production, though it is circumscribed by the "general interest" and subject to expropriation and nationalization. The Communist party does not have the preeminent status it enjoys in the U.S.S.R. As in the Soviet constitution stress is laid upon the right to work, to have leisure, and to receive an education; civil liberties, freedom of the press and of speech are guaranteed, but clearly for proletarian purposes; the right of association may not be directed against the democratic order established by the constitution. The supreme organ of the state is the unicameral Grand National Assembly, headed by a Presidium; the executive branch of the government is the Council of Ministers.[14]

Since the adoption of the constitution there have been few important structural changes in the government but rather a consolidation of the regime, the reorganization of the administration and the army (which apparently now exceeds treaty limits), and a running fight to eliminate the remnants of political opposition and to subdue sporadic uprisings brought about by the extensive new economic activities. A series of well-advertised public trials continued through 1948 and 1949, against Liberals, industrialists, military officers, students, Catholic and Uniate clergy, and Zionists, all categories that might cause the regime trouble or embarrassment. The new legal apparatus, including the addition of "people's assessors" to assure

14. For a recent study of constitutional developments within the Soviet sphere, see Andrew Gyorgy, *Governments of Danubian Europe* (New York, 1949).

proletarian justice and the introduction of the death penalty for treason, espionage, and economic sabotage, proved an efficient weapon in this attack. The creation, announced in January, 1949, of People's Councils as the organs of local government was to provide the basic unit for the administrative hierarchy and to pave the way to a socialist society. In September, 1949, a State Control Commission was formed "to develop the spirit of responsibility toward public property, to wipe out bureaucracy, to verify the carrying out of government decrees, and to prevent sabotage in the work of building socialism." Avram Bunaciu, Pătrășcanu's tougher successor at the Ministry of Justice, became head of this commission, which promised to be a very formidable instrument.

Along with the consolidation and coordination of the political and administrative apparatus came a marked shift in the party line from what it had been at the end of the war. The original program sought a government friendly to the U.S.S.R. and in which the workers' front would operate in coalition with middle-class parties. After 1947 not only the fact but even the pretense of collaboration was dropped. At the end of that year Gheorghiu-Dej said,

The resignation of Tătărescu and his group means the removal of the last representatives of the reactionary bourgeoisie from the government; it means that the proletariat and its allies no longer share state power with the representatives of the exploiting classes. . . . The proletarian vanguard, in close alliance with the peasants and the progressive intelligentsia, is the backbone of the government.[15]

By 1949 the People's Democracy was explicitly defined as fulfilling the functions of the dictatorship of the proletariat. It was distinguished from the Soviet form because it was possible, through the assistance of the U.S.S.R., to establish the dictatorship without civil war. In the People's Democracy, unlike the Soviet, the old state apparatus was not immediately smashed; bourgeois elements were retained for a time.

But only with the establishment of People's Councils—local organs of state power built on broad democratic lines—will the new state apparatus be created, corresponding from top to bottom in every way with the aims and tasks of the new state and adjusted to the tasks of building Socialism. . . . The establishment of the People's Councils signifies

15. *For a Lasting Peace, for a People's Democracy* (January 1, 1948). (Published in Belgrade until December, 1948; subsequently in Bucarest.)

that in form the People's Democracy is approaching the higher form of the dictatorship of the proletariat—the Soviet form.[16]

Vasile Luca even read this view into the earlier tactics of the party, stating that in 1944 the Rumanian Communists had realized that the only road forward was the one mapped by the October revolution: "There was no third path, and there can not be one." [17]

Hence by the beginning of 1950 the Rumanian government was openly recognized as a proletarian dictatorship, well on the way to the Soviet form and in full pursuit of socialism. It might seem from these statements that this program had been planned all along; certainly Georgescu and Luca, in their current stress upon the regime's revolutionary origins, sought to give that impression. Yet there is evidence that this renewed Leftist line of international communism was causing some confusion in the cadres.

For example, an article appearing in 1949 in a Hungarian Communist periodical pronounced the same general line, which is that of all eastern European Communist parties today, but in greater detail.[18] The new People's Democracy was identified with the dictatorship of the proletariat; this identity did not exist at first but was created in the course of a developing struggle, first against fascism and big business but later against all capitalist elements including the rich peasantry. The article was frank in granting that this advance was rendered possible through the initiative and continuing aid of the Soviet Union.

Significantly, however, it went on to say that the Hungarian party did not have a clear view of all this until it received clarification from the Communist party of the Soviet Union and the Cominform in the autumn of 1947 and the summer of 1948. As a consequence, the party membership had fallen into a number of errors: it was inclined to forget that the People's Democracy was really more than just a plebeian variety of bourgeois democracy; it stressed the differences rather than the similarities between the Soviet system and the People's Democracy; it believed that the transition to socialism could be made without the dictatorship of the proletariat, or, if not, that the dic-

16. *Ibid.* (June 1, 1949).

17. *Ibid.* (November 4, 1949). In this same vein Luca proceeded to congratulate the party for wrecking all the coalition cabinets after August, 1944: "Before March 6, 1945 not a single government had been able to consolidate itself. The pressure of the masses led by the Communist Party and the work of the Communist Ministers inside the government brought about the fall of all these governments."

18. This article was translated into English and appears as "The Character of a 'People's Democracy,'" *Foreign Affairs, 28*, No. 1 (October, 1949), 143–152.

tatorship would follow the People's Democracy and was not contained within its form; it believed that power might be shared with the peasants.

But what, it should be asked, was the source of these errors? Surely not an independent, uninformed, "soft" mood on the part of the Hungarian party. The hard line now enunciated was no new discovery; it was the familiar revolutionary message all Communists had been brought up on. Quite obviously all these mistakes were likewise, at an earlier date, the official line emanating from Moscow in support of popular fronts, and while it may be that the Moscow leadership never really subscribed to this line, the article itself would indicate that party membership had been sufficiently indoctrinated in the more moderate tactic that it was now necessary to make a special effort to redirect its views. Given the tight coordination of all Communist parties in the Soviet sphere, there is no reason to doubt that this interpretation also applies to the Rumanian case.

On the international level, Rumania's relations deteriorated steadily after 1946; the American and British governments repeatedly wrote notes of protest against the violation of Allied agreements and the peace treaty; the Rumanian government responded sharply with charges of American imperialism and espionage. In 1949 the issue of the Bulgarian, Hungarian, and Rumanian violation of human rights was brought before the General Assembly of the United Nations, which recorded its disapproval of the completely uncooperative attitude displayed by these states and resolved to refer the issue to the International Court of Justice for definition and clarification.[19] It was not clear by the end of the year that this action could achieve any important results under existing circumstances.

Since the creation in 1947 of the Cominform, which signalized the return to a hard line, and especially with the transfer of its headquarters to Rumania after the break with Tito, Bucarest has become one of the principal centers of international communism. At the same time the country has been increasingly isolated from the Western world. In April, 1949, even diplomatic representatives were prohibited from traveling in the Banat, Bucovina, Moldavia, or Dobrogea.

It is idle to speculate whether or when Rumania will enter the Soviet Union as a member republic, although rumors anticipating that event have not been lacking in the last two years. It would appear to be a question of relatively little practical importance, since the U.S.S.R.

19. United Nations, *Official Records of the Fourth Session of the General Assembly. Resolutions, 20 September–10 December 1949* (Lake Success, N.Y.).

already enjoys virtually complete control over the country. Moreover, while the Rumanian political and economic structure is steadily approaching, and probably not asymptotically, the Soviet model, the final decision on incorporation will be based—apart from considerations of expediency—on political definitions which a mind not steeped in Leninism-Stalinism would have small chance of foreseeing.[20]

Economic Conditions

Economic developments since 1945 may be divided into two periods: two years, 1945–47, of confusion and distress resulting from the war, Russian withdrawals, severe drought, the agrarian reform, monetary inflation, and the unsettled political situation; since 1947, a period of greater stability, an apparent increase in production, and the beginning of a directed and planned economy. In neither period can one obtain a very satisfactory picture of economic conditions. In the first months there was much administrative disorganization, and the government itself frequently lacked accurate information. The Groza regime has not hesitated from the outset to manipulate statistics for political and propagandistic purposes. Since the tightening of the administration in 1948, Rumania has been as reluctant as the Soviet Union, more reluctant than the other satellites, to publish any measurable economic data. Today, the few figures that appear are given as percentage gains for which it would be exceedingly difficult to supply a reasonably accurate base.

In general, it may be said that Rumania was slower than the other eastern European states to recover from the war, in somewhat the same way it lagged in coming out of the depression. Agricultural production fell off seriously in 1945 and 1946, partly because of the disorganization attendant upon the agrarian reform, but largely because of two years' serious drought. Both the acreage sown and the crop yields, especially in maize, the peasant's source of food, were exceptionally low; in 1946 the level of agricultural production was only 59 per cent of the 1934–38 average.[21] The production of indus-

20. This point is not very important but it is of interest to note that in the exchange of notes leading to Tito's expulsion from the Cominform in 1948, the Central Committee of the Communist party of the Soviet Union, after referring to Kardelj's hope, expressed in 1945, that the Yugoslav government would be regarded as the representatives of one of the future Soviet republics, rather scornfully dismissed his "primitive and fallacious reasoning . . . about Yugoslavia as a future constituent part of the USSR." It did not, however, vouchsafe its own authoritative views on the subject. Cf. Royal Institute of International Affairs, *The Soviet-Yugoslav Dispute* (London; New York, 1948), p. 39.

21. United Nations, Department of Economic Affairs, *Economic Survey of Europe in 1948* (Geneva, 1949), p. 17.

trial and food crops fell successively in 1945 and 1946, and it is to be noted that the soybean, so extensively advertised in the 1930's, virtually disappeared as a crop when the peasants were left to their own devices.

The absence of accumulated stocks of grain, the large deliveries to Russia under the armistice, and the failure of the maize harvest in 1946 produced a disastrous and tragic famine, above all in Moldavia, in the winter and spring of 1947. Relief shipments had to be brought in from abroad, including substantial assistance from the United States.

The livestock position, while improving over the situation immediately after the war, was still weak by 1948. There were, in that year, 30 horses and 138 oxen (including buffaloes) per 100 agricultural exploitations as against 56 and 150 respectively in 1941; in terms of cultivation, there were 21 draft animals per 100 hectares of arable land in 1948 as against 27 in 1941. The quantity of agricultural equipment showed less diminution: an increase in the total number over 1941 was matched by a slight decline in the amount of equipment per exploitation, a result presumably of the increase in small holdings after the 1945 reform.[22]

Rumanian industry, which had expanded under wartime demands, registered a decline in 1944 and 1945, but a slight recovery in 1946. According to the Ministry of Finance, total industrial production was 80 per cent of the 1941 level in 1944, 60 per cent in 1945, and 77 per cent in the first ten months of 1946.[23] The chemical, metallurgical, and food industries were the most severely hit. The petroleum industry, which appears to be facing an exhaustion of the tapped fields, had already showed signs of decline before the war; in 1947 the output of crude petroleum was 3.8 million tons as against 8.7 million in 1936 and 5.8 million in 1940.

In addition to the slump in agricultural and industrial production, the Rumanian economy suffered from the flow of goods to the Soviet Union. The total value of Rumanian wealth transferred officially or unofficially, as restitution, reparations, or war booty has been the

22. A. Golopenţia and P. Onica, *Recensământul agricol din Republica Populară Română, 25 Ianuarie 1948. Resultate provizorii,* Institutul Central de Statistică (Bucarest, 1948).

23. Rumanian Ministry of Finance, *Expunere de motive la bugetul 1947/48,* p. 338. The validity of these figures is uncertain, and they may represent an inflated estimate. Tătărescu is reported to have said in 1947 that after two years of the Groza regime the general level of production was only 48 per cent of the 1938 output. *New York Times,* June 6, 1947.

subject of a number of heated disputes at international conferences, and it would be very difficult to make a reliable estimate.[24] That the drain was serious is indicated by the fact that as early as 1945 some Rumanian Communists, with more than the average amount of economic insight and less than the usual blind devotion to the Soviet Union, were in despair over the effect of the Russian withdrawals upon the country's economy and their own political position. The glaring contradiction between Russia's efforts to woo Rumania and to secure some measure of popularity for the Communist party and its rather frantic removal of goods and equipment has puzzled many observers. The explanation may simply be that the policy of this monolithic state was not consistent, or rather, that two different policies were here overlapping.

Rumania's foreign trade was greatly reduced after the war; by 1948 the value of its exports was only 50 per cent of the 1938 figure (in 1947, 21 per cent), and its imports 69 per cent (in 1947, 57 per cent).[25] The bulk of the trade was with the generally similar economies of the other eastern European states, which were being increasingly linked by a network of trade agreements.

The combination of low output, armistice obligations and war costs, and the general political uncertainty of the postarmistice months led to a fearful inflation. Rumanian currency had never been sound since the First World War and had showed a tendency toward inflation in the 1930's and the war years; between 1945 and the summer of 1947, when a drastic stabilization was achieved, prices rose to dizzying heights. The cost of living index increased from a base of 100 in 1938 to 145.0 in 1940, 413.9 in 1943, 3,678.7 in 1945, 46,140 in December, 1946, and 525,688 in July, 1947.[26]

24. At the time of the Paris Peace Conference the American delegate, Willard L. Thorp, complained that the Rumanian delegation had been of no assistance in supplying information on this point, but he estimated that the total cost to Rumania of its defeat would be about $2,000,000,000. As of 1946 he estimated that about $1,050,000,000 had already been transferred: $325,000,000 for the maintenance of occupation troops, $100,000,000 for reparations based on the 1938 price level, $175,000,000 for property restitution, and $450,000,000 for requisitions. U.S. Department of State, *Bulletin, 15,* No. 379 (October 6, 1946). In July, 1948, General Radescu, in exile in the United States, stated that since Thorp's estimate Rumania had paid an additional $735,000,000. *New York Times,* July 18, 1948. Some attempts have been made to relate these withdrawals to Rumania's national income, but both figures would by necessity be exceedingly uncertain.

25. United Nations, Department of Economic Affairs, *Economic Survey of Europe in 1948,* Table XVI.

26. Institutul Central de Statistică, *Comunicări statistice, No. 19* (Bucarest, January 31, 1948).

The Change in Economic and Agrarian Policy

With regard to economic policy, the first two years after the war might be regarded as an induced and foreshortened NEP; not a retreat from war communism as the Soviet New Economic Policy had been, but, in form at least, the creation of a transitional economy between the older Rumanian capitalism and the drive toward socialism. This concept is closely related in the Communist mind to the functions of the People's Democracy and is embodied in the Constitution of 1948, though by that time the actual economic policy was moving beyond it.

For all the fanfare accompanying the 1945 agrarian reform, the organization of Rumanian farming in the first two or three years after its application showed little change. In the planting year 1946/47 much the greater part of the working force was engaged in family farms. About 181,000 persons (2.3 per cent of those active in agriculture) were permanent farm laborers, about 783,000 were engaged in seasonal work, and 1.4 million persons did some work on farms other than their own.[27] Payment for work continued to be a mixture of money and produce, only one-third of the work being paid solely in money.

The type of cultivation was much the same, though there was a retrogression from mixed agriculture. If the figures are comparable, some 61 per cent of the exploitations in 1948 were devoted to cereal cultivation as against 51 per cent in 1941; only 1.2 per cent of the exploitations concentrated on raising livestock as against 12 per cent in 1941, a reflection of the wartime loss of animals and the breaking up of large estates.

About two-thirds of the exploitations obtained their money income through sale of produce, the other third through outside labor. Two-fifths of the exploitations in 1947 were obliged to buy agricultural produce to supplement their own deficient production.

In 1945 the Groza regime announced that the agrarian reform was but the initial step in a whole series of projected reforms which would transform Rumanian agriculture, but at this time there was no mention of collectivization as the general goal. On the contrary, any mention of collective farming was frowned upon, and the whole emphasis was on assisting the independent peasant. Actually, the list of

27. *Recensământul agricol din Republica Populară Română, 25 Ianuarie 1948*, p. 35. The relation between the last two categories is not clear, but the figures on permanent and seasonal workers are quite similar to those of 1941. See above, p. 52

proposed measures was very similar to those brought forward repeatedly by various Rumanian governments in the preceding twenty-five
years. Great publicity was given to state-operated agricultural machine stations which were to enable the peasant to mechanize his
cultivation; from the beginning, however, this measure was regarded
as a powerful potential lever in the hands of the state to direct agriculture. The promise of an agricultural machine industry was also a
familiar item of earlier programs. Other recognizable projects were
land reclamation, the creation of better experimental stations, improved agricultural education, more credit, a vigorous cooperative
movement, development of agricultural industries, a scientific land
survey, and the encouragement of animal husbandry.[28]

In 1945 the government created a National Cooperative Institute
to assist agriculture, but its principal function appears to have been
grain collection.[29] In November, 1946, appeared a new organ, RE-
AZIM, an autonomous administration for developing agriculture,
animal husbandry, and the use of agricultural machinery. REAZIM
took over most of the state functions for agrarian improvement, rationalizing cultivation, supplying seeds and equipment, executing
production plans, and managing agricultural machine stations.

Although many of these projects resembled those proposed by
earlier regimes, it was obvious that the Communists had no intention
of permitting Rumanian agriculture to proceed in its traditional rut.
Even in the first phase of ostentatious silence about collective agriculture, the nature of the reforms, or rather the absence of certain reforms, provided an indication of developments to come. In its plans
for agricultural improvement, the regime appears to have laid little
stress on the desirability of consolidating holdings in private ownership, and the 1948 census showed the fragmentation of properties to
be just as extreme as in 1941. The emphasis was upon increasing
cereal output through mechanization rather than upon the intensified
and diversified cultivation suitable to peasant farming. When, as a
consequence of the 1946–47 famine, poor peasants began to sell their
holdings, the government took steps to cancel sales to rich farmers.
All these moves showed that it had no intention of fostering the
growth of an independent, potentially capitalist peasantry on the

28. See, for example, the two pamphlets outlining the government's plans for intensifying livestock raising and for land reclamation: *Intensificarea creşterii animalelor
in cadrul refacerii economice* (Bucarest, 1946), and *Imbunătăţirile funciare în agricultura românească* (Bucarest, 1946).

29. In 1945 INCOOP was granted 57 billion lei for the collection of grain, of which
13 billion was for deliveries to the U.S.S.R., 8 billion to supply Soviet troops, 1 billion
to supply the Rumanian army, and 35 billion for the civil population.

Western model, but during this first period, to avoid alienating the
peasants, it held its hand.

A somewhat similar situation obtained in the question of industrial
policy, though here official propaganda was much more hostile to
exploiting industrialists. So long as the Tătărescu Liberals were in
the government, it called for the cooperation of private capital, and
the only important step taken in this first phase was the nationalization of the National Bank. As late as March, 1947, Mihail Ralea,
Rumanian Minister to the United States, protested against rumors
that the government was proceeding against private enterprise and
maintained, either disingenuously or without information (Ralea
was not a member of the Communist party), that one of the main
goals of the Groza regime was to "foster private initiative," to which
it granted complete freedom.[30] Nevertheless, in practice the sphere
of private industrial activity was increasingly circumscribed and restricted by a number of devices: obstructive action by the workers,
appeals to the national interest, or simply charges of inefficiency and
sabotage.

Perhaps the most significant economic innovation in the months
after the armistice was the creation of a number of joint Soviet-
Rumanian enterprises. On May 8, 1945, the Rumanian government
signed an agreement with the Soviet Union providing for extensive
economic collaboration. The U.S.S.R. was to assist Rumanian agriculture by supplying tractors, seed, and agricultural experts. A
number of SOVROM companies were set up in the important fields
of river and air transport, banking, lumbering, and oil production
and refining. (A 1948 trade agreement created two new SOVROM
companies for the manufacture of tractors and chemical products.)
Participation in the companies was on a 50–50 basis, and the Rumanian state was to grant them special privileges and monopolies.
Much of the Soviet capital was quite easily obtained from the German assets in Rumania, awarded to the U.S.S.R. in the Potsdam
agreement. These concerns clearly gave the Soviet Union a controlling
position at key points in the Rumanian economy.

This form of economic collaboration was reminiscent of the
Rumanian-German trade agreement of 1939. The principal difference lay less perhaps in the agreements themselves than in the
structure of the Soviet and German economies. Under the German-
Rumanian agreement the two economies were seen as complementary,
and the major function of Rumania was to provide raw materials; the
Germans showed some hostility to the further development of Ru-

30. See his letter to the *New York Times*, March 12, 1947.

manian industries, especially secondary industries. Both Russia and Rumania, however, are still industrializing economies and there seems to be little evidence, in the Rumanian case at least, of a desire to check the industrialization of the latter.[31]

The turning point in the economic policy of the immediate postwar period was the stabilization of the currency in August, 1947, which more or less liquidated the old financial structure and served as a vast economic leveler. On the fifteenth of that month, the leu was devalued (to 150 to the dollar) and the old money was ordered to be exchanged immediately at the rate of one new leu for 20,000 old lei. Peasants were limited to exchanging 5,000,000 lei; workers to 3,000,000; and other persons to 1,500,000. That is, at the official new rate, peasants could receive in exchange $1.67, workers $1.00, and others $0.50. Gold and foreign currency were entitled to full value but had to be declared under penalty of life imprisonment. This drastic measure, which came at a time of continued commodity shortages, inevitably caused widespread hardship. There were numerous reports of resistance by the peasants who felt as usual that they were being sacrificed to the benefit of the towns. The government hurled many charges of speculation and exchange violation, and part of the brutal behavior of the regime in the course of 1947 is to be associated with, if not explained by, this Draconian financial reorganization.[32]

Along with the tightening of political control the Groza government now entered a new phase of economic policy marked by the progressive nationalization of industry, collectivization of agriculture, and the beginning of economic plans. In 1947 pressure against private industry consisted primarily in assuming control over certain specific enterprises, supervising industrial activity, and making accusations of sabotage against foreign-owned concerns. At the beginning of 1948 Gheorghiu-Dej launched a general attack on private capital, which dominated industry, banking, and insurance: "Our democratic regime has been very patient with private enterprise, but private owners do not make capital investment, nor do they renew equipment. They transfer capital abroad and openly sabotage reconstruction." In January the concession of the Rumanian match monopoly to the Swedish firm (this concession had been granted at the time of the stabilization loan of 1929) was declared invalid and

31. See also below, pp. 327–329.
32. A defense of the stabilization, written by the National Bank, is published as "La Réforme monétaire en Roumanie, 15 août 1947," in *Les Archives internationales*, Doc. 664.

annulled. In the following months government administrators were appointed to supervise the British and American-owned oil companies, which action, in effect, put these firms in a state of forcible dissolution. The Rumanian industrialist, Nicolae Malaxa, who had made great efforts to accommodate himself to the Russians and the Groza regime, was unable to ride this new wave and his factories, the most important in the country, were also taken over. While, as has been seen, the Rumanian government has always worked in close conjunction with Rumanian industry—fostering desirable undertakings and even setting up state-owned enterprises—this new advance was under quite different auspices and had a far more ambitious intent.

The decisive step came in June, 1948, with a bill providing for the nationalization of all industrial, mining, banking, insurance, and transport concerns. The law at the outset affected some 1,068 enterprises, including 132 heavy industries, 20 coal mines, 25 oil and natural gas companies, 56 building material companies, 163 textile factories, 15 insurance companies, and 4 shipping concerns. While the law did not, in theory, deny compensation, it was to be based on profits, its amount was to be determined by a government commission, it was to be paid in state bonds, and would not be given to persons who "have enriched themselves illegally or left the country illegally." The motives given for the bill were largely political: the new situation demanded changes in the national economy; the bourgeoisie, which had been disarmed politically, must not be permitted to retain its potent economic weapons.

In November all privately owned health institutions, hospitals, sanatoria, and the film industry were nationalized. In April, 1949, the state took over a new batch of private companies, pharmacies, laboratories, drug and cosmetic factories. Thus, by the end of the year, a significant and certainly decisive sector of the economy was directly controlled and managed by the state.

The switch in agrarian policy came at a somewhat later date, though in 1946 and 1947 one finds mounting criticism of the predatory activity of the rich peasants and the sabotage committed by estate owners on the land remaining to them. A foreshadowing of a change in eastern European agriculture was given in a Russian broadcast of February 9, 1948, to Soviet farmers: "Today the governments of the new democracies know that the present small peasant holdings are not a paying proposition and that the peasants' road to wealth lies in co-operation and the uniting of small holdings into large collective estates. . . . The movement for setting up co-operative agriculture is growing apace."[33] Nevertheless, in the spring of 1948 Gheorghiu-Dej was denying rumors that the land would be taken back from the peasants, and a decree in March permitted peasants possessing more land than they could till to employ day laborers.[34]

By the summer, however, the government was emphasizing the need of "sharpening the class struggle in the countryside, organizing agricultural laborers, and fighting the rich peasant." It introduced progressive scales of taxation and forced grain delivery aimed at preventing accumulation of grain or wealth by kulak or estate owner and ultimately undermining their economic position. It set up "village information offices" with instructions to "unmask all the dishonest kulaks and inform the farmers of their duties."

On March 2, 1949, the regime, on the simple sweeping charge of sabotage and failure to comply with regulations, seized the land, livestock, and inventory which had been left to the large landowners under the 1945 reform. In this action, carried out abruptly and without prior notification, some 17,000 families were evicted from their homes at night and sent to various resettlement areas. The government now directed all its energies against the rich peasants.[35] Lenin's dictum that "Small-scale exploitation generates capitalism and the bourgeoisie constantly, daily, hourly, in an elemental way, and on a mass scale," again made its appearance and became the leitmotiv for innumerable articles.

Embroidering on this theme, Gheorghiu-Dej marked out the party line for 1949. In 1945 the landlords had been liquidated as a class, but this act fostered small-scale economic activity in agriculture. "It follows that the complete victory of socialism is impossible so long as private property in the means of production, in the towns and in the countryside, including private property in land, continues to exist." The Communist party, therefore, had a number of important

33. *East Europe* (February 19, 1948).
34. *Ibid.* (April 1, 1948).
35. The distinction between poor, middle, and rich peasant, or kulak, is not based on size of holding or amount of wealth alone and seems to take on different meanings under different political circumstances. In simplest terms, the rich peasant is one who hires labor or charges rent for machinery and equipment; the middle peasant uses only family labor but produces enough, or more than enough, to support his household; the poor peasant is unable to support himself on his holding and is on the verge of drifting into the agricultural proletariat. In 1941, 12 per cent of the land in Rumania was farmed solely by paid labor, and 24.8 per cent by a mixture of paid and family labor. The first category, in the main, represented the properties of estate owners, the second the holdings of the richer peasants. In 1948, according to Gheorghiu-Dej, 57 per cent of the rural population belonged to the small peasantry and 33 per cent to the middle peasantry.

tasks. The first was to restrict the kulaks and dislodge them from their position. Then it would be possible "when conditions are ripe, to pass over to the policy of the complete liquidation of the kulaks." [36] He anticipated, of course, that the kulaks would resort to underground struggle, sabotage, and criminal acts in an effort to avert their approaching fate.

The second task was to undertake propaganda convincing the poor and middle peasants of the need to unite in collective farms. When that task had been achieved, when all the land belonged to the collectives in perpetuity, the goal of making the land public property and bringing about the socialist transformation of the countryside would be reached. Gheorghiu-Dej emphasized, however, the necessity of making this transition gradually, by means of persuasion, and with the voluntary support of the peasant. The poor peasants should not be driven into collectives, the middle peasant should not be identified with the kulak, and the whole process must be paced by the development of agricultural machinery, machine tractor stations, and the expansion of the network of consumer and producer cooperatives as broad mass movements.[37] These words of caution presumably reflect the wisdom gained from the Soviet experiment in collectivization.

Gheorghiu-Dej concluded his remarks with the inevitable "self-criticism": in the past the party had not provided a clear political line for work in the countryside and had failed to popularize the notion of uniting the working peasantry into collective farms, and had even ignored or denied this goal.[38] That these so-called errors were the fault of the Rumanian Communists is, of course, nonsense. The party line, emanating from Moscow, had shifted, and in this instance a strong case can be made that the change had been planned long in advance. The Communists could have had no intention of stopping at the stage of small peasant cultivation which had, in any event, reached a cul-de-sac in Rumania.

The creation of collective farms got under way in 1949, and by the end of the year, according to the glowing account of a Russian visitor, 56 *kolkhozi* comprising 4,000 peasant families had been estab-

36. As in Russia representatives of the restricted and soon to be liquidated kulak class are not to be admitted to the collective farms.

37. The cooperatives, however, must rid themselves of capitalist elements, must intensify their collaboration with the state trading organs, and must promote the spirit of "socialist emulation" among the peasants.

38. G. Gheorghiu-Dej, "Tasks of the Rumanian Workers Party in the Struggle for the Socialist Reorganization of the Countryside," *For a Lasting Peace, for a People's Democracy* (Bucarest, March 15, 1949).

lished; in addition, 55,000 households had joined producer cooperatives.[39] By the official account these collectives, which took on such
spontaneously peasant names as the Red Tractor, the Red Field,
the Victory of Socialism, and the New Way were organized through
the voluntary action of the peasants.

Take, for example, the collective farm, "1907," set up in August,
1949, in the commune of Căldărași, Județ Buzău, as described by
the enthusiastic reporter of the Communist paper, *România Liberă*.[40]
Thirty-seven families had united their land, livestock, and equipment and had received the government's permission to establish a collective. The peasants brought with them 13 carts, 7 horses, 7 oxen,
6 ploughs, and 3 harrows. On the day of its inauguration the collective received from the state one tractor, 2 tractor-drawn ploughs,
one threshing machine, one electric generator, 6 iron ploughs, one
seeder, 74 hoes, and 107 pitchforks. It also received advice on an
agricultural plan from the provisional județ committee. The collective
possessed 151 hectares of land, of which 88 had previously belonged
to the peasants, the remainder coming from the state. Six hectares
were to be distributed among the peasant households for garden plots,
most of the rest were to be devoted to a three-year rotation schedule
of mixed crops. Such, in the prospectus at least, was the promising
new life awaiting the multitude of poor peasants who would now
leave behind them the undeniable poverty and squalor of their earlier
small-holder existence.

It is too early to say what relation this promise is likely to bear
to future reality in the Rumanian countryside. Public information
from Rumania is so scanty and unreliable that one cannot ascertain
how the peasants are reacting to this new departure. In principle,
at least, collectivization is supposed to be wholly voluntary and there
is to be no bullying of the middle peasants. But since the return to
the peasant is to be based upon work performed rather than upon
the amount of land he contributed, it is difficult to see what incentive
the middle peasant will have for joining a collective unless its aggre-
gate output is exceptionally high. There have been reports, moreover,
of armed peasant resistance, especially in the Banat, a region of comparatively large and prosperous farms.

It is also too soon to tell what effect collectivization will have upon
the level of agricultural output, peasant income, and the whole of
the economy. As has been stressed throughout this study, something

39. I. Rukhadze, "Rumanian Village Yesterday and Today," *New Times,* No. 3
(1950), p. 27.
40. *România Liberă,* August 11, 1949.

unquestionably had to be done to pull Rumanian agriculture out of its ever-deepening rut; many of the criticisms raised by the Communists against the earlier order are largely valid. The attempt to create a prosperous small holder, specializing in intensive cultivation, made little headway between the wars. The richer peasant seems to have been gaining at the expense of the submerged mass of marginal producers, though he was not as wealthy nor nearly as responsible for the poor peasants' plight as Communist propaganda has made out. So long as cereals were to be the major crop, cultivation on a scale large enough to permit the amalgamation of strips and the use of mechanized equipment seemed to be called for. In brief, given the political impossibility and undesirability of returning to the old privately owned great estates and the failure of small-holding to prosper, some type of cooperative or collective agriculture would appear to be at least a partial answer to the agrarian problem.

Beyond this, however, one is inevitably faced with the Soviet example: the kolkhozi are now the inspiration of the Rumanian planners and probably provide the best clue, if one could interpret it, to the future of the Rumanian peasant. Here, of course, certain doubts present themselves. On the dark side of the picture stand the vast misery occasioned by the tempestuous collectivization of the first five-year plan, the widespread peasant resistance leading to the catastrophic destruction of livestock, the forcible uprooting not only of kulaks but of many smaller peasants, and the obvious fact that the step was taken not for the immediate benefit of the peasant but to increase and assure deliveries of grain for the towns and for export and to check any resurgence of capitalism in the countryside. It might be said that many of these hardships need not be repeated in the Rumanian case, that the transformation now can be more gradual and less jolting, and that increased grain deliveries would be more than matched by the greater efficiency of mechanized agriculture, by the removal of excess population to the rapidly industrializing towns, and ultimately by the vastly higher productivity of an industrial economy.

Unhappily, the evidence is by no means clear that such has been the result in the Soviet Union, at least to the present. The surplus which was obtained seems to have been at the direct expense of the peasant, since agricultural productivity did not increase to the degree anticipated (especially when the costs of the new agricultural machinery are deducted); peasant income ten years after collectivization was still lower than before. The task of sifting out what was exceptional and temporary in the Soviet experience and what was a natural concomitant and hence relevant for an estimate of the Rumanian future is exceptionally difficult; at the present state of our knowledge of Soviet agriculture it would be hazardous to base any Rumanian prediction upon it.[41]

In a curious way, however, this issue resembles the pre-1914 dispute in Rumania between the proponents of estate and peasant farming, and in certain respects the wheel has turned full circle. The collective farmer, with his own tiny personal plot, working on the great farm, delivering what amounts to payments in kind and performing a set number of work days, is obviously reminiscent of his grandfather under neoserfdom, with, of course, a different master and the promise contained in, if not yet realized by, the power of the tractor. Somehow, through all the changes the past century has witnessed, an apparently distinctive eastern European pattern is reasserting itself.

Both the nationalization of industry and the move toward collective agriculture are to be understood within the context of an over-all planned economy, not only for one nation but for all the eastern European satellite states. In the field of planning Rumania lagged a bit behind its neighbors, perhaps because of difficulty in creating an adequate and reliable administrative staff, but is now proceeding along the same path.

In general, after putting through a land reform and obtaining control of the industrial sector of the economy, all these states have inaugurated short-term plans of one or two years to restore their economies from the devastation wrought by the war and to pave the way for the next stage, long-term development programs. The primary aim of all the plans is, naturally, increased industrialization; agricultural development takes second place. In the view of a United Nations study, the plans "appear to aim at the development of more or less self-contained industrial economies in order to minimize their dependence on trade with the outside world. . . . The similarity in the investment pattern in the various countries suggests that the industrial plans were drawn up individually, on a national basis."[42] This presumed element of individuality is rather surprising in view

---

41. Favorable interpretations of the success of Soviet collectivization may be found in Alexander Baykov, *The Development of the Soviet Economic System* (New York, 1946), and Maurice H. Dobb, *Soviet Economic Development since 1917* (London and New York, 1948). A quite pessimistic view, based on an extensive criticism of Soviet statistics, is given in Naum Jasny, *The Socialized Agriculture of the USSR* (Stanford University Press, 1949).

42. United Nations, Department of Economic Affairs, *Economic Survey of Europe in 1948*, p. 202.

of the evidence that the Soviet Union exerts a dominating influence in the whole area.[43] It should be observed, however, that even within the countries the plans "aim at a geographical spread of industrialization throughout their individual areas by concentrating on the industrial development of the most backward regions." [44] Hence, the guiding philosophy seems to be that industrialization per se is the cure all and should therefore be spread as widely as possible. In consequence, less attention appears to be paid to the matter of economic complementarity; certainly the complementarity is not to be based on an agriculture-industry exchange.

In this respect the plans differ sharply in their outlook from Nazi Germany's schemes for southeast Europe with their emphasis upon economic exchange. The Polish economist Oskar Lange has recently stressed this fact as proof of the nonexploitative, anti-imperialist behavior of the Soviet Union. It is hard to say what economic advantages are being lost by this parallel rush to industrialization. There must be a point at which the principle of "socialization in one country" can be driven to an absurdity.

The long-term plans anticipate a steep increase in the rate of capital investment, with an annual increase of gross national product of about 10 per cent. However, employment in industry, for the four or five years of the plans, will increase by only one or 2 per cent of the total population, which itself may rise by some 5 per cent in the same period; the plans will not, in the immediate future, do much to solve the pressing problem of agrarian overpopulation. One reason for the relatively low increase in industrial employment is the concentration on heavy industry, in which the capital per worker employed is comparatively high. The prior development of light industries, which would expand employment, is apparently being avoided, perhaps because such an approach would increase dependence upon imports, perhaps because of the need to strengthen the sinews of war.

When the major Rumanian industries were nationalized in the summer of 1948 the government announced that this act rendered possible the creation of a planned economy. The first plan, a one-

43. One recent article asserts that "according to the secret protocol to the pact for the Council of Mutual Economic Assistance [the Soviet response to the Marshall Plan, established at the beginning of 1949], the Soviet State Planning Committee will 'coordinate' the economic planning of member countries for the next twenty years." "The Peasant in Eastern Europe's Economic Planning," *The World Today* (August, 1949), p. 364.

44. United Nations, Department of Economic Affairs, *Economic Survey of Europe in 1948,* p. 202.

year plan for recovery, was inaugurated in 1949. It was to involve the expenditure of 82,000 million lei, including 7,000 million for the completion of work started in 1948, and was to achieve a 40 per cent increase in the level of production over 1948. The capital expenditure was to be invested, percentage-wise, as follows: mining and manufacturing, 47; transportation and roads, 21; agriculture, 9; housing and public services, 21; other, 2. Throughout the year the government issued reports of various portions of the plan being "fulfilled and over-fulfilled," but no absolute quantities were mentioned, only percentage gains over 1948, a singularly uninformative year. In the summer of 1949 the government announced that a budget surplus rendered available several billion additional lei which would be used to begin construction of the Danube–Black Sea Canal.[45] The plan for 1950 appears to be still a preliminary rather than a long-term development program.

Viewed abstractly, and hence, as all Leninists know, incompletely, Communism has three aspects which might commend it to the Rumanian situation: its emphasis upon the importance of industry, its equalitarianism, and its insistence that a backward society can make meaningful progress through its own efforts. Previous Rumanian political movements lacked one or more of these aspects. The Liberals and the neoliberals of the Carolist regime saw the desirability of industrialization, but it proved to be largely for the benefit of a narrow oligarchy. The National Peasants were far more democratic but they tended to be, if not hostile to industry, at least opposed to forced industrialization, which was probably the only way to bring industry to Rumania. Feeling that their country was too weak for such an effort, they turned to foreign capital for assistance, but their hopes for international economic progress "in the spirit of Geneva" were blighted by the depression. The Iron Guard had nothing to offer in this connection. The Social Democrats recognized the importance of industry as well as the necessity of achieving a truer democracy in Rumania, but they were unable to see how their socialist goals could be gained in Rumania with its peasant economy.

The Russian Bolsheviks under Lenin's influence achieved a remarkable tour de force in uniting these elements. They were aware

45. Along with the growing similarity of the Rumanian economy to that of the Soviet Union, there have been a number of reports of forced labor, primarily in connection with the Danube–Black Sea Canal. It may be relevant to note that by a law of January 21, 1939, the Carolist regime established an Administration for the Exploitation of Penal Labor; on May 31, 1945, the Groza regime transferred this administration from the Ministry of Justice to the Ministry of Interior.

of the political importance of the peasantry, but refused to accept the rural ideals of populism; they saw the need for industrialization but were not going to let industry fall into the hands of a capitalist oligarchy. Having achieved their revolution they set about to prove that it was possible to achieve socialism in one state, be it a backward state such as Russia. Whether this revolution and this socialism were what Karl Marx had in mind is a different matter.

The question remains, of course, whether the Bolshevik achievement was anything more than a tour de force. One can maintain that it succeeded simply because it has survived and expanded under exceptionally difficult circumstances. On the other hand, the shadow of repression which darkens the Soviet state, the heavy weight of a bureaucracy forming its own hierarchy, and the vast extension of forced labor, under whatever guise, would indicate that the Leninist synthesis did not reveal a magical solution for the economic problems of a backward state and that the Soviet Union has paid dearly for its ambition to build socialism in a single and relatively retarded country.

Aside from these problems of the Soviet economy, the installation of a Communist regime in Rumania involves additional difficulties. The mere fact that the Groza government was externally imposed has stigmatized it as an alien intruder. To say that this is of no moment except to the nationalist middle classes is but casuistry. It is significant that while one may find certain justifications for the Soviet action in Rumania—in the strategic importance of the area, in the pronounced hostility displayed by Rumanian regimes since 1917, in the advantages of coordinating the eastern European states in one large economic region—Soviet and Rumanian Communist apologists unfailingly fall back upon the one explanation which simply is not true, that the Groza government represents and is supported by the overwhelming majority of the Rumanian people. This does not mean that it will be vigorously and permanently resisted; alien domination is an old familiar in eastern Europe, and history tends to overlook the many cases when national independence, crushed to earth, remained there. But it does mean, for the near future at least, the blighting of whatever democratic tendencies may be contained in the theory of communism. Those Rumanian Communists who were known to have a Rumanian rather than a Soviet point of view were dropped from their posts and eliminated from the political scene well before the Titoist heresy became a public issue.

As to the economic prospects, there is, of course, the general advantage of participating in a large economic space. People of nearly all political outlooks have felt that the multitude of small states created in eastern Europe after the First World War did not represent a rational economic solution. The principal, and decisive, differences arose over the nature of the union or federation which should be inaugurated.

On the other hand, Rumania is now in the position of being a junior partner in a belt-tightening association. There is no question that in blatant contrast to the Soviet political aim of creating an eastern European coprosperity sphere, the actual Soviet activities, largely under the terms of the armistice, have thus far constituted a heavy drain on the Rumanian economy. There is no need to attribute malevolent intentions to this drain. The Russians were badly in need of supplies and equipment to restore their economy, and it is altogether natural that they should have accorded a higher priority to their needs than to Rumania's, and given the power relations they were perfectly able to do so. Unfortunately, this pressure in one form or another, most probably in relation to military requirements, may last for an indefinite period of time.

Ultimately, the development of the Rumanian Communist party and the fate of the People's Republic will depend upon the Soviet Union's relations with the Western powers. The Groza government was installed for reasons of international policy and its future rests with the fruits of that policy.

XV

CONCLUSION

THE agrarian problem is but one aspect of a crisis that has persisted in the economic, political, and intellectual life of Rumania since the impact of Western capitalist civilization began to make itself felt. Various disrupting effects of this protracted influence have been considered earlier. The society it has produced is a hybrid, monstrous in some respects. This statement should not be taken to imply that the earlier society was better. Nor is it constructive to suggest solutions to any of Rumania's problems in terms of going back to old ways. Modern Rumania must be dealt with as it is.

Although the record of peasant-boyar conflict extends much farther into the past, a new source of tension appeared with the growing commercial importance of cereals and the consequent increased cultivation which strained the traditional forms of agricultural organization based on a relatively self-sufficient economy. Labor servitudes, always a focus of discontent, became increasingly so under the pressure of export requirements. After the emancipation peasant land hunger was the major problem, despite the rapid extension of the area under cultivation. From 1864 to 1917, under the system called neoserfdom, the redistribution of land in one manner or another became the principal preoccupation of reformers. The full complexity of the agrarian problem become apparent after the 1918–21 reforms when estate land had been substantially, though by no means wholly, expropriated and redistributed. The dream of a prosperous peasantry on the Western model failed to materialize, and throughout the years 1922–45 successive governments experimented with one remedial measure after another, with no significant results.

The principal features of the agrarian problem in the period under review may be stated simply: low productivity; too many peasants on too little land, in parts of the country at least; and inadequate capital accumulation to permit of improvement. Proposed remedies included: a) technological changes, i.e., improved methods of cultivation, mechanization of agriculture, soil conservation, use of fertilizers, seed and livestock improvement, rational crop rotation, diversification and intensification of production, as well as improvements in internal transport; b) financial and economic reforms, including more and cheaper credit, and the development of cooperative activity in purchasing, marketing, and cultivation; c) demographic changes, including emigration and birth control; d) changes in property and tenure relations, including further redistribution of land, consolidation of strips, and regulation of alienation, inheritance and subdivision of land; e) and finally, industrialization, a solution based on the assumption that reforms in agriculture alone would be inadequate. It was variously believed that industrialization would increase the value of agricultural produce through the development of agricultural industries, be a source of employment for excess agricultural labor, provide agricultural equipment and fertilizers, increase total national output and expand the internal market, and, eventually, create a different mode of living, bringing with it, among other things, a declining birth rate.

These proposed reforms are really a catalogue of the points wherein the Western economies differ from the Rumanian and Western agriculture is superior to Rumanian. It has been shown in the preceding chapters how in one way or another there were more or less serious obstacles to the successful application of any of these measures. Purely technical reforms would have been of limited advantage to Rumania so long as the land was cultivated in minute strips. Besides, in most cases they presupposed available capital, and to be economically successful they required a more extensive market than Rumania possessed. As for credit and cooperatives, the poor peasant was not in a position to benefit greatly from the one or to participate effectively in the other. What credit facilities did exist were directed into fields other than agriculture, but Rumania did not in any case have much credit to provide. Emigration, which was not seriously considered because it ran counter to the whole national idea of a Greater Rumania, would have been difficult because of general world restrictions on immigration after 1918 and because of the physical difficulty of transporting enough people to provide substantial relief.

There was certainly room for reform in land tenure. The predominance of large latifundiary estates before 1914 had, however, centered attention on the question of large-scale versus small-scale agriculture, which was not the main problem in Rumania. After the 1918–21 land reforms there still remained more large property than was generally admitted, but it was not enough to relieve the peasants' need for land. Moreover, even where further redistribution would provide at least temporary relief for the peasants, it would not benefit the country as a whole unless accompanied by other reforms, since it would extend the area of properties subject to the process of fragmentation. Of far greater importance was the need to consolidate peasant farms and to find some means of preventing their continual degeneration into uneconomic dwarf holdings.

Consolidating peasant holdings, partially evacuating the villages, and establishing separate farmhouses on the holdings were undoubtedly prerequisites to efficient peasant farming on the Western model. The peasants, however, were indifferent to, if not actually suspicious of, a consolidation which would involve their giving up strips of their own land, no matter how inadequate or widely separated. There was no natural or spontaneous movement toward consolidation; it would have required government action. In this respect, the operation of expropriating the estate owner and distributing his land to the peasants, for all its appeal as an act of social justice, was an oversimplified solution representing the path of least resistance.

Conversion of estate land to peasant land was not accompanied in Rumania, as it had been in western Europe, by the creation of an intensive mixed farming. The emphasis upon extensive cultivation of grain persisted after the land had been transferred to the small holder, partly because of economic inertia, but largely because grain remained the means by which Rumania could obtain foreign industrial products. The produce of intensified agriculture usually requires a nearby market, and the internal Rumanian market was too limited to provide an adequate stimulus.

In recent years the agrarian problem has been intensified by the emergence of a surplus agricultural population. To a degree, real overpopulation has come to replace the apparent overpopulation of pre-1914 Rumania, which to a considerable extent was the result of unequal distribution of land. The so-called "vital revolution" had quite different consequences in eastern and in western Europe. In the West the expansion of population was matched by the industrial revolution which greatly increased productivity, absorbed labor, and also created new social patterns characterized by a declining birth rate. Extending to eastern Europe the vital revolution completely unsettled the old equilibrium without substituting a new.

Western Europe had become the workshop of the world, and the expansion of population in the East was not followed by those other developments which counteracted its effect in the West. Through channels of commerce an economic complementarity was established between the East and the West, whereby agricultural products were exchanged for industrial goods. It cannot be said that this was without advantage to the eastern European states since it did open the door to accelerated material progress by bringing them into the world economy. But it fostered the continuation of a relatively low degree of productivity and a rural economy which did not provide for the rapidly increasing population.

It has only been fairly recently that Western economists have recognized that there may be sound economic reasons for the industrialization of the more backward agrarian areas. The peoples of these areas, however, have long resented the real or apparent advantages accruing to the industrial states. In 1879, the Rumanian writer Xenopol said bitterly,

Western Europe throws upon us the heavy and fatiguing work of agriculture while reserving to itself the nobler work of industry, which saves energy as well as being better recompensed. In other words, in the great European society, we Rumanians are charged with rude debasing labor akin to that of the animals; we are reduced to the status of being the helots of civilization.[1]

The fact that Rumania lacked the special combination of circumstances which initiates the process of self-propelling industrialization was not in itself a necessary disadvantage; practically all states, except for Great Britain and the urban areas in western Europe which actually started the industrial revolution, began industrialization by borrowing techniques which had already been developed. Nor was it to be expected that the development of Rumanian industry should have been a telescoped and foreshortened version of the history of Western industrialization. It was obviously an advantage to be able to import at the outset a modern locomotive rather than start off with Stephenson's "Rocket." Nevertheless, the advantages to the latecomer who is able to make use of the industrial experience and techniques of the more advanced states have their price. Adopting modern industry involves taking over a vast technological and economic structure and superimposing it upon the traditional economy; the less developed a society and the later it undertakes industrialization, the greater the shock resulting from this superimposition.

Hence, while it may be conceded that some form of industrialization was necessary to extricate Rumania from its impasse as an agrarian society, it was bound to bring very serious problems. The "natural" play of economic forces would not be conducive to rapid industrialization, if for no other reason because the countries which had already

1. Quoted in N. Razmiriţa, *Essai d'économie roumaine moderne, 1831-1931* (Paris, 1932), p. 80.

achieved a higher degree of industrialization could more than compete with initial local efforts. From the very outset Rumania pursued a protectionist policy. Tariff debates were not concerned with free trade versus protection but with the advisability of protecting even those industries which showed little sign of ever being able to fend for themselves without assistance. Even protection was not sufficient, since the potentialities of the Rumanian market were so limited that the elimination of foreign competition was not enough to provide a powerful stimulus to industry. Consequently, the state engaged in a variety of more positive actions: subsidies, special exemptions, and state purchases.

Up to the present, however, Rumanian industrialization has not notably benefited agriculture either in providing it with equipment, absorbing surplus labor, or increasing the local market. On the contrary, the intensive drive toward industrialization in the 1930's was at the expense of agriculture. The reason is obvious. Although industrialization was often advocated as a means of remedying the agrarian situation, industries actually grew up where there were opportunities for profit or where the government took the initiative in the national interest, which was conceived of in terms of defense and prestige. Most foreign investment was directed toward the exploitation of natural resources or toward export industries. Internal investment moved to those industries which gave the best promise of gaining a monopolistic position, either through tariffs and import regulations or through positive state support. While the state participated in a variety of undertakings, it was, especially in the later years, primarily interested in heavy industry for armaments. European industry as a whole was becoming a network of cartels, and inevitably Rumanian industry followed this trend. Moreover, the sudden leap into industrialization in the face of powerful foreign competitors naturally promoted internal combinations and agreements.

The pattern of Rumanian industry showed the effect of its forced growth. In 1937, capital goods industries were almost as important as consumer goods industries, usually a sign of a relatively advanced industrial economy, but here indicating rather the lack of integration of industry with the older sectors of the economy. Rumania did not have that complex of intermediate activities, including what Colin Clark calls tertiary industries—the vast variety of services connected with marketing, distributing, and selling—which can be taken as evidence of an advanced economy and a high per capita income. There is an impression of disparateness throughout Rumania. In Bucarest one is startled by the abrupt transitions from modernity to backwardness. The oil wells and refineries at Ploești spring out of a peasant landscape. Discussions of Rumanian industry revolve not around branches of industry but around specific large enterprises— Reșița, Malaxa, I.A.R.—isolated spots in the economy. In both Rumanian agriculture and industry there is lacking a "middle ground," a diversified, intensive peasant farming and the complex of intermediate industrial activities.

It is frequently held that the distortions of the Rumanian economy, and especially the continued misery of the peasantry, cannot be ascribed solely to the working out of economic forces. Indeed, it is a commonplace to maintain that the real trouble has been the deplorable corruption in politics which has thwarted all reforms; the bureaucrat, not the capitalist, has been the real exploiter. This contention has a good deal of truth; attempts to borrow institutions and programs from the West proved as disturbing in the political and administrative fields as in the economic.

There is no denying the programs not carried out, the persistence of corruption in one regime after another, the ineradicable proclivity for *șmecherie*,[2] which lead one to dismiss Rumanian politics as vicious nonsense and to consider the government and administration a huge trough in which successive cliques take turn in wallowing. Nevertheless, these features of Rumanian public life are symptoms rather than the cause of Rumania's basic difficulties.

The two outstanding characteristics of Rumanian political institutions are the failure of the adopted Western constitutional and political forms to produce Western results in political and administrative behavior and the growth of "bureaucratism." In bringing out the contrasts between theory and practice in Rumania there is a danger, of course, of idealizing Western forms and of attributing to them virtues which have never been realized in the Western states themselves. But even with that reservation, there is no question that the venality of Rumanian politics is exceptional. It was scarcely to be expected, however, that forms developed in a quite different social and economic milieu should have been taken over wholesale and applied to Rumanian society without maladjustment. The Byzantine and Phanariot traditions in Rumanian public life, for all their unpleasant qualities, were at least long-standing modes of social and political behavior closely integrated with the life of the country. Consequently, at those points where the new constitutional forms came into conflict with traditional institutions—above all with the oli-

2. Usually a term of half-admiration for fraudulent actions performed with a degree of poise and dexterity.

garchic structure of society, in which the landed boyars held power over a mass of backward and long-subjugated peasants—habitual relationships persisted within the new framework.

The resultant, however, was neither the traditional boyar society nor a replica of Belgium or France, but something new. Despite the temptation to call Rumanian politics Phanariot, one has only to look at the strangely exotic portraits of the early nineteenth-century Rumanian boyars to realize the vast change which has occurred since the term was really applicable. The mingling of Western forms and traditional practices has, in the course of time, created a distinctive political amalgam.

A phenomenon more difficult to explain is what Dobrogeanu-Gherea called "bureaucratic hypertrophy," that excessive expansion of government activity accompanied by all the evils customarily associated with the eastern European bureaucrat. The principal explanation appears to be that in suddenly entering the modern world, the Rumanian state simply could not wait to evolve gradually from the simple boyar court to a modern government. A nation attempting to affirm its national independence and to modernize in the midst of powerful and more advanced states and empires was hardly in a position to experiment with a passive government. Since neither the boyars nor the peasants, who made up most of the nation, were equipped to take the initiative, whatever was to be done had to be done by the state. Once it had assumed the modernizing role, its administrative machinery tended to be self-expanding and self-perpetuating.

The state was obliged to create agencies for internal and external security. The armed forces, to be effective, had to keep abreast with the technical demands of modern warfare, which was being perfected by states of much greater power and wealth. A gendarmerie to preserve order in the countryside—for all the evil reputation it enjoyed among the villagers—had a necessary and positive function in superseding the hired bullies maintained by the old boyars.

Economic activity, as has been seen, was undertaken to a large degree through the state or with its official or unofficial support. Business success and political maneuvering were intimately related. Since the most lucrative field for professional men—lawyers, economists, men with a Western education—was in the state service, an exceptionally high percentage of them worked for the government or engaged in politics. Since Bucarest was the place for advancement, doctors, agrarian experts, and other trained men clustererd in the capital, though there was a desperate need for their services in the countryside. Practically all the political parties promised to reduce the obviously overstaffed bureaus and to induce bright young men to study less law and more public health and useful technical arts, but since the parties themselves were products of the same process, these promises were not carried out: "One crow does not peck out the eyes of another." The resulting civil and military bureaucracy, built on the model of states with a much greater national income, was beyond the means of Rumanian society to support; rank and file civil servants and police officers were perennially underpaid and had no recourse but to corruption and bakshish.[3]

A more subtle crisis, one which greatly increases the difficulty of understanding the Rumanian situation, has occurred in the realm of ideas and political theory. Just as Western economic, institutional, and political forms were superimposed, so most of the coherent and organized ideas on politics, society, and economics have been adopted from the West and applied to Rumania. The result is particularly confusing to the Western student, for the Rumanian writer is using terms and concepts—whether historical categories, economic theories, or political axioms—which are familiar to the Westerner but which describe the Rumanian reality only approximately and may indeed be quite inapposite. It is understandable why this should have happened. Rumanian society lacked the conceptual apparatus to provide an adequate explanation of what was occurring in and to Rumania, so Rumanian students looked to the West, primarily to France and Germany, not only for scientific instruction but for the whole content of modern secular thought. In Rumanian writings one is continually struck by the frequency with which quotations from Western authorities are inserted to bolster an argument on some phase of Rumanian life.

Ever since their emergence as an independent nation the Rumanians have been preoccupied, almost obsessed, with the nature of their relation to the West. Broadly, this relationship has been interpreted in four ways. There is first the belief that, whatever the superficial differences, Rumanian society is essentially a part of Western society and while suffering certain handicaps is moving along with it. This has been the position of those who have stressed Rumania's Latinity and French connections, who like to regard Bucarest as the

3. A study undertaken in May, 1941, of a group of state employees in the Central Institute of Statistics—one of the first studies made of the actual conditions of the Rumanian civil servant—revealed that on the average 62.3 per cent of the personal budgets of employees was devoted to food alone, 13 per cent to housing, and 11 per cent to clothing. Cf. G. Retegan, *Condiţiile de viaţa ale oamenilor de serviciu*, Institutul Central de Statistică, Biblioteca statistică No. 21 (Bucarest, 1945).

little Paris of the Balkans, and Rumanian civilization as the outpost of Western culture against a Slavic and barbaric East. Curiously enough, it has also been, for quite different reasons, the view of the Communists, who have contended that Rumania was participating in the worldwide era of capitalist imperialism. The difficulty of this view is that it ignores the obvious differences between Rumanian and Western society or denies their significance.

A second interpretation, a modification of the first and upheld by Zeletin, is that Rumania is repeating the historical evolution of the Western states but at a later date, that Rumania today is passing through the phase of mercantilism. While this concept has the apparent advantage of assuring the Rumanians that they are really Westerners and also of explaining the marked differences, it is based on doubtful premises. It assumes that the constant external influences are not so great as to make any such repetition impossible and it puts excessive faith in the idea that certain definite stages in historical development are universally necessary. Its political effect was a rather ingenious justification of the status quo.

A third interpretation, expounded by the populist Stere, is that Rumania has its own unique course to follow, a view which borrows from the German romantics as well as from the Russian narodniki and has a strong national emotional appeal. This concept recognizes the fact that societies do have a life of their own and that institutions, like literature, are a reflection of the society which created them. But it does not accept the fact of the interactions between societies. Stere is able to show as an illustration of Rumania's individuality that the rich connotations of the Rumanian word *mioriţă* (diminutive from *mioară*, young sheep) are untranslatable because of their old association with Rumanian shepherd life, but fails to note that Rumania has long since been torn from a pastoral existence and is now using the *dinamo-electric* and the *motor cu benzină*, which notably lack bucolic overtones.

A fourth interpretation, formulated by Dobrogeanu-Gherea, is that Rumanian social development is a hybrid between Western and local forms. In general, this seems to be the most satisfactory in providing an explanation of the various anomalies of Rumanian society, although as has been observed Dobrogeanu-Gherea, perhaps because of his Marxism, viewed this relationship too mechanically and in terms of a "normal" development from which Rumanian development unhappily deviated.

The passion with which the Rumanians have argued these various views for the last half century derives from the urgency of the very difficult problem of adjustment to modern Western society as well as from the fact that the sides taken in the dispute often reflected the social and economic interests of their proponents. In turning to the political movements which have been examined in the preceding chapters, one finds in their party ideologies, in their economic policy and practices, and in their political behavior all the elements of crisis and distortion associated with Western influence and inspiration.

The National Liberal party, which was in power far longer than any other party and has left a deep mark on Rumanian politics, took as its inspiration the two nineteenth-century forces it incorporated in its name, nationalism and liberalism. In the twentieth century these two terms have come to be regarded as antithetical rather than complementary, but in the national independence movements liberalism was generally seen as the ally of nationalism in the struggle against the prevailing conservatism of the post-Napoleonic era. The Liberals considered themselves in the Western tradition and the bearers of enlightenment to their benighted land, as indeed they were in 1848. Nationalism, however, was always the dominant force. Historically, liberalism was associated with the development of capitalism and a middle class, but capitalism advanced in Rumania not under the aegis of Manchester but through the state. The entrepreneurial function was not carried on by a middle class in the broad Western sense of the word but by the so-called financial oligarchy, which was socially attached to the landed gentry.

Briefly, the Liberals in looking to the West saw the national state and capitalism as the keys to progress, but when these were translated into Rumanian terms they produced a strident nationalism, economic xenophobia, a tutelary state, and a controlled, if not regulated, economy. Although a Liberal government had introduced universal suffrage and the 1918 agrarian reform, the Liberals were unable to face the consequences of free elections and sacrificed agriculture to the interests of industry. These contradictions resulted in their defeat, which they could have staved off, not by a return to liberalism, which for them was impossible, but by a total denial of it. But the Brătianus, while willing to pervert the parliamentary form of government, were not the men to overthrow it.

In considering the peasantist movement and the National Peasant party, one must distinguish three distinct political philosophies which were not integrated but were, in fact, opposed on certain points: populism, radical agrarianism, and a liberal capitalism. Populism in its purest form advocated a nonindustrial democracy, holding that Rumania should not attempt to pursue the course of Western capitalist development but should nourish its agrarian economy. It was faced, however, by an impossible dilemma: if it remained constantly hostile to industry it condemned Rumania to a backward, primitive level; on the other hand, once it made concessions to industry, either in respect to internal development or to foreign commerce, it undermined its own premises. As a matter of fact, these concessions had been made—for the most part unconsciously and gradually but irrevocably—long before the populists put forward their philosophy, which was a rather belated reaction to a process already devouring the old society.

A less philosophical and more practical peasantism is found in the speeches of Mihalache in 1920 and also in the early literature of the Ploughmen's Front, formed in 1933. It arose from the active discontent of the poor peasant cultivator, and as such quite authentically reflected his demands, much more so than populism, which was rather an intellectual's view of what the peasant wanted or ought to want. Unfortunately, the demands of the hard-pressed peasant, while indicative of the ills of Rumanian society and of the failure of other political movements to provide any relief, were by their very origin too limited to provide an adequate total response to the political and economic problems of Rumanian society. As a result, these radical peasant currents in the course of time fatally became attached to more comprehensive movements—in one case to the National Peasants and in the other to the Communists—which quickly overbore them.

The actual political philosophy of the National Peasants, as displayed in their actions, was not really peasantist—though they were interested in the peasants—but a form of liberal capitalism. It probably had the closest affinity of any Rumanian political movement with Anglo-America economic and political traditions. Although the National Peasants often spoke of the peasant state's having a positive function, the tendency of the party while in power was toward decentralization and removing the Liberals' economic controls and restrictions to permit a natural course of development. They opposed the Liberal policy of protecting "artificial" industries and hoped that a process of "natural selection" in the countryside would produce an economically healthy peasantry.

People who use the term natural selection are apt to forget that the selection is brought about by elimination, that it destroys as well as creates. Rumanian agriculture and Rumania as a nation were in weak positions to gain from natural selection, even in the polite form of free trade and free competition. If the Rumanian peasantry had come into full possession of the land seventy-five years ago, when the pressure of population was less acute—that is, if Rumania's history had been quite different—competition among proprietors might have aided in establishing a more prosperous peasant agriculture.[4] But in the interwar period, with over half the proprietors living on the margin of subsistence, with increasing pressure of population, and with limited alternate means of employment, natural selection would have a principal effect of dispossessing the poorer peasants.

Attacking excessive protectionism, the National Peasants counted on the international division of labor plus the assistance of foreign capital to remedy Rumania's industrial deficiencies. Rumania's position in international commerce and finance was, however, that of the last man in a game of crack-the-whip, and when the international regime showed its instability, as in 1929–31, the effects in Rumania were disastrous. In general, the National Peasants had an unwarranted confidence in the immediate applicability of liberal capitalism to the Rumanian situation and in the stability of the liberal-capitalist system itself. In 1940 Virgil Madgearu, who had been a leading advocate of the "spirit of Geneva," reluctantly decided that "the road of a pure liberal capitalist economy, in light of the experience of the whole world, appears utopian." But by 1940 the phase of liberal capitalism in Rumania had long since passed.

Under Carol, especially after 1933, there was a reaction against the National Peasant policy, a reaction initiated by the exigences of the depression. The Carolist regime developed a form of corporatism as a means of rescuing Rumania from the quagmire of agrarian backwardness. There was a vigorous drive to industrialization, an emphasis upon a directed economy, and the establishment in the 1938 Constitution of what amounted to a corporatist state.

It seems doubtful, however, whether the royal dictatorship was equipped to achieve its avowed aims, even had there been no war. In theory a corporatist economy envisages a harmonious and coordinated development of the whole economy in the interests of the state, but in Rumania the policy which developed in the Tătărescu administration and was climaxed by Carol's dictatorship was largely that of furthering industry—above all heavy industry—by whatever means possible, with very little regard to its effect upon agriculture.

4. The somewhat more intense and diversified form of cultivation practiced by Bulgarian peasants on the south bank of the Danube indicates the advantage of having escaped the semiservile conditions under which Rumania lived after the emancipation. On the other hand, in its broad lines the agrarian problem in Bulgaria is similar to that in Rumania, as both suffer from low productivity, surplus agricultural population, and a limited local market.

The only agrarian measure followed consistently and requiring the outlay of important government funds was the maintenance of wheat prices, which was of commercial advantage and assisted the wheat grower but which did not touch the problem of the small peasant. Nor was the industrial drive accompanied by the other measures which should reinforce such an effort. A program of forced industrialization may involve forced saving and a diversion of labor and capital to industry, but it should not have the effect of crippling the other sectors of the economy. With all the maze of controls and regulations which multiplied as the Carol regime progressed, there is little evidence that it had any comprehensive policy. On the positive side, the rate of industrial development did increase, though industrial production as a whole remained quite small, and an increasing percentage of Rumanian industry was financed by local rather than by foreign capital.

After 1939, under the influence of the German trade agreement and the direct menace of war, there were signs of a more integrated economic program. It is to be noted, however, that in a very important respect the goals under the terms of the German trade agreement were not those which had been pursued in the preceding years of the regime. The Germans disapproved of the attempt of the Balkan states to industrialize themselves and advocated rather a European complementarity, by which Germany should provide them with manufactured goods, while they undertook a diversified and intensified agriculture and exploited their natural resources. (They were permitted, however, to undertake initial processing of raw materials.)

Carol's corporate state completed the breakdown of parliamentary government in Rumania. At the same time, the increasing corruption of Rumanian political life fostered a one-sided economic expansion. While the general desirability of increasing industry may be admitted, it is doubtful that industrialization dictated by pressure groups and extraparliamentary influences, including the royal industrialist Carol, best served the interests of the nation as a whole. Of course, if one assumes that the personal interests of an Auşnit or a Malaxa have a preestablished harmony with those of Rumania, no difficulty arises. But from the coincidence that Rumania required a greater degree of industrialization and that Malaxa and Ausnit were aggressive industrialists, it did not follow syllogistically that all was for the best. The span of the Carolist regime in its dictatorial phase was too brief to permit a definitive judgment, but it would appear that under it the Rumanian people were not paying temporarily for the establishment of industries which would benefit them subsequently but were instead being drained of their resources for the profit of a small group of industrialists, politicians, and court favorites in no way responsible to them.

Thus, the borrowing of corporatism failed, as had the borrowing of national-liberalism and liberal capitalism, to solve Rumania's social and economic problems. The Carolist regime did, however, introduce an explicit dictatorship, which under different auspices has continued to the present. Although dictatorships are nothing new, they appear increasingly to have become in the twentieth century the instrument for the forced modernizing of backward countries. In this respect, Carol's break with parliamentary government implies more than a borrowing from the West.[5]

The emergence of the fascist Iron Guard, which differed from other political movements in having—for all its German and Italian trappings—a strong indigenous impulse, was a sign of the crisis of Rumanian society. The Guard's wholesale denial of parliaments, parties, and programs, its glorification of the untouched peasant, were clearly a revulsion against all the mimicry, simulation, and hypocrisy of Rumanian public life. But while it represented a native and widespread reaction to the dislocations of Rumanian life, it did not come into being spontaneously. Perhaps the only purely spontaneous political actions in Rumania have been peasant uprisings such as that which took place in 1907. In a less violent and more reasoned form, the creation of the Peasant party after the First World War and of the Ploughmen's Front in 1933 may be regarded as spontaneous, in that they were direct expressions of the dissatisfaction of the peasantry.

The Legionary movement was obviously quite different. It was not an immediate reaction against poverty and oppression but was rather an almost esthetic reaction against the distortions of Rumanian society. It took its most violent form and gained the most rabid of its adherents precisely in those parts of Rumanian society where there would be the greatest awareness and feeling of anomaly: among the

5. In this connection F. Borkenau (*The Communist International*, p. 43), speaking of backward countries, suggests the necessity of a "modernizing dictatorship" if they are to advance: "In all those countries the impact of Western capitalism has shattered the *ancien régime* without creating modern classes which could take the lead in reconstruction and they are therefore compelled to choose either interminable and futile convulsions or the establishment of some sort of dictatorship to execute the task in which the bourgeoisie fails, namely to modernize the country. Whether the dictator calls himself Lenin, Ataturk, or Chiang Kai-Shek matters less than may sometimes appear; it is not decisive whether originally he starts from a dogma of proletarian revolution, of national or of religious revival. The fact of a modernizing dictatorship is decisive."

students, unemployed intellectuals, discharged civil servants, and, in
a more general way, among those who had been uprooted from the old
agrarian society but who lacked a secure place in the new.

The Iron Guard failed utterly to solve any of Rumania's difficulties or even to master the problem of gaining and maintaining power.
It has been suggested above that the basic reason for this failure
was the unadulterated quality of Legionary fascism. Most successful
fascist movements have allied themselves with or taken over one or
more of the positive forces of modern society, industry and the army
being perhaps the most important. But the Guard did not adopt corporatism; in 1938 Carol was able to win over industrial circles against
them; in 1941 Antonescu used the army to defeat them. By its ultimate failure the Guard demonstrated the fact that Rumania was
fatally attached to the modern world. This is not to say that Rumanian fascism was not dangerous. The savagery displayed by the
Guard during its brief spell in power is ample evidence of its vicious-
ness. Nor should it be forgotten that many of the emotional appeals
of fascism were employed to an important extent in both the Carol
and Antonescu dictatorships.

In sharp contrast to the Iron Guard, the ideas of the Rumanian
Social Democratic party, in the years after 1922, seemed almost
wholly un-Rumanian. To be sure, in Dobrogeanu-Gherea's writings
the Rumania Social Democrats thought they saw a means of relating
Marxism to an agrarian country, but this was only in the limited sense
of recognizing that the agrarian issue in Rumania had not been between peasant and capitalist farming but between feudal latifundia
and a peasant agriculture which contained the seeds of subsequent
capitalist development. But as the Social Democrats said repeatedly
their real goal—the inauguration of the socialist society—could not
be sought in Rumania until it had been achieved by the advanced capitalist countries in western Europe. Thus they were put, despite their
protests to the contrary, in the odd position of having little to work
for except the unimpeded advance of capitalism. It may be said that
unlike the other parties, the Social Democrats bred no monsters but
remained sterile.

The Communists had a doctrine which had already been borrowed
and altered before it reached Rumania. In the preceding chapters
mention has already been made of the numerous social and economic
problems which Rumania and Russia had in common and of Lenin's
unique interpretation of Marx for the purpose of bringing about
the Bolshevik revolution. It seems evident that the Communist use of
Marxism is but another example of the same process by which po-

litical theories and ideologies taken from the West have been warped and somehow transmuted in the course of their application in eastern Europe. Despite the Communist contention that under the conditions of "capitalism in the period of imperialism" it is logical that the socialist revolution should have occurred first in backward Russia, the weakest link in the chain of world capitalism, one is left with the feeling that the situation which Marx envisaged as leading to the proletarian victory and the conditions under which the Bolshevik revolution took place are worlds apart.

Although Marx had expected the revolution to come in advanced industrial states where the contradictions of capitalism had reached their culmination, parts of his message had a profound appeal to backward lands on the periphery of the capitalist world. Agrarian countries, resenting the superior situation of the industrial states and yet envying their prosperity, could be attracted by his corrosive critique of capitalism and his prophecy of its doom. Not only would the present holders of power and wealth be overthrown, but the down-trodden would inherit the earth. The task, however, was to make this Marxist promise applicable to a backward nation.

This was Lenin's achievement. He saw that if there was to be a Marxian revolution in Russia—his basic premise—he must find interpretations of party organization, the peasant question, and the state that would be relevant to the Russian situation. It is to be noted that where he most strongly influenced Marxist theory he was introducing Russian elements: the clandestine organization of the earlier revolutionaries, the land aims of the narodniki, and much of the old state apparatus. It may be maintained, as the Social Democrats have done, that for all his dialectical skill Lenin misapplied Marx when he undertook the Bolshevik revolution and distorted him to justify it. The important fact is that, in addition to a number of accidental and contingent factors working to his advantage—the shock of the First World War, the incapacity of the tsarist regime in its last days—Lenin succeeded in the revolution because he had modified his doctrine to fit his country instead of trying to apply it in its purely Western form to be blunted and paralyzed by the uncompromising differences of Eastern agrarian society.

After the overthrow of Antonescu on August 23, 1944, the Rumanian Communists, especially upon the return of the Moscow group, set about their work in the best Leninist tradition: openly and underground, within the Radescu government and against it, rousing the workers to demonstrations, and seeking to attract the peasant masses by a campaign for radical land reform. But there is no evidence that these tactics would have succeeded if the Red Army had not been in Rumania. Indeed, it was the Soviet emissary, Vyshinsky, who obliged King Michael to accept the Groza cabinet. The communism thus installed in Rumania in 1945 was even farther removed than Lenin's from Marx. In the first place, it had evolved considerably in twenty years of Stalin's application of Lenin's principles to a rapidly growing and developing nation. In the second, it was not a political system arising from the actions of the Rumanian people or even from the Rumanian proletariat, but one imposed by a foreign power.

Hence, in estimating the consequences of the victory of Soviet communism in Rumania, it is necessary to consider two facts: 1) that Leninism is a political-economic system created for and developed in a type of society resembling Rumania's; 2) that its coming to power in Rumania was a Russian decision connected with the eminently worldly interests of the Soviet Union. From the first fact it follows that Leninism is relevant to Rumania. This does not mean that Leninism provides a final answer to Rumania's difficulties nor that it will gain popular support for its program, but that the problems with which it is primarily concerned, the social and economic milieu which it presupposes are to be found in Rumania.[6] The sense of maladjustment and inappropriateness one feels when Leninist concepts are placed in a western European context is far less jarring in the case of Rumania. The ultimate question arises, however, whether for all its relevance Leninism can in fact resolve the complex of refractory problems which have been the subject of the preceding chapters. It has been suggested above that Leninism did not unravel the tangle of economic and social difficulties besetting a backward state but, perhaps by necessity, slashed through them violently and brutally. It remains to be seen whether such practices as the widespread use of forced labor are to continue as an integral part of the Communist pattern and whether Soviet industry will in time be able to raise the per capita income of the Russian citizen to the western European level. Here, the Rumanian proof must be found in the Soviet pudding.

With respect to the second fact, supporters of the present regime in Rumania and in the other eastern European states have contended that the "controlled revolution," or "revolution from without," which the Russians brought to Rumania, is really a blessing since it en-

6. There is, of course, the one important political difference which the Rumanian Social Democrats have always and correctly pointed out: Rumania did not have a background of tsarism but of constitutional, parliamentary government, however poorly it may have functioned.

ables the Rumanians to benefit from the lessons of the Russian Revolution without having to pass through all its tribulations; the progress from capitalism to socialism and thence ultimately to communism can take place by a series of orderly, planned steps that avoid the mistakes and disasters Russia encountered as pathfinder.[7]

Admittedly the Soviet experience has instructive lessons to teach, and thus far the eastern European states have not suffered the tremendous throes of the Russian Revolution or the first years of collectivization. Further, it may be granted that no particularly promising answers seemed to be forthcoming from native Rumanian leadership in the 1930's and early 1940's. The correspondent, Leigh White, reports a remark made to him by a Rumanian—presumably of the Left—at the time of the Iron Guard revolt in 1941: "The day will come when the Red army will have to save us from ourselves. Then we'll be able to make a decent revolution." [8] Nevertheless, the controlled revolution not only assumes the total correctness of the whole series of stages to be covered but involves complete political death since it means the surrender of any Rumanian voice in setting the course to be followed. Finally, it provides no guarantee that Rumania will not continue to be exploited for the benefit of the senior partner, the Soviet fatherland, whether as a quasi-independent People's Republic or as a member of the U.S.S.R.

A general question remains: how is a backward country to advance? How is a society, whose own pattern of life, government, and economic organization has been irrevocably altered, if not destroyed, by the inroads of the advanced material civilization of the West to adjust itself to that civilization? In view of the experience not only of Rumania and the agrarian states of eastern Europe but also of the colonial areas of Africa and Asia, the optimistic hopes of the nineteenth century for a natural, automatic, and progressive readjustment must be abandoned. Nor in most cases is the hurdle to be overcome merely by installing Western procedural techniques, whether economic or political. Rumanian history shows only too clearly how easily these fail to take root or else produce disconcertingly un-Western results.

The answer would seem to be that a healthy, constructive, and peaceful readjustment is possible only with the active and enlightened help of the advanced countries; failing this, the backward state

7. See, for example, Paul M. Sweezy's discussion of the advantages of the "peaceful transition to socialism" of the eastern European states since 1945, in his recent study, *Socialism* (New York, 1949), pp. 66–69 and 130.
8. Leigh White, *The Long Balkan Night* (New York, 1944), p. 145.

is compelled to seek a compensation, rather than a solution, in a modernizing dictatorship, which may, if it has adequate material to work with, give the appearance of advance, but only at the expense of internal liberties and amicable foreign relations. In the case of Rumania, the Western democracies provided no real assistance during the interwar period; after the great depression, which seriously increased their difficulties, the Rumanians were driven to just such a substitution of compensation for solution: the dictatorial regimes of Carol and Antonescu.

Three courses are open to advanced states, which by necessity carry a heavy responsibility in the conduct of their relations with backward areas. First, they can refuse to see the problem until forced by it to take strenuous defensive action. Second, they may do everything in their power to keep the backward states weak and helpless. The danger of this course, apart from its moral obliquity, is that it is likely merely to stave off the reckoning. Eternal vigilance is also the price of repression. The third and perhaps obvious course is consciously to aid the backward countries. The decision to follow this course is made extremely difficult, however, for two reasons.

In the first place, it means the adoption of policies—especially in the field of foreign trade and foreign investment—which are departures from the habitual economic mores of the Western states and may in fact run counter to a number of commercial and financial interests. It is not easy in any case to supplant the long-standing complementarity between producers of raw materials and producers of industrial goods by a new pattern of international trade, or to undertake long-term development programs in place of investments based on the prospect of relatively quick and high returns.

In the second place, even if such policies are carried out, there is no certainty that they will succeed in their purpose of improving the relations between advanced and backward states. Unfortunately, the dislocation of the traditional society has by now a long history in most areas and has produced a deeply ingrained heritage of tension and frustration. Since a nation suffering a long-felt sense of frustration may well become more rather than less truculent as its power and prosperity increase, there is the danger that the well-intentioned actions of the Western nations might serve only to promote the strength of hostile powers. Here, indeed, is a risk and one which the nations of the West must recognize and be prepared to meet.

The risk today is intensified by the fact that the Soviet system was founded upon and has made enormous capital of the distortions besetting a backward society. The sense of resentment has become identified with and consecrated by the Marxist prophecy of the ultimate collapse and destruction of world capitalism; the compensation—socialism in one country through a stern dictatorship—has become an implement of great power. The leaders of the Soviet Union have recognized the dynamic effects of frustration and appear to have no intention of depriving themselves of the energy it can evoke. Thus, the U.S.S.R. has not only brought a large part of eastern Europe, including Rumania, under its direct control, but it is able to cast a shadow over most of the colonial and semicolonial world, realizing that the beginnings of an economic advance may heighten rather than diminish social friction and ready with its answer if the Western states should fail.

The danger of this third course is, nevertheless, a risk, not a certainty, and it is preferable to the other two: the first involves a blind renunciation of any control over the course of events; the second is morally unacceptable. The individual citizen of a Western state may be tempted to close his eyes to the plight of the backward areas; he may further rightly feel that he bears no personal, causal responsibility for the wretched conditions obtaining in other lands. Yet he has a moral responsibility: if he is not to make Cain's denial, he must face that disturbing question:

> "Who has given to me this sweet,
> And given my brother dust to eat?
> And when will his wage come in?"

APPENDIX

TABLE 1. POPULATION OF COMPONENT PARTS OF RUMANIA, 1860–1948

	1860 (Census)	1899 (Census)	1912 (Census)	1920 (Estimate Based on 1930 Census)	1930 (Census)	1939 (Based on 1930 Census)	1941 (Census)	1948 (Provisional Census Figures)
Oltenia			1,414,737		1,513,175		1,673,255	1,717,982
Muntenia			3,297,139		4,029,008		4,904,712	4,991,289
Dobrogea			(662,000)[3]		815,475		519,297[5]	503,217
Moldavia			2,131,527		2,433,596		2,769,380	2,598,258
Total Old Kingdom	3,917,541[1]	5,956,690[2]	7,160,682		8,791,254		9,866,644	9,810,746
Transylvania			(2,977,608) (1910)		3,217,988		1,781,038[6]	3,420,859[9]
Banat			(968,947)		939,958		957,957	948,596
Crişana-Maramureş			(1,314,409)		1,390,417		648,903[6]	1,391,672[9]
Bessarabia		(1,985,412) (1897)			2,864,402		......[7]	
Bucovina			(807,262) (1910)		853,009		336,215[8]	300,751
Total Greater Rumania				15,541,424[4]	18,057,028	19,933,802	18,535,757	15,872,624

355

1. Including districts of Cahul, Ismail, and Bolgrad in Bessarabia, lost in 1879.
2. Including the northern part of Dobrogea.
3. This figure includes the acquisition of Southern Dobrogea in 1913, not included in total figure for Old Kingdom.
4. Showing acquisition of Transylvania, Banat, Crişana and Maramureş, Bucovina, and Bessarabia after First World War, and Southern Dobrogea acquired in Second Balkan War.
5. Showing loss of Southern Dobrogea to Bulgaria, 1940.
6. Showing loss of Northern Transylvania to Hungary, 1940.
7. Showing loss of Bessarabia to U.S.S.R., 1940.
8. Showing loss of Northern Bucovina to U.S.S.R., 1940.
9. Showing recovery of Northern Transylvania, 1945.

SOURCES: Anuarul statistic al României, 1939–40. Recensământul general al României din 1941, 6 aprilie, date sumare provizorii (Bucarest, 1944). A. Golopenţia and D. C. Georgescu, Populaţia Republicii Populare Române la 25 ianuarie 1948—rezultatele provizorii ale recensământului (Bucarest, 1948).

TABLE II. DEMOGRAPHIC CHARACTERISTICS OF RUMANIA AND SELECTED EUROPEAN STATES

	Area, Population, and Density			Average Annual Interwar Per Cent Growth	Average Vital Rates 1930–31			Reproduction (a) Rates *ca.* 1930	
	Area (1,000 km.2)	*Popu-lation* (1,000's)	*Density* (*per* km.2)		*Birth*	*Death*	*Natural Increase*	*Gross*	*Net*
RUMANIA	295.0	18,057	61	1.27	34.2	20.1	14.1	2.16	1.40
Bulgaria	103.0	6,078	59	1.30	30.4	16.5	13.9	1.70	1.20
Greece	130.2	6,205	48	1.93	31.2	17.1	14.1	1.80	1.26
Yugoslavia	247.5	13,934	56	1.43	34.6	19.4	15.2	2.09	1.45
Hungary	93.1	8,688	93	.76	24.6	16.1	8.5	1.34	1.01
Poland	388.6	32,107	83	1.44	31.6	15.6	16.0	1.70	1.25
Ukrainian SSR (1926)	451.6	29,018	64	.53	41.2	18.0	23.2	2.49	1.70
Austria	83.9	6,760	81	.36	16.4	13.8	2.6	.80	.66
Czecho-slovakia	140.5	14,730	105	.71	22.1	14.3	7.8	1.22	.95
Italy	310.2	41,177	133	.85	25.8	14.5	11.3	1.59	1.15
Germany	468.8	65,218	139	.67	16.8	11.1	5.7	.80	.70
France	551.0	41,835	76	.44	17.8	16.0	1.8	1.10	.93
Denmark	42.3	3,551	84	.82	18.4	11.1	7.3	1.10	.96
England and Wales	151.1	39,952	264	.49	16.1	11.9	4.2	.93	.81

(a) Since birth and death rates fail to take into account the differences of age and sex in the composition of the population and are therefore not precise measures of the manner in which the population is growing, a more accurate device, the "reproduction rate," is employed. The "gross reproduction rate" measures the extent to which women of childbearing age are replacing themselves with girl babies, in the absence of mortality between birth and the end of the childbearing period. The "net reproduction rate" takes into account the average mortality experience of females between birth and the childbearing years. It is thus a ratio of successive female generations. In both rates 1.00 equals simple replacement. "Thus a net reproduction rate of 2.00 indicates that at current fertility and mortality the population would double in each generation. A rate of 1.00 would ultimately yield a stationary population; a rate of .50 indicates a decline of 50 per cent per generation."

SOURCE: Dudley Kirk, *Europe's Population in the Interwar Years* (League of Nations, 1946), p. 263.

TABLE III. REGIONAL DEMOGRAPHIC CHARACTERISTICS IN RUMANIA

	Area (1,000 km.²)	Population (1,000's)	Density (per km.²)	Vital Rates, 1930			Reproduction Rates	
				Birth	Death	Increase	Gross	Net
RUMANIA	295.0	18,057	61	34.2	20.1	14.1	2.16	1.40
Oltenia	24.1	1,513	63	33.7	20.4	13.3	2.11	1.37
Muntenia	52.5	4,029	77	35.4	20.1	15.3	2.22	1.44
Dobrogea	23.3	815	35	39.2	23.7	15.5	2.70	1.75
Moldavia	38.0	2,434	64	39.9	21.4	18.5	2.48	1.61
Bessarabia	44.4	2,864	64	38.3	20.8	17.5	2.57	1.67
Bucovina	10.4	853	82	31.3	19.0	12.3	1.88	1.22
Transylvania	62.2	3,218	52	30.1	18.5	11.6	2.01	1.30
Banat	18.7	940	50	21.3	18.7	2.6	1.25	.81
Crişana and Maramureş	21.3	1,390	65	28.8	19.1	9.7	1.77	1.15

SOURCE: *Ibid.*

TABLE IV. VITAL RATES IN RUMANIA

A. The Old Kingdom, 1859–1915

Period	Vital Rates per 1,000 Inhabitants		
	Births	Deaths	Excess of births over deaths
1859–63	31.3	21.4	9.9
1864–68	33.4	28.2	5.2
1869–73	33.3	28.0	5.3
1874–78	35.4	31.3	4.1
1878–83	42.0	27.7	14.3
1889–93	40.2	30.4	9.8
1894–98	40.7	28.0	12.7
1899–1903	42.1	27.6	14.5
1904–08	40.5	25.7	14.8
1909–13	41.7	25.3	16.4
1914–15	41.3	24.0	17.3

B. Greater Rumania, 1920–46

Year	Vital Rates per 1,000 Inhabitants (U = Urban; R = Rural)		
	Births	Deaths	Excess of births
1920	34.7	26.7	8.0
U	19.7	18.3	1.4
R	39.0	29.1	9.9
1921	39.4	23.7	15.7
U	22.7	16.3	6.4
R	44.2	25.7	18.5

Year   Vital Rates per 1,000 Inhabitants (cont.) (U = Urban; R = Rural)

	Births	*Deaths*	*Excess of births*
1922	38.4	23.5	14.9
U	22.5	17.5	5.0
R	42.9	25.3	17.6
1923	37.6	23.0	14.6
U	22.3	17.2	5.1
R	41.8	24.6	17.2
1924	37.9	23.3	14.6
U	22.2	16.8	5.4
R	42.1	25.0	17.1
1925	36.3	21.7	14.6
U	20.7	15.7	5.0
R	40.5	23.3	17.2
1926	35.9	22.0	13.9
U	21.6	17.5	4.1
R	39.7	23.2	16.5
1927	35.2	22.9	12.3
U	21.4	17.4	4.0
R	38.8	24.4	14.4
1928	35.9	20.2	15.7
U	22.3	17.0	5.3
R	39.4	21.1	18.3
1929	34.0	21.4	12.6
U	21.4	18.4	3.0
R	37.3	22.2	15.1
1930	35.0	19.4	15.6
U	23.6	17.7	5.9
R	37.7	19.8	17.9
1931	33.4	20.9	12.5
U	22.3	18.8	3.5
R	36.1	21.4	14.7
1932	35.9	21.7	14.2
U	22.3	18.9	3.4
R	39.1	22.3	16.8
1933	32.0	18.7	13.3
U	20.8	17.2	3.6
R	34.7	19.1	15.6
1934	32.4	20.7	11.7
U	20.9	17.9	3.0
R	35.0	21.3	13.7
1935	30.7	21.1	9.6
U	20.7	19.3	1.4
R	33.0	21.5	11.5
1936	31.5	19.8	11.7
U	21.4	19.4	2.0
R	33.8	19.9	13.9

Year   Vital Rates per 1,000 Inhabitants (cont.)

	Births	Deaths	Excess of births
1937	30.8	19.3	11.5
1938	29.6	19.2	10.4
1939	28.3	18.6	9.7
1940	26.5	19.1	7.4
1941	23.0	19.3	3.7
1942	21.5	19.0	2.5
1943	20.3	16.7	3.6
1944	21.7	19.6	2.1
1945	19.9	19.3	0.6
1946	23.7	18.0	5.7

SOURCES: Sabin Manuila, *Structure et évolution de la population rurale* (Bucarest, 1940), p. 45; Sabin Manuila and D. C. Georgescu, *Populaţia României* (Bucarest, 1938), pp. 83–84; Institutul Central de Statistică, *Comunicări statistice*, No. 18 (August 15, 1947).

TABLE v. AGRICULTURAL POPULATION, 1941

	Total Population	Rural Population	Agricultural Population	Active in Agriculture	Passive in Agriculture
RUMANIA	13,535,757	10,238,255	9,690,423	6,504,291	3,186,132
Plain of Siret and Prut	2,037,892	1,601,094	1,572,169	1,030,235	541,934
Moldavian Carpathians	949,617	747,918	749,741	489,178	260,563
Muntenian and Oltenian Carpathians	2,577,913	2,190,766	2,117,182	1,379,258	737,924
Plain of the Danube	3,781,925	2,377,906	2,354,502	1,576,694	777,808
Dobrogea	519,297	365,585	331,740	210,714	121,026
Bucovina	336,215	266,619	273,545	185,685	87,860
Transylvanian Plateau	1,731,038	1,376,353	1,186,546	819,298	367,248
Western Transylvania	1,601,860	1,312,014	1,104,998	813,229	291,769

SOURCE: Roman Cresin, *Recensământul agricol al Romăniei din 1941, date provizorii*, Biblioteca Statistică, No. 10 (Bucarest, 1945), Table 20.

TABLE VI. AGRICULTURAL POPULATION, 1941: PERCENTAGE
AND DENSITY

	Agricultural Population as Per Cent of:		Percentage of Agricultural Population:		Total Population per 100 Ha. Total Area	Agricultural population per 100 Ha. Agricultural Surface (a)	Active per 100 Ha. Agricultural Surface (a)	Active per 100 Ha. Arable Surface (b)
	Total population	Rural population	Active in agriculture	Passive in agriculture				
RUMANIA	71.4	94.4	67.1	32.9	69.5	94.3	63.3	71.9
Plain of Siret and Prut	77.2	98.2	65.5	34.5	81.4	87.7	57.5	64.4
Moldavian Carpathians	79.0	100.2(c)	65.2	34.8	65.7	112.8	75.0	101.0
Muntenian and Oltenian Carpathians	82.1	96.6	65.1	34.9	77.2	121.5	79.2	103.6
Plain of the Danube	61.7	98.1	67.1	32.9	96.7	89.7	60.1	64.7
Dobrogea	63.9	90.7	63.5	36.5	31.2	48.8	31.1	32.4
Bucovina	81.4	102.6(c)	67.9	32.1	47.2	108.3	73.5	84.8
Transylvanian Plateau	68.5	86.2	69.0	31.0	58.1	98.5	68.0	75.0
Western Transylvania	69.0	84.2	73.3	26.7	55.4	84.0	61.8	66.5

(a) Agricultural surface (i.e., arable, meadows, pastures, vineyards, and orchards) in the 1941 census includes only land under private exploitation, or approximately 73 per cent of the total agricultural area of the country.

(b) Arable surface included in the 1941 census represents approximately 87 per cent of the total arable.

(c) The figure of over 100 per cent merely means that part of the urban population was also engaged in agriculture.

SOURCE: *Ibid.,* Table 21.

TABLE VII. AGRARIAN OVERPOPULATION, BY REGION, IN RUMANIA

	1 Population Dependent on Agriculture (1,000's)	2 Output in Crop Units per Ha. ――――― Density of Agricultural Population	3 = Output in Crop Units per Cap.	4 Agricultural Production in Crop Units (1,000's)	5 European Output per Ha. ――――― European Density	6 = European Output per Cap	7 Standard Population Assuming European per Cap. Output (1,000's)	8 "Surplus" Population Number (1,000's)	9 "Surplus" Population Per Cent
RUMANIA	13,000	$\dfrac{17}{.80}$	= 21	273,000	$\dfrac{24}{.56}$	= 43	6,300	6,700	51
Old Kingdom	6,400	$\dfrac{17}{.80}$	= 21	133,000	$\dfrac{24}{.56}$	= 43	3,100	3,300	51
Bessarabia	2,400	$\dfrac{14}{.70}$	= 20	48,000	$\dfrac{24}{.56}$	= 43	1,100	1,300	54
Bucovina	600	$\dfrac{28}{1.46}$	= 20	12,000	$\dfrac{24}{.56}$	= 43	280	320	53
Transylvania	3,600	$\dfrac{18}{.81}$	= 22	80,000	$\dfrac{24}{.56}$	= 43	1,900	1,700	48

COMMENT: This table, adapted from the computations made in Wilbert E. Moore, *Economic Demography of Eastern and Southern Europe* (League of Nations, 1945), can be used only for purposes of general illustration. Output and area are given in terms of "crops units" and "arable equivalent" hectares, statistical devices to make possible a comparison of different types of agricultural land and different agricultural products. Cols. 1 to 4 give the agricultural population of Rumania and its four major regions as of 1930; the total agricultural production; and the relations between output per unit of area, density of population, and per capita output. Col. 7 gives the population which would be required to achieve this total production on the basis of the average European (excluding Russia) per capita output (Col. 6), which in turn is determined by the European output per unit of area and the European density of agricultural population (Col. 5). Col. 8 then shows the resulting "surplus" population, and Col. 9 this surplus as a percentage of the total Rumanian agricultural population.

TABLE VIII. DISTRIBUTION OF AGRICULTURAL PROPERTY IN THE
OLD KINGDOM, 1907

Categories (hectares)	Number of Holdings	Per Cent of Total Properties	Area (hectares)	Per Cent of Total Area
0–½ ha.	62,832	6.60	26,426	0.34
½–1	81,039	8.50	72,757	0.93
1–2	147,900	15.20	237,029	3.01
2–3	131,630	13.60	337,000	4.30
3–4	172,446	17.90	631,964	8.08
4–5	148,717	15.40	711,033	9.08
5–7	131,145	13.50	743,486	9.50
7–10	45,230	4.70	393,950	5.05
Total, 0–10 ha.	920,939	95.40	3,153,645	40.29
10–50	36,318	3.70	695,953	8.89
50–100	2,405	0.26	166,847	2.13
100–500	3,314	0.41	816,385	10.43
500–1,000	1,122	0.13	803,084	10.26
1,000–3,000	771	0.09	1,236,420	15.80
3,000–5,000	112	0.01	434,367	5.55
Over 5,000	66	0.00	520,095	6.65
Total	965,047	100.00	7,826,796	100.00

SOURCE: G. D. Creangă, *Grundbesitzverteilung und Bauernfrage in Rumänien*, in
Staats- und sozialwissenschaftliche Forschungen, Heft 129 (Leipzig, 1907),
p. 93.

COMMENT: This table includes private properties, land owned by religious and other
public foundations, state land, and crown domains. With regard to type of land, it
includes arable, meadows, and pasture, but not vineyards, orchards, or forests. Creangă
estimated that there were in Rumania some 74,000 hectares of orchards and 98,000
hectares of vineyards, belonging mostly to small holders, and 2,422,000 hectares of
forest (not including swamp land), belonging almost entirely to large proprietors,
either public or private. His figure for the area of holdings under 10 hectares is too
low, as it was based on data from 1896, and about 153,000 hectares of state land were
distributed to the peasants between 1897 and 1905.

TABLE IX. LEASING OF AGRICULTURAL PROPERTY IN THE
OLD KINGDOM, 1907

Category of Property (hectares)	Amount Leased (hectares)	Percentage of Land Leased
50–100	40,184	24.09
100–500	409,608	50.17
500–1,000	467,819	58.23
1,000–3,000	721,198	58.33
3,000–5,000	318,628	73.36
Over 5,000	376,708	72.43
Total over 50 ha.	2,334,145	56.86

SOURCE: *Ibid.*, p. 140.

TABLE X. DISTRIBUTION OF LAND BY FARM UNITS IN THE
OLD KINGDOM, 1913

Categories of Farms (hectares)	Number	Percentage of Total Number	Total Area Covered (hectares)	Percentage of Total Area	Average of the Category (hectares)
0–2	476,649	42.0	572,169	9.7	1.20
2–5	441,336	39.0	1,546,311	26.5	3.50
5–10	161,550	14.3	1,118,409	19.2	7.34
10–25	42,996	3.8	622,174	10.7	14.47
25–50	5,697	0.5	193,128	3.3	33.91
50–100	1,554	0.1	107,182	1.8	68.96
100–500	2,377	0.2	587,549	10.1	247.50
Over 500	1,043	0.1	1,093,699	18.7	1,047.10
	1,133,202	100.0	5,840,621	100.0	5.15

Categories of Farms	Owner-cultivated		Tenant-cultivated	
	Area (hectares)	*Per Cent*	*Area (hectares)*	*Per Cent*
0–2	421,712	73.7	150,457	26.3
2–5	1,045,525	67.6	500,786	32.4
5–10	647,518	57.9	470,891	42.1
10–25	396,764	63.8	225,410	36.2
25–50	141,263	73.1	51,865	26.9
50–100	74,408	69.4	32,774	30.6
100–500	281,871	48.0	305,678	52.0
Over 500	495,860	45.3	597,839	54.7
	3,504,921	60.0	2,335,700	40.0

SOURCE: Rumanian Ministry of Agriculture, *Agricultorii și repartizarea pământului cultivat in 1913* (Bucarest, 1915), quoted in David Mitrany, *The Land and the Peasant in Rumania* (New Haven, Yale University Press, 1930), pp. 241–242.

COMMENT: Unfortunately this table and Table VIII, on the distribution of properties, appear to defy comparison, and in certain important respects they are in serious contradiction. The total area for properties is some 2,000,000 hectares larger than that for farms. Probably a large part of this difference is attributable to grazing lands and fallow, which are not included in the statistics for farms. According to figures for 1905, pasture and fallow amounted to about 1,400,000 hectares. L. Colescu, *Progresele economice ale României îndeplinite sub domnia M.S. Regelui Carol I, 1866–1906* (Bucarest, 1907), p. 51. Owner-cultivated farms under 100 hectares are given as some 1,300,000 hectares less than properties under 100 hectares (2,727,000 hectares as against 4,016,000 hectares). It seems impossible to explain this difference either by the absence of grazing land, which belonged mainly to large properties, or by mutual interleasing among peasants, which could scarcely have achieved such a magnitude. The figure for farms over 100 hectares is some 2,100,000 hectares less than that for properties over 100 hectares (1,681,000 hectares as against 3,810,000 hectares). This difference is to be explained by the absence of grazing land in the farm statistics, by the fact that land was leased from the large estates to peasant farms, and by the sale of estate land between 1907 and 1913, but the relative importance of these factors is not clear. The total area leased from properties over 100 hectares is given by Creangă at about 2,300,000 hectares; the total farm area under tenant cultivation, for both large and small farms, is about 2,336,000 hectares, but this similarity is misleading because the figure for leased properties presumably includes grazing land.

The only point in mentioning these inconsistencies—especially in statistics which are known to be of uncertain reliability—is that repeated attempts have been made to reach too definite conclusions through a collation of these tables or a selected part thereof.

TABLE XI. PRE-1914 DISTRIBUTION OF LAND IN BESSARABIA

A. By Type of Property

Categories		Number of Properties	Total Area (hectares)	Average Area (hectares)	Per Cent of Total Area
	Nobles	1,474	818,744	555.4	20.1
Private	Priests	126	4,308	34.2	0.1
1. individual	Merchants, etc.	1,944	253,867	—	6.7
properties	Peasants	7,718	135,384	17.5	3.2
	Foreigners	13	30,390	2,337.6	0.8
	Various	10,102	94,157	9.0	2.3
	Large owners	275	169,416	616.3	4.3
		21,652	1,506,266	69.4	36.8
2. Joint holdings		540	201,591	373.3	4.9
3. Nadyel lands		2,209	2,111,940	956.0	50.7
4. State domains		—	53,648	—	1.3
5. Churches and monasteries		—	204,190	—	5.0
6. Town properties		—	23,600	—	0.6
7. Private institutions		—	30,362	—	0.7
		24,401	4,131,597	166.3	100.0

SOURCE: E. Giurgea in *Buletinul Statistic*, No. 2 (1919), pp. 324–327, quoted in Mitrany, *op. cit.*, p. 201.

B. By Size of Property

Properties (hectares)	Area	Per Cent of Total Area	Number of Proprietors	Per Cent of Total Number
0–10	2,156,827	51.6	285,663	98.4
10–100	180,984	4.3		
Over 100	1,844,539	44.1	4,480	1.6
	4,182,350	100.0	290,143	100.0

SOURCE: Alexander Nasta, "La Réforme agraire en Roumanie," report presented to the Fourteenth Congress of the International Congress of Agriculture (Bucarest, June 7–10, 1929).

COMMENT: These figures must be regarded as very approximate, since they involve, among other things, a translation of Russian returns which were based upon types of ownership rather than size. The number of proprietors in Table B, which is much greater than the number of properties in Table A, includes the peasants cultivating nadyel (allotted) land, which had been granted to the peasant commune rather than to the individual under the Russian emancipation.

TABLE XII. PRE-1914 DISTRIBUTION OF LAND IN BUCOVINA

A. Distribution of Total Area

Categories (hectares)	Number of Properties	Per Cent	Area (hectares)	Per Cent
0–10	191,737	96.27	270,730	25.92
10–100	6,606	3.32	134,115	12.84
100–500	585	0.29	130,939	12.53
Over 500	257	0.12	508,674	48.71
	199,185	100.00	1,044,458	100.00

SOURCE: Livius Lazar, *La Mise en oeuvre de la réforme agraire,* p. 64, quoted in Mitrany, *op. cit.,* p. 204.

B. Distribution of Agricultural Land (Arable, Meadows, and Pasture, but Excluding Forests)

Categories (hectares)	Area (hectares)	Per Cent
0–10	264,673	48
10–100	152,094	27
Over 100	140,560	25
	557,327	100

SOURCE: Ifor L. Evans, *The Agrarian Revolution in Roumania* (Cambridge, 1924), p. 87, from information provided by Rumanian authorities in Bucovina.

TABLE XIII. PREREFORM DISTRIBUTION OF LAND IN TRANSYLVANIA

Category (hectares)	Number of Owners	Per Cent	Area (hectares)	Per Cent
0–10	843,448	87.6	2,536,738	34
10–100	113,887	11.8	2,153,117	29
Over 100	4,601	0.6	2,751,457	37
	961,936	100.0	7,441,312	100

SOURCE: Nasta, *op. cit.*, p. 24.

COMMENT: The reliability of this official estimate is extremely doubtful. The table appears to be only an approximate conversion into hectares of figures compiled in cadastral yokes by the provisional Transylvanian government in 1919. The reliability of the latter compilation has been challenged. According to Hungarian critics "no exact figures are or ever have been available for the land distribution in 1919 in the total area annexed by Rumania." C. A. Macartney, *Hungary and Her Successors* (Oxford University Press, 1937), p. 316, n. 2.

TABLE XIV. LAND EXPROPRIATED UNDER THE AGRARIAN REFORMS OF 1918 AND 1921, AS OF 1927

	Old Kingdom (hectares)	Transylvania (hectares)	Bucovina (hectares)	Bessarabia (hectares)	Total (hectares)
Arable	2,269,192.27	470,389.56	48,544.64	1,210,627.20	3,998,753.67
Meadow	27,386.94	80,745.60	9,742.63	—	117,875.17
Pasture	442,988.68	398,257.50	8,296.69	—	849,542.87
Forests	19,156.10	663,967.24	8,420.54	198,404.60	889,948.48
Orchards, Vineyards	2,466.18	12,114.07	—	—	14,580.25
Building land, farmyards, etc.	360.11	14,006.35	357.16	—	14,723.62
Barren	14,851.15	24,328.71	605.69	82,888.44	122,673.99
Total	2,776,401.43	1,663,809.03	75,967.35	1,491,920.24	6,008,098.05

SOURCE: Nasta, *op. cit.*, p. 16.

COMMENT: Despite the confident calculation to two decimal places, the accuracy of this table is rather uncertain. In 1937 the figure given for the total amount of expropriated land was somewhat less: 5,811,827 hectares. G. Ionescu-Sişeşti and N. Cornăţeanu, *La Réforme agraire en Roumanie et ses conséquences* (Bucarest, 1937), p. 36. In 1940 it was officially announced that 3,900 estates were still in possession of land which was to have been expropriated. Moreover, there seems to have been a good deal of circumvention of the expropriation laws through the reconstitution of estates by a variety of semilegal or illegal means. According to Mitrany, *op. cit.*, p. 223, the Ministry of Agriculture confirmed that in the steppe region of the Bărăgan newly formed estates, running up to 3,000 hectares, could be found.

TABLE XV. DISPOSITION OF LAND EXPROPRIATED UNDER AGRARIAN REFORMS OF 1918 AND 1921, AS OF 1927

	Old Kingdom (hectares)	Transylvania (hectares)	Bucovina (hectares)	Bessarabia (hectares)
Distributed to peasants	2,037,293.04	451,653.96	42,832.25	1,098,045.50
Communal pastures	524,720.87	418,361.43	5,831.85	—
Communal forests	—	484,805.24	4,377.72	—
Forests administered by state to be distributed	21,027.90	179,162.00	8,523.84	198,404.60
Land unfit for distribution	17,677.44	36,442.78	605.69	82,888.44
Reserved for general needs	175,682.18	93,383.62	13,796.00	112,581.70
Total expropriated	2,776,401.43	1,663,809.03	75,967.35	1,491,920.24

SOURCE: Nasta, *op. cit.*, p. 19.
COMMENT: The reliability of this table depends upon that of Table XIV.

TABLE XVI. LAND RECEIVED BY THE PEASANTS UNDER THE AGRARIAN REFORMS OF 1918 AND 1921

A. As of 1927

	Number of Peasants Entitled to Land	Number of Peasants Receiving Land	Area Distributed (hectares)	Area Distributed as Communal Pasture (hectares)	Area Distributed as Communal Forests (hectares)
Old Kingdom	1,053,628	630,113	2,037,293.04	524,720.87	—
Transylvania	490,528	310,583	451,653.96	418,361.43	484,805.24
Bucovina	77,911	71,266	42,832.25	5,831.85	4,377.72
Bessarabia	357,016	357,016	1,098,045.50	—	—
Total	1,979,083	1,368,978	3,629,824.75	948,914.15	489,182.96

SOURCE: *Ibid.*

B. As of 1938

	Number of Peasants with Right to Land	Number Receiving Land — Number	Number Receiving Land — Per Cent of those with right	Land Distributed (hectares)	Average Area per Peasant Receiving Land under Reform
Old Kingdom	1,075,330	648,843	60.3	2,286,740	3.4
Transylvania	490,528	310,583	63.3	489,043	1.6
Bucovina	82,603	76,941	93.2	49,179	0.6
Bessarabia	357,016	357,016	100.0	1,098,045	3.1
Total	2,005,477	1,393,383	69.5	3,923,007	2.8

SOURCE: *60 Sate româneşti* (5 vols., Bucarest, 1941–43), II, 10.

TABLE XVII. DISTRIBUTION OF AGRICULTURAL PROPERTY FOLLOWING THE AGRARIAN REFORMS OF 1918 AND 1921, AS OF 1927

Before the Reform:

	Small Property (under 100 ha.)	Per Cent	Large Property (over 100 ha.)	Per Cent
Old Kingdom	4,593,148	57.5	3,397,851	42.5
Bessarabia	2,337,811	55.9	1,844,539	44.1
Transylvania	4,689,855	63.0	2,751,457	37.0
Bucovina	405,000	78.0	115,000	22.0
	12,025,814		8,108,847	

or:

Small Property: 12,025,814 ha. or 59.77%
Large Property: 8,108,847 ha. or 40.23%
                20,134,661 ha.

After the Reform:

	Small Property	Per-Cent	Large Property	Per Cent
Old Kingdom	7,369,549	92.22	621,450	7.78
Bessarabia	3,829,731	91.57	352,619	8.43
Transylvania	6,353,664	85.38	1,087,648	14.62
Bucovina	480,967	92.49	39,033	7.51
	18,033,911		2,100,750	

or:

Small Property: 18,033,911 ha. or 89.56%
Large Property: 2,100,750 ha. or 10.44%
                20,134,661 ha.

SOURCE: Nasta, op. cit., pp. 26–27.

COMMENT: Although these figures have been used as the basis for most studies of Rumanian agriculture, they are misleading and incorrect. The area estimated as having been expropriated from properties over 100 hectares (Table XIV) was simply subtracted from estimates of the prereform extent of such property and added to the estimates of properties under 100 hectares. The results are naturally quite impressive but unacceptable. The prewar figures for the Old Kingdom were based upon G. D. Creangă's estimate for 1905 (Table VIII) (except that the figure for properties under 10 hectares was taken from the somewhat higher estimate of the Ministry of Finance for 1905, a justified substitution). An estimated reduction of properties over 100 hectares between 1905 and 1918 (amounting to 412,500 hectares) was added to the 1905 figure for those below 10 hectares. As a result of this method of computation, the total area of medium properties, between 10 and 100 hectares, is assumed not to have changed at all between 1905 and 1927. All the land expropriated is considered to have been transferred to the small peasants, when, in fact, of the 2,776,000 hectares reported expropriated in the Old Kingdom, only 2,037,000 hectares of arable had been distributed to the peasants by 1927, and 525,000 hectares of communal grazing land established.

It has already been noted that the accuracy of estimates of prereform land distribution in Transylvania was doubtful. Only properties of over 100 hectares are reported to have suffered expropriation, although in Transylvania there were undoubtedly numerous cases where land under that figure was taken. In Bucovina, of the 75,967 hectares expropriated, some 23,000 were reported in 1927 to be either unfit for settlement or held as state-administered forest, and therefore cannot be regarded as having increased peasant holdings. In Bessarabia, all properties over 100 hectares were to have been expropriated; of the 1,845,000 hectares in this category, 1,492,000 were expropriated, and only 1,100,000 distributed to the peasants.

Finally, forest land is handled ambiguously. In Transylvania about 40 per cent (664,000 hectares) of the area expropriated from large estates was forest; in the Old Kingdom, however, the forests of large landowners—which were not expropriated but which in 1905 amounted to over 800,000 hectares in private ownership alone—were not included in the figures (this seems also to have been the case with the extensive forests of Bucovina). To have made the statistics consistent either all forest properties in all regions should have been included, which would have increased considerably the area shown as remaining to large properties after the reform, or they should have been omitted, which would have reduced the size of the area reported expropriated by nearly 900,000 hectares. In general, then, the conclusions were artificially established and certainly represent an inflated picture of the redistribution of property.

TABLE XVIII. FISCAL CENSUSES ON LANDHOLDINGS, 1923 AND 1928

Hectares	1923			1928		
	Number of Taxpayers	Area (hectares)	Average Size (hectares)	Number of Taxpayers	Area (hectares)	Average Size (hectares)
0–5	3,154,211	5,745,921	1.8	3,408,503	6,653,801	2.0
5–10	458,534	2,618,824	5.7	455,934	3,000,859	6.6
10–50	181,494	2,359,075	13.0	139,807	2,286,413	16.4
50–250	16,557	1,425,053	86.0	13,163	1,308,121	99.4
Over 250	3,168	1,537,046	485.1	1,834	861,299	469.4
Total	3,813,964	13,685,919	3.6	4,019,241	14,110,493	3.5

SOURCE: *60 Sate românești*, II, 12–15.

COMMENT: Although these tables, prepared by the Ministry of Finance for tax purposes and using different categories of size of landholding, cannot be compared with earlier or later figures, they are of use in showing certain trends in land distribution in the 1920's. The 1928 figure for properties over 250 hectares seems very low, however, since a Ministry of Finance estimate for 1927 (given in Mitrany, *op. cit.*, p. 247) listed 2,597 owners in this category with an area of 1,305,672 hectares.

TABLE XIX. DISTRIBUTION OF AGRICULTURAL LAND ACCORDING TO
SIZE OF EXPLOITATION, 1930 CENSUS

Categories of Exploitations (hectares)	Exploitations		Total Area		Cultivated Area	
	Number	*Per Cent*	*Hectares*	*Per Cent*	*Hectares*	*Per Cent*
0–1	610,000	18.6	320,000	1.6	275,000	2.1
1–3	1,100,000	33.5	2,200,000	11.1	1,850,000	14.4
3–5	750,000	22.9	3,015,000	15.3	2,475,000	19.3
0–5	2,460,000	75.0	5,535,000	28.0	4,600,000	35.8
5–10	560,000	17.1	3,955,000	20.0	3,110,000	24.2
10–20	180,000	5.5	2,360,000	12.0	1,715,000	13.3
20–50	55,000	1.7	1,535,000	7.8	1,015,000	7.9
50–100	12,800	0.4	895,000	4.5	540,000	4.2
100–500	9,500	0.3	2,095,000	10.6	920,000	7.2
Over 500	2,700	0.1	3,375,000	17.1	950,000	7.4
Total	3,280,000	100.0	19,750,000	100.0	12,850,000	100.0

SOURCE: Institutul Central de Statistică, *Statistica agricolă a României în 1938*
(Bucarest, 1939), p. 94.

COMMENT: This table, the only general summary published for the 1930 census, presents certain difficulties. The figure for the total cultivated area corresponds with the 12,857,112 hectares of arable (cereals, artificial meadows, fallow, alimentary and industrial crops) reported under cultivation in 1930. It is less easy to determine what the 19,750,000 hectares include. Since in 1930 arable land plus grazing, orchards, and vineyards amounted to only 17,525,000 hectares, the figure must include some 2,000,000 of the 7,134,000 hectares of forest land. Some sources (e.g., *Bréviaire statistique de la Roumanie, 1940*) state that the 1930 figures refer to properties rather than exploitations.

TABLE XX. DISTRIBUTION OF AGRICULTURAL PROPERTIES AND
EXPLOITATIONS ACCORDING TO SIZE, 1941 CENSUS

Category of Size (hectares)	Properties		Exploitations		Extent of Properties		Extent of Exploitations	
	Number	*Per Cent*	*Number*	*Per Cent*	*Hectares*	*Per Cent*	*Hectares*	*Per Cent*
Total	2,257,050	100.0	2,263,963	100.0	10,419,000	100.0	10,419,570	100.0
Under 0.1			83,815	3.7				
0.1–0.5			172,709	7.6				
0.5–1.0			211,337	9.3				
Total under 1	524,549	23.3	467,861	20.6	230,000	2.2	190,883	1.8
1–3	792,969	35.1	757,646	33.5	1,559,000	15.0	1,446,627	13.9
3–5	415,921	18.4	439,919	19.5	1,680,000	16.1	1,704,211	16.4

Category of Size (hec- tares)	Properties		Exploitations		Extent of Properties		Extent of Exploitations	
	Num- ber	Per Cent	Num- ber	Per Cent	Hec- tares	Per Cent	Hec- tares	Per Cent
5–10	381,444	16.9	448,188	19.8	2,707,000	26.0	3,072,676	29.5
10–20	100,932	4.5	115,481	5.1	1,340,000	12.9	1,489,895	14.3
20–50	31,479	1.4	26,167	1.1	883,000	8.5	713,360	6.8
50–100	4,891	0.2	4,789	0.2	315,000	3.0	317,842	3.1
100–200	2,544	0.1	2,099	0.1	349,000	3.3		
200–500	1,690	0.1	1,286	0.1	521,000	5.0	1,484,076	14.2
Over 500	631	0.0	527	0.0	835,000	8.0		

SOURCE: Roman Cresin, *op. cit.*, p. 17.

COMMENT: This census, which did not cover Northern Transylvania, Bessarabia, Northern Bucovina, or Southern Dobrogea, was limited to land in private cultivation and did not include state, public, or communal holdings. It did, however, include forests and other nonagricultural land if these were in private hands.

The area covered by the census comprised a little over half the total area of Rumania:

Type of Terrain	Total Area (1,000 ha.)	Area Covered in Census (1,000 ha.)	Difference	
			In 1,000 hectares	In per cent
Arable	8,578	7,486	1,090	12.7
Meadow	1,069	831	238	22.3
Pasture	2,209	368	1,841	83.3
Vineyards	209	167	42	20.1
Orchards	195	145	50	25.6
Forest	4,789	803	3,986	83.2
Other land	2,476	387	2.089	84.4
Total	19,525	10,187	9,338	47.8

The difference of 9,338,000 hectares between the total area and the area covered by the census was accounted for as follows:

	Hectares
Individual exploitations omitted from the census but included subsequently, and in Table XX	232,000
Communal pastures	1,600,000
State forests	1,500,000
Forests belonging to various institutions	ca. 2,500,000
Lakes, ponds, etc. from the floodable regions of the Danube	ca. 900,000
Areas occupied by communications, cities, industries, etc.	ca. 1,000,000
State farms, land belonging to Ministry of Agriculture, crown domains, and undeclared areas	ca. 1,600,000
	9,332,000

TABLE XXI. DISTRIBUTION OF AGRICULTURAL EXPLOITATIONS ACCORDING TO USE OF LABOR, 1941

	Number	Per Cent	Per Cent	Area (hectares)	Per Cent	Per Cent	Average Size (hectares)
General total	2,258,530	100.0		10,187,003	100.0		4.51
Dwarf exploitations (a)	471,618	20.9		318,965	3.1		0.68
Exploitations remaining after leasing (b)	54,882	2.4		45,856	0.4		0.83
Exploitations proper (c)	1,732,030	76.7	100.0	9,822,182	96.5	100.0	5.67
Exploitations worked by hired labor only	25,466	—	1.5	1,188,015	—	12.1	46.65
Exploitations worked by family and hired labor	265,906	—	15.3	2,438,642	—	24.8	9.17
Exploitations worked by family labor only	1,009,031	—	58.3	4,667,089	—	47.5	4.63
Exploitations worked by only part of family labor	431,627	—	24.9	1,528,436	—	15.6	3.54

(a) Very small exploitations cultivated by peasants with little or no land; exploitations not the principal occupation of the cultivator.

(b) Land remaining after the proprietor has rented out more than 80 per cent of the total property, the remainder representing only limited agricultural activity—a few animals, a garden, etc.

(c) Exploitations of at least two hectares, or one hectare of arable, or 0.5 hectares of land devoted to vineyards, orchards, etc.

SOURCE: *Ibid.*, pp. 24–25.

TABLE XXII. DISTRIBUTION OF AGRICULTURAL EXPLOITATIONS ACCORDING TO USE OF LABOR AND TYPE OF TENURE, 1941

	Number	Per Cent of Total	Per Cent of Subgroup
Total exploitations proper	1,732,030	100.0	—
A. Worked by hired labor only	25,466	1.5	100.0
1. On own land	16,294	0.9	64.0
2. On own and rented land	4,716	0.3	18.5
3. On rented land only	4,456	0.3	17.5

	Number	Per Cent of Total	Per Cent of Subgroup
B. Worked by hired and family labor	265,906	15.3	100.0
1. On own land	192,674	11.1	72.5
2. On own and rented land	70,775	4.1	26.6
3. On rented land only	2,457	0.1	0.9
C. Worked by family labor only	1,009,031	58.3	100.0
1. On own land	720,013	41.6	71.4
2. On own and rented land (a)	289,018	16.7	28.6
D. Worked by part of family labor	431,627	24.9	100.0
1. On own land	315,167	18.2	73.0
2. On own and rented land (a)	116,460	6.7	27.0

(a) Peasant exploitations using family labor on rented land only were too infrequent to warrant inclusion as a separate category.

SOURCE: *Ibid.*, p. 28.

TABLE XXIII. PREVALENCE OF TYPES OF CULTIVATION (BY PERCENT-AGE) ACCORDING TO SIZE OF EXPLOITATION IN THE JUDEȚ OF ARGEȘ, 1941

Categories of Size (hectares)

	Total	Under 0.1	.1–.5	.5–1	1–3	3–5	5–10	10–20	20–50	50–100	Over 100
Total	100	100	100	100	100	100	100	100	100	100	100
Total exploitations proper	70.5	1.9	3.0	10.9	78.9	99.8	99.9	99.8	100.0	97.5	97.6
A. With hired labor only	1.3	—	—	0.1	0.3	0.9	2.2	7.3	23.4	53.7	97.6
B. With hired and family labor	11.7	0.1	0.1	0.6	6.8	14.9	25.9	50.6	65.9	43.8	—
C. With family labor only	30.9	0.2	1.0	3.9	34.6	47.4	47.0	27.2	8.1	—	—
D. With part of family labor	26.6	1.6	1.9	6.3	37.2	36.6	24.8	14.7	2.6	—	—
Remaining after leasing	1.2	23.4	5.0	1.3	0.3	0.2	0.1	0.2	—	2.5(a)	2.4(a)
Holdings of agricultural workers with little land	24.3	33.3	73.8	78.7	19.3	—	—	—	—	—	—
Holdings of agricultural workers without land	0.5	15.5	2.4	—	—	—	—	—	—	—	—
Dwarf exploitations whose cultivator has nonagricultural occupation	3.5	25.9	15.8	9.1	1.5	—	—	—	—	—	—

(a) The unexplained presence of exploitations of over 50 hectares in the category "Remaining after leasing" (i.e., remaining after 80 per cent of the property has been let out) presumably indicates a few large properties of little agricultural value, since according to the census this category was unimportant agriculturally.

SOURCE: Roman Cresin, *Agriculture din județul Argeș* (Bucarest, 1945), p. 11.

TABLE XXIV. EXPROPRIATION AND REDISTRIBUTION OF LAND UNDER 1945 AGRARIAN REFORM, AS OF JANUARY 8, 1947

Regions	Number of Proprietors Expropriated	Area Expropriated (hectares)	Area Distributed (hectares)	Area Reserved by the State (hectares)	Peasants Having right to land	Peasants Having received land
RUMANIA	143,219	1,443,911	1,057,674	387,565	1,114,888	796,129
Plains of Siret and Prut	1,542	196,130	162,486	33,644	198,603	160,334
Moldavian Carpathians	349	47,529	32,615	14,914	87,542	50,171
Muntenian and Oltenian Carpathians	1,802	115,065	71,214	51,851	178,618	99,083
Danube Plain	2,787	309,886	241,213	68,673	248,720	220,181
Dobrogea	1,122	62,333	52,089	3,562	34,795	18,165
Bucovina	79	4,610	4,412	198	17,707	8,518
Transylvanian Plateau	62,157	345,598	215,956	129,642	206,054	123,938
Tisa Plain	73,381	362,760	277,689	85,071	142,849	115,737

SOURCE: Institutul Central de Statistică, *Comunicări statistice*, No. 17 (March 15, 1947), p. 9.

TABLE XXV. DISTRIBUTION OF AGRICULTURAL PROPRIETORSHIP AND EXPLOITATIONS AFTER 1945 AGRARIAN REFORM, AS OF JANUARY, 25, 1948

Categories of Size (hectares)	Proprietors Number	Proprietors Per Cent	Exploitations Number	Exploitations Per Cent
0–0.5	901,016	16.4	233,153	7.5
0.5–1	1,100,852	20.0	296,321	9.6
1–2	1,472,785	26.8	1,106,754	35.7
2–3	838,286	15.2		
3–5	697,318	12.7	707,001	22.8
5–10	363,678	6.6	551,090	17.8
10–20	88,335	1.6	153,516	5.0
20–50	23,698	0.4	34,222	1.1
Over 50	15,170	0.3	14,120	0.5
Total	5,501,138	100.0	3,096,177	100.0

SOURCE: A. Golopenția and P. Onica, *Recensământul agricol din Republica Populară Română, 25 ianuarie 1948, rezultate provizorii* (Bucarest, 1948), pp. 11–16.

COMMENT: The value of this census is greatly reduced by the failure to publish the amount of land comprised in the various categories of properties and exploitations. Of a total area of 23,730,000 hectares, 20,661,000 were declared as properties and 19,199,000 hectares as exploitations (of which 94 per cent were declared as owned by the cultivator). The fact that there were 1.8 proprietors to each exploitation (5,501,000 proprietors and 3,096,000 exploitations) is explained, presumably, by the numerous cases of joint proprietorship: husband and wife, parents and children, etc.

TABLE XXVI. COMPARISON OF DISTRIBUTION OF EXPLOITATIONS BY SIZE IN 1941 AND 1948 (EXCLUDING NORTHERN TRANSYLVANIA)

Categories of Size	1941		1948	
(hectares)	Number	Per Cent	Number	Per Cent
0–0.5	277,500	12.0	190,169	7.3
0.5–1	213,088	9.3	246,016	9.5
1–3	760,700	33.0	933,383	35.9
3–5	441,213	19.2	604,540	23.3
5–10	449,716	19.5	462,607	17.8
10–20	116,537	5.1	122,262	4.7
20–50	27,845	1.2	26,607	1.0
Over 50	16,873	0.7	11,316	0.4
Total	2,303,472	100.0	2,596,900	100.0

SOURCE: *Ibid.*, p. 20.

COMMENT: Although the geographic regions covered in these two tables are the same, the comparison sheds little light and may be misleading, because the amount of land included in each category is not given. In 1941, according to the census of that year, the 2,300,000 exploitations occupied only 10,419,000 hectares, of which about three-fourths was arable. According to the 1948 census the 2,600,000 exploitations occupied approximately 17,000,000 hectares, of which less than one-half was arable. Because of this great difference in the amount of land involved, it would be fallacious to use these tables as a demonstration of the effects of the 1945 agrarian reform.

TABLE XXVII. PRINCIPAL BRANCHES OF AGRICULTURAL ACTIVITY
A. Percentage of Arable Devoted to Different Crops

	Cereals	Wheat	Maize	Barley	Oats	Rye	Alimentary Plants	Industrial Plants	Forage Crops	Fallow
1921–25	87.1	25.5	31.7	15.6	11.3	2.5	3.3	2.2	4.2	3.2
1926–30	85.4	24.4	34.7	14.4	8.8	2.5	3.3	3.1	5.1	3.1
1931–35	83.9	24.0	36.8	13.4	6.2	2.9	3.6	2.8	5.5	4.2
1936	83.3	24.6	37.7	11.6	5.8	3.0	3.8	3.5	5.6	3.8
1937	82.4	25.7	36.5	10.8	5.6	3.3	3.7	3.6	5.2	5.1
1938	82.1	28.3	36.3	9.0	4.7	3.4	3.6	3.5	5.3	5.5

SOURCE: *Statistica agricolă a României în 1938,* pp. xiv–xv.

B. Distribution of Agricultural Exploitations According to Type of Farming

Percentage of Total Number of Exploitations

	1941	*1948*
Cereals	50.7	60.7
Animal husbandry	12.5	1.2
Viticulture	1.4	1.3
Fruits	0.7	0.7
Mixed, and other	34.7	36.1

SOURCES: *Recensământul agricol din 1941; Recensământul agricol din Republica Populară Română.*

TABLE XXVIII. PERCENTAGE OF LAND DEVOTED TO DIFFERENT CROPS ACCORDING TO SIZE OF PROPERTY, 1938

Size of Property (hectares)

	0.1–1	1–3	3–5	5–10	10–25	Over 25	Total
Cereals	51.37	62.61	64.61	72.94	73.14	50.42	66.05
Alimentary plants	4.21	3.59	3.17	2.27	2.75	2.40	2.75
Intercropped plants	2.64	2.36	1.86	1.14	0.86	0.90	1.35
Forage crops	4.27	6.63	7.58	5.00	3.97	3.06	5.03
Industrial plants	1.12	1.77	2.46	1.84	1.29	1.44	1.73
Fallow	0.90	1.77	2.33	2.46	1.90	0.71	1.90
Natural meadow	10.53	7.90	5.36	3.42	3.12	7.62	5.11
Pasture	0.25	1.09	1.67	1.87	1.70	2.22	1.73
Orchards	5.50	1.75	1.19	0.77	0.76	0.53	1.00
Vineyards	10.29	4.61	3.91	3.43	2.99	0.79	3.22
Forests	5.60	3.83	3.61	2.67	3.95	25.43	7.18
Barren	0.15	0.59	0.23	0.38	0.49	0.52	0.42
Not utilized	3.16	1.56	2.02	1.83	3.07	3.96	2.47

SOURCE: *60 Sate româneşti*, II, 97.

COMMENT: These figures were reached through a sampling investigation of some 60 villages.

TABLE XXIX. PRODUCTION OF PRINCIPAL GRAINS

	Output in 1,000 Quintals				Area Covered
	Wheat	Maize	Barley	Oats	
1921–25	24,377	35,613	12,083	9,118	
1925–30	30,138	46,071	19,139	11,047	
1931–35	26,285	53,672	13,122	6,553	71 *judeţe*, frontiers
1936	35,031	56,120	16,119	8,471	as of January, 1938
1937	38,098	46,560	9,463	5,158	
1938	49,124	52,231	8,232	4,605	
1935–39	25,960	39,020	5,500	4,010	
1940	13,758	37,432	4,963	3,707	
1941	19,862	33,472	3,911	3,830	40 *judeţe*, frontiers
1942	8,549	21,816	3,323	3,372	as of January, 1941
1943	23,287	22,283	5,165	4,526	
1944	26,529	32,649	3,821	3,502	
1945	10,885	13,138	2,441	2,334	
1945	12,745	18,196	3,376	3,567	58 *judeţe*, postwar
1946	16,087	10,040	2,334	2,823	frontiers

SOURCES: *Statistica agricolă a României în 1938*, p. xvii; *Statistica agricolă a României în 1941–1944*, p. xiii; *Expunere de motive la bugetul general al statului* (Bucarest, 1946, 1947).

TABLE XXX. WHEAT AND MAIZE YIELDS, 1892–1946

Yield in Quintals per Hectare

	Old Kingdom		Rumania	
	Wheat	*Maize*	*Wheat*	*Maize*
1891–95	10.9	9.7		
1896–1900	8.9	9.6		
1901–1905	12.5	8.8		
1906–1910	11.3	11.6		
1911	13.5	14.1		
1912	11.8	13.3		
1913	14.1	14.2		
1914	6.0	13.2		
1915	12.8	10.9		
1921	10.1	8.5	8.6	8.1
1922	10.2	9.0	9.5	8.9
1923	10.7	12.3	10.3	11.3
1924	6.8	10.9	6.1	10.9
1925	9.5	11.1	8.6	10.5
1926	8.5	13.3	9.1	14.4
1927	8.4	7.4	8.5	8.4
1928	9.1	5.6	9.8	6.2
1929	8.5	12.4	9.9	13.3
1930	12.5	10.3	11.6	10.2
1931	12.4	13.1	10.6	12.7
1932	5.2	12.1	5.1	12.5
1933	9.8	9.8	10.4	9.4
1934	6.2	9.1	6.7	9.6
1935	7.2	11.0	7.6	10.4
1936	10.0	9.9	10.2	10.7
1937	10.8	8,1	10.7	9.6
1938	13.4	8.6	12.5	10.4
1939			11.7	13.7
1940			6.4	10.4
1941			8.7	10.9
1942			5.5	6.5
1943			10.7	7.9
1944			11.4	12.8
1945			5.7	5.0
1946			5.9	2.9

SOURCES: *Statistica agricolă a României în 1938,* pp. 41, 96; Traian Săvulescu, *Problema alimentării populaţiei* (Bucarest, 1947), Annex 1.

TABLE XXXI. RUMANIAN INDUSTRY

A. Distribution of Industries with More than Twenty Employees, 1938

	Number	Capital Invested (1,000 lei)	Horse-power	Personnel	Salaries (1,000 lei)	Value of Output (1,000 lei)
Food	974	10,773,000	137,018	38,736	789,919	15,577,444
Textile	640	8,230,382	79,561	74,077	1,798,766	14,691,948
Chemical	397	12,325,308	183,393	28,298	1,196,853	14,154,605
Metallurgic	366	8,466,368	152,147	51,321	1,847,665	11,362,803
Wood	713	2,273,553	64,121	43,326	860,423	3,583,563
Leather	158	1,025,357	13,415	13,366	450,351	3,437,533
Paper	157	3,577,369	53,366	15,222	656,410	3,088,518
Construction materials	258	2,493,447	56,563	15,104	421,624	1,959,621
Electrotechnic	31	199,837	2,958	2,684	94,281	674,620
Glass	39	561,446	3,216	5,691	141,109	527,135
Ceramic	34	143,322	1,031	1,652	39,592	148,948
Total	3,767	50,069,389	746,789	289,117	8,301,610	69,206,738

SOURCE: Virgil Madgearu, *Evoluţia economiei româneşti după războiul mondial* (Bucarest, 1940), p. 146.

B. Expansion and Concentration of Rumanian Industry, 1927–38

	Number of Enterprises	Horsepower	Personnel	Index of Production (1929 = 100)
1927	4,097	463,436	214,052	85.2
1928	3,966	472,271	206,547	94.9
1929	3,736	497,963	201,184	100.0
1930	3,646	492,715	174,227	97.3
1931	3,524	498,059	152,309	96.7
1932	3,557	514,743	152,198	81.8
1933	3,487	529,963	184,777	100.9
1934	3,509	558,468	208,240	126.0
1935	3,613	582,946	280,717	123.8
1936	3,553	579,543	260,934	131.0
1937	3,512	722,638	278,918	137.4
1938	3,767	746,789	289,117	156.3

SOURCE: *Ibid.*, p. 148.

TABLE xxxII. RUMANIAN FOREIGN COMMERCE: BALANCE OF TRADE

	Imports (metric tons)	Value (1,000 lei)	Exports (metric tons)	Value (1,000 lei)		Difference (1,000 lei)
Average 1901–05	534,622	298,923	3,054,871	360,651	+	61,728
Average 1906–10	805,574	408,939	3,804,380	501,274	+	92,335
Average 1911–15	1,002,056	526,969	3,765,234	605,320	+	78,351
1919	413,939	3,762,300	109,140	104,385	—	3,657,915
1920	304,485	6,980,290	1,467,118	3,447,848	—	3,532,442
1921	615,451	12,145,405	2,713,138	8,263,009	—	3,882,396
1922	583,668	12,325,366	4,069,963	14,039,296	+	1,713,930
1923	699,124	19,516,026	4,900,734	24,594,129	+	5,078,103
1924	825,754	26,264,582	4,833,419	28,361,044	+	2,096,462
1925	899,925	29,912,645	4,663,892	29,126,824	—	785,821
1926	924,442	37,195,415	6,117,781	38,264,805	+	1,069,390
1927	1,008,069	33,852,131	7,337,087	38,110,810	+	4,258,679
1928	952,808	31,640,956	5,886,405	27,029,728	—	4,611,228
1929	1,101,992	29,628,038	7,064,619	28,960,005	—	668,033
1930	805,233	23,044,163	9,214,754	28,522,028	+	5,477,865
1931	560,366	15,754,569	10,047,002	22,196,914	+	6,442,345
1932	449,980	12,011,325	9,056,959	16,721,593	+	4,710,268
1933	446,962	11,741,850	8,777,730	14,170,828	+	2,428,978
1934	635,868	13,208,543	8,854,096	13,655,734	+	447,191
1935	533,268	10,847,530	9,276,009	16,756,223	+	5,908,693
1936	630,443	12,637,698	10,548,913	21,703,391	+	9,065,693
1937	709,415	20,284,748	9,637,497	31,568,357	+	11,283,609
1938	820,603	18,767,830	7,409,084	21,532,580	+	2,764,750
1939	739,039	22,890,474	7,564,146	26,809,349	+	3,918,875

SOURCE: *Bréviaire statistique de la Roumanie, 1940*, p. 188.

TABLE xxxIII. RUMANIAN FOREIGN COMMERCE: IMPORTS

Value of Imports, by Per Cent

	Animals	Food	Raw materials and semifinished	Finished goods	Gold and silver
1920	—	10.4	1.9	87.6	—
1921	—	9.8	3.2	87.0	—
1922	—	11.0	4.8	84.1	—
1923	—	10.3	4.3	85.3	—
1924	—	7.7	5.4	86.9	—
1925	—	8.1	6.1	85.8	—
1926	0.1	5.7	7.0	87.0	0.2
1927	0.2	6.0	10.1	83.7	—
1928	—	6.5	9.7	83.8	—

TABLE XXXIII. RUMANIAN FOREIGN COMMERCE: IMPORTS (*cont.*)

Value of Imports, by Per Cent

	Animals	Food	Raw materials and semifinished	Finished goods	Gold and silver
1929	—	8.9	10.6	80.5	—
1930	0.1	6.4	10.6	83.0	—
1931	—	7.2	9.9	82.7	0.2
1932	—	7.4	10.3	77.6	4.7
1933	—	6.9	12.6	80.5	—
1934	—	5.3	14.3	80.3	—
1935	—	6.6	14.1	79.5	—
1936	0.1	5.1	14.5	80.2	—
1937	—	4.4	17.5	77.5	0.6
1938	—	4.9	20.2	74.4	0.4

SOURCE: N. Georgescu Roegen, *Comerțul exterior al României în perioada 1920–1938*, quoted in Madgearu, *op. cit.*, p. 272.

TABLE XXXIV. RUMANIAN FOREIGN COMMERCE: EXPORTS

Value of Exports, by Per Cent

	Animal	Vegetable	Cereals (as per cent of total vegetable)	Wood	Mineral (almost entirely petroleum)	Other
1919	4.4	28.4	—	—	66.8	0.4
1920	1.3	78.9	85.2	4.6	19.6	0.2
1921	12.8	62.8	80.3	9.1	24.1	0.4
1922	15.0	63.9	59.9	29.0	20.1	0.9
1923	9.0	76.0	65.2	21.9	14.1	0.8
1924	14.7	71.4	60.6	27.4	13.0	0.9
1925	20.8	56.5	44.9	38.8	21.5	1.2
1926	14.0	59.6	61.7	26.1	25.8	0.5
1927	10.4	68.3	73.1	17.7	20.5	0.8
1928	12.9	54.9	51.5	32.8	31.1	1.1
1929	12.4	52.5	58.9	30.8	34.2	0.9
1930	11.6	50.5	69.4	21.5	37.4	0.5
1931	12.0	55.2	71.6	19.4	32.1	0.7
1932	8.3	47.0	72.9	15.7	44.1	0.6
1933	6.8	36.3	63.5	19.8	56.3	0.6
1934	9.6	36.3	48.1	29.7	53.6	0.5
1935	9.7	37.6	52.1	23.1	52.1	0.5
1936	10.6	47.3	66.6	16.4	41.6	0.4
1937	9.3	48.7	66.2	18.4	41.7	0.3
1938	10.6	44.8	54.5	25.5	44.2	0.4

SOURCE: *Anuarul statistic, 1939–40*, pp. 577, 590–593.

BIBLIOGRAPHICAL NOTE

THIS note is not an exhaustive bibliography but includes only those sources employed or consulted in the preparation of this study. A useful bibliography of material on Rumania has been prepared by the Division of Bibliography, Library of Congress: *The Balkans, a Selected List of References: I. General and IV. Rumania* (mimeographed, Washington, D.C., 1943). Other extensive bibliographies are Leon Savadjian, *Bibliographie balkanique, 1920–1938* (2 vols., Paris, 1931–39), and Mario Ruffini, "Introduzione bibliografica allo studio della Romania," *L'Europa orientale* (Rome) *15* (May–June, 1935), 236–289. Paul Henry has written two historiographical articles which include discussions of post-1918 works: "Histoire roumaine," *Revue historique* (Paris), *176* (July–December, 1935), 486–537, and "Histoire de Roumanie," *ibid., 194* (1944), 42–65, 132–150, 233–252.

Works which have been used extensively or which have a special interest are discussed briefly. Other sources—technical aids, general studies, and minor Rumanian works—are listed without comment at the end.

OFFICIAL AND SEMIOFFICIAL SOURCES

Most of the statistical information in this study has been obtained from the publications of the Rumanian Central Institute of Statistics (Institutul Central de Statistică), which has issued a variety of censuses, periodical reports, and special studies. Among the more important are:

Censuses:

Recensământul general al populației României din 29 decemvrie 1930 (10 vols., Bucarest, 1938).

Recensământul general al României din 1941, 6 aprilie, date sumare provizorii (Bucarest, 1944). A collection of articles on the national significance of the 1941 census was published as *Recensământul României din 1941, lamurirea opiniei publice* (Bucarest, 1941).

Roman Cresin, *Recensământul agricol al României din 1941, date provizorii,* Biblioteca Statistică No. 10 (Bucarest, 1945).

A. Golopenția and D. C. Georgescu, *Populația Republicii Populare Române la 25 ianuarie 1948, rezultatele provizorii ale recensământului* (Bucarest, 1948).

A. Golopenția and P. Onica, *Recensământul agricol din Republica Populară Română, 25 ianuarie 1948, rezultate provizorii* (Bucarest, 1948).

Periodical reports:

Anuarul statistic al României. An annual statistical survey; before 1914 it was prepared by the Ministry of Industry and Commerce.

Bréviaire statistique de la Roumanie. An abbreviated French version of *Anuarul.*

Statistica agricolă a României. An annual statistical survey of the agricultural situation. Included under this title are certain special surveys: Vol. IV, *Inventarul agricol în Anul 1943* (Bucarest, 1946), and Vol. V, *Inventarul agricol în Anul 1945* (Bucarest, 1947).

Comunicări statistice. Since 1945 the institute, to make up for the lapses during the war, has published fortnightly a selection of miscellaneous statistics to be issued later in more detail. Very useful for recent developments.

Analele Institutului Statistic al României. A publication started during the war and containing articles on statistical methods.

Special studies:

Roman Cresin, *Agricultura din Județul Argeș* (Bucarest, 1945). A detailed study of one district, based on the 1941 census. Extremely useful so long as the complete results of the census are not published.

Petre Onica, *Statistica agricolă* (Bucarest, 1945). A guide to the preparation of agricultural statistics in Rumania.

G. Retegan, *Condițiile de viată ale oamenilor de serviciu,* Biblioteca Statistică, No. 21 (Bucarest, 1945). One of the few pieces of precise information about the living conditions of government employees and their reasons for leaving the village to work in the capital.

Nicolae M. Dunăre, *Fii de țarani vânzători ambulanți în capitala,* Biblioteca Statistică, No. 22 (Bucarest, 1945). A survey of street vendors who have emigrated from the villages to Bucarest; touches on the question of agricultural overpopulation.

Sabin Manuila, *Demografia rurală a României* (Bucarest, 1940).

Sabin Manuila, *Studiu etnografic asupră populației României* (Bucarest, 1940).

Sabin Manuila and D. C. Georgescu, *Populația României* (Bucarest, 1938).

Official texts of laws are published in the government gazette, *Monitorul oficial.* The first part is devoted to laws and decrees, the second to legal notices, and the third to parliamentary debates.

The Ministry of Agriculture (Ministerul Agriculturii și Domeniilor) published a monthly *Buletinul agriculturii* (sometimes appearing under the French title, *Bulletin de l'agriculture*), devoted largely to technical studies but including economic and regional surveys. Among these were R. C. Stere, "Particularitățile economice ale micilor gospodării țărănești" (April–June, 1927), pp. 33–64; R. Cresin, "Agricultura in Basarabia" (March–April, 1929), pp. 132–151; Mihai Șerban, "Les Conséquences de la réforme agraire sur l'état social et économique de la Roumanie" (May–June, 1929), pp. 21–27. The ministry also published, on the occasion of the Fourteenth Congress of the International Congress of Agriculture in Bucarest (June 7–10, 1929), *L'Agriculture en Roumanie: atlas statistique* (Bucarest, 1929), which is filled with

charts and diagrams; the accuracy of some of the information is doubtful
however. At the same conference A. Nasta presented a paper, "La Réforme
agraire en Roumanie," which contained the official though not very reliable
statistics on the application of the 1918–21 agrarian reforms.

The Ministry of Industry and Commerce (Ministerul Industriei și Com-
erțului) published a quarterly periodical in French and English, *Correspondance économique roumaine,* containing articles on Rumanian economic life,
texts of laws, and summaries of the economic situation. Designed to present
Rumania in the best possible light, it suffered from chronic overoptimism.

The Ministry of Finance (Ministerul Finanțelor) published an annual
Expunere de motive la bugetul general al statului, which in addition to information on the budget contained a summary of economic developments.

The Rumanian National Bank (Banca Națională) published a monthly
Bulletin d'information et de documentation, containing financial and economic
studies. A somewhat similar publication was the semiofficial *L'Économiste roumain (Organ de l'Institut Économique Roumain et de l'Association des Banques Roumaines),* which discussed most of the economic laws and agreements
of the Liberal regime. In economic policy it followed Vintilă Brătianu.

The semiofficial *Enciclopedia României* (4 vols., Bucarest, n.d.) was
started as a monument to the Carol regime but was completed under Marshal
Antonescu. It contains many articles, some of them excellent, on all aspects
of Rumanian life. The last two volumes are devoted to economic and commercial affairs. As a whole, however, it reflects the political bias of the years
of the Carol and Antonescu dictatorships and strives to gloss over the unpleasant parts of the political and economic scene.

Since the advent of the Groza government, its propaganda ministry has
issued a number of publications, of rather low quality, on economic developments. *La Réforme agraire en Roumanie* (Bucarest, November, 1946) contains the text of the 1945 agrarian reform, but the commentary is worthless.
The periodical *Rumanian Review* (French edition, *Revue roumaine*) has a
number of articles on economic and political life, but they are all tainted with
propagandist aims. Of somewhat greater value, though also containing a
good deal of propaganda, is a series of pamphlets put out by Oficiul de Studii
și Documentare, Biblioteca Economică: *Imbunătățirile funciare în agricultura
românească* (Bucarest, 1946); Cornel Irimie, *Centrele de mașini agricole*
(Bucarest, 1946); *Intensificarea creșterii animalelor în cadrul refacerii
economice* (Bucarest, 1946); Traian Săvulescu, *Problema alimentării populației* (Bucarest, 1947). The last work has some useful data on the severe
famine of the winter of 1946–47.

An extremely valuable source of information is the work carried on by the
semiofficial Institutul de Științe Sociale al României, under the direction of
the sociologist D. Gusti; *60 Sate românești* (5 vols., Bucarest, 1941–43)
presents the results of a sampling investigation in a number of Rumanian
villages in the summer of 1938. It is especially useful for its data on peasant
agriculture, land relations, and the standard of living in the countryside. Detailed studies have been made of certain villages selected as representative of

a particular aspect of Rumanian peasant society. *Nerej, un village d'une région archaïque* (3 vols., Bucarest, 1939) investigates a community in a region of traditionally free peasants. *Dâmbovnicul, o plasă din sudul Județului Argeș* (Bucarest, 1942) was chosen as a representative Wallachian peasant community under the impact of modern economic pressures. A more general study of the forms of village landholding was prepared by H. H. Stahl, *Sociologia satului devălmaș românesc* (Bucarest, 1946). The institute also published two periodicals which have articles on a wide range of social, political, and economic topics: *Arhiva pentru știința si reforma socială* (occasionally issued in French as *Archives pour la science et la réforme sociales*) and *Sociologie românească*.

GENERAL HISTORIES

There is, in English, only one extensive history of Rumania from its origins: R. W. Seton-Watson, *A History of the Roumanians from the Roman Times to the Completion of Unity* (Cambridge University Press, 1934). It does not extend to the period covered in the present study but gives a useful outline of Rumania's activities in the First World War and the acquisition of the new territories. The two most extensive histories of Rumania in Rumanian are Constantin C. Giurescu, *Istoria Românilor* (4 vols., Bucarest, 1935–37) and Nicolae Iorga, *Istoria Românilor* (10 vols., Bucarest, 1936–39). (For a recent appraisal of Iorga's work as a historian see John C. Campbell, "Nicholas Iorga," *The Slavonic and East European Review, 26*, No. 66 [November, 1947], 44–59.) Neither of these works, however, treats the interwar period.

Although he is primarily concerned with the agrarian reforms of 1918–21, David Mitrany, *The Land and the Peasant in Rumania: the War and Agrarian Reform (1917–1921)*, Economic and Social History of the World War, Rumanian Series, published for the Carnegie Endowment for International Peace, Division of Economics and History (London; New Haven, Yale University Press, 1930), provides much the best background to the agrarian question. It studies the period of reform in the greatest detail and analyzes the consequences of the reforms up to the fall of the Brătianu government. Prepared in the 1920's, this book expressed optimistic hopes regarding the future of the peasant movement in eastern Europe which have not been realized. In some cases the wealth of statistical material leads to confusion rather than clarity, but in its general sweep it is a very impressive study. Of much less importance are two other books in the Carnegie war history series: G. Ionescu-Sișești, *L'Agriculture de la Roumanie pendant la guerre*, and Gr. Antipa, *L'Occupation ennemie de la Roumanie et ses conséquences économiques et sociales* (Paris; New Haven, Yale University Press, 1929).

There are no satisfactory histories of Rumania in the interwar period. Joseph S. Roucek, *Contemporary Roumania and Her Problems: a Study in Modern Nationalism* (Stanford University Press, 1932), attempts a general survey up to 1931, but it is largely a chronicle and a compendium; analysis is very weak. Roucek also devoted a chapter to Rumania in his later study, *The*

Politics of the Balkans (London; New York, McGraw-Hill, 1939), but a far more adequate treatment of Rumania in the general setting of eastern Europe is given by Hugh Seton-Watson, *Eastern Europe between the Wars, 1918–1941* (2d ed., Cambridge University Press, 1946), a work of great insight and originality. George Clinton Logio, *Rumania, Its History, Politics, and Economics* (Manchester, Sherratt and Hughes, 1932), is a very uneven book but is useful where it reflects Logio's own experiences in Rumania. Charles Upson Clark, *United Roumania* (New York, Dodd, Mead, 1932), is an enlargement of the earlier study, *Greater Roumania* (New York, Dodd, Mead, 1922), but neither work is outstanding. C. G. Rommenhöller, *Gross-Rumänien, seine ökonomische, soziale, finanzielle, und politische Struktur, speziell seine Reichtümer* (Berlin, Puttkammer und Mühlbrecht, 1926), is mainly concerned with Rumania's industrial potentialities; the political and historical sections are very brief. Norman L. Forter and Demeter B. Rostovsky, *The Roumanian Handbook* (London, Simpkin, Marshall, 1931) is a loosely organized collection of information on Rumania. Pavel Pavel, *Why Rumania Failed* (London, Alliance Press, n.d.) is an anti-Carol, pro-Maniu apology for Rumania's participation in the Second World War; it is factually unreliable. Convenient as a brief handbook is C. Kormos, *Rumania,* British Survey Handbooks (Cambridge University Press, 1944).

REGIONAL STUDIES

The Royal Institute of International Affairs prepared a number of Balkan studies, with a special emphasis on economic questions, which include some useful information on Rumania: *The Balkan States. I. Economic* (Oxford University Press, 1936); *South-Eastern Europe, a Political and Economic Survey* (Oxford University Press, 1939); and *South-Eastern Europe, a Brief Survey,* Information Department Papers, No. 26 (Oxford University press, 1940). A recent study of post-1945 constitutional developments in this region is Andrew Gyorgy, *Governments of Danubian Europe* (New York, Rinehart, 1949).

A good survey of the economic policy of the Danubian states in the early 1920's is provided by Leo Pasvolsky, *Economic Nationalism of the Danubian States* (New York, Macmillan, 1928). Especially valuable for the 1930's and the period of German economic penetration is Antonin Basch, *The Danube Basin and the German Economic Sphere,* International Library of Sociology and Social Reconstruction (London, Kegan Paul, 1944). Frederick Hertz, *The Economic Problem of the Danubian States* (London, Victor Gollancz, 1947), is mainly concerned with Austria and Hungary; the material on Rumania is scanty and in some cases inaccurate. The PEP study (Political and Economic Planning), *Economic Development in S. E. Europe* (London, 1945), contains some helpful comparative information on economic conditions but is chiefly interested in future plans. N. Momtchiloff, *Ten Years of Controlled Trade in South-Eastern Europe,* National Institute of Economic and Social Research, Occasional Papers, Vol. VI (Cambridge University Press, 1944), is a brief examination of the trade policy pursued in the 1930's and suggests that certain of the controls developed in those years may have a useful function in the proper context.

A number of League of Nations studies have been of value, above all Wilbert E. Moore, *Economic Demography of Eastern and Southern Europe* (Economic, Financial and Transit Department, League of Nations, Geneva, 1945), which has an excellent analysis of agricultural overpopulation in its relation to the agrarian problem in eastern Europe. Also to be mentioned are *Industrialization and Foreign Trade* (1945); *Agricultural Production in Continental Europe during the 1914–18 War and the Reconstruction Period* (1943); *Final Report of the Mixed Committee of the League of Nations on the Relation of Nutrition to Health, Agriculture, and Economic Policy* (1938), which has a section on the Rumanian peasant diet; *The Agricultural Crisis* (2 vols., 1931); Dudley Kirk, *Europe's Population in the Interwar Years* (1946); *Memorandum on Public Finance, 1926–28* (1929), with a section on Rumania, pp. 203–221; and *The League of Nations Reconstruction Schemes in the Inter-War Period* (1945), Appendix I, "Trade and Production in the Danubian States."

RUMANIAN ECONOMIC HISTORY

The most recent large study is Virgil Madgearu, *Evoluția economiei românești după războiul mondial* (Bucarest, Independența economică, 1940). While the organization of this work is cumbersome, it is the only extensive Rumanian interpretation of the interwar period. It contains a good deal of information which Madgearu obtained from unpublished sources. Its outlook is that of a disappointed and somewhat disillusioned National Peasant. N. Razmirița, *Essai d'économie roumaine moderne, 1831–1931* (Paris, Librairie générale de droit et de jurisprudence, 1932) is largely devoted to the pre-1914 period; its sections on the postwar years are not very good. Florin Em. Manoliou, *La Réconstruction économique et financière de la Roumanie et les partis politiques* (Paris, J. Gamber, 1931), undertakes to analyze the economic policy of the Liberal, People's party, and National Peasant governments in the years between 1920 and 1931. Not a very penetrating study, it is of value in sketching the principal economic measures of the various cabinets.

Like Razmirița and Manoliou, quite a number of Rumanian students in Paris wrote dissertations on aspects of Rumanian economic life. The quality of these is very uneven; some are worthless, others are quite good. Perhaps the best are Savel Radulescu, *La Politique financière de la Roumanie depuis 1914* (Paris, Les Presses Universitaires de France, 1923), and Nicolas C. Cristoveanu, *Essai critique sur la politique roumaine en matière de dettes agricoles* (Paris, A. Rousseau, 1933). Less useful are C. A. Tatarano, *Les Nouvelles tendances économiques de la Roumanie* (Paris, 1922); Dorin Kastris, *Les Capitaux étrangers dans la finance roumaine* (Paris, 1921); A. Theveneau, *La Roumanie économique et le change roumain au lendemain de la guerre* (Paris, Les Presses Universitaires, 1923); Alexandre-Ionescu Ivanof, *La*

Réforme monétaire roumaine (Paris, Librairie du Recueil Sirey, 1929); A. G. Georgescu, *Le Régime juridique et financier des capitaux étrangers en Roumanie* (Paris, Les Presses Universitaires, 1932); Ludovic Iavorschi, *L'Équilibre budgétaire en Roumanie de 1920 à 1932* (Paris, J. Gamber, 1933); Mihail-Dumitru N. Israil, *Le Marché monétaire roumain après la stabilisation monétaire* (Paris, Librairie L. Rodstein, 1933).

THE AGRARIAN QUESTION

As has been mentioned, David Mitrany's *The Land and the Peasant in Rumania* is the most satisfactory study of the agrarian question. Much briefer and less comprehensive is Ifor L. Evans, *The Agrarian Revolution in Rumania* (Cambridge University Press, 1924). A very informative history of the Rumanian peasant question in the nineteenth century is Marcel Emerit, *Les Paysans roumains depuis le Traité d'Andrinople jusqu'à la libération des terres, 1829–1864* (Paris, Librairie du Recueil Sirey, 1937). It was M. Emerit's intention to write a second volume on the years between the emancipation and the agrarian reform, but it has not yet appeared.

Classic Rumanian studies on the peasant question are the two works of Radu Rosetti, *Pământul, sătenii, și stăpânii in Moldova* (Bucarest, SOCEC, 1907) and *Pentru ce s'au răsculat țăranii* (Bucarest, SOCEC, 1908). Rosetti wrote from a populist point of view, and his belief in the peasants' original right to the land was challenged by his contemporary, Gheorghe Panu, in *O Incercare de mistificare istorică* (Bucarest, Brozer and Parzer, 1910). It is now generally agreed that a number of Rosetti's conclusions were based on very weak evidence.

Among other studies which date from the time of the 1907 uprising but which are still important for an understanding of the Rumanian agrarian question are those of Garoflid and Creangă. Constantin Garoflid's penetrating analysis, *Chestia agrară în România* (Bucarest, Gutenberg, 1920), was originally written in 1907 but later published with other articles and speeches. A landowner himself, Garoflid criticized the old latifundiary system of cultivation but was opposed to the creation of a multitude of small properties which would not be self-sustaining. Some of his statistics, which have been employed by subsequent authors, are clearly incorrect. His views on the postreform period may be found in two articles: *Un Program agrar* (Bucarest, 1924) and *Rolul social al proprietații mijlocii* (Bucarest, 1926), as well as in a contribution to the *Enciclopedia României*. G. C. Creangă, *Grundbesitzverteilung und Bauernfrage in Rumänien*, 3 Teile, in *Staats- und sozialwissenschaftliche Forschungen*, Hefte 129, 140 (Leipzig, 1907, 1909), is the most complete statistical analysis of Rumanian property relations before the agrarian reforms; Creangă's figures, while not wholly satisfactory, have provided the basis for most estimates of the pre-1914 situation.

The veteran agricultural economist G. Ionescu-Sișești wrote a number of works on the agrarian question. For the most part, however, they are marred by the tone of bland optimism which is the bane of much Rumanian writing of an official or semiofficial nature. *Politica agrară cu privire specială la România* (Bucarest, Libraria L. Alcalay, n.d., *ca.* 1913) has an interesting review of Rumanian writings on the agrarian question. In *Structure agraire et production agricole de la Roumanie* (Bucarest, 1924) he examined the consequences of the agrarian reforms, especially in their effect upon cultivation in metayage. He collaborated with A. Frundianescu in a contribution to *Agricultural Systems of Middle Europe, a Symposium,* ed. O. S. Morgan (New York, Macmillan, 1933), and with N. Cornățeanu in *La Réforme agraire en Roumanie et ses conséquences* (Bucarest, Académie roumaine, 1937), which provides some useful farm-accountancy statistics but is quite misleading in its interpretation of Rumanian peasant agriculture. During the Second World War, however, he wrote a very pessimistic study, "Le Nouvel Aspect du problème agraire en Roumanie,"*Archives pour la science et la réforme sociales, 16,* Nos. 1–4 (1943), 260–267.

The legal aspects of the 1918–21 agrarian reforms are discussed in Ilie S. Diaconescu, *Chestiunea țărănească în România* (Bucarest, Cultura Poporului," 1928), which gives the texts of the laws and an extended commentary; its value as a historical narrative is limited. Mitița Constantinescu, *L'Evolution de la propriété rurale et la réforme agraire en Roumanie* (Bucarest, 1925), while written at great length and with assurance, was prepared before many of the results of the reforms were known. In 1945 Constantinescu came out as a stanch advocate of intimate Rumanian-Soviet relations (see his pamphlet *Relațiile economice între România și U.R.S.S.,* Bucarest, Cartea Rusă, 1945), but in this earlier study he stressed the importance of the agrarian reform as a bulwark against bolshevism.

A number of Paris dissertations were concerned with the agrarian question; none is outstanding: C. C. Bosiano, *La Politique paysanne en Roumanie depuis la guerre* (Paris, 1920); Valeriu Bercaru, *La Réforme agraire en Roumanie* (Paris, H. Gamber, 1928); Antoniu Saki, *La Question agraire en Roumanie* (Paris, Les Presses Modernes, 1926). Of the same order is Ernest Grintzesco, *Le Problème du redressement agricole en Roumanie* (Bucarest, F. Göbl et Fils., 1931).

A good summary of Rumania's agrarian position at the outbreak of the Second World War, especially in regard to its export position, was prepared by the United States Department of Agriculture, "Wartime Agricultural Surpluses of the Danube Basin," *Foreign Agriculture, 4,* No. 12 (December 1940), 705–778. The article does, however, attribute too many virtues to the pre-1914 large estates.

A very intelligent analysis of the Rumanian agrarian problem is by the Danish specialist, M. Gormsen, *Short Introduction to the Principal Structural Problems of the Agriculture in Roumania* (Bucarest, 1945). The Rumanian text of this rather bad English translation is to be found in the volume issued by Institutul Economic Românesc, *Problema agrară* (Bucarest, Cartea Românească, 1945) which also includes an article by Valeriu Bulgariu on the subdividing of peasant property, "Divizibilitatea proprietații țărănești."

In the last decade or so there have been a number of studies on the plight of the eastern European peasant countries. Doreen Warriner, in *The Economics of Peasant Farming* (Oxford University Press, 1939), came to the negative conclusion that emigration was virtually the only solution to the problem of overpopulation. A more positive solution has been proposed by K. Mandelbaum, *The Industrialisation of Backward Areas,* Oxford Institute of Statistics Monograph, No. 2 (Oxford, Basil Blackwell, 1945). This study, which is based on the southeastern European states, draws up a formal model for their planned industrialization. Its principal limitation, as the author admits, is that it abstracts all the political difficulties. Two other works may be mentioned which reflect the same interest: S. N. Prokopovicz, *L'Industrialisation des pays agricoles et la structure de l'économie mondiale après la guerre,* trans. N. Nicolsky (Neuchâtel, 1946), and P. N. Rosenstein-Rodan, "Problems of Industrialisation of Eastern and South-Eastern Europe," *The Economic Journal, 53* (1943), 202–211.

POLITICAL MOVEMENTS

A useful guide for political developments up to 1936 is the publication of the Conférence Permanente des Hautes Études Internationales, *Chronique des événements politiques et économiques dans le bassin danubien, 1918–1936: Roumanie* (Paris, Institut International de Coopération Intellectuelle, Société des Nations, 1938). This booklet also lists and summarizes the principal laws and decrees of the period. A symposium of lectures on political theories current in Rumania at the beginning of the interwar period was published by Institutul Social Român as *Doctrinele partidelor politice* (Bucarest, Cultura Națională, n.d.). The book includes lectures on nationalism by Iorga, peasantism by Virgil Madgearu, liberalism by I. G. Duca, conservatism by Al. Marghiloman, neoliberalism by M. Manoilescu, and socialism by Șerban Voinea. No Communist was invited to speak. While one may feel that a number of these lectures had little or nothing to do with Rumanian realities, the collection is most interesting in showing the eagerness with which the Rumanians were attempting to relate their society to the West. A much less interesting work is *Politics and Political Parties in Roumania* (London, International Reference Library Publishing Co., 1936), which includes the programs of the principal parties and a political "Who's Who."

a. *Liberals*

Istoricul Partidului Național Liberal de la 1848 și până astazi (Bucarest, 1923) is a rather conventional official history of the party. It is of little use for the interwar period. A biography of Vintilă Brătianu was written by C. Georgescu, *Vintilă Brătianu ca om de stat, economist, și financiar* (Bucarest, 1936). Brătianu's economic views found frequent expression in the above-mentioned *L'Économiste roumain;* they were also clearly displayed in a parliamentary address which was translated into French: *La Situation financière de la Roumanie; discours tenu à la Chambre des Députés les 1 et 2 février 1923* (Bucarest, Imprimeria "Indépendance," 1923). Some information on the banking activities of the Liberals is to be found in Alfred Bonafous, "Les Grandes Banques d'affaires de Roumanie," *Revue d'économie politique* (Paris), *36* (1922), 323–340. The darker side of the Liberal regime is seen in the somewhat sensational exposé of the methods employed by the secret police: C. G. Costa-Foru, *Aus den Folterkammern Rumäniens* (Vienna, Kulturpolitischer Verlag, 1925).

The most brilliant defense of the role of the Rumanian Liberal party was made by St. Zeletin, who propounded a highly ingenious though probably untenable theory of Rumania's historical development in his two studies, *Burghezia română, origina și rolul ei istoric* (Bucarest, Cultura Națională, 1925) and *Neoliberalismul* (Bucarest, Editura "Pagini agrare și sociale," 1927). His quasi-Marxist approach was bitterly attacked by the Social Democrat, Șerban Voinea, in *Marxism oligarhic, contribuție la problema desvoltarii capitaliste a României* (Bucarest, Editura I. Brănișteanu, 1926).

b. *National Peasants*

The best exposition of the principles of Rumanian populism is Constantin Stere's series of articles entitled "Socialdemocratism sau poporanism," *Viața românească* (August, 1907–April, 1908). Stere's views, somewhat modified, are also to be found in his pamphlet *Naționalizarea industriei de petrol* (Bucarest, 1921). The issue between Marxism and populism is also examined in David Mitrany, "Marx vs. the Peasant," *London Essays in Economics: in Honour of Edwin Cannon*, eds. T. E. Gregory and H. Dalton (London, Routledge, 1927). J. Delevsky, "Les Idées des 'narodniki' russes," *Revue d'économie politique, 35* (1921), 432–462, gives a brief history of Russian populism and is a source frequently cited by Rumanian peasantist writers. A biting criticism of Rumanian populism is to be found in the essays of H. Sanielevici, collected as *Poporanismul reacționar* (Bucarest, SOCEC, 1921). For a recent exposition of populism by a well-known Bulgarian politician see George M. Dimitrov, "Agrarianism," *European Ideologies. A Survey of Twentieth Century Political Ideas,* ed. Felix Gross (New York, Philosophical Library, 1948), pp. 396–451.

The most vivid and intelligent expressions of the radical agrarianism of the early Peasant party are Ion Mihalache's parliamentary speeches, which were published separately as political pamphlets: *Proectul legei de improprietarirea tăranilor, intocmit de țăranul I. Mihalache* (Bucarest, Tipografia "Lupta," 1920); *Dreptul țăranilor la pământ, izlazuri, și păduri* (Bucarest, Tipografia Berbecaru, 1922); and *Partidul Țărănesc în politica țărei* (Bucarest, 1925).

The move away from populism and toward a form of liberal capitalism is seen in the writings of Virgil Madgearu: *Țărănismul* (Bucarest, "Reforma Socială," n.d.); "Doctrina Țărănistă," in *Doctrinele partidelor politice; Revoluția agrară și evoluția clasei țărănești* (Bucarest, 1923); *Agrarianism—un discurs parlamentar* (Bucarest, Imprimeria Statului, 1927); *Rumania's New Economic Policy* (London, P. S. King, 1930); *La Politique économique extérieure de la Roumanie, 1927–1938,* Conférence Permanente des Hautes

Études Internationales, xiie session, Mémoire roumaine, No. 1 (Paris, Institut International de Coopération Intellectuelle, Société des Nations, 1939).

An attempt to unite peasantism with a revived conservatism was made by C. Rădulescu-Motru, *Ţărănismul, un suflet şi o politică* (Bucarest, Cultura Naţională, 1924). While one may doubt the feasibility of this attempt, the essay is excellent in its portrayal of all the anomalies in Rumania's political life.

The modifications in the outlook of the Peasant party appear clearly in the successive programs of 1921, 1922, 1924, and 1926: *Proectul de program al Partidului Ţărănesc din România* (Bucarest, "Viaţa românească," 1921); *Partidul Ţărănesc, Programul şi Statutele* (Bucarest, 1922); *Partidul Ţără-nesc, Programul general şi Statutele* (Bucarest, 1925); and *Partidul Naţional-Ţărănesc, Principiile programul şi statutul* (Bucarest "Reforma Socială," 1926).

c. *The Carolist Era*

An "official" biography of King Carol by Baroness Helena von der Hoven, *King Carol of Romania* (London, Hutchinson, 1940), is of practically no value and shows little understanding of Rumanian politics. A more serious study, A. L. Easterman, *King Carol, Hitler, and Lupescu* (London, Gollancz, 1942), recognizes Carol's autocratic and arbitrary instincts but does not give him sufficient credit for his part in wrecking the parliamentary system. Easterman makes Antonescu, the Iron Guard, and the Germans the complete villains of the piece.

The most interesting, if also most exasperating, political economist of this period was Mihail Manoilescu, whose works are listed in Florin E. Manoliou, *Bibliographie des travaux du Professeur Mihail Manoilesco* (Bucarest, "Luceafarul," 1936). The earlier phases of Manoilescu's thought are repre-sented in his article, "Neoliberalismul" in *Doctrinele partidelor politice,* and in his critique of peasantism: *Ţărănism şi democraţie* (Bucarest, 1922). His most important study was translated into English as *The Theory of Protection and International Trade* (London, P. S. King, 1931). An expanded German edition, *Die nationalen Produktivkräfte und der Aussenhandel* (Berlin, 1937), included his rebuttals of the numerous criticisms of his theory of permanent protection.

A series of articles—obviously designed for foreign consumption—on the economic policy of the Carolist dictatorship appeared in several issues of *The Banker* (London): V. Dimitriuc, "Roumanian Exports and Agrarian Policy," *51* (July, 1939), 49–53; Valeriu Bulgariu, "Agrarian Policy in Roumania," *49* (March, 1939), 344–348; Mitiţa Constantinescu, "The Mone-tary and Credit Policy of Roumania," *44* (February, 1938), 183–189; C. Angelescu, "Banking Development in Roumania," *ibid.*, pp. 189–192; Eugene Savu, "The Financial Policy of Roumania," *ibid.*, pp. 193–194; G. Ionescu-Sişeşti, "Agriculture in Roumania," *ibid.*, pp. 197–201; Ch. Pencsco-Kertsch, "Industry in Roumania," *ibid.*, pp. 206–209.

The Germans produced a mass of official and semi-official literature in the course of their economic drive in the Balkans. One of the more important examples is Ernst Wagemann, *Der neue Balkan: altes Land—junge Wirtschaft* (Hamburg, Hanseatische Verlagsanstalt, 1939), a portion of which was translated as "The Pressure of Population as an Economic Force," *Weekly Report of the German Institute for Business Research,* Nos. 25/26 and 27/28 (June 29–July 14, 1939). Wagemann criticized the forced industrialization of the Balkan states and attempted to show that they would do better to develop their raw materials and let Germany provide the manufactured goods.

Although Grigore Gafencu's two books, *Prelude to the Russian Campaign,* trans. E. Fletcher-Allen (London, Frederick Muller, 1945), and *Last Days of Europe. A Diplomatic Journey in 1939,* trans. E. Fletcher-Allen (New Haven, Yale University Press, 1948), are chiefly concerned with diplomatic relations, they do provide some information on the last phase of the Carolist dictatorship. Also dealing with foreign relations before 1939 are two books by another Rumanian foreign minister, N. P. Comnène, *Preludi del grande dramma* (Rome, Edizioni Leonardo, 1947) and *I Responsabili* (Verona, Arnoldo Mondadori, 1949).

d. *The Fascists*

Codreanu's memoirs were published in German as Codreanu, *Eiserne Garde* (Berlin, Brunnen Verlag/Willi Bischoff, 1939). Codreanu's narrative stops at 1933, but the German edition includes some later information provided by members of the Guard. Klaus Charle, *Die Eiserne Garde* (Berlin-Vienna, Deutscher Rechtsverlag, 1939), is an enthusiastically pro-Guardist account of the movement. I. P. Vifor, *Doctrina fascismului român* (Bucarest, 1924), which contains the program of the ephemeral Fascia Națională Română, is of interest as an expression of an early imitation of Italian fascism. For a macabre account of the atrocities committed while the Iron Guardists were in power see "Blood Bath in Rumania," published by *The Record, 4,* Nos. 6–7, (New York, July–August, 1942).

Harald Laeuen, *Marschall Antonescu* (Essener Verlagsanstalt, 1943), provides an admiring biography of Germany's loyal ally. The first volume of an account of Antonescu's career by a former secretary, G. Barbul, *Mémorial Antonesco: Tome Premier, le IIIᵉ Homme de l'Axe* (Paris, Editions de la Couronne, 1950), appeared too late to be used in this study.

e. *The Marxists*

Constantin Titel Petrescu's history of Rumanian socialism, *Socialismul în România* (Bucarest, Biblioteca Socialistă, n.d., *ca.* 1945), is valuable for its inclusion of party programs, resolutions, and speeches. It is very uneven in its treatment, however; over three-fourths of the book is devoted to the years before 1919, and the interwar period is covered superficially. Some useful information on the Rumanian socialist movement before the war and in the unsettled months after 1917 is given in L. Trotsky and Ch. Rakovsky, *Ocherki politicheskoi Rumynii* (Moscow, Gosudarstvennoe Izdatelstvo, 1922). The first half of the book consists of a collection of articles written by Trotsky while in Rumania in 1913; in the second half Rakovsky interprets the political situation of postwar Rumania. An account of the final absorption of Rumanian Social Democracy by the Communists may be found in Valentin Thoma, "Wie es zur Liquidierung des rumänischen Sozialismus kam," *Die Zukunft* (July, 1949).

There is relatively little reliable information on the history of the Rumanian Communist party, largely because the party was illegal during most of its existence. However, in the issues of the organs of the Comintern, *The Communist International* and *International Press Correspondence,* there are occasional directives to the Rumanian Communists as well as comments on their activities.

Some information on conditions in Rumania, though surprisingly little, is in the publications of the Red Peasant International: *Der Weltbund der Bauern: Der Gründung des Internationalen Bauern-Rates* (Berlin, 1924); Dr. Kazescu, "Die rumänische Bauernschaft und der Europäische Bauern-Kongress," *Bulletin zum Europäischen Bauern-Kongress,* No. 4 (Berlin, 1930), pp. 39–48; *Europas werktätige Bauern schreiten zur revolutionären Tat* (Berlin, 1930); N. L. Mecheriakov, *The Peasantry and the Revolution* (Berlin, 1927); Guido Miglioli, *Bauernnot und Hakenkreuz* (Berlin, Verlag des EBK, n.d.).

The International Agrarian Institute in Moscow published a periodical, *Agrarprobleme,* which occasionally had articles on agrarian conditions in the Balkans and in Rumania: B. Boschkowitsch, "Der revolutionäre Aufschwung auf dem Balkan," Band 4, Heft 3–4, (n.d., *ca.* 1931), pp. 151–157; Tatarow, "Die Agrarkrise in Rumänien," Band 4, Heft 2, pp. 44–80; S. Timow, "Wird Rumänien agrarsiert oder industrialisiert?" Band 2, Heft 2 (1929), pp. 310–346.

The outstanding Marxist thinker in Rumania was undoubtedly C. Dobrogeanu-Gherea, whose book *Neoiobăgia* (1st ed. 1910, 2d ed., Bucarest, Viața românească, n.d.) is still extremely valuable for an understanding of Rumania. During the Second World War the Communist Lurețiu Pătrășcanu, until 1948 Minister of Justice in the Groza cabinet, wrote a trilogy of studies on Rumanian history and society: *Un Veac de frământări sociale, 1821–1907* (Bucarest, Cartea Rusă, 1945); *Problemele de bază ale României* (3rd ed., Bucarest, Editura de Stat, 1946); and *Sub trei dictaturi,* which has been translated into French as *Sous trois dictatures* (Paris, Editions Jean Vitiano, 1946). Although rigidly bound to the Marxist analysis, these studies are intelligently conceived and emphasize aspects of Rumanian life which are usually overlooked or concealed. It is doubtful however, whether Pătrășcanu's intellectual communism can be identified with the outlook of the present regime.

Although the Ploughmen's Front was initially an independent agrarian movement, since 1944 it has been completely under the influence of the Communist party. The most detailed account of the Front is Gheorghe Micle,

Răscoala pământului: Istoria luptelor politice ale țăranimii române, 1933–1945 (Bucarest, Editura Frontul Plugarilor, 1945).

, There is no satisfactory history of the Bessarabian question, that prolonged source of conflict between Rumania and Russia. Communist and Soviet views are to be found in Ch. Rakovsky, *Rumyniya i Bessarabiya, k semiletiyu anneksii Bessarabii* (Moscow, Izdanie Litizdata N.K.I.D., 1925); *Bessarabia . . . the Roumanian Hell* (published by the British Section of the International Class War Prisoners Aid, London, n.d.); A. Dolnik, *Bessarabiya pod vlastyu rumynskikh boyar, 1918–1940 gg.* (Ogiz-Gospoditizdat, 1945); and Akademiya nauk Soyuza SSR, Institut Geografii Akademii nauk SSSR i Moldavskii Nauchno-Issledovatelskii Institut, *Moldavskaya SSR* (Moscow-Leningrad, 1947). For the Rumanian side see Charles Upson Clark, *Bessarabia: Russia and Roumania on the Black Sea* (New York, Dodd, Mead, 1927); Andrei Popovici, *The Political Status of Bessarabia* (published for the School of Foreign Service, Georgetown University, by Ransdell, Inc., Washington, D.C., 1931); and *Facts and Comments Concerning Bessarabia, 1812–1940, Compiled by a Group of Roumanian Press Correspondents* (London, 1941).

Events after August 23, 1944, have been described by a number of American foreign correspondents, some of whom have written books: William B. King and Frank O'Brien, *The Balkans, Frontier of Two Worlds* (New York, Knopf, 1947); George Moorad, *Behind the Iron Curtain* (London, Latimer House, 1947); and Reuben H. Markham, *Rumania under the Soviet Yoke* (Boston, Meador, 1949). The last is much the most extensive, shows intimate and long familiarity with Rumania, but is marred by the author's intense personal feelings. Robert Bishop and E. S. Crayfield, *Russia Astride the Balkans* (New York, Robert M. McBride, 1948), is also a work of reportage rather than analysis; the two authors were U. S. intelligence officers in Rumania.

A bitter indictment of the.Groza regime has been prepared by a Rumanian group in exile in the United States: the Rumanian National Committee, *Suppression of Human Rights in Rumania* (Washington, D.C., September, 1949).

The Soviet view of events in Rumania in 1944–45 may be found in K. Dimitrov, "Agrarnyi vopros i agrarnaya reforma v Rumynii," *Mirovoe Khozyaistvo i Mirovoya Politika,* No. 6 (1945), pp. 15–19; and Ilya Ehrenburg's chapter on Rumania in *Dorogi Evropy* (Moscow, 1946).

PERIODICALS

The publications of the International Institute of Agriculture (Rome), especially the *International Review of Agriculture,* are quite useful, though most of the information on Rumania has an official character which often limits rather than increases its reliability. The organ of the Green (Prague) International, *M.A.B. (Mezinárodní Agrární Bureau): Bulletin du Bureau International Agraire,* contains a number of articles on Rumania in the 1920's. It is of value, too, in giving the general outlook of the eastern European peasant parties. The publications of the International Labour Office, the *International Labour Review* and *Industrial and Labour Information* have occasional items on social and labor conditions in Rumania. The first issue of the *International Journal of Agrarian Affairs* (London) (October, 1939) was entirely devoted to a series of articles on surplus agricultural population. *The Slavonic and East European Review* (London) has several articles on Rumania during the interwar period. For the years since 1945 *East Europe* (London), a periodical hostile to the present regimes behind the iron curtain, provides a weekly chronicle of events in Rumania. Among the pro-Soviet periodicals the most authoritative is the Cominform organ, *For a Lasting Peace, for a People's Democracy,* now published in Bucarest.

Among Rumanian magazines and newspapers the following have been consulted: *Viața românească,* at one time the leading periodical, containing numerous articles on social, political, and philosophical questions; *Argus* and *Finanțe și Industrie,* economic and commercial journals; the party organs: *Viitorul* and *L'Indépendance roumaine* (Liberal), *Dreptatea* (National-Peasant), *Libertatea* (Social Democrat), and *Scânteia* and *România Liberă* (Communist); and the formerly independent newspapers: *Universul, Timpul, Jurnalul de dimineața,* and *Semnalul.*

OTHER WORKS CONSULTED

a. *General or Well-known Works and Technical Aids*

Arndt, H. W. *The Economic Lessons of the Nineteen-Thirties.* Oxford University Press, 1944.

Baykov, Alexander. *The Development of the Soviet Economic System.* Cambridge University Press, 1946.

Beloff, Max. *The Foreign Policy of Soviet Russia, 1929–1941.* 2 vols., Oxford University Press, 1947–49.

Borkenau, Franz. *The Communist International.* London, Faber, 1938.

Byrnes, James F. *Speaking Frankly.* London; New York, Harper and Brothers, 1947.

Carr-Saunders, A. M. *World Population: Past Growth and Present Trends.* Oxford University Press, 1936.

Clark, Colin. *The Conditions of Economic Progress.* London, Macmillan, 1940.

Cohen, R. L. *The Economics of Agriculture.* Cambridge University Press, 1940.

Dareste, F. R., and P. *Les Constitutions modernes.* 4th ed., 6 vols., Paris, 1928–34.

David, Eduard. *Sozialismus und Landwirtschaft.* 2d ed., Leipzig, Quelle und Meyer, 1922.

Deutscher, I. *Stalin, a Political Biography.* Oxford University Press, 1949.

Dobb, Maurice H. *Soviet Economic Development since 1917.* London, Routledge and K. Paul, 1948.

Fabian Society, International Research Section. *Hitler's Route to Bagdad.* London, G. Allen and Unwin, 1939.

Fischer, Louis. *Men and Politics, an Autobiography.* New York, Duell, Sloan, and Pearce, 1941.

Gunther, John. *Inside Europe.* London, Hamish Hamilton, 1936.

Hevesy, Paul de. *World Wheat Planning and Economic Planning in General.* Oxford University Press, 1940.

Hull, Cordell. *The Memoirs of Cordell Hull.* 2 vols., New York, Macmillan, 1948.

International Institute of Agriculture. *World Trade in Agricultural Products.* Rome, 1940.

Jasny, Naum. *The Socialized Agriculture of the USSR.* Stanford, Stanford University, Food Research Institute, "Grain Economics Series," No. 5, 1949.

Keeton, George W., and Schlesinger, Rudolf. *Russia and Her Western Neighbors.* London, Jonathan Cape, 1942.

Lenin, V. I. *Selected Works.* 12 vols., London, Lawrence and Wishart, 1936–39.

Macartney, C. A. *Hungary and Her Successors: the Treaty of Trianon and Its Consequences, 1919–1937.* Oxford University Press, 1937.

Marx, Karl. *Capital,* Vol. I, English trans. by Samuel Moore and Edward Aveling. London, 1887. Vol. III, English trans. by Ernest Untermann. Chicago, 1909.

Mitrany, David. *The Effect of the War in Southeastern Europe.* New Haven, Yale University Press, 1936.

Mosely, Philip E., *Face to Face with Russia.* Foreign Policy Association, Headline Series, No. 70, July–August, 1948.

Owen, Lancelot A. *The Russian Peasant Movement, 1906–17.* London, King, 1937.

Robinson, Geroid Tanquary. *Rural Russia under the Old Regime.* New York, London, and Toronto, Longmans, Green, 1932.

Royal Institute of International Affairs. *World Agriculture, an International Survey.* Oxford University Press, 1932.

Schmidt, Paul. *Statist auf diplomatischer Bühne, 1923–45; Erlebnisse des Chefdolmetschers im Auswärtigen Amt mit den Staatsmännern Europas.* Bonn, Athenäum-Verlag, 1949.

Sherwood, Robert E. *Roosevelt and Hopkins. An Intimate History.* New York, Harper and Brothers, 1948.

Stalin, J. *Voprosy Leninizma.* 11th ed., Ogiz, Gosudarstvennoe Izdatelstvo Politicheskoi Literatury, 1945.

Stettinius, Edward R., Jr. *Roosevelt and the Russians: the Yalta Conference.* New York, Doubleday, 1949.

United Nations, Research and Planning Division, Economic Commission for Europe. *Economic Survey of Europe in 1948.* Geneva, 1949.

United States, Department of State. *Nazi-Soviet Relations, 1939–1941.* Washington, D.C., 1948.

Von Franges, Otto. *Die Bevolkerungsdichte als Triebkraft der Wirtschafts-politik der südosteuropäischen Bauernstaaten,* in *Kieler Vorträge, gehalten im Institut für Weltwirtschaft an der Universität Kiel,* No. 59. Jena, 1939.

White, Leigh. *The Long Balkan Night.* New York, Scribner's, 1944.

b. *Miscellaneous Works on Rumania*

Académie Roumaine, *La Transylvanie.* Bucarest, 1938.

——. *La Dobroudja.* Bucarest, 1938.

Antim, St. *Chestiunea socială în România.* Bucarest, "La Roumanie," 1908.

Auboin, Roger. *Rapport annuel sur la situation financière et monétaire de la Roumanie.* Bucarest, 1935.

Baerlein, Henry, ed. *The Romanian Scene.* London, Muller, 1945.

Bussot, A. "Le Bloc des états agricoles de l'Europe centrale et orientale et son programme," *Revue d'économie politique,* 47 (1933), 1544–1558.

Calinescu, Armand. *Roumania, the Country of National Renaissance and of Royal Revolution.* Pamphlet in English, translated from a speech in the Chamber of Deputies, January 28, 1939.

Ciomac, Ion Luca. *Despre starile agrare din Transilvania sub regimul maghiar, și cercetari asupră situației exploatarilor agricole după reforma agrară.* Bucarest, 1931.

Cioriceanu, Georges D. *La Roumanie économique et ses rapports avec l'étranger de 1860 à 1915.* Paris, Marcel Giard, 1928.

Claudian, Ioan. *Alimentația poporului român în cadrul antropogeografiei și istoriei economice.* Bucarest, Fundația "Regele Carol II," 1939.

Codrescu, Florin. *Essai de synthèse sur l'évolution du commerce extérieure de la Roumanie, 1918–1934.* Extract from the periodical, *Les Balkans,* Athens, 1934.

Colescu, L. *Progresele economice ale României îndeplenite sub domnia M.S. Regelui Carol I, 1866–1906.* Bucarest, 1907.

Dugdale, Mrs. Edgar. *The Hungaro-Rumanian Dispute. The Optants' Case before the League.* London, The Association for International Understanding, 1926.

Filitti, I. C. *Clasele sociale în trecutul românesc.* Bucarest, 1925.

Georgescu, C. C. *La Réforme agraire en Roumanie.* Paris, 1908.

Ghyka, Matila. *A Documented Chronology of Roumanian History from Pre-Historic Times to the Present Day.* Oxford, B. H. Blackwell, 1941.

Giannini, Amadeo. *La costituzione romena.* Rome, 1923.

——. *Le Vicende della Rumania, 1878–1940.* Milan, 1940.

Giurescu, C. *Despre boieri.* Bucarest, Cartea Românească, 1920.

Graf, O. P. *Die Industriepolitik Alt-Rumäniens und die Grundlagen der Industrialisierung Gross-Rumäniens.* Bucarest, 1927.

Hausknecht, Louis. *Politica impozitară a României după răsboiu.* Cernăuți, 1931.

Hoffmann, Walter. *Südost-Europa: Bulgarien-Jugoslavien-Rumänien.* Leipzig, 1932.

Hoffmann, Walter. *Rumänien von Heute. Ein Querschnitt durch Politik, Kultur, und Wirtschaft.* 2d ed., Leipzig, 1942.

Issacenco, A. G. *La Roumanie inconnue.* Berne, 1917.

Jaszi, Oscar. "The Economic Crisis in the Danubian States," *Social Research* (February, 1935), pp. 98–116.

Lémonon, Ernest. "La Situation économique de la Roumanie, 1918–1928," *Journal des économistes* (March 15, 1931), pp. 264–273.

Leon, Gh. N., *Struktur und Entwicklungsmöglichkeiten der rumänischen Volkswirtschaft.* Jena, 1941.

Lovrin, C. D. *Rumania Today.* London, 1945.

Micșuinescu, Emil Gr. *Die rumänische Getreideausfuhr.* Nürnberg, 1914.

Mitrany, David. "The New Rumanian Constitution," *The Journal of Comparative Legislation and International Law*, 3rd ser., *6*, Pt. 1 (February, 1924), 110–119.

Obedenare, M. G. *La Roumanie économique d'après les données les plus récentes.* Paris, Ernest Leroux, 1876.

Raducanu, Mircea I. *Die Genossenschaftsbewegung in Rumänien.* Dresden, 1941.

Rădulescu-Motru, C. *Cultura română și politicanismul.* Bucarest, n.d.

Rambaud, Benoit. *La Question des fermiers généraux en France et à l'étranger* (Paris, 1913).

Reithinger, Anton. "Grossdeutschland und Südosteuropa im Lichte der Statistik," *Allgemeines Statistisches Archiv, 29* (1939), 129–139.

Rumanian Democratic Committee. *How Rumania Was Surrendered: Statements Made by M. Juliu Maniu, Leader of the National Peasant Party, and M. Constantin Bratianu, Leader of the National Liberal Party.* London, Favil Press, 1941.

Rumania, Ministry of Agriculture. *La Roumanie, 1866–1906.* Bucarest, SOCEC, 1907.

Rumer, Willy. *Die Agrarreformen der Donau-Staaten.* Innsbrück, 1927.

Schiff, Walter. *Die grossen Agrarreformen seit dem Kriege.* Vienna, 1926.

Sollohub, W. A. "The Conversion of Agricultural Debts in Roumania," *The Economic Journal, 42* (December, 1932), 588–594.

Strat, George. *Industria românească în cadrul economiei europene.* Bucarest, "Remus Cioflec," 1945.

Tătărescu, G. *Quatre années de gouvernement, 1933–1937, exposé fait devant le comité central du Parti National-Liberal le 1 novembre 1937.* Bucarest, 1937.

Thomas, P. J. *Les Roumains nos alliés?* Paris, F. Sorlot, 1938.

Tilea, V. V. *Iuliu Maniu, der Mann und das Werk.* Hermannstadt, 1927.

Union des Chambres de Commerce et d'Industrie de Roumanie. *La Roumanie économique en 1926.* Bucarest, F. Göbl et Fils, n.d.

Vararu, M. *Le Métayage en Roumanie.* Paris, M. Giard et E. Brière, 1915.

Waldeck, R. G. *Athene Palace Bucarest: Hitler's New Order Comes to Rumania.* London, Constable, 1943.

Year-Book of Agricultural Co-operation, 1930 (London), "Rumania: the State as Co-operator," pp. 404–428.

Zăroni, Romulus. *De ce nu trebue să fie plugarul român fascist.* Cluj, Vieaţa Creştină, n.d.

INDEX

ADMINISTRATION, attempted decentralization of, 132, 173; *see also* Bureaucracy

Agrarian bloc of eastern European states, 164, 184–185

Agrarian policy and programs: Communist party, 262, 292–293, 322; Liberal party, 123; Peasant party, 27, 153–154

Agrarian problem: and Carolist dictatorship, 206–207; characteristics of, v–vi, 6, 57–59, 332–333; and Rumanian fascism, 223; *see also* Agricultural property, Agriculture, Farming, Overpopulation

Agrarian reform: contrasted with agricultural reform, 63; and strip cultivation, 58; 1917 amendment to Constitution, 24; of 1918–21, 26–30, 34, 36–39, 95, 290, 332, 366–367, Carolist criticism of, 211, effects on production, 62, and Marxist parties, 246, 250, 281, unreliability of official accounts of, 48–49; of 1945, 54, 62, 157 n., 292–299, 316, 318, 374; confiscation of remaining estate land in 1949, 323; *see also* Agricultural property, Expropriation

Agricultural associations, laws concerning, 186, 237–238

Agricultural contracts: laws of 1866 and 1872, 12–13; reform of, 21

Agricultural cooperatives. *See* Cooperatives

Agricultural credit. *See* Credit

Agricultural crisis. *See* Depression

Agricultural debts: in the depression, 178–180; moratoria and reductions of, 181–183, 210; of peasants, 79, 84, 138

Agricultural education, 159, 160 n.

Agricultural exports. *See* Commerce

Agricultural labor: after 1945, 318; number of hired laborers, 52, 291 n.; and types of tenures, 51, 372–373; wartime mobilization of, 237

Agricultural machinery, 159, 186, 239, 319

Agricultural Mortgage Institute (Credit Agricol Ipoteca), 181

Agricultural population. *See* Overpopulation, Population

Agricultural property: alienation and sale of, laws regulating, 29–30, 125–126, 156–157, 165, 204, 288, 295, political views

concerning, 157 n., National Peasant program advocates freedom of, 154, state control over, 212; consolidation of, 29, 63, 156, 319, 334; distribution of, before 1914, 6, 362–363, in Bessarabia, 33, 364–365, in Bucovina, 36, 365, in Transylvania, 37, 366, between 1921 and 1945, 49–52, 367–371, after 1945, 297, 374–375; as factor in overpopulation, 46, 53–54; leasing of, on large estates before 1914, 14–15, 363, in metayage, 238, after First World War, 53; subdivision and fragmentation of, through inheritance and sale, 11–12, 49, 65, creating dwarf holdings, 46, 54, efforts to check, 29–30, 154; *see also* Expropriation

Agriculture: condition of in interwar period, 83; economic planning in, 213–214; and industrialization, 201; investment in, 58; losses to in Second World War, 220; means of production in, 15, 58; mechanization of, 319; production in, 15 n., 55–57, 133, 239, 315–316; productivity in, 43–44, 57–62; protection of, 76, 177, 183–186, 202–203; *see also* Tariffs

Alba Iulia, 37, 97, 107, 168

All for the Fatherland party (Totul pentru Țara), 188, 227; *see also* Iron Guard

Allied Control Commission, 259, 268, 301

Amsterdam International Federation of Trade Unions, 247; *see also* Trade Unions

Angelescu, I. N., 113

Animal husbandry, 13, 45, 239, 316, 318

Anti-Semitism, 97 n., 101, 116, 145, 176, 190, 224–226, 234, 243; and absentee ownership, 14 n.; and Codreanu, 228; and Iron Guard dictatorship, 236; and 1907 uprising, 3, 4; in 1937 elections, 229 n.

Antonescu, Marshal (also Gen.) Ion, 92, 93, 219, 241, 305, 308, 347, 350; in Goga cabinet, 192; advent to power, 209–210; nature of his dictatorship, 223; as dictator, 233–235; relations with Hitler, 233 n.; and Iron Guard, 235, 346; agrarian policy of, 236–240; overthrow of, 242, 258

Antonescu, Mihai, Foreign Minister, 258–259

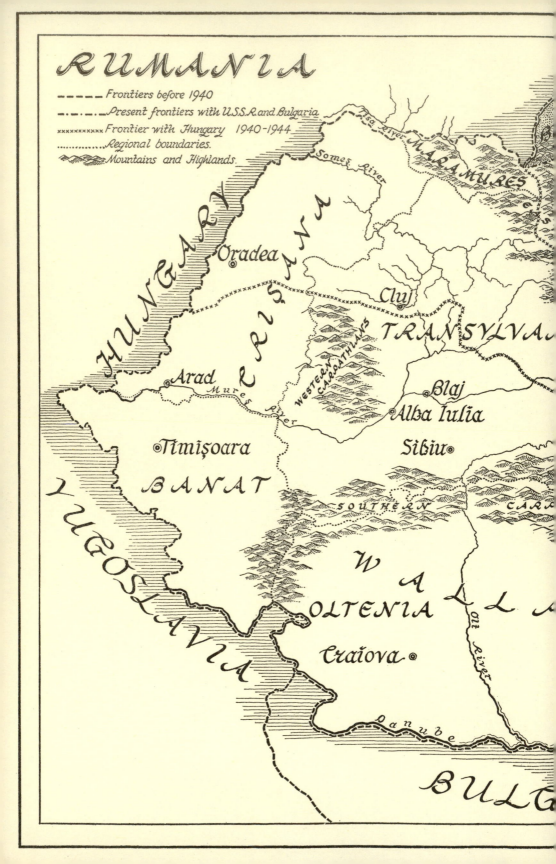

RUMANIA

----- Frontiers before 1940
-·-·-·- Present frontiers with U.S.S.R. and Bulgaria
xxxxxxxxxx Frontier with Hungary 1940-1944
.... Regional boundaries.
Mountains and Highlands.

HUNGARY

Someş River

Tisa River

MARAMUREŞ

Oradea

Cluj

TRANSYLVA

CRISANA

WESTERN CARPATHIANS

Arad

Mureş River

Blaj

Alba Iulia

Timişoara

Sibiu

BANAT

SOUTHERN

CARP

YUGOSLAVIA

W A L L A

OLTENIA

Olt River

Craiova

Danube

BULG